STACKS

A VISITOR'S GUIDE
to Colonial *&* Revolutionary

New England.

A VISITOR'S GUIDE
to Colonial *&* Revolutionary

New England.

INTERESTING SITES TO VISIT.
Lodging ❋ Dining ❋ Things to Do

Patricia & Robert Foulke

The Countryman Press
Woodstock, Vermont

Library of Congress Cataloging-in-Publication Data has been applied for.

ISBN-13: 978-0-88150-688-4
ISBN-10: 0-88150-688-5

Book design and composition by Joseph Kantorski
Cover photograph by Richard Pasley
Maps by Paul Woodward, © The Countryman Press
Interior photographs by the authors
Illustration on page 64 excerpted from *Handbook of Early Advertising Art*,
© 1947 by Clarence P. Horning; © 1953 and 1956 by Dover Publications.
Reprinted by permission.

Published by The Countryman Press, P.O. Box 748, Woodstock, VT 05091

Distributed by W. W. Norton & Company, Inc.,
500 Fifth Avenue, New York, NY 10110

Printed in the United States of America

10 9 8 7 6 5 4 3 2 1

Contents

Introduction

People who travel walk through human history, whether they are conscious of it or not. In this book we hope to enhance the pleasure of your travel throughout New England by developing and refining a sense of place. Heightened awareness of what happened where we walk now and whose footsteps preceded ours satisfies not only curiosity but also a natural longing to be connected with our surroundings.

Those who profess to live only in the present—a persistent mythical state in American popular culture—forget how disturbed they are when revisiting childhood sites that have changed almost beyond recognition. Constructing the past, and often idealizing it in the process, creates an orientation in time that is inseparable from the sense of place that defines who we are, both individually and collectively. Just as we rewrite our own internal autobiographies year by year, each generation recasts the past in its own molds.

Colonial and Revolutionary history is a kaleidoscope of movement and change, but it is clearly tied to many places that still remain. Rediscovering those places and expanding their meaning is the aim of this book. It is not designed for committed antiquarians or for those who reduce the past to a prologue of the present. It is designed for travelers with a persistent curiosity, those who like to build contexts around what they see.

This book explores colonial and Revolutionary sites, forts, government buildings, churches, inns, houses, historic districts, museums, and living-history museums, as well as reenactments and festivals throughout the six New England states. The time span begins in the early 1600s and extends into the early 1800s.

A Visitor's Guide to Colonial & Revolutionary New England combines the features of travel guides and historical narratives to recreate the conditions and ambience of colonial life for hit-the-road travelers and armchair travelers alike. As avid travelers of both sorts ourselves, we hope to bring you a vivid sense of place, time, and character.

Some of the stories are about historical figures you may already know, and others may tickle your fancy. You may enjoy reliving trips already taken, or you may be considering a new venture and want specific information on potential activities and sites within various regions.

A time line at the beginning of each chapter sets the stage for your personal orientation. An introduction describes the founding and development of what became each New England state. Then the focus shifts to places that can still be seen by visitors who want to walk into their heritage to understand it better. Throughout the remainder of each chapter the focus remains on specific places, linking each town and building or site with the events that occurred there. In some cases we may mention the dates of early settlement in a village even if there is little or nothing left to see except the topography. In other cases the process of expanding and modernizing buildings has left a remnant of a colonial home or inn intact after two or three hundred years of addition and change. Those with observant eyes may be able to reconstruct what a place might have looked like in the colonial era and get some sense of how its inhabitants lived.

Our emphasis is less on memorializing important political and military events than understanding the context in which they occurred, so the book includes much material on the social and cultural history of everyday life—architecture, clothing, food, transportation, occupations, religious practices, customs, folklore, and the like. The early groups of colonists left Europe and endured the hardships of living in the wilderness of the New World to attain religious freedom and maintain their own cultures. Often such groups defined religious and social practices narrowly, expelling those who would not conform. And sometimes rigid rules in one colony created another, as in the case of Massachusetts Bay spawning Rhode Island.

Thus the idea of a quintessential colonial America is itself more a convenience for historians than a reality. In fact there were many disparate settlements that gradually and often reluctantly banded together for limited common purposes. Since the New England colonies were quite diverse in topography and economic activity, with peoples drawn from different ethnic, regional, and religious traditions in Europe, the story has to be retold for each within the larger framework of American expansion. The process of their amalgamation lasted through the Revolution and beyond, eliciting much controversy and sometimes bumptious behavior. Regionalism, by no means dead today, persisted throughout the colonial and Revolutionary eras and blocked many attempts at cooperation among the colonies.

Also, many early European attempts to establish colonies in America were dismal failures, often because the entrepreneurs and adventurers who came were bent on exploiting the new land. Those with money to invest in shares were not used to hard work and often ill equipped for the rigors of living in the wilderness. Some of these failed ventures in New England, like the 1607 Popham colony at the mouth of the Kennebec River in Maine, became footnotes in the history of colonization. Even among the settlements that survived and prospered, some were abandoned later as economic or political conditions changed. Permanence, order, and stability were envisioned in royal charters but seldom realized in the early history of colonies.

One of the destabilizing forces was the constant flow in and out of colonies. People uprooted from their European homelands to escape religious persecution, political suppression, or the devastation of wars continued to migrate within and between the colonies searching for better land or other opportunities. Many moved on simply to find a new place with topography reminiscent of their native regions, whether flat land, rolling hills, mountains, or river valleys.

The cultural diversity that we prize today also fragmented American experience. Succeeding waves of immigrants—English Puritans, French Huguenots, Welsh Quakers, German Mennonites, Moravians, and Lutherans, Scotch-Irish Presbyterians—clung together in enclaves united by religious principles, ethnic origins, language, and folk traditions. They maintained their identity through forms of worship and customs from home—precious objects from the past, Christmas or festival decorations, and clothing worn on special occasions.

Colonial America, then, is no single fabric but a patchwork quilt of many pieces, each with its own distinctive character and design. As you explore its many wonderful places, keep an eye out for change, instability, transience, variety, and anomaly, and be prepared for surprises. During our research for this book, most of the generalizations we had harbored from American history courses were shattered, to be replaced by sharper images and a keener sense of the many stories that are never fully or conclusively told. When you discard preconceptions and look closely at the places you visit, you too will begin rewriting colonial history in your own mind.

Trip Planning

We have grouped geographically rather than chronologically in history places you may want to visit since you will be traveling in literal space and imaginative time. Each colony has its unique character, and we have tried to reflect that in the order of presentation.

Sometimes we choose to begin with the earliest settlement, branching out in various directions to follow people as they moved to new locations; in other cases we are more strictly geographical, moving from the sea inland or along the coast, according to patterns of migration.

In no case do we survey the whole state that developed from the original colony, for both practical and historical reasons. Among them, the most important is the limited transportation available to settlers. The sea was the primary means of movement, followed by navigable rivers like the Penobscot, Kennebec, Merrimack, and Connecticut and long lakes like Champlain. Settlement clung to these waterways throughout most of the 1600s and slowly moved to other inland areas with the development of roads during the 1700s. Even so, only small portions of the New England colonies had been settled before 1760.

Although the colonial settlements of particular interest are listed within their current states and grouped geographically, we cannot pretend to establish travel patterns that will match each reader's interests and timetable. Some may want to spend a week in greater Boston, while others will shoot up the whole New England coast in the same time. Therefore we do not suggest stock itineraries that "cover" the colonial high points in any region, though any reader so inclined could construct one from this book. Most people will want to browse through a region without a rigid schedule, pausing to enjoy the unexpected glimpses of daily life two or three centuries ago.

The Internet can provide you with valuable information if you can separate out the advertorials luring people to specific sites or places. Some Web sites of regional and town tourist authorities are very helpful, and links may provide more detail. Yet guidebooks like this one are the most efficient starting place for objective and informed descriptions of the places you may want to visit, with follow-up on the Web to check seasons and opening hours of sites, special exhibits and events, and other current information. For the latest updates contact the state tourist offices or local convention and visitors bureaus, which often offer detailed maps of towns and regions, guides to historic sites, locations for outdoor recreation, and lists of accommodations and restaurants. For your convenience, we list addresses, telephone numbers, and Web sites (when available) of state, regional and town tourist offices.

Because many historic sites are staffed by volunteers, their hours and seasons change frequently. It is always wise to call or check the Web site while planning your trip. And while we also list some of the traditional festivals, their dates change and some are not held every year, so it is always wise to check before making your plans.

Accommodations and Restaurants

In a country where plentiful wood was the primary building material, restricting suggestions for lodging and food to authentic colonial inns and restaurants makes little sense, because most of these establishments have been torn down, burned down, or simply rotted away—you would be out in the cold and hungry in many regions of historic interest.

But you can find wonderful accommodations from former eras for an overnight stay if you are not too fussy about the date the structure was first built. This policy makes sense for another reason: Many inns and houses, especially in New England, grew with the trade or the family as addition by addition formed an elongated T at the back of the original structure. Those who restore such buildings have to decide which era will set the pattern. Architectural purists may reject the additions that keep the house alive and full of people, but social historians understand such processes of growth and adaptation. Discriminating travelers usually find colonial, Federal, or Victorian lodgings preferable to larger but less interesting modern hotel and motel rooms, so we list the former, but seldom the latter unless there is a special reason to do so.

Restaurants present another problem not so easily resolved. Only a handful of inns have survived from the colonial era, and most of them serve a melange of contemporary cuisines with a few colonial specialties. Others listed are located in authentic historic buildings or have succeeded in recreating the ambience of former eras. Although we have at some time enjoyed a meal in the restaurants we list, in no case can we guarantee the current quality of the food. Menus change by the season and the year, and good chefs are notoriously peripatetic.

We do not pretend to be comprehensive in our suggestions for a pleasant place to spend the night or eat a good meal. We like the establishments we list but know there are many others of equal quality that we have not yet discovered. For your convenience, we list whenever possible the phone numbers and Web sites of recommended inns, bed & breakfasts, and restaurants so you can make reservations and get current information.

Acknowledgments

We are particularly grateful for the advice and help of three scholars, all historians who have written about aspects of colonial and Revolutionary New England:

Professor John B. Hattendorf, Chairman of the Maritime History Department at the Naval War College; Professor Emeritus Tadahisa Kuroda of Skidmore College; and Professor Emeritus Benjamin W. Labaree of Williams College. They are not responsible for any errors or omissions, but they led us to important sources and solved a number of specific historical problems.

We also extend our gratitude to many persons who helped us plan our travels through colonial New England, provided maps, arranged appointments, and sometimes reviewed our text. They include directors of local and regional visitors bureaus and chambers of commerce, media specialists in state tourist authorities, public relations representatives and guides at historical sights, friends and a host of others who went out of their way to give us information and lead us to important sites in their communities.

We also thank Kermit Hummel, editorial director of The Countryman Press for his interest in this book and the two to follow on the Middle Atlantic States and the South, managing editor Jennifer Thompson for her patience as the manuscript grew, and especially Glenn E. Novak for his editorial acumen, knowledge of history, and substantive contributions to the text.

Massachusetts

Historical Introduction *to the* Massachusetts Colony

I n the struggle for religious uniformity that raged in England throughout much of the 17th century, a group of separatists from Scrooby in Yorkshire became weary of discrimination against them and sailed for Holland in 1608. (Separatists were Puritans who chose to separate from the Church of England rather than work within the church to reform it.) The Scrooby congregation found greater religious tolerance in Leiden and formed close ties with the Dutch community and Leiden University. However, their status as permanent aliens was troubling. Despite hard work, they failed to prosper, and they were uneasy about their children absorbing too much Dutch culture, regarding Sunday as a day for pleasure rather than worship, for example, or marrying Dutch youngsters. And because the treaty between Holland and Spain was about to expire and the resumption of war threatened, they feared being trapped if Spain invaded.

In July of 1620, after prolonged and sometimes disintegrating negotiations, a group of London merchants and the Leiden separatists organized a joint stock company to finance a colonizing expedition to the New World. The Pilgrims, as they were to be called, were supposed to farm, build houses, and fish, with the profits from their communal labors flowing back to the London merchants who had provided the financing.

The Pilgrims who embarked on this voyage would endure a series of frustrations and delays, a miserable transatlantic crossing in autumnal gales, uncertainties about their eventual destination, and a winter of starvation. After tearful farewells with those who remained in Leiden, they sailed for England on board the *Speedwell* on July 22. In Southampton they found the *Mayflower* already inhabited by many so-called "Strangers"—adventurers not sharing their religious val-

Overleaf: Boston Tea Party Ship

ues—who had been recruited by the English investors. After further delays and some disputes about the costs of provisioning, the assembled company of colonists set sail on the *Mayflower* and the *Speedwell* on August 5, but when the *Speedwell* began to leak seriously they had to put into Dartmouth for repairs. They set out again on August 23 and got well beyond Land's End when the *Speedwell's* fresh leaks convinced the master that she might sink. Both ships put back to Plymouth to face some tough decisions—abandoning the *Speedwell*, cutting the colonists' number by 20, and crowding 102 persons (35 Pilgrims and 67 other English men, women, and children) into the *Mayflower* for a third and final departure on September 6, 1620.

But the clock had been ticking as the summer sailing season passed, and a passage that might have been completed in five or six weeks took nearly ten. Francis Higginson wrote, "The wind blew mightily, the sea roared and the waves tossed us horridly . . . besides, it was fearful dark and the mariners made us afraid with their running here and there and loud crying one to another to pull at this and that rope."

Landfall

Although the Pilgrims thought they were coming to the vicinity of the Hudson River (then described as the northern fringe of Virginia), they actually sighted land much farther north, off Cape Cod, on November 9. They started to coast southward but wisely turned back when they "fell amongst dangerous shoals and roaring breakers"—the still notorious Pollock Rip off Monomoy at the elbow of the Cape. Yet there was dissension from Strangers who wanted to split off because they were not going to Virginia. They were more interested in acquiring land than "the advancement of the Christian Faith," a stated objective of the Pilgrims.

So on the voyage back north along the Cape the leaders began to discuss and draft the Mayflower Compact to regulate their new life ashore. It was designed to insure law and order, an agreement for the development of "such just and equal Laws, Ordinances, Acts, Constitutions, and Offices . . . as shall be thought most meet and convenient for the general Good of the Colony." Although the compact assured that authority would be held by a few men, its full implications would emerge more than a century and a half later in the assumption that government originates in the consent of those governed.

Anchored off what is now Provincetown on November 11, the Pilgrims were finally sheltered from the rigors of a difficult Atlantic crossing, which they saw as a deliverance, associating it symbolically with the Exodus from Egypt to the Promised Land. Yet their prospects were bleak. In the words of later longtime Plymouth governor William Bradford, "Being thus passed the vast ocean, and a sea of troubles before in their preparation . . . they had now no friends to welcome them nor inns to entertain or refresh their weatherbeaten bodies; no houses or much less towns to repair to, to seek for succour . . . For summer being done, all things stand upon them with a weatherbeaten face, and the whole country, full of woods and thickets, represented a wild and savage hue. If they looked behind them, there was the mighty ocean which they had passed and was now as a main bar and gulf to separate them from all the civil parts of the world."

Forty-one adult males signed the Mayflower Compact before going ashore to replenish wood and to begin the search for their plantation site. They explored the shores of Cape Cod Bay in their shallop, a small boat brought for that purpose, and stole some corn from an Indian cache—which led to later attacks. Finally, on the third discovery expedition, after many misadventures in the shallop, they reached a site with a large harbor, a hill for defense, fresh water, even some cleared fields. They returned to the ship, and the *Mayflower* set sail for Plymouth Bay on December 15. Three days later the men began further exploration ashore.

Foothold in the New World

On December 25 the Pilgrims started building a common house to store their goods ashore and later dwellings for each of nineteen families, but they were entering the grimmest months of their ordeal. Bradford called it the "starving time." Weakened by scurvy and other diseases during the long voyage, half of the group died during that first harsh winter. They had already buried four, including Bradford's wife, in future Provincetown and two more in Plymouth before Christmas. In January the "General Sickness" took eight more, seventeen in February, and thirteen in March. Among the eighteen couples, only four women survived. Worried about what the loss of their numbers might tell surrounding Indians, colonists took to burying their dead on Coles Hill under cover of darkness. And the crew of the *Mayflower* fared no better, losing nearly half its men before returning to England in April.

Then assistance from Indians revived the distressed colony. In March, first Samoset, an English-speaking Abenaki chief from Pemaquid in Maine, and then Squanto, the only surviving Patuxet from their abandoned settlement at Plymouth, arrived. Samoset and Squanto began delicate negotiations with Chief Massasoit of the Wampanoags—the Indian people who inhabited the region—which led to a treaty with the Pilgrims to maintain peace and provide mutual assistance if either

---

MASSACHUSETTS *Time Line*

1620	1626	1629	1630	1635
The *Mayflower* sails into Plymouth Harbor, December 16	Naumkeag (later Salem) founded	The Massachusetts Bay Company formed	The Puritans found Boston and ten other settlements	Roger Williams banished from Massachusetts Bay

---

Pilgrims or Wampanoags were unjustly attacked. This treaty enabled the Pilgrims to grow and harvest their crops without fear of Indian attacks, and Squanto also helped them plant corn and squash and showed them how to catch eels. After the first harvest in October, the Pilgrims held a feast for three days in appreciation of their good fortune, with Massasoit and ninety of his braves as guests.

The population in Plymouth rose steadily from 124 in 1624 to 300 in 1630 and 550 in 1637. When the Massachusetts Bay Company arrived in 1630, the Plymouth colonists gained a new market for their grain and livestock. Plymouth Colony formally united with Massachusetts Bay in 1691.

The Massachusetts Bay Company Arrives

In contrast to the Pilgrim adventure, which was beset by problems and near disasters at every stage, the Massachusetts Bay story seems tame. The company was far larger and more diffuse, having evolved from other ventures in the 1620s. It had better financing, both from wealthy Puritans and a larger group of London merchants, and control established through an agreement that vested all interest in Puritans who were actually going to America. The Mayflower Compact was an expedient to provide some regulation on land that had not been granted to the Pilgrims, while Puritan organizer John Winthrop had insisted on a court order ceding company control to the colonists before agreeing to lead the expedition. A single ship established Plymouth partly by accident, but the Puritans came in a fleet that landed in waves during two years. The Massachusetts Bay Company sent five ships to Naumkeag (Salem) with two or three hundred passengers in 1629. Then the central emigration in March of 1630 brought seven hundred more in ten ships following the *Arbella*, and six more ships arrived in the summer. That adds up to more than twelve hundred emigrants by the end of 1630. And the flow continued for another eleven years, by which time about 21,000 emigrants had left England for Massachusetts.

Although there were large differences in financing and scale between the two colonies, the motives for emigration were similar. Like the Pilgrims, John Winthrop and his followers felt beleaguered where they were. Charles I had dismissed Parliament in 1629 and ruled without it. Economic conditions in East Anglia, where

1637	1675–76	1691	1692	1704
Anne Hutchinson banished from Massachusetts Bay	King Philip's War	Massachusetts Bay and Plymouth combined into the royal colony of Massachusetts	Witchcraft trials in Salem	Indians and French attack Deerfield during Queen Anne's War

most of Winthrop's followers lived, were deteriorating, and Puritans had suffered increasing harassment under King Charles and Bishop Laud. They also shared a religious fervor to establish a righteous "City upon a Hill," to serve as a moral example, in the New World. In a mid-Atlantic sermon, Winthrop stressed two covenants, the first with God to purify a church rent by separatists, the second to establish a community based on "brotherly affection." Ashore in the next four years absolute control of that community gradually shifted from a small group of leaders to a broader constituency of male freemen who could vote, and when that status required church membership a limited theocracy was born. Close linkage between church and state would build that ideal city upon the hill, even though clergy were not allowed direct political power.

The group on the *Arbella* stopped briefly in Salem and continued to a site on the Charles River, which they named Boston. With more financial support than the Pilgrims, they arrived with tools, livestock, and other provisions. Their Puritan vision, both personal and communal, led them to follow a strict list of rules in daily conduct. In addition, they felt obliged to make others conform to their rules or be banished from the colony—a tenet that sowed seeds for the rapid expansion of New England.

Relations with the Mother Country

In England during the eleven years without a Parliament, grievances about taxation and the authority of the church hierarchy grew. When Charles I finally called the Short Parliament in April 1640 and dismissed it in three weeks, he was forced to reconvene it in November by a defeat at the hands of the Scots, who had rebelled against his imposition of a prayer book modeled on the English version. Religious discontent was evident as Thomas Hooker remarked, "God is packing up His gospel because nobody will buy His wares, nor come to His price." The opposition took control of the Long Parliament in 1640, which was not dissolved for twenty years. Two years later Charles I called his men to arms and civil war began. The king was executed in 1649, and England had a decade of Puritan rule under Oliver Cromwell until his death in 1658, which was followed by the restoration of Charles II in 1660.

MASSACHUSETTS *Time Line*

1734	**1756-63**	**1765**	**1768**	**1770**	**1773**
Preaching of Jonathan Edwards begins Great Awakening in New England	French and Indian War (Seven Years War)	Massachusetts convenes Stamp Act Congress in New York City	Massachusetts denounces Townshend Acts	Boston Massacre	Boston Tea Party

Through these thirty years of turmoil in England, the Massachusetts Bay Colony was largely neglected. It suffered from the loss of immigrants and financial support after 1640 but experienced little direct interference with its business affairs. Parliament did enact mercantile regulations in 1651, but they were seldom enforced. The crucial right to self government obtained by Winthrop found its practical forms in the establishment of elected town authorities, means for dividing land and providing deeds, and the first appearance of the cherished New England town meeting. In 1648 Congregational ministers did petition for a synod to provide some uniformity in doctrine and clearly rejected toleration of dissenters. Yet, although the church held wide influence in the conduct of daily life, each congregation managed its own affairs and only occasionally requested adjudication of local disputes by the General Court of the colony.

In this context of growing independence, the Restoration brought immediate shocks—reminders that England regarded Massachusetts Bay and other American colonies as subject to the will of the mother country. First was the Navigation Act of 1660, which in colonists' eyes unreasonably declared that goods could be brought to England from America only in English ships, with an English captain, and in addition three-quarters of the crew had to be English. The 1663 Staple Act ordered that all European goods headed for the colonies must be sent first to England. In addition, the 1673 Plantation Duty Act ordained that colonials pay duty on goods shipped from one colony to another.

Of course, these acts caused a great deal of friction between governors and merchants within the colonies. As a result the Crown sent Edward Randolph to Massachusetts in 1676 for the specific purpose of checking up on the colonists' adherence to the various acts. He reported that Massachusetts was disobeying just about everything England had demanded. Since trade was the major engine of economic activity in the colony, the grievances that would lead to revolution in the next century were already rankling.

King Philip's War

What seemed like a peaceful situation between the Indians and the English in the middle of the 17th century was deceptive. As Plymouth Colony expanded,

1774	**1775**	**1776**	**1780**	**1788**
England closes Boston Harbor with the Coercive, or Intolerable, Acts	Fighting at Lexington and Concord begins Revolutionary War	British evacuate Boston after siege by Continental Army	Commonwealth of Massachusetts constitution ratified	Massachusetts ratifies U.S. Constitution

the Wampanoags lost territory and tensions grew. Massasoit knew that he needed the support of Plymouth as an ally against the powerful Narragansetts to the west. Although the United Colonies' commissioners smoothed over crises, the Narragansetts and the other tribes continued to feud. When Massasoit's son, Metacomet (called King Philip), became sachem in 1662, he found that the white settlers were aggressively taking more land. In 1671, just half a century after the treaty with Massasoit had saved Plymouth from extinction, Metacomet was arrested on charges of plotting against the colony. Morale had deteriorated among his braves, and four years later some of them began harassing and looting settlers on the fringes of the colony. When they murdered a family in Swansea, King Philip's War erupted and spread throughout New England, eventually affecting Connecticut and Rhode Island as well as Massachusetts.

When King Philip got the Nipmucs involved, attacks reached the western and northern fringes of the colony in the Merrimack and Connecticut valleys. Northfield and Deerfield were abandoned, and Springfield was burned by attacking Indians. Alarmed that the Narragansetts might be getting involved, some of the Puritan

The GREAT AWAKENING

✲ Jonathan Edwards, a Congregational minister who had succeeded his grandfather as minister in the Connecticut River valley town of Northampton, Massachusetts, noticed a great increase in religious enthusiasm among the townspeople in 1735. Most of the colonies responded to waves of revivalism, especially between 1740 and 1742.

George Whitefield, one of the founders of Methodism, arrived from England in 1738 and proceeded to call the colonists to repent their sins and confess their faith in Jesus Christ. During a tour of Massachusetts in 1740, when Whitefield visited Ipswich, Salem, Newbury, Northampton, and Boston, huge crowds gathered, both in churches and in fields, to learn how they could be saved.

Edwards's sermons, like Whitefield's, were directed at raising emotions as well as ideas. His most famous sermon, delivered in 1741, "Sinners in the Hands of an Angry God," painted a picture of hell that was graphic to the senses. (Edwards, however, did not subscribe to the heresy that salvation could somehow be earned, adhering to the Puritan doctrine that it would come only to the "elect" through God's grace.)

Edwards' renown, though earned and genuine, was to prove ephemeral. In 1742 he insisted that those who took communion had to make a profession of faith. An uproar followed, eventually leading to his dismissal from the Northampton church in 1750. As the enthusiasm of parishioners waned, their focus returned to worldly interests, but one unintended aftereffect of the Great Awakening was greater toleration of diversity in religious beliefs.

governments organized an expedition to secure their neutrality but succeeded only in arousing their hatred. In mid-December the combined army of Massachusetts Bay, Plymouth, and Connecticut attacked the Narragansetts' winter fort in Rhode Island, killed hundreds of men, women, and children, and destroyed their food supply. More than seventy militiamen lost their lives in that Great Swamp Fight. In the winter of 1676, raids occurred in the heart of the Massachusetts Bay Colony, as far east as Medfield, Sudbury, and Weymouth. But by late spring the colonists, who outnumbered the Indians and had greater resources, began defeating their opponents in a series of successful raids. And in August a group of colonists and allied Indians led by Captain Benjamin Church tracked down King Philip in his home territory and killed him.

The war was over, but only at enormous cost. It had destroyed thirteen English settlements, while six others were partially burned. More than one thousand colonists and countless more Indians had been killed. Commerce had been halted and settlement of the frontiers pulled back. An aftermath of the war was hatred on both sides—of Indians, even those who had remained neutral, by the colonists, and of the white intruders who had taken their land and destroyed their people by the Indians. In that sense it was a cataclysmic confrontation with lasting and irreparable consequences. Relations between colonists and Indians never reached comity again.

The French and Indian War

France and England both wanted to control North America, and both sides were necessarily allied with Indian inhabitants of the disputed territories. The French and Indian War was perhaps the most important part of a larger conflict, the Seven Years War, a struggle for world empire. In North America the French wanted to connect their control of Canada with their colonies in Louisiana to prevent the westward expansion of British colonies in New England and the Middle Atlantic region. As a result the important battles occurred outside Massachusetts, especially in the Ohio valley and along the Champlain-Hudson waterway. Although the northern and western fringes of Massachusetts were frequently in danger, especially in the Connecticut River valley, the colony's main role was in providing experienced leaders and troops to fight battles elsewhere, and in helping to pay for a very expensive war.

Massachusetts leaders and troops were essential in opposing French incursions both before and during the war. Massachusetts militia had earned a reputation back in 1745, during King George's War, when William Pepperell led a New England contingent in a famously successful siege against the French fortress at Louisbourg on Cape Breton Island, to prevent harassment of New England shipping and fishing. In 1755 some five thousand Massachusetts men joined in Governor Shirley's unsuccessful campaigns against the French at Crown Point and Niagara in New York. In 1758 Massachusetts men were part of James Abercrombie's armada on Lake George to assault Fort Carillon at Ticonderoga, again unsuccessfully. And

Massachusetts men were part of Wolfe's victory at Quebec and Amherst's at Montreal in the following two years.

But the last war had been especially costly for England, raising its national debt from 75 to 140 million pounds, and only a small part of that expense had been borne by the colonies. Although Massachusetts' war debt had reached 300,000 pounds by 1758, legislatures in other major colonies like Pennsylvania and Virginia had at first refused to vote funds to support the war and were slow in providing men and supplies. Moreover, the contempt for provincial officers and soldiers frequently expressed by British commanders and officers soured relations and increased the unwillingness of the colonies to contribute men or money to the war effort. Because the English need was strong and the situation delicate, levying taxes on the colonials was held in abeyance during the war. After the Peace of Paris in 1763, it did not take long for that reluctance to disappear.

Revolutionary Rumblings

George Grenville became George III's chancellor of the exchequer in 1763 and quickly addressed the war debt by creating streams of colonial revenue. Throughout succeeding years, acts of Parliament and royal mandates continued to spawn

George Washington, later to command the Continental Army in the siege of Boston at the outset of the Revolution, learned about military tactics in two events that provoked the war in North America.

In May of 1754, at the age of twenty-two, he led a party of forty Virginians in an encounter with French troops from Fort Duquesne. During a fifteen-minute skirmish, the Virginians killed the French commander, Joseph Coulon de Villiers de Jumonville, and twelve others. Two months later Jumonville's half brother, leading a force of 600 French and about 100 Indians, attacked Washington and his main force of 400 in the temporary Fort Necessity he had constructed. Outnumbered and unable to respond effectively to fire from unseen enemies in the surrounding woods, Washington was forced to surrender.

In the following summer Washington became a guide to General Edward Braddock, commander-in-chief of all British forces in North America, in a campaign to take over Fort Duquesne, strategically located at the confluence of the Allegheny and Monongahela Rivers (modern Pittsburgh). However, a group of French and Indians ambushed them in the woods a short distance from the fort, mortally wounding Braddock and killing 900 of his 1,400 men.

Thus two defeats suffered at the outset of the French and Indian War—both the result of unconventional tactics in British eyes—contributed to the military education of the young Washington. During the Revolution, he would persist through many more defeats, as well as lack of money, supplies, and troops, to lead the Continental Army to ultimate victory.

resistance and sometimes rebellion among affected colonials, who were not especially committed to reducing the mother country's debt load. A decision to maintain ten thousand British troops in the colonies after the war to defend the frontiers against further French incursions seemed illogical to colonials, and it created greater need for their financial support. Knowing that customs enforcement had been lax, Grenville demanded that appointed customs collectors reside in America rather than leaning on deputies, and the Sugar Act of 1764 was designed specifically to plug loopholes in enforcement and provide legitimate revenue to support the troops, by taxing New England's lucrative trade with the West Indies. Merchants, shipowners, and others engaged in maritime trade protested, especially in Boston, where Sam Adams raised what was to become a mantra of rebellion—no taxation without representation.

> ✦ Another punch aimed directly at merchants in the home country was delivered by the Daughters of Liberty, a group of city women. They stopped buying goods from English merchants and made their own clothing and household items, refusing to patronize merchants who did not approve of their boycott. They boycotted tea with great zeal, instead serving "liberty tea" made from dried raspberry or currant leaves.

Another attempt to raise revenue in support of troops had wider scope. The 1765 Stamp Act mandated that duty was to be levied on business papers, licenses, newspapers, almanacs, printed sermons, even playing cards and dice. In Boston the Sons of Liberty, a group of shopkeepers, artisans, seamen, unskilled workers, and apprentices, took it upon themselves to quash this newly imposed tax by targeting highly placed officials responsible for collecting it. When they enlisted the help of Ebenezer Mackintosh, leader of a South End gang, mob action followed. First they ripped apart the home of Andrew Oliver, then secretary of the colony, who had not yet accepted an appointment as stamp distributor. When Thomas Hutchinson, the lieutenant governor, tried to intervene, they took revenge by destroying and looting his mansion. Others turned to political action.

Massachusetts convened the Stamp Act Congress, which met in New York in October 1765. The congress concluded that "no taxes ever have been, or can be constitutionally imposed on them [the colonies] but by their respective Legislatures." Nine colonies met together in the congress, and feelings ran high enough for them to proclaim this rebellious position. In January 1766 William Pitt, a member of Parliament sympathetic to the colonists, argued that if Americans gave in to this kind of taxation they would be like slaves, not Englishmen. He said that Parliament could use its power over the colonists in many ways, including the regulation of manufacturing and trade, "except that of taking their money out of their pockets without their consent." Parliament repealed the act but simultaneously passed the Declaratory Act, which affirmed its power over the colonies "in all cases whatsoever." It was soon busy creating even more offensive levies.

The Townshend Acts

In the spring of 1767, Charles Townshend, then chancellor of the exchequer, proposed taxes on lead, paint, paper, glass, silk, and tea coming into the colonies from England. Under the provisions of the Townshend Acts, this revenue would defray the cost of maintaining British troops in America. In protest, Sam Adams wrote the so-called Circular Letter of February 11, 1768, for the Massachusetts legislature, and it was sent to all the colonies. Lord Hillsborough, secretary of state for the colonies, demanded that Massachusetts rescind the Circular Letter, which it refused to do by a vote of 92 to 17, lionized as the "Glorious 92." When Hillsborough received that negative reply, he ordered Governor Bernard to dissolve the legislature and send troops into Boston. In response Boston merchants drew up agreements against importing English tea and other taxed goods. The agreements were voluntary and never totally effective, but they did succeed in cutting imports by half from 1768 to 1770.

Nevertheless, by 1770 the air was thick with resentment over these accumulating attempts to pay for troops and colonial administration by taxing the colonies. Friction between troops and citizens exploded on the evening of March 5, when an apprentice argued with a sentry in front of the customs house, leading the sentry to strike the apprentice with the butt of his musket. As the alarm was spread, other youths began to throw things at the sentry, and a crowd of several hundred gathered. When the sentry called for help, Captain Thomas Preston sent in six grenadiers and a corporal to protect him, but the mob continued to throw things at the soldiers. When a club bowled over one of the grenadiers he got up and fired a shot, apparently into the air, and more shots were fired into the mob by the soldiers. In the confrontation five citizens were killed. Although Governor Hutchinson promised that the perpetrators of the "Boston Massacre" would be punished, sentiment was running high for the removal of British troops. Hutchinson asked the commanding officer to depart, and within a week the troops had withdrawn from the city to Castle William in Boston Harbor.

On the day of the Boston Massacre, in London Parliament repealed all the provisions of the Townshend Acts but one—the tax on tea. Lord North, the new chief minister, wanted to impress on the colonies that Parliament still had the right to levy taxes on them. That insistence would come to haunt him three years later.

The Explosive Tea Act

That relatively quiet interim in the disputes between Massachusetts and its colonial governors, though not devoid of colonial suspicions and pamphlets that retailed the list of old grievances, let trade between England and the colony resume. That calm evaporated when Lord North urged Parliament to relieve an East India Company surplus and create a British monopoly in the Tea Act of 1773. Although the reduced tax from the Townshend Acts remained, the wholesale arrangements in the act assured that Americans would be able to purchase tea at reduced prices. Lord North apparently overlooked the accumulated annoyance that the former levies had created, as well as the stocks of smuggled Dutch tea that colonial merchants had acquired from other sources. When the *Dartmouth*, the first of the ships loaded with surplus tea, had come into port on November 27, soon to be followed by the *Eleanor* and *Beaver*, a confrontation in Boston seemed inevitable. It had been avoided in other colonial ports receiving the consignments—Charleston, Philadelphia, New York—by either sending the ships laden with tea back or putting it in storage. But the situation in Boston was more explosive because the consignees refused sending the tea back and Governor Hutchinson insisted that it be unloaded and marketed, against the will of the citizenry.

There was a deadline of twenty days to solve the impasse, filled with many complex negotiations. Sam Adams and other patriots, at one time numbering an estimated five thousand, met more than once in Old South Meeting House to determine what to do about the tea. As the last meeting broke up on the night of December 16, 1773, some were heard to say: "Boston Harbor a teapot tonight!" and "The Mohawks are come!" That referred to about sixty young men disguised as Indians who had converged with those leaving the meeting that night, heading for the three tea ships moored at Griffins Wharf. Some of them were sailors who knew exactly what to do, opening the hatches, hoisting out the tea chests, breaking them open, and throwing some forty-five tons' worth of tea into the harbor.

When the news reached England in January 1774, a year of turmoil began. By March Parliament had passed the first of four Coercive Acts—in the colonies they were to become known as the Intolerable Acts. Called the Boston Port Bill, it closed the port of Boston to all but shipments of food or fuel, effective June 1 until the East India Company was compensated for its losses. Three other Coercive Acts followed before the end of June. The Administration of Justice Act allowed officials who killed citizens while suppressing riots to be tried in England. A third act, perhaps the most important in the long term, amended the 1691 Massachusetts charter to give the governor power to select council members, appoint and remove judges and sheriffs—powers formerly enjoyed by the legislature— and limited town meetings to one a year to elect local officials. The fourth act gave the governor increased power to billet troops in colonial towns. If this quartet were not enough, Parliament also passed the Quebec Act in June, extending the borders of that Canadian province south and west to the Ohio and Mississippi Rivers, thereby forestalling westward expansion by the colonies.

The powder keg was ready, waiting for a match, but it wouldn't be lighted for another ten months. In the interim General Gage, now appointed governor, moved the capital to Salem in May and then moved it back to Boston in August. In September he fortified Boston Neck, controlling access to the city.

The Massachusetts Assembly responded. Before the governor dissolved it in June, it secretly selected delegates to the Continental Congress, and an unofficial Provincial Congress met in Salem in October and set aside 20,000 pounds to arm local militias. The Provincial Congress met again in Cambridge in February 1775 and in Concord in March. The rest of the story is engraved in Massachusetts and

American history and hardly need be repeated here. (See Boston, Lexington, and Concord sections, beginning on page 77.) The shots fired in Lexington and Concord on April 19, 1775, were the overdue legacy of the cost of the French and Indian War and of Parliament's effort to renew its control of Massachusetts, a colony that had managed most of its own affairs from the outset.

Birth of the Continental Army

In the series of armed encounters on April 19 perhaps as many as 4,000 American minutemen and militiamen were involved, with 49 killed and 46 wounded or missing. The British expedition of 1,800 suffered 273 casualties, including 73 men killed. In the first encounter, Captain John Parker lined up about 70 men on Lexington Green, in European style on open ground; but as colonials harassed the British column returning to Boston, they exacted their greatest toll fighting in the style of the French and Indian War, firing from the cover of trees and buildings along the way.

But the outbreak of armed conflict against a highly trained and disciplined army called for more than militia sorties. The committee of safety appointed by the Provincial Congress replaced the minutemen and militias with a unified army enlisted for eight months' service. Remembering the food and supplies that had been contributed to Boston after the port was closed, they also asked for help from other New England colonies. And looking ahead to wider conflict, the Provincial Congress asked the Continental Congress to take over the new army gathering around Boston.

Before that occurred, that army took offensive action in June by occupying Breed's Hill overlooking the Charles and Mystic Rivers. The British responded immediately with bombardment from ships and an amphibious assault. But before they drove a smaller American force off the hill, they would suffer more than 1,000 casualties among the 2,400 troops involved, while American casualties stood at just over 400. The Battle of Bunker Hill showed that the newly formed, inexperienced army could stand its ground.

Washington and the Siege of Boston

After Lexington, Concord, and Bunker Hill, newly commissioned general George Washington arrived in Cambridge on July 2 to take over the New England army. He had been appointed commander in chief by the Second Continental Congress in June, with Charles Lee, a former British officer, as second in command. Washington had inherited four separate armies from Massachusetts, Connecticut, Rhode Island, and New Hampshire, and he was appalled at the lack of discipline and order within the collected ranks. Apart from the need for training, the men also lacked adequate supplies, ammunition, and artillery to effectively attack regular British troops. Yet Charles Lee advised Washington, "To you they look for decision, by your conduct they are to be inspired by decision. In fact, your situation is such that the salvation of the whole depends on your striking, at certain crises, vigorous strokes, without previously communicating your intention." Washington first addressed the need for training and discipline.

The Continental Congress had faith in Washington's integrity and accepted his initiatives even when it did not order them. It had refused to create an American navy in the spring of 1775, but Washington developed a fleet of six ships to harass British supply ships coming to Boston during the siege. He also clamped down on Tories, ordering the seizure of all officers of the Crown who were "acting as enemies of their country." He encouraged Governor Trumbull of Connecticut in the same vein: "Why should persons who are preying upon the vitals of their country be suffered to stalk at large, whilst we know they will do us every mischief in their power?" By the end of 1775 Washington had persuaded the four New England colonies to commit to achieving independence.

Yet as the four armies merged into one and tightened the noose around Boston, Washington was frustrated by his inability to attack the city directly. Getting through the heavily fortified neck was risky, and attacking across the shallow marshland of Back Bay even riskier. And even if artillery had been available, prolonged destructive bombardment of New England's premier city was not a viable option. What "vigorous stroke" could he take to bring the impasse to an end?

The Reverend William Emerson from Concord visited the encampment and wrote, "There is great overturning in camp as to order and regularity. New lords, new laws . . . Orders from his Excellence are read to the respective regiments every morning after prayers. The strictest government is taking place, and great distinction is made between officers and soldiers. Everyone is made to know his place and keep in it, or be tied up and receive not 10, but thirty or forty lashes according to his crime. Thousands are at work every day from four till eleven o'clock in the morning. It is surprising how much work has been done."

The answer came in the successful completion of an extraordinary mission undertaken by Colonel Henry Knox, a former Boston bookseller. In November he had led an expedition to retrieve the guns of Fort Ticonderoga, captured by Ethan Allen and Benedict Arnold in May. Arriving at the fort in early December, Knox faced a 300-mile journey dragging heavy artillery across thin ice, through deep snow and mud, across mountains, and through unsettled territory, much of it roadless. When he arrived in Boston with fifty-eight mortars and cannon in late February, a new strategy emerged. The army would occupy the hills of Dorchester Heights and place cannon there, within range of Boston's defenses and harbor. With utmost care for secrecy, one of the most brilliant plans of the Revolution required moving the cannon and erecting prefabricated defenses on the frozen ground of Dorchester Heights in a single night, March 4. It worked, and British commander William Howe, who had succeeded Gage, found his fortified town and the British fleet so vulnerable that he immediately set plans for an attack in motion, but a winter gale thwarted him. He chose the only alternative available, a mass evacuation of soldiers and Loyalists, which finally set sail on March 17. The siege of Boston was over, and a tacit agreement that Howe would not burn the town if his forces were not attacked during the evacuation saved Boston. For eleven months Massachusetts had been the center of conflict between England and the colonists. Now the war moved south to Long Island and New York City.

Regions *to* Explore

SOUTHERN MASSACHUSETTS

Southern Massachusetts offered a series of fine natural harbors on Buzzards Bay to settlers who wanted to engage in fishing—Wareham, Marion, and Mattapoisett, Fairhaven/New Bedford, South Dartmouth, and Westport. Among them Fairhaven/New Bedford became a major commercial port as whaling developed from a local enterprise into a worldwide industry. Now many of those harbors are chock-full of sailing yachts and the land around them with elegant summer homes and estates. The area as a whole contains industrial cities like New Bedford and Fall River, which reached their peak as manufacturing centers in the late 19th century and fell into decline during the 20th. But there are still corners that remain almost untouched by time or development, like the pastoral area south of the cities between the Rhode Island border and South Dartmouth.

NEW BEDFORD

Less than fifteen miles west of where the arm of Cape Cod is attached to the shoulder of the mainland, the Acushnet River flows into Buzzards Bay. Eighteen years before the Pilgrims landed on the opposite side of the Cape in Plymouth, Bartholomew Gosnold sailed the *Concord* along this shore and landed near the mouth of the Acushnet. Although he found a good supply of cod, he didn't stay long.

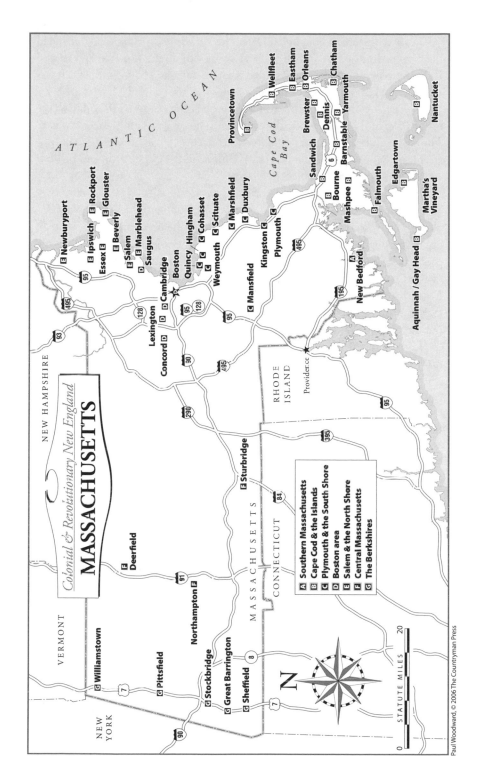

MASSACHUSETTS

Colonial & Revolutionary New England

A Southern Massachusetts
B Cape Cod & the Islands
C Plymouth & the South Shore
D Boston area
E Salem & the North Shore
F Central Massachusetts
G The Berkshires

ATLANTIC OCEAN

Cape Cod Bay

NEW HAMPSHIRE

VERMONT

NEW YORK

MASSACHUSETTS

CONNECTICUT

RHODE ISLAND

Provincetown
B Wellfleet
B Eastham
B Orleans
B Chatham
B Nantucket
B Brewster
B Dennis
B Yarmouth
B Barnstable
Sandwich
B Bourne
B Mashpee
B Falmouth
B Edgartown
Martha's Vineyard
B Aquinnah / Gay Head

E Newburyport
E Ipswich
E Rockport
E Glouster
E Essex
E Beverly
E Marblehead
E Salem
Saugus
D Cambridge
D Boston
D Quincy
C Hingham
C Cohasset
C Scituate
C Marshfield
C Duxbury
C Weymouth
C Kingston
C Plymouth
A New Bedford

Lexington **D**
Concord **D**
C Mansfield

Providence

F Sturbridge

F Deerfield

Northampton **F**

G Williamstown
G Pittsfield
G Stockbridge
G Great Barrington
G Sheffield

95
495
93
128
128
95
128
90
495
290
91
7
8
84
395
195
495
6
95

N

STATUTE MILES
0   20

Paul Woodward, © 2006 The Countryman Press

In 1652 the settlers bought land from the Wampanoag Indians that included the New Bedford area, originally called Dartmouth. In the 1740s Joseph Russell III founded Bedford Village and started what became the whaling industry. It was originally an inshore fishery using small sloops that towed whales into beaches for "trying out"—extracting the oil from the blubber. But before the Revolution the installation of try pots on board vessels led to larger ships and longer voyages. Among the chief whaling ports, Nantucket concentrated on the sperm whale fishery in southern waters, while Boston, Wellfleet on the Cape, and New Bedford sought the right whale in northern waters.

Bedford Village was burned in a British naval raid during the Revolutionary War. But in the following century New Bedford became the center of New England whaling and prospered with that industry as the need for oil grew with an expanding population. A sign of that prosperity in the older sections of town is the profusion of buildings that were designed as banks. Although petroleum had been discovered in Pennsylvania in 1859, the whale fishery remained economically viable. It wasn't until as late as 1871, when thirty-three New Bedford whaling ships became locked in Arctic ice, that the end appeared inevitable. The ships' crews survived, but the whaling industry suffered a real setback that hastened its demise.

Dying industries have a way of ravaging town after town as sources of wealth move elsewhere. Some communities prove resilient, like New Bedford. You could drive through town forty years ago without seeing much but decaying buildings, but now the core historic district has been beautifully rejuvenated.

When the British burned Bedford Village in 1778, many of its colonial buildings were destroyed. Only the Seth Russell House (1765) on Union and North Water Streets survives. The town was rebuilt starting in 1787, and the walking tour of the Waterfront Historic District will take you by a number of buildings from the early Federal era. They include the Tallman Warehouse (ca.1790), the Bryant-Washburn Building (ca. 1790), the Mariner's Home (ca. 1790 and still in operation for visiting sailors), the Benjamin Taber Building (1792), Captain Cornelius Howland's Store (ca.1792), and the Caleb Spooner House (1806). You can get a map and description of buildings for this walking tour at the visitor center of the New Bedford Whaling National Historical Park.

HISTORICAL SITES *and* MUSEUMS

The best place to start is the visitor center of the **New Bedford Whaling National Historical Park** (508-996-4095), 33 William St. Open daily. Established in 1996, the park covers 34 acres spread over 13 city blocks and includes the visitor center, the New Bedford Whaling Museum, the Seamen's Bethel, the schooner *Ernestina*, and the Rotch-Jones-Duff House and Garden Museum.

The **New Bedford Whaling Museum** (508-997-0046), 18 Johnny Cake Hill. Open daily. New Bedford, once the center of America's whaling industry, now has the world's most comprehensive whaling museum. The centerpiece of the National Historical Park, this expanded museum covers every aspect of the whaling industry, including its history and practices, with maps, books and logbooks, documents, paintings, and prints from around the world, photographic images, and artifacts of all kinds related to whaling. Here you will find the largest scrimshaw collection in the world, as well as the largest whaling-ship model, the 89-foot-long *Lagoda*. You can't miss the three whale skeletons and a wealth of information about blue, humpback, and sperm whales. Navigational instruments and figureheads are also featured in the museum's galleries.

In 2001 the museum acquired the Kendall Whaling Museum of Sharon, Massachusetts, with its stunning collections of whaling artifacts, art, and research materials. Now the Kendall Institute, located in a spacious former bank building on Purchase Street, houses 23,000 books and pamphlets on whaling, the world's largest collection of logbooks and journals, and 160,000 images in its photo archives. Home of the Whaling History Symposium since 1975, the Kendall Institute also sponsors the Scrimshaw Collectors' Weekend and maintains the archives of the Herman Melville Society and the New Bedford Port Society.

LODGING

CAPTAIN HASKELL'S OCTAGON HOUSE BED & BREAKFAST
347 Union St.,
New Bedford, MA 02740
508-999-3933; theoctagonhouse.com
This 1848 house, built by John Venal for a master of New Bedford's whaler *Mercury,* has a conservatory and a cupola.

DAVENPORT HOUSE BED & BREAKFAST
124 Cottage St.,
New Bedford, MA 02740
508-999-1177;
www.bbonline.com/ma/davenport/
This 1912 home is one of the few examples of neo-Jacobean architecture in New Bedford.

MELVILLE HOUSE BED & BREAKFAST
100 Madison St.,
New Bedford, MA 02740
508-990-1566; www.melvillehouse.net
During the 1860s Herman Melville visited his sister's home here. This 1855 Italianate house was built by a sea merchant for his daughter.

THE ORCHARD STREET MANOR
139 Orchard St.,
New Bedford, MA 02740; 508-984-3475;
www.the-orchard-street-manor.com
Whaling captain Benjamin Clark built this handsome home in 1845; features Pairpoint chandeliers and leaded glass windows.

RESTAURANTS

THE CANDLEWORKS
72 N. Water St., New Bedford, MA
02740; 508-997-1294
Italian and American cuisine in a historic 1810 Rodman Candleworks building.

EVENTS

June: Whaling Festival; 508-993-2517
July: Summerfest and Blessing of the Fleet; 508-999-5231

INFORMATION

SOUTHWESTERN MASSACHUSETTS CONVENTION AND VISITORS BUREAU
70 N. Second St.,
P.O. Box 976, New Bedford, MA 02741
800-288-5253, 508-997-1250;
www.bristol-county.org

CITY OF NEW BEDFORD OFFICE OF TOURISM AND MARKETING
www.ci.new-bedford.ma.us/
DestinationNewBedford.htm

WATERFRONT VISITOR CENTER
Wharfinger Building,
52 Fisherman's Wharf, Old City Pier #3,
New Bedford, MA 02740
800-508-5353, 508-979-1745

**NEW BEDFORD WHALING NATIONAL
HISTORICAL PARK VISITOR CENTER**
33 William Street,
New Bedford, MA 02740
508-996-4095; www.nps.gov/nebe

CAPE COD AND THE ISLANDS

When Bartholomew Gosnold first landed on Cape Cod in 1602 and was duly impressed with the plenitude of cod in the surrounding waters, it would have been difficult for him to imagine the role this big curved glacial moraine would play in New England history. Its harbors would attract many early settlers and produce a breed of hardy seafarers who hunted whales in all the world's oceans. In later centuries, blessed with the most beautiful beaches in New England and an equable climate, it would become a magnet for vacationers and summer residents. Offshore to the south, Martha's Vineyard and Nantucket, part of the same glacial moraine, developed the same seafaring traditions and, like most islands, developed their own distinctive cultures.

The Cape was the stepping-off point in the very earliest European settlement of Massachusetts. On November 11, 1620, the *Mayflower* made landfall at the tip of the Cape and anchored in what is now Provincetown Harbor, then sent expeditions out for about five weeks along the Cape and around the bay before its passengers decided to settle in Plymouth. That colony opened a trading post at Aptucxet (now in Bourne), at the base of the Cape, in 1627 for barter with Indians and Dutch traders from New Amsterdam (New York). The Council for New England annexed Cape Cod to Plymouth in 1630, and four towns were established: Sandwich, Yarmouth, Barnstable, and Eastham. During the 1630s and 1640s many Plymouth colonists moved onto the Cape. By 1644 Governor William Bradford of Plymouth announced that he felt lonely, as if children had left their mother.

You can circle the Cape on a counterclockwise route that heads outward along the ocean-side perimeter (Nantucket Sound and the Atlantic) and returns along Cape Cod Bay. On the bay side, MA 6A between Orleans and Sandwich takes you by many colonial sites, while US 6, the mid-Cape highway, simply zooms around them. But the distances are small, and you can also choose to enjoy the smaller roads by crisscrossing the mid-Cape highway from ocean to bay and back.

It's easy to travel from the Cape out to Martha's Vineyard and Nantucket. Ferries leave from Wood's Hole, Hyannis, and Falmouth (summer only), but in season you need to plan ahead and book tickets. Taking your car is nice but is not encouraged on the Vineyard and actively discouraged on Nantucket. On both islands, rental bikes will take you anywhere too far to walk.

BOURNE

Bourne is the first town that travelers encounter upon crossing the Cape Cod Canal from the "mainland." The canal, opened in 1914, linked two tidal rivers to enable coastal maritime traffic to avoid the long, often hazardous journey around the Cape—a dream held early on by Myles Standish.

HISTORICAL SITES and MUSEUMS

The trading post built in 1627 by the Pilgrims from Plymouth Plantation has been called the "cradle of American commerce." The **Aptucxet Trading Post Museum** (508-759-9487; www.bournehistoricalsoc.org), 24 Aptucxet Rd., is a replica built on the original foundation. Open May–Columbus Day. The Pilgrims needed a place to trade with the Indians from Cape Cod and with the Dutch from New Amsterdam. The replica of the original building contains 17th-century furnishings, Indian artifacts, and pieces used during colonial times.

An interpreter has samples of the items used in trading, including beaver and otter skins, as well as wampum, which was used as money and was also important for ceremonies. Wampum was also given as a special gift and not considered to be jewelry.

From the Dutch traders, Pilgrims received dry goods, sugar, candles, ceramics, pots, lead spoons, dried peas, and molasses. Clothing needed included shifts, which women wore all year long, bloomers, pantaloons, petticoats, and wool bodices. The grounds of the trading post include a windmill and an herb garden.

> Wampum beads were made from quahog shells; the holes were made with a small bone dipped in sand and spun. Beads made from the purple part of the shell were worth twice those made from the white part. A fathom (240 beads) was used as a method of measurement in trade. Native Americans might spend a year making a fathom.

A saltworks was one of the main moneymakers. The Sears family had huge evaporation tanks. The heat of the sun evaporated the seawater, leaving crystalline salt.

RESTAURANTS

LOBSTER TRAP
290 Shore Rd., Bourne, MA 02532;
508-759-3992
The restaurant overlooks the water, is decorated in a nautical theme, and serves all sorts of seafood, of course.

SAGAMORE INN
1131 MA 6A, Sagamore, MA 02561;
508-888-9707
The restaurant looks like "old Cape Cod" and there's an anchor in front. Seafood is on the menu.

FALMOUTH

Falmouth remains one of our favorite towns on the Cape. It is loaded with history and has managed to keep its colonial architecture intact in the midst of later development, especially in the center and along the shore. And it's a great base for exploring the Cape, with a wonderful selection of B&Bs, many of them in former captains' houses.

Suckanesset, as it was then known, became home to the Cape's first European settlers, who arrived in 1660 and bought land from the Indians. Jonathan Hatch, Isaac Robinson, and 11 others left Plymouth Colony because of its strict church-state decrees. They established religious tolerance for those who had been persecuted in other parts of Massachusetts.

Suckanesset means "place where the black wampum is found." By 1694 the name was changed to Falmouth to honor Bartholomew Gosnold, who had arrived here in 1602 from Falmouth, England.

The first meetinghouse was built in 1670, adjacent to what is now the Old Burying Ground. A memorial stone there commemorates Gosnold's 1602 voyage. A new meetinghouse was built in 1756, and it had a bell tower with an iron bell, cast by Paul Revere, installed in 1796. By 1800 the meetinghouse became the First Congregational Church and was moved to its present site on the village green.

HISTORICAL SITES *and* MUSEUMS

The **Falmouth Historical Society Museum** (508-548-4857; www.falmouth historicalsociety.org), Palmer Ave., owns and operates a 2-acre complex on the town green. Open June–Sep. The **Julia Wood House** was built in 1790 by Dr. Francis Wicks. It has one of the few "widow's walks" in town. The house contains pieces from Falmouth's early history, period furnishings, paintings, and china.

The **Conant House,** Palmer Ave., dates from 1770 and has a marvelous collection on the development of coastal trade, shipbuilding, and whaling. It explains how young boys often went to sea on long voyages and sometimes came back as captains. One room is full of mementos from Falmouth families involved in seafaring.

The property also has a colonial flower garden, an herb garden, and a memorial garden. Some of the original boxwood plants in the garden were planted in the late 1790s.

The **Old Burying Ground,** just off Mill Rd., is one of the most remarkable on the Cape, so secluded that it's hard to find. That isolation gives it a special charm as a place unaffected by later development. As you stroll through you can pick out names on tombstones of those you may have heard about, like Jonathan Hatch, one of the founders of the town. You'll also see a memorial to Falmouth mariners celebrating the 1602 voyage of Bartholomew Gosnold.

During the War of 1812 the British frigate *Nimrod* harassed a number of ports in Buzzards Bay and Vineyard Sound. On January 14, 1814, she bombarded Falmouth from a mile offshore, some of her cannonballs reaching Main Street. In fact, some of the balls remain in the Nimrod Restaurant and the Elm Arch Inn. Six months later the *Nimrod* trapped 17 Falmouth ships in Wareham Harbor, destroyed them, and ransacked the town. The next day she ran aground on a reef between New Bedford and Quick's Hole in the Elizabeth Islands. The crew tossed some of her cannons overboard to lighten the vessel and get off the reef, creating a legend and mystery that survived in local lore, enticing divers in the 20th century. Henry Kendall, an MIT scientist and Nobel Prize winner in physics, found the cannons after a careful search of Buzzards Bay, recovering them for the Kendall Whaling Museum, now merged with the New Bedford Whaling Museum. One was donated to the Falmouth Historical Society, and two others to Wareham and Stonington, Connecticut, other sites of the *Nimrod's* depredations.

LODGING

CAPTAIN TOM LAWRENCE HOUSE
BED & BREAKFAST
75 Locust St., Falmouth, MA 02540
800-266-8139, 508-548-9178;
www.captaintomlawrence.com
Tom Lawrence left home at 17 and sailed with his wife and daughters until 1862, when he built this house with a circular stairway and high ceilings.

CHAPAQUOIT INN
BED & BREAKFAST
495 MA 28A,
West Falmouth, MA 02574
800-842-8994, 508-540-7232;
www.chapoquoit.com
The house dates from 1739 and was one of the first homesteads in Falmouth. Original owner Lydia Dinningham apparently was the last local woman to give up wearing her Quaker bonnet.

COONAMESSETT INN
Jones Rd. and Gifford St.,
Falmouth, MA 02540
888-281-6246, 508-548-2300;
www.capecod.com/coonamessett
The inn dates from 1796 and has fireplaces built from "ballast brick" carried on schooners. A popular full-service restaurant offers contemporary regional cuisine.

ELM ARCH INN
Elm Arch Way, Falmouth, MA 02540
508-548-0133; www.elmarchinn.com
The inn was built in 1810 for whaling cap-
tain Silas Jones, and was bombarded by the British frigate *Nimrod* during the War of 1812.

INN AT ONE MAIN
BED & BREAKFAST
1 Main St., Falmouth, MA 02540
888-281-6246, 508-540-7469;
www.innatonemain.com
This house dates from 1892, when it was built for Amelia Lawrence and her husband, a local hardware merchant.

INN AT WEST FALMOUTH
BED & BREAKFAST
66 Frazar Rd., West Falmouth, MA 02574; 508-540-7696;
www.innatwestfalmouth.com
This attractive 1898 cedar-shake mansion features a widow's walk and wraparound porch.

INN ON THE SOUND
BED & BREAKFAST
313 Grand Ave., Falmouth, MA 02540
800-564-9668, 508-457-9666;
www.innonthesound.com
The 1875 inn is located on a bluff overlooking the beach and Vineyard Sound.

MOSTLY HALL BED & BREAKFAST
27 Main St.,Falmouth, MA 02540
800-682-0565, 508-548-3786;
www.mostlyhall.com
The house has a "widow's walk room" at the top. It was built in 1849 by Captain Albert Nye as a wedding gift for his bride.

RESTAURANTS

LA CUCINA SUL MARE
237 Main St., Falmouth, MA 02540
508-548-5600;
www.lacucinasulmare.com
An attractive eatery with murals and a
lengthy menu of Italian specialties.

THE NIMROD RESTAURANT
100 Dillingham Ave.,
Falmouth, MA 02540
508-540-4132; www.thenimrod.com
The Nimrod was once two homes: the
smaller, dating from the 17th century, was
on a site by the ocean, and was struck by
cannon fire from the British frigate *Nimrod*
in 1814; the larger was built in the 18th
century. The cuisine is memorable, often
accompanied by music.

THE QUARTERDECK
164 Main St.,
Falmouth, MA 02540;
508-548-9900
Lobster and other seafood specialties.

THE REGATTA OF COTUIT
4613 MA 28, Cotuit, MA 02635
508-428-5715; regattaofcotuit.com
Not far away from Falmouth is this lovely
1790 Federal mansion, once a stagecoach
stop and now its historic rooms welcome
dinner guests. Seasonal menus feature
New England, Asian, and European dishes.

EVENTS

July 4: Blessing of the Fleet
December: Christmas by the Sea;
508-548-4709

MASHPEE

Mashpee means "Land of the Great Cove." Descendants of the Mashpee Indians
still live in the area, and some of them gather cranberries in the local bogs. The
center of town is off MA 28 on MA 130, away from the heavy traffic.

Mashpee Indians, belonging to the Wampanoag federation, had lived here
long before the settlers arrived. In 1620 the Mashpee Wampanoag tribe welcomed
the Pilgrims to the New World in the spirit of peace and taught them how to survive the first winter. Richard Bourne appealed to the Massachusetts legislature on
their behalf, and in 1682 they received a land grant. Yet in 1752 the Mashpee tribe
sent a petition to the Massachusetts General Court seeking relief because nonna-
tive people were encroaching on their land.

HISTORICAL SITES *and* MUSEUMS
The **Mashpee Wampanoag Indian Museum** (508-477-1536), located on MA
130, displays traditional tribal articles and traces the tribe's history during the colonial era.

EVENTS

July: Annual Mashpee powwow. The local
tribe celebrates its heritage in full Indian
regalia at the tribal grounds at 483 Great
Neck Rd., with dances, handicrafts,
demonstrations, and refreshments.
508-477-0208

CHATHAM

On the exposed elbow of the Cape, Chatham is surrounded on three sides by the sea, with Nantucket Sound to the south, the Atlantic to the east beyond a barrier island, and Pleasant Bay to the north. Long, ever-shifting Monomoy Island extends southward from the elbow, separating the sound from the ocean. Once busy with shipbuilding, whaling, saltworks, and shoemaking, residents now support themselves largely with fishing and tourism. The town has retained many lovely colonial homes and traditional Cape Cod beach homes with exteriors of weathered cedar shingles.

South of Monomoy, Pollock Rip Passage, tricky with riptides and shoals, is the shortest route into Nantucket Sound from the east. These treacherous and shifting shoals played a role in determining the history of our country, forcing the *Mayflower* to turn back northward, abandoning its original destination near the mouth of the Hudson.

The shifting sands of the region make these feared shoals difficult to chart, and they have taken a deadly toll in wrecks and lives through four centuries. As an illustration, in October 1770 a number of ships foundered during a violent storm: A sloop returning from a whaling trip was wrecked near Eastham, another at Race Point, and a whaling schooner foundered off Chatham.

> Chatham and its neighboring town, Harwich, have had a running rivalry for years. One tall tale about a Harwich ship that foundered says the crew paddled toward shore on planks and hatch covers. As they got near land, one of them asked the crowd on shore where they were. When someone yelled "Chatham," the sailors turned around and headed back out to sea.

HISTORICAL SITES *and* MUSEUMS

The **Old Atwood House** (508-945-2493), 347 Stage Harbor Rd., is the home of the Chatham Historical Society. The 1752 house was built for Joseph C. Atwood, a sea captain. It stayed in the Atwood family for at least 175 years and contains a collection of items from the Chatham Light, as well as antique household pieces.

LODGING

THE CAPTAIN'S HOUSE INN
369-377 Old Harbor Rd.,
Chatham, MA 02633
800-315-0728, 508-945-0127;
www.captainshouseinn.com
Captain Hiram Harding built this home in 1839 for his bride.

THE CHATHAM BARS INN
Shore Rd., Chatham, MA 02633
800-527-4884, 508-945-0096;
www.chathambarsinn.com
The resort is on a hill overlooking a beautiful beach.

CHATHAM WAYSIDE INN
512 Main St., Chatham, MA 02633
800-391-5734, 508-945-6660;
www.waysideinn.com
Renovated in the mid-1990s, this 1860 inn
is right on the main street.

THE CRANBERRY INN
359 Main St.,
Chatham, MA 02633
800-332-4667, 508-945-9232;
www.cranberryinn.com
The inn dates from the 1830s. Bedrooms
offer four-poster, canopy, and antique
brass beds; several also have fireplaces.

THE QUEEN ANNE INN
70 Queen Anne Rd.,
Chatham, MA 02633
800-545-5667, 508-945-0394;
www.queenanneinn.com
The 1840 inn has a view of Oyster Pond
Bay. Guests are offered a complimentary
cruise around the harbor and the use of
bicycles.

**WEQUASSETT INN RESORT
AND GOLF COURSE**
2173 MA 28, Chatham, MA 02633
800-225-7125, 508-432-5400;
www.wequassett.com
Set in landscaped grounds are 22 buildings,
including historic houses from other sites.

RESTAURANTS

THE CAPTAIN'S HOUSE INN
369-377 Old Harbor Rd.,
Chatham, MA 02633
800-315-0728, 508-945-0127;
www.captainshouseinn.com

The inn serves afternoon tea every day,
which includes both sweets and savories in
the English manner.

CHATHAM BARS
Shore Rd., Chatham, MA 02633
800-527-4884, 508-945-0096;
www.chathambarsinn.com
This inn offers several restaurants,
including a tavern.

CHATHAM WAYSIDE INN
512 Main St., Chatham, MA 02633
800-391-5734, 508-945-6660;
www.waysideinn.com
The restaurant is open for all meals.

IMPUDENT OYSTER
15 Chatham Bars Ave.,
Chatham, MA 02633
508-945-3545
The building has a peaked ceiling with
exposed beams and hanging greenery;
order daily specials or from the menu.

TWENTY-EIGHT ATLANTIC
Wequassett Inn, 2173 MA 28,
Chatham, MA 02633
800-225-7125, 508-432-5400;
www.wequassett.com
The restaurant has a water view and the
menu is both American and Continental.

EVENTS

July: Independence Day Parade
508-945-5199
October: Seafest; 508-945-5199

ORLEANS

Orleans is situated conveniently between the quieter coves of Cape Cod Bay and
the exposed beaches of the Atlantic. Surfers flock to some of the latter, like Nauset Beach, which is known for its rollers when conditions are right. Skaket Beach
on the bay side is a favorite of those who just want to enjoy a day at the beach.

Bartholomew Gosnold found Nauset Beach—one of the finest on the Cape—
in 1602, and Champlain reached it in 1605. But like the whole outer arm of the
Cape, it is also dangerous, the site of many shipwrecks. One of the first on record
occurred there in 1626 when the *Sparrow Hawk* ran aground.

HISTORICAL SITES *and* MUSEUMS

The **Jonathan Young Windmill** (508-240-3700), Town Cove Park, is open from late June through early September. The gristmill dates from 1720. Exhibits inside detail the milling process that was so essential to colonial life.

LODGING

SHIP'S KNEES INN
186 Beach Rd., P.O. Box 756,
East Orleans, MA 02643
888-744-7756, 508-255-1312;
www.shipskneesinn.com
An interesting place nearby to stay the night is this former home of a sea captain. A "ship's knee" is a piece of wood cut that braces deck beams to the frames, preferably cut from sections of trees with curved grains.

RESTAURANTS

ACADEMY OCEAN GRILLE
2 Academy Place, Orleans, MA 02653
508 240-1585
The building is historic and the menu is classic French.

THE BARLEY NECK INN
5 Beach Rd., Orleans, MA 02653
508-255-2364
The 1857 captain's house offers contemporary French cuisine with an Asian touch.

CAPTAIN LINNELL HOUSE
137 Skaket Beach Rd.,
Orleans, MA 02653; 508-255-3400
This handsome 1850 sea captain's

mansion is enhanced by gardens. The cuisine is Continental.

THE LOBSTER CLAW
MA 6A, Orleans, MA 02653
508-255-1800
The restaurant is family owned and seafood is the prime focus of the menu.

THE JAILHOUSE TAVERN
28 West Rd.,
Orleans, MA 02653
508-255-5245
In the 1800s this was a jail, now it's a tavern with a flair. The atmosphere is casual and the food varied.

EVENTS

Fall for Orleans; 508-255-1386

INFORMATION

ORLEANS CHAMBER OF COMMERCE
44 Main St., P.O. Box 153,
Orleans, MA 02653
800-865-1386, 508-255-1386;
www.capecod-orleans.com

EASTHAM

With our mouths watering for one of the best lobster rolls on the Cape in Eastham, we nevertheless head for the **Cape Cod National Seashore Salt Pond Visitor Center** (508-255-3421) to earn our special lunch. Take a look at the schedule for the day or week and plan on attending some of the programs in the evening as well. The center has three self-guiding trails: Nauset Marsh Trail, which circles the marsh and is one mile long; Buttonbush Trail, which is a quarter-mile long with a guide rope for the blind and text in braille; and the Fort Hill Trail, which passes the mansard-roof home built there by whale ship captain Edward Penniman and leads to the Red Maple Swamp.

The *Mayflower* Pilgrims met their first Indians in Eastham; a marker on Samoset Road describes the attack on Myles Standish's scouting group. These Indians were not friendly because earlier some of their people had been captured and taken to Spain. Squanto was one of them, but he managed to get to England and then back home, where he became very helpful to the Pilgrims.

The **Old Windmill**, on US 6, is the oldest working windmill on the Cape, built in 1793. It was actually built in Plymouth, then moved to Truro, and finally to Eastham. You can see the old handmade machinery—wooden gears, a 7-foot peg wheel, and a full set of sails. Some Pilgrims from the *Mayflower* were buried in **Old Cove Cemetery** on US 6.

LODGING

WHALEWALK INN
220 Bridge Rd., Eastham, MA 02642
508-255-0617; www.whalewalk.com
A whaling master built this home in the 1830s. The property now includes the main inn, a barn, a guest cottage, and a saltbox cottage.

RESTAURANTS

EASTHAM LOBSTER POOL
4380 US 6, North Eastham, MA 02651
508-255-9706

For years we have always stopped for a lobster roll when anywhere close. Other seafood is available.

EVENTS

September: Windmill Weekend
508-240-5900

INFORMATION

EASTHAM TOURIST INFORMATION
US 6 at Governor Prence Rd.,
Eastham, MA 02642 508-255-3444;
www.easthamchamber.com

WELLFLEET

Cape Cod National Seashore maintains its park headquarters in South Wellfleet on Marconi Site Road. Did you know that the very first wireless message was sent to Europe from near here in 1903? An interpretive shelter and a bust of Marconi mark the site.

The Atlantic White Cedar Swamp Trail begins at the headquarters and winds through thick bushes and tall cedars before entering the swamp, a remnant of glaciation. Part of the trail is on a boardwalk through the swamp, so bring insect repellent.

Colonists of Plymouth and Duxbury found rich fishing grounds in what is now Wellfleet Harbor, which had long been known for its oysters—Champlain had named it "Port aux Huitres." The English colonists called this area Billingsgate, from the London fish market of the same name, and the town's name itself is believed to come from England's famed Wellfleet oysters. Permanent settlers arrived in the 1650s. By 1707 the whaling industry in Wellfleet was thriving. A fleet of ships cruised as far as the coast of Africa. Residents prospered, until the British blockade during the Revolutionary War idled their ships.

HISTORICAL SITES *and* MUSEUMS

The **Wellfleet Historical Society** (508-349-9157; www.wellfleethistorical society.com) is at 266 Main St. Open June–Sep. The collections include photographs, maps, documents, marine artifacts, Indian artifacts, and lifesaving equipment. The small cannon on the lawn is actually a Lyle gun, which was used by lifesavers on the Back Shore. When a ship foundered on the sandbars, the Lyle gun shot a line to the rigging of the vessel. That line was used to pull over a larger line holding a breeches buoy—a life buoy with a pair of canvas breeches attached. A stranded sailor could climb into the oversize trousers and be hauled to land.

INFORMATION

WELLFLEET CHAMBER OF COMMERCE
P.O. Box 571, Wellfleet, MA 02667
508-349-2510;
www.wellfleetchamber.com

INFORMATION BOOTH
US 6, South Wellfleet, MA 02663

PROVINCETOWN

"P-town" is a walking town with narrow, sometimes congested, streets. For many decades an artists' colony and more recently a mecca for those with alternative lifestyles, it has plenty to offer for everybody, including great Portuguese food from some of its old whaling families. Come early and park your car, then tackle the town on foot. The waterfront has its own fascination, especially in summer, when a large fishing fleet and visiting yachts keep the harbor busy.

The Pilgrims anchored off what is now Provincetown and stayed in the harbor for five weeks. By the mid-18th century it had become a whaling seaport.

HISTORICAL SITES *and* MUSEUMS

The **Pilgrim Monument**, on High Pole Hill, off Bradford St., is a granite tower, in Italian Renaissance style, that serves as a memorial to the Pilgrims' first contact with the New World on November 11, 1620. We always like to climb up the tallest tower we can find in any place to get oriented and survey the surrounding coun-

The SANDS *of* HISTORY

In 1778, during the Revolution, the *Somerset*, a 64-gun British man-of-war, ran aground on Peaked Hill Bars off Truro, just south of Provincetown. (Longfellow wrote about an earlier brush with history by the *Somerset* and her captain, George Curry, in the third verse of "Paul Revere's Ride.") The captain surrendered himself and his crew to men from Provincetown who had come to salvage the wreck. Revolutionary history records the winter-long march of the five hundred prisoners across the Cape to Boston. More than a hundred years later the *Somerset's* timbers reappeared in the sands of Peaked Hill Bars, and in June of 1973 her bones appeared again.

tryside. This 252-foot-high challenge had us huffing by the time we climbed the 60 ramps and 116 stairs to the top. But the view is worth the effort as you take in the panorama of the sea and the Cape. Copied from the Torre del Mangia in Siena, Italy, the Pilgrim Monument is the tallest granite monument in the United States.

The Pilgrim Room in the adjacent **Provincetown Museum** (508-487-1310) contains *Mayflower* mementos, ship models, and collections of colonial china, silver, and pewter. The Pilgrim wing has a stunning collection of murals such as "First Landing," "First Washday," "Discovering Fresh Water," "First Encounter (with Indians)" and "Finding Corn." There is also a replica of part of the *Mayflower*. One display case contains letters, medals, a piece of fabric from Priscilla Mullin's dress, and a doll in its cradle depicting Peregrine White, the first child born to the Pilgrims in the New World.

LODGING

THE RED INN
15 Commercial St.,
Provincetown, MA 02657
866-473-3466, 508-487-7334;
www.theredinn.com
Part of this waterfront building dates from 1805 and part from 1915.

RESTAURANTS

FRONT STREET
230 Commercial St.
Provincetown, MA 02657; 508-487-9715
The restaurant is in the brick cellar of a Victorian house and offers Mediterranean cuisine.

MARTIN HOUSE
157 Commercial St.
Provincetown, MA 02657; 508-487-1327
A captain built this home in 1750 and it still has its colonial attributes. The cuisine is memorable.

THE RED INN
15 Commercial St.,
Provincetown, MA 02657
866-473-3466, 508-487-7334;
www.theredinn.com
The menu is American.

EVENTS

June: Portuguese Festival and Blessing of the Fleet; 508-487-0086
July: Independence Day; 508-487-7000, x 536
November–December: Festival of Lights, 508-487-1310

INFORMATION

PROVINCETOWN CHAMBER OF COMMERCE
307 Commercial St., P.O. Box 1017,
Provincetown, MA 02657
508-487-3424;
www.ptownchamber.com

OLD KING'S HIGHWAY

From Orleans you may want to return to the base of the Cape on the Old King's Highway, MA 6A. This thirty-four miles of road curves and winds through seven Cape Cod towns, and there are historic sites all along the way to visit. This may have been the Cape Cod Trail used by Native Americans in between Provincetown and Plymouth. Early settlers used this path as their east-west route. After earlier agrarian settlement, the 18th-century maritime industry produced many captains' homes.

BREWSTER

Brewster is just about at the center of Cape Cod on MA 6A. A number of early 19th-century sea captains' homes line the streets. Visitors enjoy the art galleries and antiques shops in town.

HISTORICAL SITES and MUSEUMS

The **Old Higgins Farm Windmill** (508-896-9521), Drummer Boy Park, Brewster, is one of the few 18th-century windmills on the Cape. Windmills were used both for grinding grain and pumping salt water for evaporation in the saltworks.

The **Stony Brook Grist Mill and Herring Run** (508-896-6194), Stony Brook Rd., was the first water-powered mill, built in 1663. The mill there today dates from 1873.

LODGING

**BREWSTER BY THE SEA
BED & BREAKFAST**
716 MA 6A, Brewster, MA 02631
800-892-3910, 508-896-3910;
www.brewsterbythesea.com
This Greek-revival farmhouse dates from 1846; there is also a newer carriage house.

**PEPPER HOUSE INN
BED & BREAKFAST**
2062 Main St., Brewster, MA 02631
888-896-2062;
www.pepperhouseinn.com
The inn dates from 1793 when it was home to a sea captain by the name of Bangs Pepper.

RESTAURANTS

CHILLINGSWORTH
2449 MA 6A, Brewster, MA 02631
508-896-3640; www.chillingsworth.com
The building is three centuries old and the restaurant offers a seven-course, prix fixe French/California menu at two seatings; a bistro is in the greenhouse.

EVENTS

Mid-April–early May: Herring Run

INFORMATION

BREWSTER CHAMBER OF COMMERCE
2198 Main St. (Town Hall), P.O. Box 1241, Brewster, MA 02631; 508-896-3500; www.brewstercapecod.org

DENNIS

Located at the center of the north shore of Cape Cod, Dennis offers many lovely old homes, artists' studios, and the Cape Museum of Fine Arts (508-385-4477), which displays the work of Cape Cod artists. Visitors enjoy the popular Cape Playhouse (508-385-3911), which serves up plays, mysteries, and musicals on the playbill every summer.

HISTORICAL SITES and MUSEUMS

Josiah Dennis Manse Museum (508-385-2232), 77 Nobscusset Rd. Open late June–Sep. The Reverend Dennis built this saltbox house in 1736. It is decorated as it would have been in his time.

LODGING

**THE ISAIAH HALL
BED & BREAKFAST INN**
152 Whig St., Dennis, MA 02660;
508-385-9928;
www.bbonline.com/ma/isaiah
This 1857 Greek-revival farmhouse was
built by a cooper. Rooms are furnished
with antiques.

EVENTS

August: Dennis Festival Days;
800-243-9920, 508-398-3568

INFORMATION

DENNIS CHAMBER OF COMMERCE
242 Swan River Rd., P.O. Box 1001,
West Dennis, MA 02670
800-243-9920, 508-398-3568;
www.dennischamber.com

YARMOUTH

The town of Yarmouth, including South Yarmouth and Yarmouth Port, extends from Nantucket Sound in the south to Cape Cod Bay in the north. The area is noted for its family orientation, and there is a lot to enjoy. Besides visiting historic sites, you can choose to go to a zoo, the beach, play minigolf, take the boardwalk over a marsh, or walk on botanical trails.

Yarmouth was the third village to be founded on the Cape, in 1639.

HISTORICAL SITES *and* MUSEUMS

The **Winslow-Crocker House** (617-227-3956; www.historicnewengland.org), 250 MA 6A. Open the first Saturday of every month in the afternoon. The house was built in West Barnstable, then taken down and moved to Yarmouth in 1935. Mary Thacher's collection of furniture, hooked rugs, ceramics, and pewter displays early American styles from Jacobean to William and Mary, Queen Anne to Chippendale.

The **Captain Bangs Hallet House Museum** (508-362-3021; www.hsoy.org), 2 Strawberry Lane. Open mid-June through mid-Oct. It was built in 1740 by Thomas Thacher and enlarged by Captain Henry Thacher in 1840. It is maintained by the Historical Society of Old Yarmouth.

The **1791 Judah Baker Windmill** (508-362-3021), on the shore of Bass River at Willow St., is a "smock" windmill (one with eight sides). It was originally on the top of a large hill with a view of packets landing from Boston. When the miller saw a packet, he hoisted a flag on a pole so people would know it was arriving. The day before a packet left, the miller hung out a black ball as a signal to travelers that the boat was about to leave. In 1865 the windmill was moved to South Yarmouth, then to Main Street, and finally to "the House of Seven Chimneys" by the Davis family.

The **Baxter Grist Mill** (508-398-2231), off Mill Pond Rd. and MA 28, West Yarmouth. Open June–Sep. The mill was built in 1710 and renovated in 1989. In 1850 the water was so low that the wheel froze, so an indoor water turbine was constructed. It is in operation today, producing flour and meal with the same natural nutrients as it did a hundred years ago.

LODGING

CROOK JAW INN BED & BREAKFAST
186 Main St./MA 6A,
Yarmouth Port, MA 02675
508-362-6111;
www.CrookJawInn.com
The inn dates from 1790 and is decorated with antiques and braided rugs.

LANE'S END COTTAGE
BED & BREAKFAST
268 Main St.,
Yarmouth Port, MA 02675
508-362-5298
This cape, with a white picket fence, is 300 years old.

LIBERTY HILL INN BED & BREAKFAST
77 Main St.,
Yarmouth Port, MA 02675
800-821-3977, 508-362-3976;
www.libertyhillinn.com
The Hallet family built this home in 1825 on the site where the Sons of Liberty put up the first liberty pole.

OLDE CAPTAIN'S INN
101 Main St.,
Yarmouth Port, MA 02675
888-407-7161, 508-362-4496
This sea captain's home was built in 1812.

RESTAURANTS

THE OLD YARMOUTH INN
223 MA 6A, Yarmouth Port, MA 02675
508-362-9962; www.oldyarmouthinn.com
The inn dates from 1696 and is the halfway point between Plymouth and Provincetown, a welcome respite for colonial (and modern-day) travelers. On long-ago Sundays, the inn offered warmth and refreshment after lengthy services in an unheated church; during the Revolutionary War, it was a gathering place for the exchange of news. Reportedly, ghosts have wafted in and out of the inn but they are friendly. Menus are creative.

EVENTS

September: Open House All Around the Common; 508-362-3021
October: Seaside Festival; 508-778-1008
December: Christmas Stroll; 508-362-3021

INFORMATION

YARMOUTH AREA
CHAMBER OF COMMERCE
424 MA 28, West Yarmouth, MA 02673;
P.O. Box 479, South Yarmouth, MA 02664;
800-732-1008, 508-778-1008;
www.yarmouthcapecod.com

BARNSTABLE

Barnstable Village provides a welcome escape from the congestion of Hyannis. Its harbor offers fishing opportunities as well as whale watching, and the village has antiques shops to visit.

HISTORICAL SITES and MUSEUMS

The **Sturgis Library** (508-362-6636; www.sturgislibrary.org), 3090 MA 6A, Barnstable Village. Open daily except Sun. Reportedly it is the oldest library in the United States. This 1644 building was home to John Lothrop, the founder of Barnstable. He went to sea after his father died, sailed in the Northwest and China trades, and returned a captain. The collections include maritime and genealogical materials.

RESTAURANTS

DOLPHIN
3250 MA 6A, Barnstable, MA 02630; 508-362-6610
This restaurant has been in the chef-owner family for three generations. Seafood is king here.

East Sandwich

By chance we happened to arrive just as the curator of the Benjamin Nye Homestead was about to leave. She is a Nye descendant and graciously opened the house for us.

HISTORICAL SITES *AND* MUSEUMS

The **Benjamin Nye Homestead** (508-888-4213; www.nyefamily.org), 85 Old Country Rd., was built by Benjamin Nye in 1681. Open July–Oct. Nye was one of the first 50 men to settle in Sandwich. He also built a gristmill on his property. A Nye descendant, Rosanna Cullity, who is the curator of the homestead, gave us a tour. She had just completed stenciling the borning room. And she showed us the "bugaboo," a room behind the fireplace where children liked to play.

Inside, the house had two rooms up and two down with more rooms added on the back, changing the shape to a saltbox. More rooms were later added on the second floor. There are five fireplaces and old wide-board floors. The Nye coat of arms as well as a copy of the original deed are there. Six generations of Nyes lived in the house.

> A 1677 grave on Wilson Road, that of Edmund Freeman, is unusual because his stone is a saddle and that of his wife a pillion, or chair that can be attached to a saddle so that two persons could ride at once.

The Marine Room contains memorabilia including a gold chronometer and a sea chest full of items brought back from the South Seas. Thomas Nye had twelve children, and seven of them became sea captains.

Sandwich

Sandwich has a stunning town center, with the old gristmill reflected in a lake on one end and the Hoxie House on the other. You can visit a number of colonial buildings, as well as the extensive grounds of the Heritage Museum, which offers a range of exhibits, gardens, and an impressive collection of antique cars.

Sandwich is the oldest permanent settlement on the Cape, with the first group arriving in 1627 from Plymouth and another in 1637 from Saugus. The historic district contains a number of houses from the 17th century.

HISTORICAL SITES *and* MUSEUMS

Dexter Mill (508-888-1173), Water St., conducts milling demonstrations. Open June–Oct. The mill dates from 1640 and was rebuilt in 1654. The location is lovely, with Shawme Pond on one side and a rushing stream turning the wheel. Walk inside and you will be in the midst of the old-fashioned milling process. Organically grown corn is ground either coarse or fine here, and you can purchase some if you wish.

Thornton Burgess, the naturalist and author of children's books, wrote a poem,

"The Honest Miller," in honor of the reopening of the mill in 1962. Leo Manning is the town miller, and he is there to talk with visitors.

Hoxie House (508-888-1173), Water St., a restored saltbox, may be the oldest house on Cape Cod. Open Memorial Day–Oct. The house dates from 1640 and stands on a bluff overlooking Shawme Pond. It was named for Abraham Hoxie, a whaling captain who owned the house in the mid-1800s. John Smith came to Sandwich in 1675 and lived in the house with his wife and 13 children. Take a look in the large fireplace to see various cooking pieces, including a gridiron, spider, rotating grill and toaster, and pots. Some of the pewter pieces were poisonous, with a high lead content, a fact unknown at the time.

The **Wing Fort House** (508-833-1540), 69 Spring Hill Rd. Open June–Sep., except Sun. and Mon. Built in 1641 by a Quaker and partially fortified, it was owned and occupied by members of the Wing family through three centuries until 1942. The rooms now contain period furnishings.

 These sayings came from a colonial house. Can you guess the objects they came from?
- **Raining cats and dogs** (a cat sliding on a steep roof)
- **Upper crust** (bread was sliced sideways and the upper crust was the best)
- **Spinster** (wool spinning was often done by single ladies)
- **Sleep tight; don't let the bed bugs bite** (strung-rope bed that could be retightened if it sagged; straw mattresses conducive to critters)
- **Burning the candle at both ends** (rush lamps could be burned that way)
- **Dead as a doornail** (a familiar inanimate object)
- **Little shavers** (children grating sugar)

The **First Parish Meeting House**, Main St., is known for its bell and town clock given by Titus Winchester. He was a slave who received his freedom when his master, Abraham Williams, died in 1749. Winchester specified that the bell was to ring on the hour in memory of Williams.

Heritage Museums and Gardens (508-888-3300; www.heritagemuseumsandgardens. org), Pine and Grove Sts. Open May–Oct. The

The miller needs to be watchful so that the stones do not get too hot, burn the corn, and cause an explosion. Hence the phrase, "Keep his nose to the grindstone."

Dexter Mill

museum preserves and shares the history, industry, art, and horticulture of America. The land now occupied by Heritage was first settled by members of the Wing family in 1677. Their house still stands as an ell on another house at 14/16 Grove St. in the village.

The **American History Museum** is housed in a replica of the Temple of New Windsor where George Washington awarded the first Purple Heart to a wounded soldier. The military miniature collection has been reinstalled there. The museum also has an exceptional antiques firearm collection and American Indian artifacts.

Sometimes a docent will have a wonderful repertoire of stories about life in colonial houses. For example, have you ever wondered where the phrases "saved by the bell" or "was a dead ringer" came from? After someone appeared to be dead, a string was tied around a finger or toe of the corpse and the end tied to a bell, just in case he or she turned out to be alive. Furniture in colonial houses often had two uses. A table could be tilted up to form the back of a chair. When one "turns the tables" it means the evening entertainment is over.

LODGING

BELFRY INNE & BISTRO
8 Jarves St., Sandwich, MA 02563
800-844-4542, 508-888-8550;
www.belfryinn.com
Once a Victorian manse, this inn has stained-glass windows and a tower on top for the view.

THE DAN'L WEBSTER INN
149 Main St., Sandwich, MA 02563
800-444-3566, 508-888-3622;
www.danlwebsterinn.com
A parsonage, then the Fessenden Tavern, once sat on the property. It was a patriot headquarters during the American Revolution.

THE INN AT SANDWICH CENTER
118 Tupper Rd., Sandwich, MA 02563
800-249-6949, 508-888-3622;
www.innatsandwich.com
This 1750 inn has period furnishings.

RESTAURANTS

BELFRY BISTRO
8 Jarves St., Sandwich, MA 02563
800-844-4542, 508-888-8550;
www.belfryinn.com
The menu is contemporary, varied, and memorable.

DAN'L WEBSTER INN
149 Main St., Sandwich, MA 02563
800-444-3566, 508-888-3622;
www.danlwebsterinn.com
Three meals a day are offered in several locations. The conservatory is a favorite with a waterfall and greenery outside.

EVENTS

December: Christmas in Sandwich
508-759-6000
Heritage Museum Festival of Lights
508-888-3300

INFORMATION

For information on Cape Cod in general and about specific locations on the Cape, contact the following:

CAPE COD CHAMBER OF COMMERCE
888-33CAPECOD, 508-362-3225;
www.capecodchamber.org

CAPE COD WELCOME CENTER AND ADMINISTRATIVE OFFICES
US 6 and MA 132, Hyannis, MA 02601
888-33CAPECOD, 508-362-3225

ROUTE 25 VISITOR CENTER
MA 25 eastbound,
Plymouth, MA 02360; 508-759-3814

MARTHA'S VINEYARD

Visiting Martha's Vineyard today can be an adventure into the past, the chance to hike or bike on quiet country roads and visit distinctive villages. Although there are six towns on the island, Edgartown and Vineyard Haven are the largest centers for shopping, restaurants, and lodging. The other, more rural towns are Aquinnah (formerly Gay Head), Oak Bluffs, West Tisbury, and Chilmark. Four large harbors offer cruises and fishing charters, as well as moorings for yachts. If you arrive without your car, there are shuttle buses and bicycle rentals to get you around, and first-time visitors may also want to take a sightseeing tour to get oriented.

According to tradition, Leif Eriksson stopped on the island in the 11th century, calling it Straumey, which means island of currents. Verrazano arrived in 1524 and called it Louisa. But the name that stuck came from Bartholomew Gosnold, who stepped ashore in 1602 and named the island after his daughter Martha and the wild grapes that grew there.

In 1642 Thomas Mayhew purchased Martha's Vineyard, Nantucket, and the Elizabeth Islands—not from the native inhabitants, but from the English grantees.

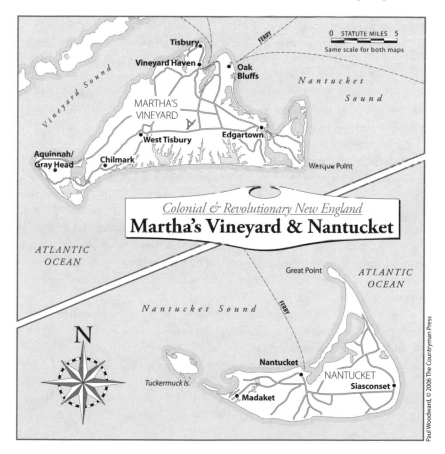

Mayhew's son, of the same name, settled at what is now Edgartown and brought Christianity to the Wampanoag Indians there. Christiantown Cemetery in Vineyard Haven has a large plaque stating that the "Ancient township of the praying Indians" was set apart in 1660 by Josias, the sachem of Takemmy, and was later called Christiantown. Mayhew Chapel in West Tisbury was built as an Indian chapel in 1910.

Gay Head, renamed Aquinnah in the 1990s to reflect its Indian heritage, caps the high southwestern tip of Martha's Vineyard. Its varicolored cliffs are a national monument. Each colored layer records a part of geological history before the last ice age. The layer of black at the bottom indicates buried forests; red and yellow layers are clay; a layer of green sand that turns red when exposed to the air contains fossils of crabs and clams; the gravel-like layers contain sharks' teeth, whale bones, and animal skeletons. To get a closer look at this geological wonder, you can walk on marked paths but are not allowed to wander off them.

Many of the inhabitants of Gay Head are of Indian descent. In September 1981, after four years of negotiations, the town agreed to return 238 acres of shorefront property to the three hundred members of the Wampanoag tribe. The land, which is worth millions, will be kept in its natural state. Part of the agreement allows the Indians to apply for federal funds to buy 175 acres for housing on the island.

Moshop, a mythical hero to the Indians, was said to have built the Devil's Bridge, a reef of glacial boulders reaching out from the Gay Head cliffs toward distant Cuttyhunk Island. On January 18, 1884, the steamship *City of Columbus* crashed into the reef; 121 passengers and crew lost their lives that night. The English thought of Moshop as the devil. You can drive along Moshop's Trail with its wind-battered vegetation, but you can't stop to swim or walk the dunes because of possible damage to the environment.

Oak Bluffs on the northern shore of the island offers strollers the rare chance to wander through a colony of Victorian cottages painted in all colors and often decorated with gingerbread carvings. The town was settled in 1642, but there was not much activity until 1835 when it was used as a Methodist assembly ground by "Reformation" John Adams. He delivered passionate sermons and tearful praying that won converts away from the Congregationalists. The original tents were replaced with the Trinity Park Tabernacle, which is still in use today. This assembly ground, perhaps the best preserved in the nation, represents an important national religious movement in the 19th century.

Vineyard Haven is a commercial center where longtime residents of the island live and work. It is the primary year-round ferry terminal for the island and a base for workboats, with a protected inner harbor. In recent decades, national celebrities have taken to building second homes in Tisbury, the larger town surrounding Vineyard Haven. The harbor was harassed by a British fleet of eighty-three ships during the Revolution. They pulled into port and almost destroyed the town. Hearing that the British wanted to use the flagpole standing in town for a mast, three young ladies got rid of it.

EDGARTOWN

Edgartown, the principal and oldest town on the island, is an architectural delight. On its tree-lined streets you can stroll past colonial and Greek-revival homes built by prosperous ship captains and perhaps find lodging in some that have become B&Bs. In the town center, galleries and shops are interspersed with restaurants. The harbor is the yachting center of the island, hosting one of the most famous regattas in the region. Edgartown was founded in 1642 by the Mayhew family, who named it Great Harbor.

HISTORICAL SITES and MUSEUMS

The **Thomas Cooke House** (508-627-4441; www.marthasvineyardhistory.org), Cooke and School Sts. Open in winter Tue.–Fri. afternoons; summer Tue.–Sat. It was the home of the customs keeper. The 1765 house is furnished with period Vineyard pieces. A maritime gallery offers scrimshaw, mementos from whaling trips, and whaling logbooks.

The oldest surviving house on the island, dating to the 1670s, is the **Vincent House** (508-627-4441), Pease's Point Way. Open spring through fall, Mon.–Fri. Some of the walls are left exposed to show the original construction. The spinning wheel found in the attic may have belonged to the Vincents. The Blue Parlor is decorated in the Federal style. During the 19th century, furnishings changed from colonial to Federal in some homes. The house is owned by the Martha's Vineyard Historical Preservation Society.

When we visited we heard the story about Susanna Vincent, who purportedly was seen as a ghost in the Blue Parlor around 3 PM by three of the junior staff. Apparently Susanna likes to have people enjoying her house, so the girls spent the night there and felt comfortable.

LODGING

THE ASHLEY INN
129 Main St., Edgartown, MA 02539
508-627-9655; www.ashleyinn.net
Dating from 1860, the inn was the home of a sea captain.

THE COLONIAL INN
OF MARTHA'S VINEYARD
38 N. Water St., Edgartown, MA 02539
800-627-4701, 508-627-4711;
www.colonialinnmvy.com
Established in 1911, the inn overlooks the harbor.

THE HARBOR VIEW HOTEL
131 N. Water St.,
Edgartown, MA 02539
800-225-6005, 508-627-7000;
www.harbor-view.com

This hotel offers 130 guest rooms, suites, and two-bedroom townhouses.

THE KELLEY HOUSE
Kelley St., Edgartown, MA 02539
800-225-6005, 508-627-7900
Also owned by the Harbor View Hotel, this former tavern dates from 1742.

RESTAURANTS

ATRIA
137 Main St., Edgartown, MA 02539
508-627-5850; www.atriamv.com
Dinners are served in the garden or inside.

L'ETOILE
N. Water St., Edgartown, MA 02539
508-627-5198; www.letoile.net
Contemporary French cuisine.

SQUARE RIGGER
225 State Rd. at the Triangle,
Edgartown, MA 02539;
508-627-9968
Watch the cooks in action.

Vineyard Haven also offers lodging and restaurants, including the following:

1720 HOUSE BED & BREAKFAST
152 Main St.,
Vineyard Haven, MA 02568
508-693-6407; www.1720house.com
A 300-year-old copper beech tree
shades this historic house.

BLACK DOG TAVERN
509 State Rd.,
Vineyard Haven, MA 02568
508-696-8190;
www.theblackdog.com/
Located on the harbor, the Black Dog's
specialty is seafood.

EVENTS
June: Oak Bluffs Harbor Festival
508-693-3392
August: Edgartown House Tour
508-693-4645
December: Holiday events; 508-693-1151

INFORMATION
**MARTHA'S VINEYARD
CHAMBER OF COMMERCE**
Beach Rd., P.O. Box 1698,
Vineyard Haven, MA 02568
800-505-4815, 508-693-0085;
marthasvineyardchamber.com

FERRY SERVICE
STEAMSHIP AUTHORITY
508-477-8600, 508-693-9130;
www.steamshipauthority.com

HI-LINE
888-778-1132; www.hi-linecruises.com

NANTUCKET

Islands have always been associated with legend and romance; they appeal to the imagination through the mixed signals they give us. They are exposed to the hazards of the surrounding ocean, yet provide respite from its rigors. Their beaches have been littered with wrecks, but draw swarms of swimmers and sun seekers. They are wonderful places to get away from it all, although sometimes hard to reach or almost impossible to leave in bad weather.

Among Atlantic islands off the southern New England coast, Nantucket fills this bill perfectly. It is much farther offshore than Block Island or the Vineyard— some thirty miles—and a modest fifteen miles long and four miles wide, not counting projecting sand spits.

The old town is much as the same as it was in the early 18th and 19th centuries, with newer buildings conforming to the older architecture. Some houses are left to weather so that their cedar shingle sid-

Have you heard of "laning"? Nantucket residents like to wander through their many narrow lanes during the early evening. Visitors can do the same, perhaps losing their way among the saltbox houses with flowering gardens, turning onto a grassy path and eventually finding a familiar street again. From the lanes it is perfectly acceptable to gaze inside windows at lovely antique pieces inside. It seems to be the practice for owners to leave some lights on for the benefit of laners.

ing eventually turns silvery gray in the salt air. Elegant homes built from the proceeds of whaling front on cobblestone streets. The stones are unfriendly to cyclists or even walkers, but you can cross the streets on large flat stones placed as if you were about to cross a little brook. Streetlights look like 19th-century gas lanterns, and there are many benches for weary walkers. Dogs snooze on the brick pavement in front of shops to complete the picture of a former era.

Nantucket was settled by early colonists who learned from the Indians how to capture whales; they watched for whales coming close to shore and harpooned them. In 1712 Captain Christopher Hussey's ship had been blown farther out to sea in a gale. He nabbed a sperm whale and found that it gave more oil than the right whales that swam near shore. Nantucketers began using larger ships that could accommodate offshore work. By 1740 the island was considered the whaling capital of the world. Merchants sold oil in Europe and became wealthy enough to build grand homes on the island.

Visitors new to Nantucket will enjoy taking **Gail's Tours** (508-257-6557), offered by a seventh-generation native. This is a good way to survey the island and then choose where you want to spend more time.

HISTORICAL SITES *and* MUSEUMS

The **Nantucket Historical Association** (508-228-1894) maintains 11 buildings on the island, including houses, museums, a gaol, and a mill.

The **Oldest House** (1686), Sunset Hill, was built by Jethro Coffin. The horseshoe pattern on the brick chimney was thought to protect the family from witches. This wooden saltbox has a secret hiding place in the closet.

The Oldest House in Nantucket

The **Macy-Christian House** (1745), 12 Liberty St., was built by Nathaniel Macy, a merchant on the island. The Reverend George P. Christian and his wife, Ruth, bought the house and filled it with their collection of American antiques.

The **Old Mill** (1746), 50 Prospect St., is the oldest American windmill in continuous operation. The original hand-crafted gears are still in use today.

Thomas Macy House (1770), 100 Main St., was remodeled in 1834 by Thomas Macy, an auctioneer, postmaster, and blacksmith. This house is owned by the Historical Association but is not open to the public. It is used for special events.

The **Nantucket Whaling Museum** (508-228-1736), Broad St., is housed in a former candle factory. Open Apr.–Oct. William Rotch built the first candle factory in 1770. Nantucket controlled the whale-oil supply to the colonies and England. The museum documents every aspect of the major economic enterprise on Nantucket in the colonial period and beyond. Here visitors will find an outstanding collection of whaling gear, a whaleboat, models, paintings, and some fine examples of scrimshaw. You can't miss the skeleton of a 46-foot sperm whale! The whale died on a Siasconset beach in 1998; the bones were buried in a pit for several months and later submerged in the harbor in cages to finish the cleaning.

There are several legends describing the birth of Nantucket, but our favorite is the story of Moshop, the first inhabitant of Martha's Vineyard. One day an Indian maiden came to him with an appeal: She was from a poor family, and the parents of the boy who wanted to marry her would not allow it. Moshop promised to meet the young lovers on Sampson's Hill, on Chappaquiddick. As they were trying to think of some way to marry, he took out his pipe and began to smoke. Because he was a giant, his pipe was filled with many bales of tobacco. When he knocked the ashes out into the sea, clouds of smoke and vapor filled the air. The fog lifted to reveal an island—Nantucket—gilded by the rising sun. With this island as a dowry, the young people were allowed to marry.

The romanticized "Nantucket sleigh ride" was an endurance contest between the whale and men in the whaleboat as the whale dove and plunged madly after being harpooned, towing the whaleboat behind it. Our guide related an apocryphal tale of one such trip: While traveling rapidly to leeward on a "sleigh ride," the crew looked back and saw an empty whaleboat following in their wake. A wave eventually smashed her to pieces, but the crew was still curious, wondering where she had come from. When they arrived back on board their ship and hoisted up their own whaleboat, the mystery was solved. The whale they had harpooned had traveled so fast that the paint had stripped off the whaleboat. What they had seen was their own shell of paint following them!

LODGING

No one should have trouble finding accommodations of historic interest on Nantucket.

THE ANCHOR INN
66 Centre St., Nantucket, MA 02554
508-228-0072; www.anchor-inn.net
Once owned by a whaling ship captain, this 1806 building is in the historic residential district.

THE CARLISLE HOUSE INN
26 N. Water St., Nantucket, MA 02554
508-228-0720; www.carlislehouse.com
This 14-room inn dates from 1765.

THE JARED COFFIN HOUSE
29 Broad St., Nantucket, MA 02554
800-248-2405, 508-228-2400;
www.jaredcoffinhouse.com
The three-story mansion, built in 1845, was a private residence for Jared Coffin, a successful ship owner.

THE MARTIN HOUSE INN
6l Centre St.,
Nantucket, MA 02554; 508-228-0678;
www.martinhouseinn.net
In the historic district, the inn was built in 1803 as a sea captain's home.

CLIFF LODGE
9 Cliff Rd., Nantucket, MA 02554
508-228-9480;
www.clifflodgenantucket.com
Under the same ownership as the Martin House Inn, the house was built for a whaling master in 1771.

THE ROBERTS HOUSE INN
11 Indian St., Nantucket, MA 02554
800-588-0087, 508-228-9009;
www.robertshouseinn.com
This Greek-revival inn dates from 1846.

THE MANOR HOUSE INN
31 Centre St., Nantucket, MA 02554
800-588-0087, 508-228-0600;
www.robertshouseinn.com/
manorhouse
Part of a family of inns, including the Roberts House, the house was also built in 1846.

THE PERIWINKLE GUEST HOME
9 N. Water St., Nantucket, MA 02554
800-837-2921, 508-228-9267;
www.oneweb.com/nantucket/pgh.html
This B&B is near the dock and the center of town on a quiet side street.

THE WAUWINET
120 Wauwinet Rd.,
Nantucket, MA 02554
800-426-8718, 508-228-0145;
www.wauwinet.com
This gray-shingled building dates from 1860 with later additions.

THE WOODBOX INN
29 Fair St., Nantucket, MA 02554
508-228-0587; www.woodboxinn.com
Built as a private residence in 1709, it is the oldest inn on the island.

RESTAURANTS

AMERICAN SEASONS
80 Centre St.,
Nantucket, MA 02554; 508-228-7111;
www.americanseasons.com
American specialties from all over the country are served.

JARED COFFIN HOUSE
29 Broad St., Nantucket, MA 02554
508-228-2400
Have dinner in Jared's or the Tap Room. Ask about the seafood buffet on special nights.

21 FEDERAL
21 Federal St., Nantucket, MA 02554
508-228-2121
Dine inside or outside in the garden from a bistro menu.

TOPPER'S
120 Wauwinet Rd., in the Wauwinet, Nantucket, MA 02554
508-228-8768; www.wauwinet.com
The dining room offers a varied menu at dinner and for lunch you can choose a sampler plate.

THE WOODBOX INN
29 Fair St., Nantucket, MA 02554
508-228-0587
Three dining rooms with a Continental menu.

EVENTS

May: Historic Preservation Week;508-228-1700
July 4: Independence Day; 508-228-0925
August: House Tour; 508-228-0888
November–December: Holiday events

INFORMATION

NANTUCKET CHAMBER OF COMMERCE
48 Main St., Nantucket, MA 02554;
508-228-1700; www.nantucketchamber.org

FERRY SERVICE

STEAMSHIP AUTHORITY
508-477-8600, 508-693-9130;
www.steamshipauthority.com

HI-LINE
888-788-1132,
www.hi-linecruises.com

PLYMOUTH AND THE SOUTH SHORE

The South Shore stretches from Sagamore Beach, at the base of the Cape, along the coast to Plymouth and up to Quincy, right outside Boston. Although much of it is in commuting distance of the Boston metropolitan area, this region has the air of being off the main line of suburban or exurban development, with cranberry bogs and attractive shore towns that maintain their own integrity. You can take yourself back to the year 1620 by visiting Plymouth Rock and a replica of the *Mayflower*, relive the lives of our first settlers at Plimoth Plantation, spend time on quiet sandy beaches, visit a church built like a ship, tour the homes of two presidents who were born in Quincy, and follow the Patriot's Trail through many South Shore towns.

PLYMOUTH

Plymouth, the spot where it all began, is still the best place to imagine what life must have been like for the Pilgrims in 1620. Their story, like that of Columbus, has been overloaded with patriotic myths and clichés for centuries, but with the help of replicas and reenactments it can be visualized more realistically here.

Today a visit to Plymouth can bring back the history you may have enjoyed in school. A short walking tour in the heart of town, site of the original settlement in 1620, is unusually rewarding, with many colonial houses and monuments to see. After visiting the *Mayflower II* you can stroll along the waterfront to Plymouth Rock. Although it has been moved several times and cracked, this piece of rock remains symbolic as the landing spot of the Pilgrims.

After bouncing in the *Mayflower* for over two months in North Atlantic fall gales, amidst very cramped and unpleasant conditions, these steerage passengers probably walked on dry land with great expectations. But hard work followed, with severe struggles for their very existence. Half of them died during that first harsh winter ashore.

HISTORICAL SITES *and* MUSEUMS

First-time visitors usually want to take a look at **Plymouth Rock.** Located off Water St. in the center of town, it commemorates the spot where the Pilgrims landed to establish the plantation. Don't be disappointed—the rock is small. The date engraved on the stone—December 21, 1620—is accurate for this landing but not for the Pilgrims' first contact with the New World, since they had reached Provincetown on November 11. The rock is now protected from the weather by a large, columned granite building.

Across the street stands the **Pilgrim Mother**, a fountain built in honor of the women who sailed on the *Mayflower.* They must have been courageous indeed to undertake a dangerous voyage to an unknown land with little hope of returning home. Gardens surrounding the statue thrive, and the language of herbs symbolizes the virtues of these women: basil for love, thyme for courage, and sage for immortality. At the top of the hill stands the statue of **Massasoit**, the sachem who helped the Pilgrims survive.

A statue of **William Bradford,** the second and longtime governor as well as the colony's historian, stands on the shore.

Town Brook offered both pure water and water power to the Pilgrims. Now a

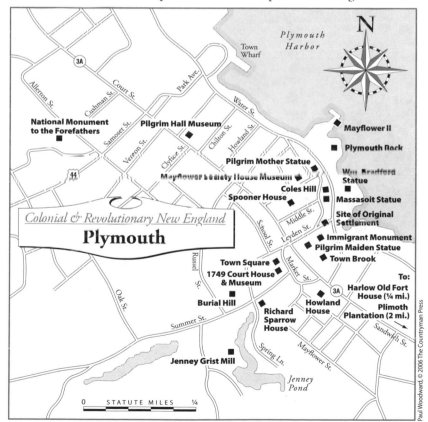

paved path along its south side provides a fine walk upstream all the way to **Jenney Grist Mill**. Surrounding the brook in Brewster Gardens you'll find the **Immigrant Monument** and the **Pilgrim Maiden** statue.

When you have looked at the monuments, you can head for another living-history conversation on board the *Mayflower II* (508-746-1622; www.plimoth.org), moored at State Pier. Open Apr.–Nov. This accurate replica was built in England and sailed to America in 1955 under the command of Alan Villiers, a renowned sailing captain and maritime historian. It is a three-masted, square-rigged bark 106 feet overall on deck with a beam (width) of 25 feet; its headroom belowdecks is a foot higher than on the original vessel, but don't let that keep you from ducking as you head down.

As you step aboard you may be greeted by Master Christopher Jones, an interpreter dressed as Jones would have been. He might tell you about the 100 passengers aboard with six and twenty crew and "there you be—tossing about all being seasick with pigs and goats beside you." Seaman Smith told us about the voyage in very heavy weather, how he steered a course of southwest by west, and how the ship behaved.

Down below we met a young lady who was sitting on a bunk, sewing. She told us that the voyage was very hard on her children—not much room to roughhouse and let off steam down there. In nice weather she took her children up on deck for fresh air and exercise.

Interpreters and a compass on the Mayflower II

Back on deck you may want to ask the master about the navigating system and the seaworthiness of the vessel. Also glance over the starboard side at the ship's shallop, another accurate replica moored alongside; it was essential to the month of exploration in Cape Cod Bay that preceded the landing at Plymouth.

If the *Mayflower II* has roused your curiosity about the ships of the era, you can see the only surviving remains of one early 17th-century ship, the *Sparrow Hawk,* in the **Pilgrim Hall Museum** (508-746-1620; www.pilgrimhall.org), Court and Chilton Sts. Open Feb.–Dec. She was wrecked off Cape Cod in 1626, silted over by sand for many years, and brought up more than 200 years later.

Among other exhibits in the museum is the sampler Lora Standish, a daughter of Myles Standish, stitched in 1653. The museum also contains collections of Pilgrim furniture, pewter, textiles, books, tools, weapons, and personal treasures, including Peregrine White's cradle, swords belonging to Myles Standish and John Carver, and the Bibles of John Alden and William Bradford.

One Thanksgiving we remember watching a procession winding through town and into the **First Parish Church** (508-746-3026), on Town Square. This structure was actually built in 1899, but the congregation dates back to a group that first met in Scrooby, England, then at Leiden in the Netherlands, and finally in Plymouth. The church resembles one in Austerfield, England, where William Bradford was baptized. The figure in the window over the choir loft portrays John Robinson as he spoke to his congregation before they left the Netherlands for the

Daily life in colonial times reenacted at Plimoth Plantation

New World. He intended to follow, but died first.

Climb up beyond the church to **Burial Hill**, the site of a 1622 fort and meetinghouse. A number of colonists, including Governor Bradford, John Howland, and the last woman survivor, Mary Cushman, lie there. If you are fascinated by the inscriptions in old cemeteries, here is the place to wander and read the tales of courageous folk on their headstones.

Coles Hill, closer to the water, was where the dead were placed in unmarked graves during the first winter. The

Plymouth's Burial Hill

colonists did not want the Indians to know how many of them had died. A granite sarcophagus now holds the remains of those who were uncovered through erosion. Its inscription reads: "In weariness and painfulness, in watchings often, in hunger and cold they laid the foundations of a state wherein every man through countless ages, should have liberty to worship God in his own way"—suggesting a religious toleration beyond the Pilgrim's grasp at that time. Massasoit's bronze monument is there too, commemorating the friendship with Indians that enabled the struggling settlement to survive.

> The stone for John Howland reads, "Here was a godly man and an ancient professor in the wayes of Christ. Hee was one of the first comers into this land and was the last man that was left of those that came over in the Shipp called the Mayflower that lived in Plymouth."
> Elizabeth Savery's stone reads:
> *Remember me as you pass by,*
> *As you are now so once was I;*
> *As I am now so you must be,*
> *Prepare for death to follow me.*

Plymouth is lucky to have a concentration of later colonial homes that didn't go up in flames. Edward Winslow, a great-grandson of Governor Edward Winslow, built his home at 4 Winslow St. in 1754, and it is now owned by the **Mayflower Society House Museum** (508-746-2590; www.mayflowersociety.com). Open Memorial Day–Columbus Day.

Nine rooms are furnished with period pieces from the 17th to the 19th centuries. *Mayflower* descendants have given family treasures including clocks, Wedgwood china, quilts, and a 1670 court cupboard belonging to the Brewster family. The flying staircase is a highlight of the Georgian section of the house.

The oldest original house in town is the 1640 **Richard Sparrow House** (508-747-1240; www.sparrowhouse.com), 42 Summer St. Open Apr.–Nov. A large fireplace dominates the original downstairs room; upstairs there was another room for sleeping. Over the years Sparrow added rooms at the back, and the next owner built the entire right side of the house as it stands today. Stoneware pottery has been made in the house for years.

Five generations have lived in the 1749 **Spooner House** (508-746-0012), 27 North St. Open June–early Oct. It contains oriental rugs, period furniture, and wallpaper that once lined tea boxes, as well as blue Canton and rose medallion china. As the family prospered, the left side of the house was added later. James Spooner could open up a window on the harbor side to watch the wharf below, essential in his maritime business. The family company, Plymouth Cordage, was the largest rope company in America.

John Howland, who was saved by the "Grace of God" when he was almost washed overboard on the voyage to America, lived in the 1667 **Howland House** (508-746-9590; www.pilgrimhall.org), 33 Sandwich St. Open Memorial Day weekend–Columbus Day, and Thanksgiving weekend. The house has many interesting 17th-century pieces, including a chest thought to have belonged to the family. Ask to see the "Murphy" bed and look carefully at the stools with curved holes that fit the shape of a hand for easy carrying.

> If you've wondered about the source of the potent lifestyle phrase "burning the candle at both ends," it may have come from the rush reeds that were dragged through tallow, placed in a holder, and then lit at one or both ends. The choice between more light for a shorter time or less for a longer time quite naturally represents spendthrift and conservative human impulses. The rushlight both smoked and smelled, and it had to be watched, because when the reed was consumed the light went out. Some holders had hooks for hanging, some had legs so they could stand on the floor, and others a heavy bottom to be placed on a table or shelf.

By 1700 the family had added a kitchen, a borning room, and two more rooms above. The left side of the house, another addition, was built around 1750.

One more house to see before you leave Plymouth is the 1677 **Harlow Old Fort House** (508-746-0012), 119 Sandwich St. Open July and Aug. William Harlow built the house for his family of ten. He worked as a cooper, farmer, and soldier. When the Old Fort was dismantled after 1676, some of its beams were reused to support this house—a recycling practice common in colonial times. Inside, docents may be engaged in spinning, weaving, candle making, and other household tasks.

To top off your visit (pun intended), take a look at the 81-foot granite monument, called **The National Monument to the Forefathers**, on Allerton St. Open Mar.–Nov. The names of all 102 *Mayflower* colonists are etched on the statue's base. The figure that symbolizes Faith is 36 feet tall, and other figures depict liberty, morality, law, and education. The memorial honors the Pilgrims for their "labors, sacrifices and sufferings for the cause of civil and religious freedom."

After exhausting the sites in town, you may wish to head out to visit the popular living-history plantation, just 3 miles away: **Plimoth Plantation** (508-746-1622; www.plimoth.org), MA 3A/Warren Ave. Open daily. The site re-creates the original village established by the Pilgrims in 1620. Archaeological research, descriptions recorded by members of the group, and study of the documentation have provided an authentic reproduction of the village's structures as they would have appeared in 1627.

Imagine yourself in this setting 375 years ago as you walk into the visitor center to prepare for your trip backward in time. The orientation video begins with prelanding images of inhabitants in tune with nature—a pristine sunrise complete with birds wheeling, waves splashing, and a grassy cliff. The "People of the Dawn" were the Wampanoags, who introduced their beautiful land to the Pilgrims. The stage is set for you to arrive as a Pilgrim.

After seeing the video, walk through the Carriage House Crafts Center, where artisans make baskets, furniture, and pottery and weave. A short walk along the path outside will take you to the entrance of the 1627 Pilgrim Village.

We were lucky enough to visit Plimoth Plantation on Thanksgiving Day for a number of years. Cold, blustery winds blowing down the hill, swirling the smoke from chimneys and bursting into houses through cracks, brought us back into the harsh environment of daily life during the colder months.

Every year interpreters in colonial dress play the part of Myles Standish, John and Priscilla Alden, Governor William Bradford, and other historical persons in

ᴀ TASTE of a PILGRIM THANKSGIVING

The following material and recipes are by permission from *Giving Thanks: Thanksgiving Recipes and History, from Pilgrims to Pumpkin Pie*, by Kathleen Curtin, Sandra L. Oliver, and Plimoth Plantation (Clarkson Potter, October 2005).

☞ *Thanksgiving recipes, old and modern, can be found on the next two pages.*

Docents are always willing to engage with visitors at Plimoth Plantation

the plantation. If you ask them questions appropriate to the year 1627 they will answer in the dialects and accents of that day. Interpreters welcome give-and-take, even if they pretend not to understand anachronistic questions, so don't be bashful in talking to them.

Women interpreters wear a shift (like a shirt), petticoat, gown (or waistcoat and skirt), apron and coif (linen cap covering hair). Men wear a shirt, breeches, stockings, and doublet (close-fitting jacket). Both wear a cape, hat or cap, and low shoes tied with lappets fastened in front.

Stewed Turkey *with* Herbs *and* Onions

If you have never thought to boil a turkey, this 1623 recipe will make a believer out of you. The sauce with its spices, onions, and sweet/sour balance of sugar and vinegar is quite lovely.

This recipe could be used for any wildfowl. Turkey is in fact not even mentioned in the original, but it is ideally suited to the dish. While the notion of boiling a whole turkey may seem odd, the cooking technique was common into the first few decades of the 20th century. Boiling was by far the most common method used by American cooks of the past for just about any meat. Boiling required less time, fuel, and attention than roasting; it was economical, resulting in broth as well as cooked meat; and it tenderized tougher or older cuts of meat

While the original recipe calls for a whole bird, the modern recipe is adapted to use with prepackaged turkey pieces. If you would like use a small whole bird (10–12 pounds), cut it into 10 pieces before boiling—it is really difficult and potentially dangerous to lift a whole steaming turkey from a pot of boiling broth. For this larger amount of turkey, you will need to double the other ingredients. The original recipe also uses mutton broth. In England in the 17th century, mutton was very common, so the broth was readily available. In this version, we will use the broth from the turkey. Purists can certainly use mutton broth (4 cups) to experience the recipe as written.

Inside the thatched-roof dwellings, the inhabitants are baking bread, stirring up Thanksgiving dinner, spinning, and preserving food. Outside others are harvesting crops, sheering sheep, salting fish, chopping wood, planing clapboards, and hoeing gardens. On our last visit, after a heavy rain, many men were digging small ditches to control water flow and others were trying to drain a muddy pigpen—all with the tools of 1627. The interpreters actually do the work of the plantation.

THANKSGIVING DINNER—Old *and* Modern

Boiled Fowl, 1623 Recipe

To boile any wild Fowle, as Mallard, Teale, Widgeon, or such like: First boile the Fowle by it selfe, then take a quart of strong Mutton broth, and put it into a pipkin, and boile it; then put into it good store of sliced Onions, a bunch of sweete pot-hearbes, and a lump of sweete butter; after it hath boiled well, season it with verjuice, salt and sugar, and a little whole Pepper; which done, take up your Fowle and break it up according to the fashion of Carving, and sticke a few Cloves about it; then put it into the broth with Onions, and there let it take a walme or two, & so serve it and the broth foorth uppon Sippets, some use to thicken it with toasts of bread steept and strained, but that is as please the Cooke.

Gervase Markham, *The English Huswife*, 1623

Modern Version

4 pounds turkey parts (thighs and legs work well for this recipe)
1 teaspoon salt
2 large onions, sliced into ¼-inch rings
Bundle of fresh herbs, tied (any combination of the following are appropriate: sage, thyme, parsley, marjoram or savory), or 2 tablespoons dried

⅓ cup red wine vinegar or cider vinegar
2 tablespoons (¼ stick) salted butter
2 tablespoons sugar
1 teaspoon black peppercorns
¼ teaspoon ground cloves
6 to 8 1-inch-thick slices of hearty bread, cut in half and toasted or fried until browned

Rinse the turkey pieces and place them in a pot large enough to accommodate them. Cover with cold water and add the salt. Cover the pot and bring the contents to a boil over medium-high heat. Reduce the temperature to keep the broth at a low simmer for one hour. Periodically, skim any froth that rises to the surface.

After an hour, remove the turkey pieces and set aside to cool. Raise the heat until the broth comes to a boil. Continue boiling, uncovered, until the liquid is reduced by half. This will take about an hour. When the broth is reduced, add the sliced onions, herbs, vinegar, butter, sugar, peppercorns, and cloves. Simmer for about 20 minutes, until the onions are soft. While the broth is simmering, cut the cooled turkey into serving pieces.

Before serving, taste the broth and adjust the seasoning. Place the meat into the broth and "let it take a walme or two," that is, let it simmer gently for just a minute. Pour the turkey and sauce into a serving bowl. Pass the "sippets" (toasted bread slices) to serve as a base for the turkey and to sop up the sauce. *Serves 6*

The "First Thanksgiving" feast probably included cod, sea bass, wild fowl, corn meal and wheat breads, venison, and perhaps a sallet, or vegetable dish. Beverages were beer and "aqua vitae" (strong waters).

After several hours of wandering in and out of the Pilgrim houses, take a stroll down along the water to Hobbamock's Homesite, where you will meet the Wampanoag Indian interpreters. Unlike the interpreters in the plantation, they

You Say Pumpkin, I Say Squash . . .

"Pompion" is the common 16th- and 17th-century English word for what we now call squash and pumpkins. Squash, the shortened, English version of the Narragansett Indian word *asquutasquash*, first appeared in print in 1643. Confused? It only gets worse. In reality there is absolutely no botanical difference between squash and pumpkins. William Woys Weaver, in *Heirloom Vegetable Gardening*, explains that "pumpkin is merely a term of convenience, for there are only squash . . . pumpkins are really a type of squash."

New World pumpkins and squashes were introduced into Europe in the late 15th century. By the time the colonists made their way to Plymouth, "pompions" had gained widespread acceptance in England. In New England, stewed pumpkin was common, everyday fare—a "standing dish"—particularly in the fall and winter. The lyrics to a song traditionally attributed to 1630 reveal the colonists' dependence on pumpkins:

For pottage, and puddings, and custards, and pies,
Our pumpkins, and parsnips are common supplies;
We have pumpkin at morning and pumpkin at noon,
If it was not for pumpkin we should be undone.

This recipe for stewed pumpkin comes from John Josselyn, an early traveler to New England. His description of the common dish is full of wonderful details that provide both a sense of how the finished dish should taste ("tart like an apple") and a vivid glimpse into a colonial kitchen ("stew them upon a gentle fire a whole day"). "The Ancient New England standing dish" is one of the earliest written recipes from New England.

The Ancient New England Standing Dish

But the Housewives manner is to slice them when ripe, and cut them into dice, and so fill a pot with them of two or three Gallons, and stew them upon a gentle fire a whole day, and as they sink, they fill again with fresh Pompions, not putting any liquor to them; and when it is stew'd enough, it will look like bak'd Apples; this they Dish, putting Butter to it, and a little Vinegar, (with some Spice, as Ginger, &c.) which makes it tart like an Apple, and so serve it up to be eaten with Fish or Flesh: It provokes Urin extreamly and is very windy.

John Josselyn, *New-Englands Rarities Discovered,* 1672

Modern Version

4 cups cooked squash or pumpkin, mashed
4 tablespoons butter
1 to 2 tablespoons of cider vinegar
1 to 2 teaspoons of ground ginger (or any combination of nutmeg, cloves, cinnamon, and/or pepper, to taste)
1 teaspoon salt

Place the squash, butter, vinegar, and spices in a saucepan over low heat. Stir and heat until all the ingredients are well combined and hot. Adjust the seasonings to your liking and serve. *Serves 6* relate the contemporary world of the tribe to the history they represent. They will tell you about Hobbamock, a real Indian who lived in the area during the 1620s. He acted as a guide and interpreter for the colonists and lived with them from 1621 until he died, around 1643.

He lived in a house covered with bark called a *neesquottow.* You can creep inside one of their structures by lifting the leather covering the doorway. Inside, you'll find people sitting on animal skins around a fire to keep warm and listening to an interpreter in Wampanoag clothing. Outside we saw men burning out the inside of a log canoe.

LODGING

THE GOVERNOR BRADFORD ON THE HARBOR
98 Water St., Plymouth, MA 02360
800-332-1620, 508-746-6200;
www.governorbradford.com
This inn overlooks Plymouth Harbor and is near Plymouth Rock.

JOHN CARVER INN
25 Summer St., Plymouth, MA 02360
800-274-1620;
www.johncarverinn.com
The inn is decorated in colonial style, and some of the staff are dressed in colonial attire.

THORNTON ADAMS HOUSE BED & BREAKFAST
73C Warren Ave., Plymouth, MA 02360
888-747-9700, 508-830-1849;
www.thorntonadams.com
This colonial classic is above the bay with an ocean view.

WHITFIELD HOUSE
26 North St., Plymouth, MA 02360
800-884-2889, 508-747-6735;
whitfieldhouse.com
This Federal home was built by a wealthy merchant in 1782.

RESTAURANTS

HEARTH 'N KETTLE
John Carver Inn, 25 Summer St., Plymouth, MA 02360
508-747-7405
Traditional Cape Cod cooking is served, including Indian pudding and seafood.

ISAAC'S ON THE WATERFRONT
114 Water St., Plymouth, MA 02360
508-830-0001
Seafood is a specialty.

WOODS SEAFOOD
800-626-1011, 508-746-0261
Town Pier off US 44,
Plymouth, MA 02360
The owner also runs a seafood business so you know it is fresh. Try a lobster roll or broiled catch of the day.

EVENTS

July: Plymouth Blessing of the Fleet and Boat Parade; 508-746-0037
August–November: Pilgrim Progress 508-224-2063
November: Thanksgiving Parade 508-532-1621
Plimoth Plantation Thanksgiving 508-746-1622
December: Christmas in Historic Plymouth; 508-830-1040

INFORMATION

PLYMOUTH COUNTY CONVENTION AND VISITORS BUREAU
800-231-1620, 508-747-0100;
www.seeplymouth.com

DESTINATION PLYMOUTH
170 Water St.,
Plymouth, MA 02360; 508-747-7533;
www.visit-plymouth.com

PLYMOUTH VISITOR INFORMATION CENTER
130 Water St., P.O. Box ROCK,
Plymouth, MA 02361
800-USA-1620, 508-747-7525

THE SOUTH SHORE

Soon after Plymouth was firmly established, its first residents and others who joined them began to spread northward along the shore. Many of these communities have retained a colonial feel and look, with a plenitude of fine old houses surviving, because the big roads and industrial developments of later centuries went elsewhere. So if you have the time and inclination, poking northward up MA 3A from Plymouth toward Boston will be much more rewarding than flying by on MA 3.

KINGSTON

Christopher Jones, whose persona you may have met on the Mayflower II, was the master on the *Mayflower*, and he agreed to stay in Plymouth with his ship and crew until spring. He lived in Kingston, where the Jones River was named for him.

HISTORICAL SITES *and* MUSEUMS
The **Major John Bradford House** (781-585-6300; www.jrvhs.org), Landing Rd. at Maple St. Open July and Aug. for breakfast, 9–11:30. The 1714 house overlooks the Jones River. As the grandson of Governor William Bradford, Major Bradford was active in the town of Kingston as a selectman and moderator of the first town meeting. The west half of the house was built first, and in 1720 the Bradfords completed the other half. Governor Bradford's original manuscript of his *Of Plymouth Plantation* was once kept in the house.

Shipbuilding prospered in Kingston, beginning in 1713. The *Independence* was built there in 1776 at **Holmes Shipyard** (1765), Landing Marine on Landing Rd. This 16-gun brig was active during the Revolution.

LODGING

1760 BRADFORD HOUSE
6 River St., Kingston, MA 02364
781-585-2646;
www.1760bradfordhouse.com
Peabody Bradford, great-grandson of

Plymouth Colony's Governor William Bradford, built this home on the northern bank of the Jones River. All goods, cattle, and travelers arrived by boat at the dock and proceeded to Kingston.

DUXBURY

Just north of Kingston, South Duxbury and Duxbury are loaded with sites associated with the earliest Pilgrims. Captain's Nook Hill, Standish Street, was the homesite chosen by Captain Myles Standish and Elder William Brewster; it looks out upon both Kingston Bay and Duxbury Bay.

HISTORICAL SITES *and* MUSEUMS
Nearby in the Standish Reservation on Crescent Street, the **Myles Standish Monument** overlooks the land where he spent the last 36 years of his life. His statue

stands extending a hand in friendship and holds a royal charter for Plymouth. Visitors can walk up to the top of the monument for a fine view of Duxbury Beach, Clark's Island, and Plymouth.

William Brewster was a tower of strength for the Pilgrims during their difficult early years. The site of his home (ca. 1631), off Marshall St. at Bradford Rd., is marked with a stone. When he died in 1645 the land was inherited by his sons, Love and Jonathan.

The **Old Burying Ground** (ca. 1635), Chestnut St. and Pilgrim By-Way, is also marked as the site of the first two meetinghouses; they were built in 1635 and in 1706. Myles Standish, his daughter Lora, and daughter-in-law Mary are buried here. John and Priscilla Alden (Longfellow's poem romanticizes Priscilla's reply to John's brokered proposal: "Speak for yourself, John") rest in the Alden Corner in unmarked graves; their son Jonathan has the oldest gravestone, dated 1697.

John and Priscilla Alden built their second home, the **John Alden House,** in 1653 (781-934-9092; www.alden.org), 105 Alden St. Open mid-May–mid-Oct. Ten generations of Aldens lived in the house. The front section has a large central chimney, and the back section probably incorporated the first Alden house built in 1628, which was then moved to connect with the 1653 house. An archaeological dig confirmed this guess, and some of the excavated artifacts are displayed in the house. Look for the clam-and-oyster-shell ceiling in the great room.

LODGING

THE WINSOR HOUSE INN
390 Washington St.,
Duxbury, MA 02332; 781-934-0991;
www.winsorhouseinn.com
In 1803 Nathaniel Winsor built the house for his daughter. Although primarily a restaurant, the inn also has rooms for overnight guests.

POWDER POINT BED & BREAKFAST
182 Powder Point Ave.,
Duxbury, MA 02332
781-934-7727; www.ppbab.com
This expanded ship's carpenter Greek-revival cottage (ca.1820) is on a peninsula.

RESTAURANTS

THE WINSOR HOUSE INN
390 Washington St.,
Duxbury, MA 02332; 781-934-0991;
www.winsorhouseinn.com
The cuisine is American.

MARSHFIELD

In the next town northward, Marshfield, colonists chose to settle in widely separated sites where they had access to protected waterfront—Green Harbor just beyond Duxbury, and North River just south of Scituate. Ships wintered in the North River, and in 1645 Thomas Nichols built a ship there.

HISTORICAL SITES AND MUSEUMS

Not far from Green Harbor is the 1699 **Winslow House** (781-837-5753), Webster and Careswell Sts. Open Memorial Day–Columbus Day. It stands near the site of the earlier 1636 "Careswell" home built by Edward Winslow. After his wife, Elizabeth, died during the first winter ashore and Susanna White's husband also died, Susanna and Edward were married in 1621. Theirs was the first marriage to take place in Plymouth.

Isaac Winslow, their grandson, built the present house on the Winslow property. The common room and the kitchen each have exposed beams and a large fireplace. The parlor contains 18th-century paneling and woodwork, complete with a Delft-tile fireplace. Upstairs is the bedroom for Isaac's bride, Sarah, and also his office.

Much later Daniel Webster arrived to buy land from both the Winslow and Thomas families, on Webster Street. His office did not go up in flames when the rest of his estate did, and it has been moved onto the Winslow property.

Winslow Cemetery (1641), Winslow Cemetery Rd., is the burial site for Governor Edward Winslow, Governor Josiah Winslow, and a number of other Winslows and Thomases. Near Daniel Webster's grave a stone marks the site of the first meetinghouse in Marshfield (ca. 1641). Peregrine White, who was born on the *Mayflower* on November 20, 1620, is buried in the cemetery. We have spotted items that he once used in our travels in the area. His high chair, for one, is in the Mann Farmhouse in Scituate.

INFORMATION

PLYMOUTH COUNTY CONVENTION AND VISITORS BUREAU
800-231-1620, 508-747-0100; www.seeplymouth.com

SCITUATE

If you've approached England by ship from the Continent and found your eyes drawn to the White Cliffs of Dover, you can empathize with the early settlers who arrived in Scituate, just north of Marshfield. It has one of the finest harbors on the South Shore, and its cliffs must have reminded early colonists of their home in Kent.

Timothy Hatherly was an adventurer who wanted to sail on the *Mayflower* but was needed in London. But he did sail to Plymouth in 1623 and liked what he saw. In 1627 he again sailed to Plymouth, and by 1633 he and three friends applied for "a grant of land beginning at the mouth of Satuit Brook and running three miles northeasterly into the woods." They were called the "Conihasset Proprietors."

A number of interesting 17th-century structures have survived in town.

HISTORICAL SITES *and* MUSEUMS

The linsey-woolsey curtains were all made on a late 1600s loom in the **Cudworth House** (781-545-1083; www.scituatehistoricalsociety.org), First Parish Rd. and Cudworth Rd. Open on Sun. July–Oct. The old kitchen's fireplace was built in 1636, and there is an oven in the back.

Mordecai Lincoln, one of Abraham Lincoln's ancestors, made the gigantic pot standing on the hearth. Look for the spit with a turning lever, a device that may have been the source of the phrase "done to a turn." The unfinished room upstairs was used as a church for a number of years.

The **Mann Farmhouse and Historical Museum** (781-545-1083; www.scituate.com), Stockbridge Rd. and Greenfield Lane. Open Sun. July–Oct. Richard and Rebecca Mann came from England around 1644. Unfortunately, Richard fell into a pond and drowned: "Wee find that by coming over the pond from his owne house towards the farms that he brake through the iyce and was in soe deep that he could not get out."

Like many other colonial homes, the Mann Farmhouse has gone through

Kathleen Laidlaw weaving curtains, top, and a treasure found in the Mann Farmhouse and Historical Museum

many changes. A late-1600s foundation sits under a 1700s house, and an ell was attached in 1825. The house remained in the Mann family until the last member died. Most of the furnishings you will see belonged to the Manns, including Peregrine White's high chair, marked "PW 1620 TM 1650" after it was used by Thomas Mann.

Upstairs is a sail loft dating to 1821; see if you can find the "baggy wrinkle" up there. Also called a "bag o' wrinkle," it is used by sailors to prevent chafe between lines and sails as they rub against each other in a seaway. It was essential to keeping the rigging working on long voyages. Made from bits of old rope yarns woven into longish bunches of padding, baggy wrinkle was attached to rope stays, shrouds, and other lines that might come into contact with sails and wear holes in them.

Mystery unfolded when the last Mann heirs pulled up floorboards in 1967 and found two cans containing 18th-century coins. Also found was a bag with the name "Holmes" that could have been buried by the Scituate pirate, Holmes, who had captured a ship, taken the loot, and buried it. He was hanged for his pains, but perhaps one of the Manns found the treasure and secreted it in the attic.

Stockbridge Mill (ca. 1640) (781-545-1083), Country Way. Open Sun. July–Oct. It is the oldest operating water-powered gristmill in the country. Isaac

Stedman built this mill with equipment he brought from England. The mill has been restored and still grinds corn today.

Samuel Woodworth wrote "The Old Oaken Bucket," which immortalized the pond and the mill, after living in Scituate beginning in 1784. Later, while living in New York on a particularly hot day, Woodworth yearned, "What would I not give for a drink from the old well in Scituate." The well is still there on Old Oaken Bucket Road.

The "Old Oaken Bucket" well has a fine example of a well sweep poised above it. The sweep is a long pole leaned against a Y-shaped supporting fulcrum. The bucket hangs from the end of the pole over the well, ready to go down for water and be lifted full with minimal effort. Simple and efficient engineering of ancient lineage.

LODGING

THE ALLEN HOUSE
18 Allen Place, Scituate, MA 02066
781-545-8221; www.allenhousebnb.com
It was built by William Paley Allen in 1905 and has a view of the harbor and the ocean.

THE INN AT SCITUATE HARBOR
7 Beaver Dam Rd.,
Scituate Harbor, MA 02066
800-368-3818, 781-545-5550;
innatscituateharbor.com
This location on the sea offers views and walking along the beach.

OCEANSIDE INN
8 Oceanside Dr., Scituate, MA 02066
781-544-0002;
www.bnboceansideinn.com
You can see the flashing Minot's light with its 1-4-3 flash meaning "I Love You." The beach is right in front of the inn.

RESTAURANTS

BARKER TAVERN
21 Barker Rd., Scituate, MA 02066
781-545-6533, 800-966-6533;
www.thebarker.com
Originally built by John Williams in 1634, it was used as a garrison during King Philip's War (1675–76). Sections of the original house remain in the entrance and the room on the left.

INFORMATION

SCITUATE CHAMBER OF COMMERCE
P.O. Box 410, Scituate, MA 02066
781-545-4000

PLYMOUTH COUNTY CONVENTION AND VISITORS BUREAU
800-231-1620, 508-747-0100;
www.seeplymouth.com

COHASSET

The next town north, Cohasset, now a Boston suburb and sailing center because of its fine harbor, began with a needed industry. Mordecai Lincoln, an ancestor of Abraham Lincoln, started his ironworks here around 1704. By 1708 George Wilson and Joseph Southern began building ships.

HISTORICAL SITES *and* MUSEUMS

Colonists lived around the handsome common then just as residents do today; all the houses are private, and some of them date from the colonial period. Here's a place to feast your eyes on surviving beauties of colonial architecture: the homes of James Stutson (1750) at 3 N. Main, Adam Beal (1756) at 7 N. Main, Nehemiah Hobart (1722) at 19 N. Main, Joseph Bates (1713) at 67 N. Main, and James Hall (1750) at 3l Highland.

If you like reminders of the role of the sea in this area, visit the **Maritime Museum** (781-383-1434; www.cohassethistoricalsociety.org), Elm St. The 1760 building was once Bates Ship Chandlery at the Cove. It was moved to Elm Street in the 1950s. The maritime collections include paintings, photographs, scrimshaw, and ship models.

Also operated by the Cohasset Historical Society is the **Captain John Wilson House** (781-383-1434), Elm St. Open summers. The house has antique furnishings.

The **Captain John Smith Monument**, Town Landing, marks the place where the enterprising captain and explorer landed in 1614.

LODGING

COHASSET HARBOR RESORT
124 Elm St., Cohasset, MA 02025;
781-383-6650;
www.cohassetharborresort.com
The resort is on the harbor with views.

RESTAURANTS

**ATLANTICA AND
THE OLDE SALT HOUSE**
44 and 40 Border St., Cohasset, MA 02025; 781-383-0900
The two restaurants are connected and both serve seafood as well as pub fare. The Olde Salt House serves outdoors.

INFORMATION

COHASSET CHAMBER OF COMMERCE
P.O. Box 336, Cohasset, MA 02025
781-383-1010;
www.cohassetchamber.org

PLYMOUTH COUNTY CONVENTION AND VISITORS BUREAU
800-231-1620, 508-747-0100;
www.seeplymouth.com

HINGHAM

Just to the west of Cohasset, but protected from the open ocean by Hull peninsula, is Hingham. Twenty-eight colonists arrived here from England with the Reverend Peter Hobart in 1635, built a meetinghouse, and named their town Hingham after their hometown in England. Originally an agricultural community, Hingham diversified by adding shipyards, an ironworks, and mills.

Today, Hingham is a pleasant suburb of Boston that has not lost much of its original character in older sections of town. You can stroll the streets past many colonial homes, now in private hands. We were lucky enough to have relatives living there and spent many Thanksgiving holidays in town. After attending church services in the Old Ship Meeting House and having a traditional dinner, we drove to Plimoth Plantation to enjoy the Pilgrim interpreters with our young children.

HISTORICAL SITES *and* MUSEUMS
If you'd like to visit a church that looks like a ship, don't miss the 1681 **Old Ship**

Church (781-749-1679), 90 Main St., which remains one of the oldest wooden churches still in use in the country. Look up from the box pews to see the oak-beamed ceiling in the shape of a ship's hull upside down. The woodwork in the church is spectacular, almost guaranteed to keep you awake through a long sermon. (Did you know that colonials were kept awake in church by a tickle from the end of the tithingman's rod?)

The 1680 **Old Ordinary** (781-749-0013), Lincoln St. Open mid-June–mid-Sep., closed Sun. and Mon. This building began as a two-room house for Thomas Andrews. His son, with the same name, began to sell drinks in 1702, then Francis Barker bought it in 1740 and ran it as a tavern. Today the building contains 14 rooms of furnishings, textiles, paintings, glass, wallpaper, pewter, and clothing. The 1760 section has been kept as a taproom. Upstairs, several cradles include those of two governors: John Andrew and John Long. Frederick Law Olmsted planned the colonial-style garden in the 19th century.

The **Ensign John Thaxter House,** 70 South St., started life as a simple four-room house before the owner added more rooms. Inside, the original panels painted by John Hazlitt around 1785 are still intact. The house is now the Hingham Community Center.

Like Cohasset, Hingham is lucky to have an impressive collection of private homes dating from the colonial period. Most of them are on Main Street, including the Daniel Cushing House (ca. 1690) at 209 Main, the Hawkes Fearing House (1784) at 303, the John Tower House (1664) at 518, the Edward Wilder House (ca. 1650) at 597, the Theophilus Cushing House at 753 and also 757 Main, and the Daniel Shute House (1763) at 768. On North Street you will find the Samuel Lincoln House (1667) at 172, the Benjamin Lincoln House (1673) at 181, and the Samuel Lincoln House (pre-1740) at 182.

INFORMATION

PLYMOUTH COUNTY CONVENTION AND VISITORS BUREAU
800-231-1620, 508-747-0100; www.seeplymouth.com

WEYMOUTH

The settlement of the adjoining town, Weymouth, is complicated and intriguing. In 1622 two ships, the *Charity* and the *Swan,* arrived with men to set up a fishing station and trading post. They were financed by London ironmonger Thomas Weston, the original leader of the group that had backed the Pilgrims. They called their town Wessagussett. They built the trading post, but because they did not plant crops, the settlement failed. A second wave of settlers—including farmers this time—led by Captain Robert Gorges arrived a year later with their families and moved into the buildings left by the first group. In addition to farming, the new settlers soon engaged in fishing and lumbering. Sir Ferdinando Gorges, Robert's father, was to be governor, but when his influence faltered and questions about his right to the land arose, Robert returned to England. Some of the settlers remained, and a small group of families from Weymouth, England, joined them in 1624. The town was incorporated as the Plantation of Weymouth in 1635.

Today, Weymouth is largely a bedroom community; many of the inhabitants work outside town but enjoy coming home to this unpretentious place.

HISTORICAL SITES *and* MUSEUMS

North Weymouth Cemetery, North and Norton Sts., has graves dating to the 1600s. The parents of Abigail Adams, William Smith and Elizabeth Quincy Smith, are here.

Abigail Adams reminded her husband as he was working on the Declaration of Independence, "Remember the ladies, and be more generous and favourable to them than your ancestors. Do not put such unlimited power into the hands of the husbands. Remember all men would be tyrants if they could. If particular care is not paid to the ladies we are determined to foment a Revolution, and will not hold ourselves bound by any laws in which we have no voice, or Representation."

Abigail Adams Birthplace (781-335-4205; www.abigailadams.org), North and Norton Sts. Open July–Labor Day. The house dates from 1685. Abigail, the wife of John Adams, the second president, was born in 1744, and she also became the mother of John Quincy Adams, the sixth president. The house has been renovated and restored and is furnished with period pieces.

QUINCY

Just west of Weymouth lies Quincy, now an industrial city on the fringe of Boston but still a separate and self-sufficient port and manufacturing town. Called the City of Presidents, it was home to our second and sixth presidents. Quincy's earliest beginnings date to 1625 when Richard Wollaston arrived with male settlers. Thomas Morton, a London lawyer, took over from Wollaston and built a trading post. Morton became infamous in Plymouth Colony for erecting a maypole at Merry Mount, as he called his settlement, and extending a drinking and dancing festival for days. But the Pilgrim neighbors' main complaint was far from frivolous: He had been trading firearms and liquor to the Indians for pelts. By 1628 Morton had been sent back to England, and the maypole was cut down. (He soon returned to cause more trouble.)

The Adams and Quincy families settled here in the 1630s and began to produce outstanding leaders. Industry arrived in the form of tanneries that produced shoes and granite cut for monuments and churches. Shipbuilding prospered from the 17th century through the launching of the *Massachusetts* in 1789 and far beyond the colonial era.

HISTORICAL SITES and MUSEUMS

The **Adams National Historic Site,** 1250 Hancock St. (617-770-1175; www.nps.gov/adam. This phone number is for all sites. Stop by the National Park Service Center to purchase tickets for a trolley tour of the Adams sites. You can park in the garage behind the center. Call or check the Web site for directions.) The houses are open Apr.–Nov. The Adams National Historic Site was home to four generations of the Adams family. The complex includes the Adams Mansion and the birthplaces of John Adams and John Quincy Adams.

John Hancock, president of the Continental Congress during the American Revolution, was also born in Quincy at a site that is now the **Quincy Historical Society Museum** (617-773-1144; www.discoverquincy.com), 8 Adams St.

The **Adams Mansion**, 135 Adams St., was built in 1731, bought by John and Abigail Adams in 1787, and passed down through the Adams generations. It is now run by the National Park Service. Remarkably, all its furnishings were used by the family in the house, so you can trace the development of style from colonial times to 1927.

Look for the John Singleton Copley painting of John Adams, the Trumbull engraving, a 300-year-old grandfather clock, the Louis XV safe, and high-cushion chairs specially designed for the hoopskirts of the day. A modern library next door holds the Adams collection of manuscripts and books.

In spite of their busy and sometimes tumultuous lives, both John and Abigail Adams left a significant literary heritage. The beautifully crafted letters they sent each other when John was away are among the best in American literature. And the correspondence between John Adams and Thomas Jefferson—first patriots together, then political enemies finally reconciled through words later in their live— is a treasure. It stopped only in 1826 when they died within hours of each other on the Fourth of July.

There's a secret hiding place in the chimney in case of attack by Indians in the **John Quincy Adams Birthplace**, 141 Franklin St. The 1663 building continued to be the home of John and Abigail Adams until they returned from England, where John had been the United States minister to the Court of St. James's. John Quincy Adams was born in the house in 1767.

The Constitution of Massachusetts was drafted in John Adams's study in 1779; he promoted some of the structural features that characterize our federal Constitution, including the separation of powers among three branches of government and the inclusion of a bill of rights.

Nearby is the **John Adams Birthplace**, 133 Franklin St. This 1681 house was the home of Deacon John and Susanna Boylston Adams. John Adams was born here in 1735.

John Quincy Adams and his family sat in pew 54 at the **United First Parish Church** (1636), Hancock and Washington Sts. The church is an 1828 structure on the site of the original. Built of Quincy granite, the church is often called the Stone Temple. The Adams crypt contains the remains of John and Abigail Adams and John Quincy and Louisa Catherine Adams.

There's another etched window in the **Josiah Quincy House** (617-471-4508), 20 Muirhead St. (Phone 617-227-3956 for a schedule of opening days.) The 1770 house was home to six Quincys named Josiah. During the Revolution the family could watch the British coming and going. A windowpane upstairs contains a message etched during the siege of Boston, as Josiah watched General Gage, who had been replaced by Howe, depart: "October l0th 1775 Governor Gage saild for England with a fair wind." The house is filled with Quincy furnishings, and the fireplaces are handsome with English Sadler tiles. This house is preserved by the Society for the Preservation of New England Antiquities (SPNEA).

The **Hancock Cemetery**, Hancock St., was named for the Reverend John Hancock, whose son was the famous first signer of the Declaration of Independence. The cemetery dates from 1640, and the earliest grave, that of Henry Adams, is marked 1646. Abigail Adams's grandfather John Quincy is buried here, as well as Josiah Quincy. Sixty-nine veterans of the Revolutionary War also lie here.

> Look for a romantic inscription in the **Quincy Homestead**, 34 Butler Rd. The house was built in 1686 by Edmund Quincy and enlarged by later Quincys in 1706. Dorothy Quincy married John Hancock, who took her diamond ring and etched on a window, "You I love and you alone." Look for the secret chamber where American patriots hid during the Revolution.

LODGING

ADAMS INN
29 Hancock St., Quincy, MA 02171
800-368-4012, 617-328-1500;
bwadamsinn.com
The hotel has a gazebo and pier on the water.

INFORMATION

GREATER BOSTON CONVENTION AND VISITORS BUREAU
2 Copley Place, Suite 105,
Boston, MA 02116
888-SEE BOSTON, 617-536-4100;
www.bostonusa.com

MANSFIELD

Before entering Boston, you might want to take a short side trip southwest to Mansfield to visit the **Fisher-Richardson House** (508-339-8793), on Willow St. The house dates from 1704 and was expanded in 1800 as the family grew to nine children. This home is especially interesting because it portrays the lives of families who did not live in mansions but instead in dwellings like those inhabited by much of the population. The house was never "tampered with prior to the time of restoration after about 200 years." It is furnished with original pieces from relatives of former residents or local citizens. And there is an especially poignant doll collection, reminding us of the dolls our mothers and grandmothers played with.

Boston, Cambridge, Lexington, Concord

In many cities, looking for traces of their colonial past can be daunting, even fruitless. Sometimes major buildings have been torn down to make way for new ones; sometimes changes in street layouts obscure even the sites where these buildings once stood. Parts of Boston suffered this inevitable cycle of razing and rebuilding, but others did not. Perhaps because the city was so central to the entire colonial experience, succeeding generations of citizens may have preserved the physical evidence of their past more doggedly than was the custom in other places.

As a result, original buildings stand in the shadow of skyscrapers, and even the downtown upheavals of the Big Dig that put Interstate 93 underground has not disturbed them. You can look at the facades of buildings that colonial citizens saw, enter the rooms where important meetings were held, stand on key sites of conflict in the run-up to the Revolution. You can walk the Freedom Trail, justly the most famous historical walk in America. And surrounding towns like Cambridge, Lexington, and Concord have carefully maintained not only specific sites but also the ambience of their colonial past. Some sites, like the bridge in Concord and the USS *Constitution* in Charlestown, are national shrines, while others, like the restored Saugus Ironworks, help provide understanding of the role industry played in the development of the colony. There are enough wonderful historical sites in this region to keep you going for some time.

Boston

William Blackstone arrived with Robert Gorges in 1623 to settle in Wessagussett but moved across the bay in 1625 to a hilly neck of land that jutted into Massachusetts Bay, a place the Indians called Shawmut, or "living waters." His house overlooked the present northwest corner of Boston Common. This young minister had a Cambridge University degree but chose to live a solitary existence in Shawmut with his two hundred books.

In 1630, when John Winthrop and his newly arrived Puritan settlers just across the river in Charlestown were having trouble because they did not have pure water, an Indian carried a letter from Blackstone to Winthrop that began, "Worthy Mr. Winthrop, it grieves me to know that there hath been so much sickness in your company . . . and that . . . there is dearth of good water. It is not so here, but there are good springs, and the country is pleasant to dwell in. If you will come hither with the Indian, I will show you the land."

The Puritans arrived, liked what they saw, invited Blackstone to join their church, and then moved onto Blackstone's land. This was more than the reclusive Blackstone had bargained for, so he sold the rest of his holdings and left. The colony was called Trimountain (Tremont) until the name was changed to Boston, after the Puritans' home in Lincolnshire, England.

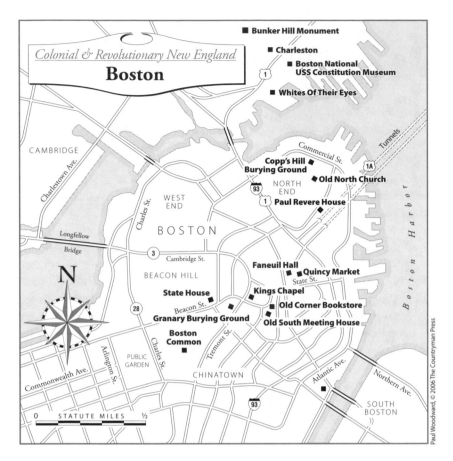

Paul Woodward, © 2006 The Countryman Press

By 1631 a ship aptly named the *Blessing of the Bay* had been built and launched for use in the Boston area. This trading vessel set the stage for Boston's auspicious future in fishing and commerce. By the 1640s Boston ships were sailing for the West Indies with cargoes of dried cod, flour, dried beef, and barrel staves; they returned with wine, sugar, and molasses. The "Sacred Cod" still hangs in the State House.

Education began early and expanded vigorously in Boston, as one might expect in a mercantile colony with strong financial backing. The Boston Latin School was founded in 1635 as the first public school in the colonies, and Harvard College became the first university in America a year later. By 1647 the General Court provided for both secondary and elementary education at public expense—but only for boys, until 1789, when girls were also included.

King Charles I planted the first seed of American rebellion when he reversed

> ✤ The warning beacon was a tall pole with an iron skillet at the top full of pitch. Someone would have to climb the pole to light it in case of an attack. It was never used, nor was a second one put in place by the Sons of Liberty in 1768.

his decision on the self-governing charter that had been granted to the Massachusetts Bay Company in 1634. When he asked for the return of the charter, the colonists gathered a militia and placed an alarm signal on top of the highest hill in Boston, Beacon Hill, to warn of English aggression. Charles II did rescind the charter in 1684 and forced Massachusetts to become a royal colony.

As a busy and growing commercial town loaded with well-educated merchants, lawyers, ministers, and shipowners, Boston led the resistance to any interference with the colony's autonomy. When England imposed one tax after the other on the colonists, Bostonians dug in their heels and refused to bend. The series of ill-advised Parliamentary mandates and taxes—the Sugar Act, Quartering Act, Stamp Act, Townshend Acts, and the Intolerable Acts—created the climate for incidents like the Boston Massacre and the Boston Tea Party. By the time patriots and redcoats faced each other in Lexington, armed rebellion had become inevitable.

HISTORICAL SITES *and* MUSEUMS

Although Boston has grown by reclaiming land from the bays and marshes that surrounded its narrow peninsula and recast itself many times since the colonial era, it has managed to preserve a past that you can still see tucked in among the skyscrapers. Begin your walk on the **Freedom Trail** at the information kiosk off Tremont Street on the Boston Common, where you can get a map. About 2 miles long through the heart of Boston, the trail is marked with a red line on the sidewalk.

Before you start, you may want to pause for a moment to appreciate where you are. No one has ever built on part of William Blackstone's land, which originally was on the water's edge of Back Bay, because it was set aside as the **Boston Common** in 1634. It was a pasture for grazing cattle, a site for militia training and public executions, and a British encampment in the years just before the Revolution. Whenever the colonists had reason to celebrate, such as the repeal of one of the oppressive British taxes, they headed for the Common. And Bostonians still use this open land in their midst for recreation.

> Massachusetts Puritans clearly believed that exposure led to deterrence, so they branded anyone who violated their code of behavior. Those who were accused of a crime had to wear a signifying letter such as *A* for adultery, *B* for blasphemy, *C* for counterfeiting, *D* for drunkenness, *F* for forgery, *R* for roguery, *S* for sedition, or *T* for theft.

The Freedom Trail's red line will lead you across the Common to the **Massachusetts State House** (617-727-3676; www.bostonhistory.org), on Beacon St., the "new" State House of 1795, designed by Charles Bulfinch. Open daily. Inside, the archives hold precious documents such as the charter of the Massachusetts Bay Company and the Massachusetts Consitution of 1780. The carved wooden "Sacred Cod" still hangs in the House of Representatives to remind visitors of one of Boston's first sources of prosperity.

Next on the trail you will pass the **Granary Burying Ground** on Tremont St. It holds the remains of many famous Americans, including John Hancock, Samuel Adams, Paul Revere, victims of the Boston Massacre, Benjamin Franklin's parents, Peter Faneuil, and some say Mother (Elizabeth) Goose.

A block farther on is the columned, stone, 1754 **King's Chapel** (617-227-2155; www.kings-chapel.org), Tremont and School Sts. Open mid-Apr.–Nov. It was built of Quincy granite on the site of a 1689 chapel, the first Anglican church in America, then became the first Unitarian Church in the country. Governor John Winthrop and William Dawes lie in the burial ground next door. A death's head was carved on the stone over Joseph Tapping's grave, and the grave of Elizabeth Pain was the inspiration for Nathaniel Hawthorne's *The Scarlet Letter.*

As you walk down School Street, a mosaic marker indicates the site of the first **Boston Latin School**. Philemon Pormont began teaching in his home in 1635, and by 1645 a building rose on the site, but it was moved in 1754. **Benjamin Franklin's Statue** was designed by Richard Greenough to honor Franklin as a printer, scientist, and signer of the Declaration of Independence and the peace treaty with Great Britain.

The next site on the trail is a major landmark of the Revolution. The **Old South Meeting House** (617-482-6439; www.oldsouthmeetinghouse.org), 310 Washington St. Open daily. The 1729 building was originally a Puritan meeting-house, which also accommodated town meetings—and, as the Revolution

approached, more ominous gatherings. All day before the Boston Tea Party, thousands of citizens met here, then the secret group slipped into the night. The Old South Meeting House is now a multimedia museum documenting the turbulent events that led to the Revolution, and it has a model of what Boston looked like in the colonial era.

Backtracking slightly, continue your walking tour from the Old South Meeting House to the **Old Corner Bookstore**, School and Washington Sts. It was the home of Thomas Crease in 1712 and later became a literary center for Boston during the 19th century. Before that it was the site of Anne Hutchinson's house, which burned in the fire that consumed much of Boston in 1711. Hutchinson was put on trial in 1637 for her nonconformity and eventually banished from the colony; she moved to what would later become Rhode Island.

If you like the sense of standing on the spot where important events occurred, look down as well as up while walking the Freedom Trail. Your eyes will be drawn to the cobblestone circles in front of the Old State House that commemorate the Boston Massacre of March 5, 1770, when five citizens were

Benjamin Franklin statue

The BOSTON TEA PARTY

No one knows exactly which citizens were involved in the Boston Tea Party, which started with the meeting here. Witnesses reported that after the meeting, one group of men gathered at Fulton's carpenter shop, another at Brewer the block maker's home, and yet another at Crane's house on the corner of Hollis and Tremont Streets during the evening of December 16, 1773. Disguised and painted as Mohawk Indians, they stormed aboard three tea ships and dumped the cargo overboard. Hawthorne used the incident as the basis for his powerful story "My Kinsman, Major Molineux."

The customs officials were removed from the vessels before the colonists attached a block and tackle to each chest so it could be hoisted up to the deck. More men splintered open the tea chests with axes, poured all 90,000 pounds of tea into the harbor, and tossed the chests in as well. The water was only 2 or 3 feet deep because the tide was low, so waterlogged tea piled up next to the ships.

After about three hours their work was done, and each man was honor-bound not to take even a pinch of the valuable tea home. When one man thrust tea into the lining of his coat, others stripped him and beat him before turning him loose. John Adams noted, "the Dye is cast: The People have passed the River and cutt away the Bridge: . . . This is the grandest Event, which has ever yet happened."

Lord North was so enraged that he supported the Coercive, or Intolerable, Acts, which started with the Boston Port Bill in 1774. This bill closed Boston Harbor to all shipping except for food and fuel until the East India Company was reimbursed for the dumped tea. The next was the Justice Act, which moved the venue of trial for any official who suppressed a riot (and therefore did not expect fairness in the colonial courts) to England. Another, the Massachusetts Government Act, abrogated the charter of the colony, and the final act forced colonists to quarter British troops at the site of any incident.

killed by British soldiers. The **Old State House** (617-720-3290: www.boston history.org), Washington St. at State St., is the oldest surviving public building in Boston. It was completed in 1713 on the site of the earlier 1657 Town House. It was here in 1761 that James Otis gave his famous speech against the "Writs of Assistance," and this was also the site of a public reading of the Declaration of Independence on July 18, 1776. Today its museum houses mementos of Boston's history as a port and center of revolutionary fervor.

A copper and gilt grasshopper adorns the top of **Faneuil Hall** (617-635-3105; www.nps.gov/bost), Congress and North Sts. The 1742 structure was donated to the city as a market by Peter Faneuil, who had made his fortune in the slave trade. The first building burned in 1761; it was rebuilt in 1763 and enlarged in 1806. James Otis called the meeting hall on the second floor the "Cradle of Liberty" because it was often filled with oratory denouncing British oppression in the decades before the Revolution. Paintings of battles hang in the hall, and a military museum, the **Ancient and Honorable Artillery Company of Massachusetts** (617-227-1638) is housed on the third floor. This museum was founded in 1638 and displays uniforms from years ago.

Facing Faneuil Hall on Merchants Row stands the popular and bustling **Quincy Market,** named after Mayor Josiah Quincy and built in the early 19th century. Although the buildings are not colonial, they retain some of the flavor of old Boston.

The **Boston Tea Party Ship and Museum** (617-269-7150; www.boston teapartyship.com), is moored at the Congress Street Bridge on Harbor Walk—a substantial excursion off the trail. The ship is open daily after a renovation in 2005. The ship is a replica of the brig *Beaver,* one of the three ships raided by the colonists. An audiovisual program shows visitors how the tea was tossed into the harbor, and there are other exhibits related to shipbuilding.

The Freedom Trail continues from Faneuil Hall, past the venerable Union Oyster House, and into the North End via a pedestrian route that as of this edition crosses a construction zone where once stood the massive I-93 elevated high-

"OLD IRONSIDES"

The USS *Constitution* is the oldest commissioned ship in the U.S. Navy, and it is a rare treat to be able to walk her decks. She is moored in the **Charlestown Navy Yard** (617-242-5670; www.ussconstitutionmuseum .org) and is open daily except Mon. Her keel was laid in 1797, and it was made of tough live oak. Paul Revere provided the copper for her bottom. Her famous nickname dates from the War of 1812 after the *Guerriere*'s shots seemed to bounce off her sides. Oliver Wendell Holmes wrote "Old Ironsides" in 1833, a poem that generated enough public sympathy to save her from condemnation. Since then she has been thoroughly restored several times. Like the cracked Liberty Bell, she has become a national symbol that needs to be preserved as long as the nation endures.

We were on board one year when she was taken out into Boston Harbor and turned around, an annual procedure to even out the sun's effect on her topsides. This happens on July Fourth, and she also receives a 21-gun salute.

A tour of the vessel brings you the flavor of sea life as you inspect the camboose (galley stove), scuttlebutt and grog tub, the bilge pumps and anchor capstan, the captain's cabin, officers' quarters, and crew's hammocks. Guides in 1812 naval uniforms are ready to answer questions.

The **USS Constitution Museum** (617-426-1812) has a number of exhibits and hands-on displays. You can swing in a sailor's hammock, raise a sail, and take a turn at the wheel. The collections include ship's logs, journals, charts, and crew members' personal gear.

way. The highway is now underground. The aftermath of the Big Dig is bringing big changes to this area, although redevelopment plans are still in flux.

The trail takes you down the main drag of the North End, an Italian-American neighborhood popular with Bostonians and tourists alike. It soon detours one block for the oldest house in Boston, the **Paul Revere House** (617-523-2338; www.paulreverehouse.org), 19 North Square. Open daily. The house dates from 1680. Revere, a silversmith and engraver, owned it from 1770 until 1800 and was active as a patriot while residing here. He created an engraving of the Boston Massacre, participated in the Boston Tea Party, and most famously, on April 18, 1775, rode to warn Lexington and Concord that British troops were coming. Exhibits include family possessions and some of Revere's work.

Next door, at 29 North Square, stands the **Pierce-Hichborn House**, built by a glass merchant, Moses Pierce. Paul Revere's cousin Nathaniel Hichborn bought the 1711 house in 1781.

The trail recrosses the main drag and heads through the leafy Paul Revere pedestrian mall to the Old North Church (617-523-6676; www.oldnorth.com), Salem and Hull Sts., where the sexton, Robert Newman, placed two lanterns in the steeple to signal Charlestown that the British were on their way across the harbor toward

Lexington and Concord. Dating from 1723, this is the oldest church building in Boston. Its formal name is Christ Church, and it is still an active Episcopal church. The bells were brought from England in 1744, and Paul Revere was one of seven boys who agreed to ring them.

A short distance up the hill is **Copp's Hill Burying Ground**, Hull and Snow Hill Sts., which has been a cemetery since the 1660s. William Copp owned the land before it was purchased by the town for this purpose; earlier, the Puritans had placed windmills here and called it Windmill Hill. Cotton Mather and his father, Increase Mather, are buried here, as is Robert Newman, the North Church sexton, and many other notables. From the hill you can get a view across the Charles River of the USS *Constitution,* from a slightly later era, and the Bunker Hill Monument, both in the city's Charlestown section.

The Freedom Trail continues across the Charles to **Bunker Hill Monument** (617-241-2258; www.nps.gov/bost), on Breed's Hill, the site of the first pitched battle of the Revolution, fought on June 17, 1775. It is open daily. During the previous night the Americans began digging a redoubt, or small fort, on Breed's Hill to defend their position. When the crew of the HMS *Lively* awoke in the morning they panicked and sent a volley of fire onto Breed's Hill, but the guns couldn't aim high enough to harm the men in the redoubt.

While the patriots continued to dig in, the redcoats were transported across the water in barges and in the afternoon stormed the hill three times before succeeding. They suffered more than a thousand casualties, including killed and wounded— more than twice the patriots' losses. When the Americans ran out of powder, they retreated north toward Cambridge, having exacted a high price from the British for the hill. A 22l-foot granite obelisk towers into the sky to mark the battle site. It was dedicated on June 17, 1843, by Daniel Webster. If you're game to climb 294 steps to the top, your reward will be a panoramic view of the city and harbor.

Here the Freedom Trail ends, but you may want to return to this side of the Charles, a bit father west, to visit Cambridge.

EVENTS June: The Battle of Bunker Hill Weekend; 617-242-5641

CAMBRIDGE

Newtown, now the city of Cambridge, was founded as a fortified town in 1630 by the Massachusetts Bay Colony. The settlers built a meetinghouse, a marketplace (now Winthrop Square), and their homes around the center.

Although Cambridge is just across the river from Boston, it has a somewhat less busy atmosphere, partly because of large tracts of land occupied by two of the country's preeminent universities, Harvard and MIT. The city's historical aspects can be enjoyed on a walking tour along Brattle Street—it was called "Tory Row"— to Harvard Yard, and then back toward Cambridge Common, where cattle once grazed. From the common you can complete the loop back to Brattle Street. Historic homes like the Hooper-Lee-Nichols House and the Longfellow House, Washington's headquarters during the siege of Boston, tell the stories that most school-children hear about. A good many academics live in the area, supporting a large number of bookstores, restaurants, and shops.

HISTORICAL SITES and MUSEUMS

Harvard College, now university, was founded in 1636 to train Puritan clergy and political leaders. If you want to get a sense of what the college looked like during the colonial era, walk around the **Old Yard** and identify some of the buildings remaining from the 18th century—Massachusetts Hall (1720), Wadsworth Hall (1726), Hollis Hall (1763), and Harvard Hall (1764). For more details stop by at the Harvard Information Center, 1353 Massachusetts Ave. (617-495-1573).

Christ Church, on Garden St. near the common, was built in 1761 by Peter Harrison, who also designed King's Chapel in Boston. In 1775 much of the Tory congregation fled to Boston, and the church became a barracks for Connecticut troops during the siege. Its organ pipes were made into bullets. But by the end of the year this temporary aberration had stopped and the church reopened for services. George and Martha Washington were present on New Year's Eve.

At the southeast corner of Cambridge Common, look down for the hoofprint **memorial to William Dawes,** the tanner who rode through Cambridge in April 1775 to spread the alarm that the British were on the way to Concord.

Cambridge Common, like its counterpart in Boston, was a center for social, political, and military events. In 1631 the land was used for grazing cattle, training soldiers, and holding public meetings. By September of 1774 patriots from other regions of New England were coming to Cambridge Common to raise their protests against the British. Three cannons taken from the British in 1775 are here. George Washington reviewed the troops and took command of the Continental Army here on July 3, 1775, an event commemorated by a bronze plaque marking what is now called the Washington Elm.

A short walk from the common through a leafy neighborhood brings you to **Longfellow National Historic Site** (617-876-4491; www.nps.gov/long), 105 Brattle St. Open daily except for Mon. and Tue. The house was built in 1759 by John Vassall Jr., one of many Tories who left Cambridge when it became a hotbed of revolt in 1774. George Washington and his family lived here during the siege of Boston from July 1775 to March 1776. Later Henry Wadsworth Longfellow and his descendants lived in the house, from 1837 until the National Park Service took over in 1974. Longfellow wrote "Paul Revere's Ride" and "The Courtship of Miles Standish" while living in this house.

There are several more interesting houses to see in Cambridge. **The Hooper-Lee-Nichols House** (1688), on Brattle St., is the oldest house in the city, now the home of the Cambridge Historical Society (617-547-4252). It is open Tue. and Thu. afternoons and by appointment.

The following houses are not open but may be viewed from the outside. The

Brattle House (1727), also on Brattle St., was built by William Brattle, another Tory who fled Cambridge. During the Revolution Major Thomas Mifflin, commissary general of the Continental Army, lived here. The Hicks House (1762), South St., was built by John Hicks, a carpenter who may have taken part in the Boston Tea Party; it is now the library of Kirkland House, a Harvard residence. **Apthorpe House** (1760), Plympton St., was built for East Apthorp, the first pastor of Christ Church. General Burgoyne and his officers lived here after their defeat at Saratoga. For more information, please call the Cambridge Office for Tourism (800-862-5678 or 617-442-2884).

LODGING

THE BOSTON PARK PLAZA HOTEL
64 Arlington St., Boston, MA 02116
800-225-2008, 617-426-2000;
www.bostonparkplaza.com
Established in 1925 by E. M. Statler, this historic hotel is in the grand style and houses several restaurants.

THE ELIOT HOTEL
370 Commonwealth Ave.,
Boston, MA 02215
800-44-ELIOT, 617-267-1607;
www.eliothotel.com
The neo-Georgian Eliot was built in the Back Bay in 1925. The restaurant Clio is in the hotel.

THE FAIRMONT COPLEY PLAZA HOTEL
138 St. James Ave., Boston, MA 02116
888-884-6060, 617-267-5300;
www.fairmontcopley.com
The hotel dates from 1912 and features large crystal chandeliers and the Oak Room restaurant.

HARBORSIDE INN
185 State St., Boston, MA 02109
888-723-7565, 617-723-7500;
www.harborsideinn.com
The building near Quincy Market was designed as a mercantile structure by 19th-century architect Gridley James Fox Bryant.

THE NEWBURY GUEST HOUSE
261 Newbury St., Boston, MA 02116
800-437-7668, 617-437-7666;
www.hagopianhotels.com
This 19th-century B&B is actually three brownstones in the Back Bay.

THE OMNI PARKER HOUSE
60 School St., Boston, MA 02108
617-227-8600; www.omnihotels.com
This historic hotel was founded in 1855 and is in the heart of downtown Boston.

THE SEAPORT HOTEL
I Seaport Blvd., Boston, MA 02210
877-SEAPORT, 617-385-4000;
www.seaporthotel.com
This waterfront hotel inspires thoughts of seafaring, and includes the restaurant Aura.

If you would rather avoid the major hotels on either side of the river, try one in Cambridge:

A BED & BREAKFAST IN CAMBRIDGE
1657 Cambridge St.,
Cambridge, MA 02138
877-994-0844, 617-868-7082;
www.cambridgebnb.com
This 1897 colonial-revival house is near Harvard Yard.

A CAMBRIDGE HOUSE, BED & BREAKFAST INN
2218 Massachusetts Ave.,
Cambridge, MA 02140
800-232-9989, 617-491-6300;
www.acambridgehouse.com
This 1892 Victorian home is a good base for sightseeing in Cambridge or Boston.

THE KENDALL HOTEL
35 Main St., Cambridge, MA 02140
617-577-1300; www.kendallhotel.com
Originally a fire station known as Engine 7, the Kendall is a member of Historic Hotels of America. The original 1874 building now includes the hotel's restaurant and displays firehouse memorabilia.

THE MARY PRENTISS INN

6 Prentiss St.,
Cambridge, MA 02140; 617-661-2929;
www.maryprentissinn.com
This historic house, now on the National
Register of Historic Places, dates from
1843, and was built by William Saunders
for his wife, Mary Prentiss.

RESTAURANTS

DURGIN-PARK

340 Faneuil Hall Marketplace,
Boston, MA 02109
617-227-2038; www.durgin-park.com
This Boston favorite has served New England cuisine for many years, including a
boiled dinner, Boston baked beans, and
Indian pudding.

NO NAME

15 Fish Pier, Boston, MA 02210
617-338-7539
This popular place provides no frills, takes
no credit cards, but serves great seafood.

UNION OYSTER HOUSE

46 Union St., Boston, MA 02108
607-227-2750;
www.unionoysterhouse.com
Established in 1846, it offers an oyster bar
and shore dinners. President Kennedy,
who had a favorite booth, was a regular.

EVENTS

March: Old State House Boston
Massacre Reenactment; 617-720-3290
April: Old North Church Lantern
617-523-6676
June: The Battle of Bunker Hill Week-
end; 617-242-5641
June–July: Boston Harborfest
617-227-1528
December: Reenactment of the Boston
Tea Party: 617-482-6439

INFORMATION

**GREATER BOSTON CONVENTION
AND VISITORS BUREAU**
2 Copley Place, Ste. 105, Boston, MA
888-SEE BOSTON, 617-536-4100;
www.bostonusa.com

LEXINGTON AND CONCORD

Although both Lexington and Concord are affluent suburbs now, legions of visitors still enjoy these towns' storied past. Revolutionary War history is around every
corner, and because woodlands have been preserved, you can almost imagine the
scenes in the 18th century. In Lexington you can begin a walking tour at the Lexington Historical Society visitor center. Lexington Road leads to Concord and the
Minute Man National Historic Park and North Bridge.

By the spring of 1775 Massachusetts was "a bonfire waiting for a match," and
the conflagration quickly erupted in Lexington and Concord and neighboring
towns. Concord was especially vulnerable to attack as both the meeting place of
the Provincial Congress and storehouse for armaments. Although General Thomas
Gage thought he would subdue the "rude rabble," the patriots were able to hear
about most of his plans in advance. Gage had secretly determined that the British
must capture the cache of military supplies at Concord. As Lieutenant Colonel
Francis Smith opened his sealed orders on April 18, the patriots had already surmised where the restless British troops were going, but they didn't know which of
two possible routes would be chosen.

Paul Revere sent the sexton of the Old North Church up into the tower armed
with two lanterns to be used as a signal to the patriots. Revere's signal: "If the British

went out by water we would shew two lanthorns in the North Church Steeple, and if by land, one, as a signal; for we were apprehensive it would be difficult to cross the Charles River, or git over Boston Neck."

HISTORICAL SITES *and* MUSEUMS

As the British troops were preparing to leave Boston in secret, two lights glowed in the Old North Church, signaling their route. Revere and William Dawes galloped off to warn John Hancock and Samuel Adams in Lexington. The two patriot leaders were sleeping in the **Hancock-Clarke House** (781-861-0928; www.lexingtonhistory.org), 36 Hancock St. Open mid-May–Oct. When Paul Revere rode up, William Munroe warned him to quiet down. Revere shouted, "You'll have enough noise before long. The regulars are out!" The 1698 house contains mementos from that day, including the drum that William Diamond used to march out the Minutemen, so called because they had agreed to fight on a minute's notice.

The **Minute Man Statue**, sculpted by Henry Hudson Kitson, greets visitors on the eastern end of the Lexington Green.

British troops arrived in Lexington in the early morning hours and were met by a group of Minutemen. Captain John Parker, known for his bravery as one of Rogers' Rangers during the French and Indian War, had told the Minutemen "not to be discovered, nor meddle, nor make with said regular troops, unless they should insult or molest us." Since the Rangers had been well known for their effectiveness in what we would now call guerrilla warfare, the advice came from experience.

British Major John Pitcairn warned his men "on no account to fire, nor even attempt it without Orders." But American witnesses noted that British officers yelled "Ye villans, ye Rebels, disperse; damn you, disperse!" Pitcairn maintained that he heard a musket fire from behind a stone wall, and then the British fired.

Revere may have been a somewhat absent-minded hero, if the stories he later told his children and grandchildren can be believed. Apparently he forgot two essential items when he left home that night—cloth to muffle the oars for crossing the Charles, and spurs for the ride itself. He dared not return and risk getting caught for violating the curfew. So one of his oarsmen got a petticoat from a girlfriend, and he sent his dog back with a message for the spurs. Or so the story goes, perhaps embellished a bit by the art of a good storyteller.

No one knows who fired the first shot, but eight Minutemen were killed in the skirmish. (A reenactment of the Battle of Lexington is held in mid-April.)

The **Lexington Visitor Center** (781-862-1450; www.lexingtonchamber.org), 1875 Massachusetts Ave., and the **Lexington Historical Society,** Meriam St., both offer dioramas of the clash on the green.

After Paul Revere rode through, the Minutemen had gathered around midnight and adjourned to **Buckman Tavern** (781-862-5598; www.lexingtonhistory.org)

on Bedford St. and the green. Open daily. Muskets from the period are on display. We also noted the mugs for serving "hot flip," a popular drink in colonial times.

Lexington Green, at Massachusetts Ave. and Bedford St., is the site of the "shot heard round the world." Couriers Paul Revere and William Dawes reported to Adams and Hancock that the regulars were coming. Captain John Parker had enough time to line his militia up on Lexington Green. Look for the large rock marking the line where the Minutemen stood. Captain Parker spoke: "Stand your ground. Don't fire unless fired upon, but if they mean to have a war, let it begin here."

Visitors can continue along Battle Road from Lexington to Concord, stopping at the **Minute Man Visitor Center** (781-674-1920). Pick up a pamphlet that maps the redcoats' route and events along the way. A stone marks the spot where Paul Revere was captured by a British patrol, who later released him without a horse. He and Dawes never got to Concord with the alarm, but a third rider who had joined them, Dr. Samuel Prescott, did.

Minute Man National Historical Park, which occupies parts of Lexington, Lincoln, and Concord, is run by the National Park Service. Open daily. In Con-

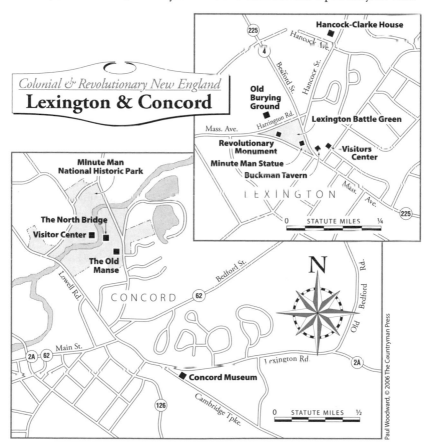

cord the NPS runs the **North Bridge Visitor Center** (978-369-6993).

By the time the British arrived in Concord, the colonists had already removed arms and ammunition by ox team. The redcoats seized the North Bridge and went on to search for munitions they thought were hidden on James Barrett's farm. In town, the British set fire to some gun carriages and, by accident, a nearby building. The Minutemen had forced the redcoats back to the west end of the bridge when they saw smoke from the fire and thought the town was being burned.

As the angered Minutemen advanced, the British withdrew over the bridge and began tearing up its planks, which further angered the Americans. In a scene of confusion, some British troops fired at the surprisingly disciplined Americans, who returned a volley with deadly effect. The panicked regulars turned and ran back toward town. The long, bloody British retreat had begun.

The British re-formed in town and started the march back to Boston, as an ever-growing patriot force sniped at them all along the way. The redcoats thought there might be a musket behind every tree. Patriots, many of them veterans of the French and Indian War, had learned how to fight behind walls, trees, and buildings. They took delight in cutting across country to ambush the British at the next angle in the road. At the end of that day the British sustained 73 dead and 26 missing, the patriots 49 dead and 5 missing.

Some of the wounded British troops were taken to the **Munroe Tavern** (781-674-9238; www.lexingtonhistory.org), 1332 Massachusetts Ave. Open daily in the afternoon. The Munroe family escaped into the woods.

The **Concord Museum** (978-369-9763; www.concordmuseum.org), is at 200 Lexington Rd. Open daily. You can learn about the history of Concord, including its original Native Americans as well as colonial and Revolutionary days. One of the two lanterns hung in the North Church in Boston is here.

Not far from Concord Bridge is the **Old Manse** (978-369-3909; www.thetrustees.org), 1269 Monument St. Open Apr.–Oct. The house was built by William Emerson in 1770. He was on hand to see the battles of the Revolution. Later Ralph Waldo Emerson, his grandson, lived in the house. Nathaniel Hawthorne rented the house as well.

LODGING

CONCORD'S COLONIAL INN
48 Monument Square,
Concord, MA 01742
800-370-9200, 978-369-9200;
www.concordscolonialinn.com
A hotel since 1889, the building dates from 1716. New England fare is served in the dining room.

HAWTHORNE INN BED & BREAKFAST
462 Lexington Rd., Concord, MA 01742
508-369-5610; www.concordmass.com
The name comes from its garden, which has larch trees planted by Nathaniel Hawthorne.

LONGFELLOW'S WAYSIDE INN
76 Wayside Inn Rd., Sudbury, MA 01776
978-443-1776; www.wayside.org
The 1716 stagecoach stop inspired Henry Wadsworth Longfellow's *Tales of a Wayside Inn* and is the oldest inn still in business in the country. The hotel and restaurant feature colonial-costumed staff.

RESTAURANTS

AGIO BISTRO
84 Thoreau St., Concord, MA 01742
978-371-1333
The restaurant is on the second floor of the old train station. Mediterranean selections are popular.

MERCHANT'S ROW
The Colonial Inn, 48 Monument Square, Concord, MA 01742; 978-369-9200; www.concordscolonialinn.com/restaurants
The cuisine is New England fare.

EVENTS

April: Patriots' Day Celebration with reenactments of the Battle of Lexington and Concord, and Paul Revere's ride.
781-862-1703, 978-369-6993

INFORMATION

CONCORD CHAMBER OF COMMERCE
15 Walden St., Suite 7,
Concord, MA 01742: 978-369-3120;
www.concordmachamber.org

CONCORD VISITOR CENTER
58 Main St., Concord, MA 01742
978-369-3120

LEXINGTON CHAMBER OF COMMERCE AND VISITOR CENTER
1875 Massachusetts Ave.,
Lexington, MA 02420; 781-862-2480;
www.lexingtonchamber.org

SAUGUS

The Saugus ironworks dates from 1646. Representing an English investment totaling more than $165,000 by current standards, it offered the first sustained production of cast and wrought iron, marking the beginning of the American iron and steel industry. Today the historic area with the ironworks has been reconstructed, a process guided by the architects of Colonial Williamsburg.

The Saugus Iron Works National Historic Site (781-233-0050), 244 Central St., is open daily. It has a reconstructed blast furnace, working waterwheels, and a forge. Enter the museum and watch a video on the process as well as see artifacts recovered from excavations. A 17th-century house, the Iron Works House, has exhibits and early American furnishings.

SALEM AND THE NORTII SHORE

Boston Harbor divides two quite distinct maritime worlds along the Massachusetts coast. To the south lie fine sand beaches and warmer water, while to the north the shore is rockbound and the water cold and often deep. To the north there is no long, sheltering cape to absorb the wrath of Atlantic gales, and harbors of refuge are an absolute need for seafarers. Many of them—Marblehead, Salem, Gloucester, Newburyport—prospered through offshore fishing and adventurous world trade, fostering skilled seamen who sustained their living from the ocean during the colonial era and later manned warships and privateers during the Revolution and the War of 1812.

The maritime heritage is still strong on the North Shore. Marblehead remains the yachting capital of Massachusetts, and Gloucester still sends fishing fleets to sea, although in reduced numbers. Fortunes made in world trade and shipbuilding created the mansions that line the streets of Salem and Newburyport. Artists who look to the sea for inspiration still choose to live and work on Cape Ann. There is much to do, from taking whale-watching tours out of Gloucester to visiting art galleries in Rockport, historic houses in Marblehead, or a major museum like the Peabody Essex in Salem.

SALEM

Like a handful of other colonial cities, Salem prospered early through its ties to the sea. Fishing was the first major industry, and early Salem trading vessels carried cargoes of dried cod, whalebone, whale and fish oil, as well as furs bartered from the Indians. Salem shipyards produced many ships for trade, and during the Revolution many of them were converted into privateers. The Continental Congress licensed these armed commerce-raiding vessels to harass British ships and to take prizes. Salem provided 158 ships for this purpose, at which it was highly successful, while it also built and manned larger warships to combat the British fleet. Between the Revolution and the War of 1812 it became one of the busiest ports in the country, pioneering trade to far regions of the world. Salem's peak of affluence came during these years, as wealthy merchants used their fleets to develop the new and extremely lucrative trade with the Far East.

As world trade in sailing ships gradually gave way to coal and steam after the Civil War, Salem turned to the leather and shoe industry and some coastal trade during the late 19th century. The city lay dormant during later eras of urban deconstruction and rapid suburban growth, sparing many of its historic buildings from demolition. In recent years Salem has shared in the resurgence of interest in heritage tourism, and not only because of witches. It is now a prize for those who want to recapture the sense of life in colonial and early Federal times.

Yet it was founded almost by accident. Roger Conant and a group of fishermen settled first on Cape Ann, which proved to be too rocky and harborless. So they sailed southwest to a cove they called Naumkeag, later renamed Salem. In 1628 a group of Puritan settlers arrived, led by Captain John Endicott. Their objective was to develop trade, including fish, timber, sassafras, and furs. Endicott was replaced as governor two years later by John Winthrop, when he arrived on the *Arbella* with a superseding charter in hand—that of the Massachusetts Bay Company. Winthrop's group was to settle a little farther south, in a place to become known as Boston.

Visitors to Salem can get oriented with a map of the **Salem Heritage Trail** (available in the Visitor Center, Essex Street Mall) and follow the red lines on the sidewalk, or take a trolley along the same route. You can begin anywhere, but perhaps the best way to appreciate the seafaring traditions of the town is by starting on the waterfront, where it all began.

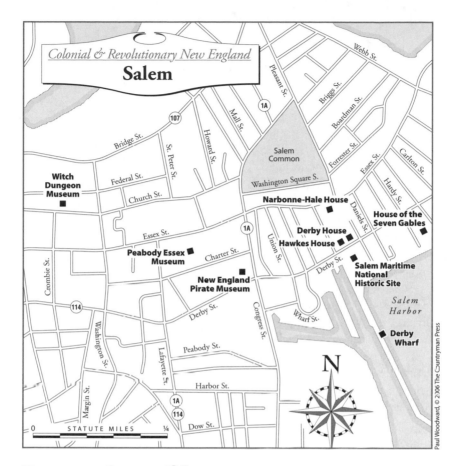

Colonial & Revolutionary New England
Salem

Witch Dungeon Museum

Salem Common

Narbonne-Hale House

House of the Seven Gables

Derby House
Hawkes House

Peabody Essex Museum

New England Pirate Museum

Salem Maritime National Historic Site

Salem Harbor

Derby Wharf

N

STATUTE MILES

Paul Woodward, © 2006 The Countryman Press

HISTORICAL SITES *and* MUSEUMS

The **Salem Maritime National Historic Site** (978-740-1660; www.nps.gov/sama), 174 Derby St., on the harbor, operates a number of buildings. They include the Central Wharf Warehouse Visitor Center (1800), where you can see an audiovisual orientation program, the Custom House (1819), the Scale House (1826), and three houses from the colonial period: Derby House, built for wealthy merchant Elias Hasket Derby and standing within sight of his many ships; Hawkes House, which was Derby's warehouse during the Revolution; and the Narbonne-Hale House, dating to the 17th century, and serving as home and shop for craftsmen and tradesmen.

A good place to begin is the massive **Derby Wharf** (1762), extending some 2,000 feet into the harbor. This wharf was once one of 50 more, all covered with warehouses where valuable spices, coffee, tea, fabrics, ivory, and gold dust were stored.

A replica of the 1797 three-masted Salem East Indiaman the *Friendship* is now moored here. We were on hand when her figurehead arrived in Salem. She is a wooden woman holding a bouquet of flowers, as shown in a painting by George Ropes in 1805. She stands 7 feet tall and weighs several hundred pounds. Her dress is in Empire-style blue and white.

The **Derby House** was built in 1762 for Elias Derby and his wife, Elizabeth, a Crowninshield. Classic but unostentatious in its lines, the house nevertheless represents the wealth of the town's two leading merchant families. It is filled with exotic imported woods, porcelain, and silver and brass collections, including a silver tankard and condiment set that belonged to the Derbys. Elias Derby's bed is at Winterthur, but a copy stands in his upstairs bedroom; it is short because people tended to sleep almost sitting up, leaning against pillows and bolsters.

When the Revolution shut down normal trade with Europe, Derby turned to privateering, then considered a patriotic and honorable profession. Half the profits from the seizure of British vessels were kept by the privateers' owners, many of whom became wealthy. A privateering commission was granted by the colonial governors and, by 1776, the Continental Congress. Of course, England considered privateers as dangerous pirates, subject to hanging if caught.

> According to legend, men who left from Salem and died at sea always returned home in spirit. In a tale reminiscent of Coleridge's *Rime of the Ancient Mariner*, a sailor on board the *Neptune* reported seeing a ship four times his own vessel's size bearing down upon him. He threw the wheel hard over to avoid a collision. The other vessel veered slightly and came along the starboard side without a sound. There was no rush of water, no crunch of wood splitting, no straining of lines and canvas—only a glowing silence. And there wasn't a seaman in sight. As the ship faded away in the distance, the sailor said, "It's the Ghost Ship. A proper Salem man has died somewhere, and the ship is bringing his spirit home to Salem, home for Christmas."

The **New England Pirate Museum** (978-741-2800), 274 Derby St. Open daily. If your children want to learn about pirates who attacked merchant ships all up and down the coast, they'll enjoy this place. They will see a model of a colonial seaport, a pirate ship, and a cave filled with treasure.

Sea captains brought back exotic curiosities from around the world, and many of them are displayed in the **Peabody Essex Museum** (978-745-9500, 800-745-4054; www.pem.org), 161 Essex St. Open daily. Only Salem captains who had sailed the seas near or beyond the Cape of Good Hope or Cape Horn were eligible for membership in the East India Marine Society. Now visitors can stroll through 30 galleries in a museum complex that documents Salem's role in New England's burgeoning world trade.

You will see ship models, paintings, figureheads, scrimshaw, navigational instruments, and a wide variety of maritime mementos. Asian collections include pottery, jewelry, weapons, and religious artifacts. The natural history collection focuses on New England's seashore, and the research library has extensive holdings of books and documents.

The Peabody Essex complex also has a number of other houses and buildings to visit:

The **John Ward House** (1684), adjacent to the museum, has a 17th-century parlor and kitchen within its clapboard walls. A lean-to houses an apothecary shop and scent shop from a later period.

Four generations of one family lived in the **Crowninshield-Bentley House** (1727), 126 Essex St. This gambrel-roof house has a symmetrical facade, anticipating later Georgian styles. You can still see the room where the Reverend William Bentley, a diarist of ordinary life in Salem, lived in the years following the Revolution.

The **Peirce-Nichols House** (1782), 80 Federal St., was designed by Samuel McIntire for Jerathmiel Peirce, who became wealthy in the China trade. Sally Peirce married George Nichols, and they lived in the house after it had been remodeled for their wedding. The house contains possessions of both the Peirce and Nichols families.

As the depot for products from all over the world, Salem's wharves occasionally saw bizarre scenes. But a drunken elephant? Yes, when the elephant arrived in 1777, it apparently had been fed beer, about 30 gallons a day, throughout the long voyage. It had become addicted to this liquid diet, and money had to be raised to support the expensive habit. So, in a move that anticipated Barnum and Bailey, people were charged admission to view the elephant.

The **Cotting-Smith Assembly House** (1782), 138 Federal St., was built as a hall for assemblies. George Washington was entertained here.

The **Ropes Mansion** (1727), 318 Essex St., was home to four generations of the Ropes family after they bought it in 1768. Although this handsome house has been architecturally altered many times, all the furniture inside belonged to the family.

The **Yin Yu Tang House**, located on the museum grounds, is a new and unusual acquisition. It was brought from China and reassembled at the museum. A late Qing dynasty merchants' house, it remained in the Huang family through eight generations, from ca. 1800 to 1982.

"Quakers" were sometimes not people but fake cannons. Some privateers mounted wooden cylinders on their vessels. As the ships closed on a British merchant vessel, the fake cannons made them look fearsomely armed. The ruse sometimes tricked the intended victim into surrender.

While you are out exploring houses on Federal and Essex Streets, it would be a shame not to return to the center of town by walking down **Chestnut Street**, adorned on both sides by mansions of merchants and shipowners. Most of these houses were built in the first two decades of the 19th century, but they represent wealth that began accumulating during the colonial era.

If you've been intrigued by Nathaniel

Hawthorne's *The House of Seven Gables,* there's a treat in store for you. A group of historic buildings—the **Hathaway House** (1682), **Retire Beckett House** (1658), and **Hawthorne's Birthplace** (1750) stand in a village setting on Salem Harbor next to the **House of the Seven Gables** (1668) (978-744-0991; www.7gables.org) at 54 Turner St. Open daily. The latter was built by Captain John Turner and later sold to the Ingersoll family. In the 1840s Nathaniel Hawthorne visited here and used the house for scenes in his novel: the parlor where Colonel Pyncheon sat dying in the oak chair, the shop where Hepzibah sold scents and candy, and the secret staircase that led to Clifford's room.

Visitors begin touring in the 17th-century kitchen where there's a beehive oven with a wooden door. We were told that the housewife would stick her hand in the oven to test for hotness before putting her food in; the length of time she could stand the heat would determine the temperature of the oven. (The U.S. Army long used the same "count" method of gauging temperature.)

> Look for the "courting" candle, which the family set in advance. When the light went out, it was time for the gentleman to go home. Climb the 20 wooden steps up into Clifford's room. You can count the seven gables on the house model in the attic. Phoebe's room is bright and cheerful, with a view of the water and of Marblehead.

When you have finished touring the house, explore the garden; there is a picturesque view of both garden and house from the seawall. Also don't miss the other open houses. Hawthorne's Birthplace, though far smaller and less complex than the House of Seven Gables, has an elegant simplicity.

Nathaniel Hawthorne's ancestor, Judge Hawthorne, was involved in the infamous Salem witch trials of the 1690s. The **Witch House** (508-744-0180) is at 310 1/2 Essex St. Open daily. This 1642 house was once the home of Jonathan Corwin, a judge in the trials. They began in 1692 when local girls had fits, which they said were brought on by hearing stories from Tituba, a slave belonging to Samuel Parris. These girls took to writhing and babbling, and accused Tituba, Sarah Good, Sarah Osborne, Rebecca Nurse, and others of casting a spell on them.

Guilty verdicts were handed down and executions took place until the governor's wife was accused—and suddenly the witchcraft hysteria stopped. Visitors to Witch House will find the room where the hearings took place upstairs.

By October 1692 more than 100 people had been accused and indicted; 50 confessed, 26 were convicted, and 19 hanged. Giles Corey was convicted

> Confessions of Sarah Carrier, age seven, 1692:
> "How long hast thou been a witch?"
> "Ever since I was six years old."
> "Who made you a witch?"
> "My mother, she made me set my hand to a book [of the devil]."
> "How did you afflict folks?"
> "I pinched them."

The House of the Seven Gables in Salem

and then crushed under a large pile of stones. By 1693 the mood had changed and the courts no longer chose to hear charges.

The **Witch Dungeon Museum** (978-741-3570; www.witchdungeon.com), 16 Lynde St. Open Apr.–Nov. Actors portray a scene from a 1692 witch trial. A re-created dungeon is also there.

Outside Salem is the **Rebecca Nurse Homestead** (978-774-8799; www. rebeccanurse.org), 149 Pine St., Danvers. Open June–Oct. Rebecca Nurse was a well-respected inhabitant of Danvers until hysterical girls shouted that she was a witch. This innocent woman was hanged in 1692.

LODGING

THE HAWTHORNE HOTEL
18 Washington Square West,
Salem, MA 01970
800-729-7829, 978-744-4080;
www.hawthornehotel.com
One of the Historic Hotels of America, dating from 1925, this hotel was named for Nathaniel Hawthorne, who spent his childhood in Salem.

**SALEM WATERFRONT
HOTEL AND SUITES**
225 Derby St., Salem, MA 01970
888-33SALEM, 978-740-8788;
www.salemwaterfronthotel.com

Although it is not old, the location on the waterfront at Pickering Wharf in Salem makes this hotel appealing.

STEPHEN DANIELS HOUSE
One Daniels St.,
Salem, MA 01970
978-744-5709
If you'd like to spend the night in a house that dates from 1667, try a room here, each with a different shape reflecting various stages of the home's evolution. There are 10 fireplaces and collections of samplers, teapots, puppets, and antique furniture.

SUZANNAH FLINT HOUSE
98 Essex St., Salem, MA 01970
800-SAY-STAY, 978-744-4080;
www.suzannahflinthouse.com
This historic B&B, now owned by the
Hawthorne Hotel, was named for an 18th-
century owner. The house has wide-board
floors and is filled with antiques.

RESTAURANTS

*Adjacent to the Maritime National
Historical Site, Salem's waterfront has
begun to develop areas that are
pleasant to wander through.* **Pickering
Wharf**, *a shopping village with a range
of restaurants, has the ambience of earlier times with the amenities of ours.*

ROCKMORE DRYDOCK
94 Wharf St., Salem, MA 01970
978-740-1001
Fresh seafood is available in the dining
room, a saloon, and the outside deck.
During the summer the **Rockmore Floating Restaurant** is out in the harbor.

**NATHANIEL'S RESTAURANT
AND THE TAVERN**
Hawthorne Hotel, 18 Washington
Square West, Salem, MA 01970
800-729-7829, 978-744-4080;
www.hawthornehotel.com
The restaurant's menu changes seasonally;
the wood-paneled tavern offers more
casual dining.

EVENTS

July: Maritime Festival
(978-740-1660).
October: Haunted Happenings
(877-725-3662), billed as "America's
Halloween Festival."

INFORMATION

**NORTH OF BOSTON CONVENTION
AND VISITORS BUREAU**
17 Peabody Square,
Peabody, MA 01960
800-742-5306, 978-977-7760;
www.northofboston.org

MARBLEHEAD

Across from Salem lies another superb harbor. Fishermen from Cornwall and the
Channel Islands arrived in Marble Harbor, now Marblehead, in 1629. The rocky
peninsula shelters a deepwater harbor with easy access to the open sea—advantages that insured its continuity as a maritime center throughout four centuries.

Marblehead's history of activity encompasses fishing, shipbuilding, privateering, blockade running, merchant voyages throughout the world, and eventually
yachting. Its townspeople were extremely active during the Revolution, both as
seamen and as soldiers, and General John Glover provided his Marblehead ship,
the *Hannah*, for the use of the Continental Congress. In 1776 Glover's experienced seamen played a crucial role in evacuating George Washington's army from
Brooklyn Heights and in ferrying it across the ice-filled Delaware to attack Tren-
ton—both times at night.

Today, visitors are treated to a wonderful collection of 18th-century buildings
and homes rivaling those in Providence and Newport. Although most of them are
not open to visitors, you can enjoy their facades as you walk the streets. The older
sections of Marblehead delight the observant eye, and walking is by far the best
way to enjoy its intricate streets and lanes. Pick up information on self-guided
walking tours from the information booth on Pleasant Street. It is open from
Memorial Day to Oct. 31.

HISTORICAL SITES
and MUSEUMS

Visitors to Marblehead are in for a treat when they see a special painting in **Abbot Hall** (781-631-0528) on Washington Square. Open daily except weekends. It's Archibald Willard's iconic *Spirit of '76*. General John Devereux gave the painting to the town, and his son was the model for the drummer boy.

The 1768 **Jeremiah Lee Mansion** (781-631-1069), 161 Washington St., has a "rusticated" exterior, that is, wood designed to look like stone. Open June–Oct. The house still has the original hand-painted tempera paper on the walls in several rooms. In the State Drawing Room the panels feature classical ruins, with each panel designed to fit the wall. Jeremiah Lee had made a fortune in shipping. His early death was thought to have been brought on by overexposure in the opening days of the Revolution. He had been involved in a meeting at the Black Horse Tavern in Arlington when the alarm was given, and he hid in the fields as the redcoats marched by on their route to Concord.

No Christmas? In the late 17th century there was a definite lack of agreement between two groups of inhabitants in Marblehead. The Puritans, who always opposed the celebration of Christmas, created an uproar when Dr. Pigot planned to hold an Anglican service. The Puritans held a lecture at the same time. Dr. John Barnard, parson of the Puritan church, argued that Christ was born in October and that Christmas was a pagan custom. Dr. Pigot published a paper entitled "A Vindication of the Practice of the Ancient Christian as well as the Church of England, and other Reformed Churches in the Observation of Christmas-Day; in answer to the uncharitable reflections of Thomas de Laune, Mr. Whiston and Mr. John Barnard of Marblehead." By 1681 the Puritan law against celebrating Christmas had been repealed.

In 1789 and 1794, Washington and Lafayette were guests in the mansion's Great Room, which is elegant indeed with its elaborately carved chimneypiece and marble fireplace. Original colonial furnishings mix with pieces collected from all over the world.

The **Marblehead Museum and Historical Society** (781-631-1069; www.marbleheadmuseum.org), 170 Washington St. It is a treat to see paintings by a Marblehead artist, John Frost, who was once a Grand Banks fisherman. Colonial samplers are there too, as well as a wooden codfish, which reminds visitors of the main industry of early Marblehead.

Another mansion to visit is the 1727 **King Hooper Mansion** (781-631-2608), 8 Hooper St. Open daily except Mon. This 1727 mansion was built by "King" Robert Hooper. Visitors can see colonial rooms, a ballroom, a wine cellar, and slave quarters. The Marblehead Arts Association has an art gallery on the third floor in the ballroom. The flower garden has been restored to its colonial design.

Here's a bell that did its job too well! One of the oldest Episcopal churches in America is **St. Michael's Church** (781-631-0657), 13 Summer St. It was constructed in 1714 with building materials sent from England. Its bell was rung so hard and long after the news of the signing of the Declaration of Independence that it cracked and had to be recast by Paul Revere.

Old Burial Hill, off Orne St., contains the graves of 600 Revolutionary War veterans—and offers a superb view. It is also the site of the first meetinghouse.

Just a few ruins remain today of **Fort Sewall** (1742), on the northeast end of Front Street. It was first built in the 17th century and then updated in 1742.

LODGING

THE HARBOR LIGHT INN
58 Washington St.,
Marblehead, MA 01945; 781-631-2186;
www.harborlightinn.com
Fireplaces and canopied beds are featured here.

RESTAURANTS

THE LANDING
81 Front St., Marblehead,
MA 01970; 781-639-1266;
www.TheLandingRestaurant.com
Seafood meals are served in the dining room and the pub.

EVENTS

December: Christmas Walk;
781-631-2868

INFORMATION

MARBLEHEAD CHAMBER OF COMMERCE
62 Pleasant St.,
Marblehead, MA 01945
781-631-2868;
www.marbleheadchamber.org,
www.visitmarblehead.com

MARBLEHEAD INFORMATION BOOTH
Corner of Pleasant, Spring, and Essex Sts., Marblehead, MA 01945
781-639-8469

NORTH OF BOSTON CONVENTION AND VISITORS BUREAU
17 Peabody Square,
Peabody, MA 01960
800-742-5306, 978-977-7760;
www.northofboston.org

BEVERLY

Beverly was founded in 1626 as an extension of Salem. It was named after a town in Yorkshire, England. Roger Conant, John Balch, and three others were each granted two hundred acres at the head of Bass River in 1636.

John Hale was called as the first minister of the church in town. He served for forty years. By 1692 he had become involved in the witchcraft trials because of his wife. She was a gentle soul, and he stood up for her and other accused witches. Because of his strong stand the witchcraft trials in Beverly were discontinued. His grandson, Nathan Hale, also is remembered for his steadfast words, before he was hanged by the British as an American spy: "I only regret that I have but one life to lose for my country."

In 1775 the *Hannah*, a local schooner, was chartered and armed by General George Washington to attack ships supplying the British army in Boston.

Today Beverly is filled with well-kept homes and estates. For visitors it offers a fine historic district with homes listed on the National Register of Historic Sites. And you can find a bench in Independence Park to gaze beyond the decorative cannons out to the sea and islands.

HISTORICAL SITES *and* MUSEUMS

Cabot House (978-922-1186), 117 Cabot St. Open daily except Sun. and Mon. It dates from 1781. John Cabot, a merchant and Revolutionary War privateer, was the first owner, and the house passed down the Cabot line for many years. A bank eventually took it over, and one of the displays in the house today is a re-creation of the 19th-century Beverly Bank. The collection includes local artifacts.

Balch House (978-922-1186), 448 Cabot St. Open May 30–Oct. except Sun. and Mon. It is on part of the land grant given to the "Old Planters" in 1635. The Balch family lived here until 1914. The house is furnished with period pieces.

GLOUCESTER

Named for Gloucester, England, and founded in 1623, this city on the southern shore of Cape Ann claims to be the oldest fishing port in the state. It is the city most closely identified with the lucrative cod fishery, the staple of exports from the New World to the Old in the colonial era. Gloucester's central role in that fishery has persisted through four centuries, but it is threatened now by the depletion of cod that has led to the closure of some offshore banks.

Today Gloucester is also a popular summer resort offering tour boats and charter vessels if you'd like to get out on the ocean to whale watch or fish. Ashore, if you are an early riser, you can watch the fish auction. At any time of day you can visit the thriving art colony on Rocky Neck, which offers an abundance of galleries, and you can watch painters at work all along the coast from Eastern Point to the adjoining town of Rockport.

Some privateers used subtle methods to fool the British. Captain Jonathan Haraden of Gloucester disguised his gunports with canvas painted the color of the hull to make his vessel look unarmed. An enemy ship might think this an easy mark and rush to capture its prize—until the real guns poked out of the canvas and fired at close range. Just the reverse of the fake "Quakers" used by some other privateers, this ruse reminds us that deception has a long history in naval warfare

HISTORICAL SITES *and* MUSEUMS

During the Revolution the town was harassed by the HMS *Falcon,* a British warship that tried to capture two colonial schooners. Gloucester men instead took 30 British sailors as prisoners; a British cannonball is on display in the **Cape Ann Historical Museum** (978-283-0455; www.cape-ann.com), 127 Pleasant St. Open Mar.–Jan. Part of the museum was the home of sea captain Elias Davis. The museum is well known for its outstanding collection of luminist Fitz Hugh Lane's paintings of the area. Other artists displayed include Jerome Elwell, Susanna Paine, Gilbert Stuart, and Alfred Wiggin. Galleries also include collections of decorative arts and antique furniture.

Gloucester Maritime Heritage Center (978-281-0470; www.glouces termaritimecenter.org), 23 Harbor Loop. Open Memorial Day–Labor Day; weekends Labor Day–Columbus Day. The Burnham Brothers Railway dates from 1849, when it fulfilled the need for those who had to haul boats out of the water for repairs. It is the oldest continuously operating marine railway in the country.

The exciting focus now is the rebuilding of two boats (one dating from the early 1900s and the other from 1936) to be turned into vessels for the Boston Tea Party Museum. They are to become the tea ships *Beaver* and *Eleanor*. They will be moved to the Boston Tea Party Museum around 2007.

> **Dogtown Common** is a ghost town in the center of the Cape Ann peninsula. The community was settled in the 1600s and was active until the Revolutionary War. Then all the men left for the war, and the women were alone with only dogs for protection. As strange derelicts and toothless crones moved in, the women moved out. Today you can see only the ruins of cellars among the bushes.

Sargent House Museum (978-281-2432; www.sargenthouse.org), 49 Middle St. Open Memorial Day–Columbus Day. Judith Sargent Murray, a writer who encouraged equality for women, lived in this 18th-century Georgian house. The collection includes art by John Singer Sargent, her great-great nephew.

Stage Fort Park was the site of the Dorchester Company Settlement, the group that sailed to Gloucester in 1623. The Gloucester Visitor Welcome Center is there now.

RESTAURANTS

THE GLOUCESTER HOUSE RESTAURANT
63 Rogers St. at Seven Seas Wharf, Gloucester, MA 01930; 978-283-1812
Seafood is a specialty in this restaurant overlooking the docks.

MCT'S LOBSTER HOUSE & TAVERN
25 Rogers St.,
Gloucester, MA 01930; 978-282-0950
There's a large selection of appetizers in this seafood restaurant.

EVENTS

September: Schooner Festival
978-283-1601

INFORMATION

CAPE ANN CHAMBER OF COMMERCE VISITOR INFORMATION CENTER
33 Commercial St.,
Gloucester, MA 01930
800-321-0133, 978-283-1601;
www.capeannvacations.com

SEASONAL INFORMATION BOOTH
Rogers St., Gloucester, MA 01930

NORTH OF BOSTON CONVENTION AND VISITORS BUREAU
17 Peabody Square,
Peabody, MA 01960
800-742-5306, 978-977-7760;
www.northofboston.org

ROCKPORT

Once a small fishing village also supported by a productive stone quarry, Rockport is now a well-known artists' colony filled with galleries, studios, and rafts of tourists during the summer. With camera in hand, many of the visitors head for Motif #1, a little red fishing shack on Bearskin Neck that has been painted many times and seems to symbolize the rugged charm of Cape Ann. Rockport's tiny artificial harbor, the only protection from the open Atlantic, is lined with houses huddled together that make a more impressive statement about the character of this place.

HISTORICAL SITES *and* MUSEUMS

James Babson Cooperage Shop (978-546-2958). Open July and Aug. The shop dates from 1658 and is probably the oldest building on Cape Ann. Exhibits include tools and furniture.

The **Rockport Art Association** (978-546-6604). Open daily. It is in a tavern dating from 1770. Many artists display their work here.

Granite Street leads out to the quarry, which is now a bird sanctuary. Granite was exported for buildings and various other purposes. (In 1710 Joshua Norwood thought of using pieces of granite for mooring-stones. He drilled a hole in the center of a slab and pushed an oak tree, roots and all, through the hole. The roots and stone sat on the bottom of the sea, and the boat was moored to the top of the tree!)

LODGING

EMERSON INN BY THE SEA
1 Cathedral Ave., Rockport, MA 01966
800–964-5550, 978-546-6321;
www.emersoninnbythesea.com
This inn opened in 1846 as Pigeon Cove House, moved to Cathedral Avenue in 1871, and became the Hotel Edward in 1913. It was named after Ralph Waldo Emerson, who stayed in room 109 in the 1850s.

THE INN ON COVE HILL
37 Mt. Pleasant St.,
Rockport, MA 01966
888-546-2701, 978-546-2701;
www.innoncovehill.com
This Historic District inn is over 200 years old.

LINDEN TREE INN
26 King St., Rockport, MA 01966
800-865-2122, 978-546-2494;
www.lindentreeinn.com
This 1850 Victorian B&B is 800 feet from the beach.

YANKEE CLIPPER INN
127 Granite St.,
Rockport, MA 01966
800-545-3699, 978-546-3407;
www.yankeeclipperinn.com
This 1929 art deco mansion has a view of the open ocean and the village. Rooms are also available in the Quarterdeck, a contemporary cape.

RESTAURANTS

THE BLUE SAPPHIRE
Yankee Clipper Inn, 127 Granite St.,
Rockport, MA 01966; 978-546-3407;
www.yankeeclipperinn.com
The restaurant offers a variety of dishes and lots of seafood.

THE GREENERY
15 Dock Square,
Rockport, MA 01966; 978-546-9593
This restaurant right on the dock specializes in seafood.

THE HANNAH JUMPER
7 Tuna Wharf, Rockport, MA 01966;
978-546-0006
The name is from an 1856 Rockport prohibitionist. Rockport is "dry," so if you wish bring your own wine or beer.

INFORMATION

ROCKPORT CHAMBER OF COMMERCE
1 Whistlestop Mall,Rockport, MA 01966
888-726-3922, 978-546-6575;
www.rockportusa.com

**SEASONAL
INFORMATION BOOTH**
Upper Main St.,
Rockport, MA 01966

**CAPE ANN CHAMBER
OF COMMERCE VISITOR
INFORMATION CENTER**
33 Commercial St.,
Gloucester, MA 01930
800-321-0133, 978-283-1601;
www.capeannvacations.com

ESSEX

Far more sheltered on a river on the north side of Cape Ann, Essex early on became a shipbuilding center. That began in 1660 when a Mr. Burnham built a boat in his house. An attic window and a wall had to be cut away so he could get the boat out. Colonial fishermen began to venture out farther and demanded larger boats of an improved design. By 1668 the town had set aside an acre on the Essex River for a shipyard, which exists to this day. Some Essex vessels were built in yards of houses a distance from the water. They would be mounted on wheels or skids and hauled to the launch site by as many as twenty yokes of oxen. The largest vessel hauled this way was fifty-five gross tons.

HISTORICAL SITES *and* MUSEUMS
The **Essex Shipbuilding Museum** (978-768-6981), 66 Main St. Open May 1–Columbus Day. The museum is in the Arthur D. Story Shipyard and another location at 28 Main St. You can learn about the history of shipbuilding and also see a collection of half-models of ships built in Essex.

RESTAURANTS

WOODMAN'S OF ESSEX
121 Main St./MA 133, Essex, MA 01929
800-649-1773, 978-768-6057;
www.woodmans.com
Although fried clams are the specialty, clam chowder, steamed clams, and lobster are also served.

INFORMATION

**CAPE ANN CHAMBER OF COMMERCE
VISITOR INFORMATION CENTER**
33 Commercial St.,
Gloucester, MA 01930
800-321-0133, 978-283-1601;
www.capeannvacations.com

IPSWICH

Beyond Gloucester and northwest of the rocky outcropping of Cape Ann lies Ipswich, on a river surrounded by salt marshes. Twelve colonists arrived here in 1633 to found a town that would become famous for shipbuilding in the colonial era and beyond. The first American female poet, Anne Bradstreet, lived here in the 1630s with her husband, Simon Bradstreet, who was a governor of Massachusetts. As the Revolution was brewing, Ipswich was the first town to denounce taxation without representation. In the 20th century Ipswich was the home of another prominent American literary figure, the novelist John Updike.

HISTORICAL SITES *and* MUSEUMS

The **Ipswich Historical Society Museum** (978-356-2811), 54 S. Main St. You can get information here on the large number of historic houses in town.

The **John Heard House** (987-356-2641), 40 S. Main St. Open May–Oct. This 1795 Federal-style mansion was home to a mercantile family active in the 19th-century China trade. The collection includes Chinese export furniture and porcelain, nautical instruments, toys, and carriages. Work by local artist Arthur Wesley Dow is also displayed.

The 1640 **John Whipple House** (978-356-2811), 53 S. Main St. Open May–Columbus Day. The house contains furnishings of the Whipple family. A colonial herb garden, including medicinal herbs, grows in back.

LODGING

**THE INN AT CASTLE HILL
ON THE CRANE ESTATE**
280 Argilla Rd., Ipswich, MA 01938
978-412-2555; www.innatcastlehill.com
The original farmhouse dates from 1886; in 1899 it was called Castle Hill Farm. Richard Crane, a plumbing magnate, bought the estate in 1910. Now the Great House is an inn with dining for inn guests. Tours of the Great House are available June–Sep. The property, as well as Crane Beach, is under the management of the Trustees of Reservations, a prominent Massachusetts organization devoted to the preservation of natural resources.

RESTAURANTS

THE 1640 HART HOUSE
51 Linebrook Rd.,
Ipswich, MA 01938; 978-356-1640;
www.1640harthouse.com
The original 1640 room is one of the dining rooms.

INFORMATION

**IPSWICH VISITOR CENTER,
HALL HASKELL HOUSE**
36 S. Main St., MA 1A,
Ipswich, MA 01938; 978-356-8540;
www.ipswichma.com

NEWBURYPORT

The town of Newbury was founded by settlers in 1635, and by 1646 they had established a port, Newburyport, on the banks of the Merrimack River. Records note a ship built here as early as 1639, and between 1671 and 1714, 117 more ships came from Newburyport yards. By 1764 the shipbuilders in Newburyport had split from the town of Newbury because their emphasis was on the sea, not farming; approximately six of every ten men in town earned their living through some trade connected with the sea. In 1776 they built two frigates for the Continental Navy, the *Hancock* and the *Boston,* and outfitted a number of privateers. But shipbuilding collapsed in the depression after the Revolution, and Newburyport launchings dropped from ninety in 1772 to three in 1788.

Today Newburyport is a place worth visiting to stroll streets lined with colonial and elegant Federal homes that are often three stories high. Along High Street you will see architecture ranging from the 17th to the 19th century. Market Square has been restored and offers antiques shops and handcrafted products.

HISTORICAL SITES *and* MUSEUMS

Newburyport has preserved the atmosphere of its maritime heritage in the **Market Square Historic District**. The centerpiece is the **Custom House Maritime Museum** (978-462-8681), 25 Water St. Open Feb.–Dec. except Sun. and Mon.

Coffin House

The museum is now located in an 1835 building but dates to an earlier era when a group of sea captains formed the Newburyport Marine Society in 1772. They collected maritime artifacts and passed them on to the Historical Society of Old Newbury after World War I. These artifacts are on display, along with ship models and navigational items.

Architecture buffs shouldn't miss a walk along Newburyport's **High Street**, where the wealth from the harbor built handsome homes through the colonial, Federal, and later eras. Among the earliest is the **Coffin House** (978-462-2634; www.spnea.org),14-16 High St. Open July–Labor Day. The 1654 house remained the home of the Coffin family until 1929, when the Society for the Preservation of New England Antiquities took it over. The house has both a 1600 and a 1700 kitchen and incorporates changes made by many generations of the family. In 1785 two Coffin brothers legally divided the building into two separate dwellings.

Less than a mile away is the 1690 **Spencer-Peirce-Little Farm** (978-462-2634; www.spnea.org), 5 Little's Lane, Newbury. Open June–Oct. The house is unusual in that it was made of stone and brick. Three centuries of Newbury and Newburyport life are displayed here, where several wealthy merchants lived.

Not far away in Amesbury is the 1793 **Lowell's Boat Shop** (978-388-0162; www.lowellboatshop.org), 459 Main St. Open daily. Lowell's claims to be the oldest active boatbuilding shop in the country. Simeon Lowell and his sons, Stephen and Benjamin, began their shop here in 1793. The fisherman's dory was their specialty, and you can still see dories and other boats being made here.

LODGING

GARRISON INN
11 Brown Square,
Newburyport, MA 01950
978-499-8500; www.garrisoninn.com
Sea captain Moses Brown built this home in 1809. It has been an inn since the turn of the century. Named for William Lloyd Garrison, it is listed on the National Register of Historic Places.

THE MORRILL PLACE INN
209 High St., Newburyport, MA 01950
978-462-2808
This 1806 inn features a staircase with six-inch risers built to accommodate women wearing hoop skirts.

RESTAURANTS

THE BLACK COW
54 Merrimac St.
Newburyport, MA 01950
978-499-8811
The restaurant, located on the Merrimack River, offers seafood and a variety of other dishes.

INFORMATION

**NEWBURYPORT
CHAMBER OF COMMERCE**
38R Merrimac St.,
Newburyport, MA 01950
978-462-6680;
www.newburyportchamber.org

CENTRAL MASSACHUSETTS

I f we imagine looking at a map of New England as it was known in the early 17th century, it would detail the inlets, bays, and natural harbors of the coastline and the rivers flowing into the sea, but no roads. To get inland efficiently, colonists had to go up a river. The Connecticut was the major river of New England in the colonial era, a waterway more than four hundred miles long leading through lands that Connecticut and Massachusetts would claim. It was navigable to above Hartford by deepwater vessels and, apart from a few portages, all the way to Turners Falls by flatboats—nearly as far north as Massachusetts would reach.

So it is not surprising that the Connecticut became the main highway to the interior. William Pynchon established Agawam, which later became Springfield, in 1636 to get closer to his source of furs. Other settlements along the river followed, including Northampton in 1653, Hadley in 1661, and Deerfield beginning in 1669. During King Philip's War in 1675-76, settlers at Springfield, Northampton, Hadley, Hatfield, and Deerfield were natural targets, and all these settlements were attacked. But the river remained a principal resource for transporting goods throughout the colonial era, and during the Revolution Springfield was chosen by General Washington as the site of the national arsenal.

Railroads lined the riverbank in the 19th century and interstate highways in the 20th as primary modes of transportation changed. But the towns that developed in the Pioneer Valley, as it is often called to recognize its origin, still retain some of their original character. In Massachusetts the valley is composed of three counties: Franklin to the north, mostly rural land with villages; Hampshire in the center, now home to five colleges; and Hampden in the south, where Springfield has become the valley's major city and transportation hub.

NORTHAMPTON

Founded as a river settlement in 1653 and granted a charter a year later, Northampton suffered Indian raids on its periphery in the fall of 1675 and turned back a major attack in March of 1676. In the early decades of the next century it became the center of a religious phenomenon that spread through the colonies. Jonathan Edwards arrived in Northampton in 1726 to help his grandfather, Solomon Stoddard, in his ministry. After Stoddard died three years later, Edwards took over the ministry and preached sermons that involved the emotions and senses as well as doctrine.

Edwards is often credited with beginning the revival known as the Great Awakening in 1734, and he welcomed popular preacher and evangelist George Whitefield to Northampton in 1740. During long rides in the woods, Edwards wrote ideas on scraps of paper and pinned them to his cloak. After he returned home, his wife, Sarah, would arrange the notes for him. He delivered his most famous fire-and-brimstone sermon in 1741, "Sinners in the Hands of an Angry God," which painted the tortures of hell in graphic terms. Edwards was a strict Puritan about doctrine and conduct, one who chastised children of local families in church. When he restricted communion to those who had publicly professed their faith, he was dismissed in 1750 and chose to become a missionary to the Indians in Stockbridge.

Nowadays the city of Northampton, home of Smith College, is one hub of the five-college consortium that includes Amherst, Hampshire, Mount Holyoke, and the University of Massachusetts at Amherst. Restaurants, craft shops, and galleries are abundant in this pleasant city, which is filled with artists and continues to attract academics, if not Puritan clergymen.

HISTORICAL SITES *and* MUSEUMS
Historic Northampton (413-584-6011; www.historic-northampton.org), Main St. The museum has three historic houses: Damon House (1813) includes a Federal-era parlor with furnishings from that Damon family. Next door, the Parsons House (1730) has interior walls exposed so that visitors can see the evolving structural and decorative changes that took place. The Shepherd House (1796) belonged to Thomas and Edith Shepherd. It has a collection of souvenirs from their turn-of-the-century travels as well as pieces from other generations.

The **Smith College Museum of Art**, in the Brown Fine Arts Center (413-585-2761), Elm St. and Bedford Terrace. This is one of the outstanding museums in western Massachusetts; in its galleries hang some of the best 19th- and early-20th-century American and European paintings. Here you'll see works by Copley, Whistler, Sargent, Homer, and Eakins, and a fine collection of prints and drawings.

INFORMATION

NORTHAMPTON CHAMBER OF COMMERCE AND VISITOR CENTER
99 Pleasant St., Northampton, MA 01060
413-584-1900; www.northamptonuncommon.com

DEERFIELD

In 1669, when Samuel Hinsdell arrived to farm, Deerfield was considered the last civilized place on the frontier of New England. Hinsdell was joined by other settlers, and within six years the population grew to 125. The Pocumtuck Indians, who had used the rich land along the Connecticut to raise corn, tobacco, and pumpkins, were enraged. They attacked during King Philip's War, when the Bloody Brook Massacre of 1675 took the lives of seventy-six persons; the village was almost abandoned after that outburst.

Deerfield's stormy history continued through the first part of the 18th century. In February 1704 the French, led by Hertel de Rouville, accompanied a group of 142 Indians who invaded the town, entered the stockade over the high snow drifts, killed 50 settlers, and set fire to homes. More than a hundred townspeople taken as prisoners were marched for three hundred winter miles into Canada. By 1706 some of them had come home, and in 1735 a peace treaty brought settlers back to Deerfield.

A little girl never forgot what happened that day in 1704. "My memories of Deerfield were of gunshots, screaming, fire and blood. I wished never to return." Eunice Williams was only seven years old when the French soldiers and Indians attacked. Eunice was wrapped in a blanket and carried on an Indian's shoulders. Her mother slogged through the ice and snow for one day and was then killed because she could not keep up the pace. Eunice lived in a Mohawk village, mar-

Allen House, one of numerous restored buildings in Historic Deerfield

ried, and remained with the Mohawks until she died in 1785.

In Deerfield, news of the Boston Tea Party pleased some but angered others. The Reverend Jonathan Ashley, who had been pastor in the parish for forty years, felt loyalty to King George III. In defiance he held a tea party in his home and sent a pound of tea to a Tory friend in nearby Greenfield. Whigs and Tories shouted vehemently from opposite sides of the street in Deerfield. In July 1774, patriots had a liberty pole ready to be erected when Tory sympathizers cut it in two during the night. The Whigs got another pole, and a replica of the liberty pole stands today.

In 1775 Deerfield men marched to Boston, and some of them fought in the Battle of Bunker Hill. Although Deerfield was isolated from the major population centers of eastern Massachusetts, the town was ready for independence and would fight for it. Citizens provided food for patriots who had fought at Fort Ticonderoga under arrangements made by Benedict Arnold.

The attractive historic town center you see today is largely the work of one family. The Flynt family restored many of the original homes and buildings in Historic Deerfield. Henry N. Flynt first came to town in 1936 when he brought his son to Deerfield Academy. He liked the town and bought an inn, followed by one home, then another and another, restoring each in turn. Over the next twenty-five years, Flynt and his wife oversaw the restoration and furnishing of twelve buildings, acquiring more than eight thousand antique pieces in the process.

Wells-Thorn House in Historic Deerfield

HISTORICAL SITES *and* MUSEUMS

Historic Deerfield (413-774-5581; www.historic-deerfield.org). Open daily. Stop first at **Hall Tavern** (ca. 1760), the visitor center, for tickets and information. Then enjoy the houses and their furnishings—among them a print shop, a tavern, a silver shop, and **Allen House** (ca. 1720), the Flynts' own home—all spread along one of the most beautiful village streets in New England. The **Frary House** (ca. 1720 and 1768) was first a home and then a tavern. The **Wells-Thorn House** (1717 and 1751) contains English ceramics, needlework, and a buttery. The **Dwight-Barnard House** (ca. 1725) was originally a merchant's house in Springfield. The **Sheldon-Hawks House** (1743) remained in the Sheldon family for two centuries, and the **Ashley House** (ca. 1730) was the home of Deerfield's Tory minister, Jonathan Ashley. And there's much more to see in the colonial village, so allow plenty of time for your visit.

   Memorial Hall Museum (413-774-3768; www.deerfield-ma.org), 8 Memorial St., in the 1798 building formerly used by Deerfield Academy. Open daily May–Oct. You will see collections of furnishings, tools, quilts, needlework, and toys. Don't miss the oak door once on John Sheldon's home—it has tomahawk marks from the night of February 28, 1704.

LODGING

THE DEERFIELD INN
81 Old Main St.,
Deerfield, MA 01342
413-774-5587;
www.deerfieldinn.com
This classic country inn, dating from 1884, is right in the center of the colonial village so you can rest in your room between spells of touring.

RESTAURANTS

THE DEERFIELD INN
81 Old Main St., Deerfield, MA 01342;
413-774-5587; www.deerfieldinn.com
A nice place with many New England specialties.

CHANDLER'S
25 Greenfield Rd.,
South Deerfield, MA 01373; 413-665-1277
Chandler's is in the Yankee Candle Company complex. New England cuisine is enhanced by candlelight.

STURBRIDGE

Living-history villages can bring alive the culture of prior eras, no matter what the century. We find Sturbridge as interesting now as it was forty years ago with our small children. The area was actually settled in 1729 as an agricultural community. Income came from orchards and dairy farms, as well as sawmills and gristmills.

   In 1730 a drawing was held for homestead lots by families, including the Bournes, Plimptons, Hardings, Gleasons, and Fiskes; the town's name was chosen because an ancestor of one of the settlers came from Stourbridge in Worcester County, England. During the Revolution the Saltonstall family gave Sturbridge Common "For Publick Use Forever," and it became the scene of great activity as militia drilled on the green. Today Sturbridge is a town within (or alongside) a town, as the re-created historical village draws tourists who often take time to visit or dine in the town itself, which has its own colonial charm.

HISTORICAL SITES and MUSEUMS

Old Sturbridge Village (800-SEE-1830, 508-347-3362; www.osv.org), 1 Old Sturbridge Rd. Although this living museum was created to depict early 19th-century life, substantial traces of the 18th century remain. Some of the buildings are from the earlier period, as is the 1780 printing office. A full-size wigwam, dated about 1760, came from a site called Chabunagungamaug in Webster, Massachusetts. Hand-carved bowls from the 1600s through the 1800s are on display.

You can wander on paths to visit typical houses, gardens, meetinghouses, a district school, mills, workshops for various trades and crafts, as well as a working farm. Costumed interpreters work on their crafts, and you can interact with them.

LODGING

PUBLICK HOUSE
MA 131 on the Common,
P.O. Box 187, Sturbridge, MA 01566
800-PUBLICK, 508-347-3313;
www.publickhouse.com
This historic inn has atmosphere as well as modern amenities. It was founded in 1771 and has rooms with period furnishings. The Chamberlain House is adjacent. The Colonel Ebenezer Crafts Inn on Fiske Hill Road, built in 1786, is also managed by the Publick House.

RESTAURANTS

THE PUBLICK HOUSE RESTAURANT
MA 131 on the Common,
P.O. Box 187, Sturbridge, MA 01566
800-PUBLICK, 508-347-3313;
www.publickhouse.com
New England fare has been served here since 1771.

THE WHISTLING SWAN
502 Main St.,
Sturbridge, MA 01518; 508-347-2321;
www.thewhistlingswan.com
The restaurant offers fine dining with a vari-

ety of dishes. Upstairs, the **Ugly Duckling** has a lighter menu and a pub atmosphere.

In *Old Sturbridge Village,* the *Bullard Tavern* cafeteria also offers meals and snacks.

SALEM CROSS INN
MA 9, West Brookfield, MA 01585
508-867-2345; www.salemcrossinn.com
Twenty minutes away from Sturbridge, this restored colonial inn offers a variety of meals as well as Sunday brunch.

EVENTS

July: Old Sturbridge Village Independence Day Celebration
800-SEE-1830
October: Sturbridge Harvest Festival
508-628-8379
November: Thanksgiving Celebration
800-SEE-1830

INFORMATION

TRI-COMMUNITY AREA CHAMBER OF COMMERCE
380 Main St., Sturbridge, MA 01566
888-STURBRIDGE, 888-788-7274,
508-347-2761; tricomchamber.org

THE BERKSHIRES

Indians traveled the **Mohawk Trail** from central Massachusetts to the Finger Lakes of New York. Colonial troops marched the same route to New York during the French and Indian War, and later settlers used the trail on their way west. Now MA 2, the trail passes through the Connecticut valley and into the Berkshire Hills, running along the banks of the Deerfield and Cold Rivers to Williamstown, in the far northwestern corner of Berkshire County and Massachusetts.

The Berkshire Hills, a north-south spine of ancient, rounded mountains located between the Taconic and Hoosac Ranges, peacefully blend the natural beauty of forests, fields, orchards, rivers, and lakes. This area remained a wilderness long after settlers had populated the Connecticut valley. The English chose not to advance into it over the granite Hoosac Range from the east, and the Taconic Range provided a barrier against incursions by Dutch settlers from the west. In the 18th century some religious leaders like Jonathan Edwards and the Shakers' Mary Lee looked upon this area as a retreat into the wilderness.

When the threat of frontier raids ended after the French and Indian War, English settlers arrived to stay. Militia from Berkshire County played a role in the Revolution, most prominently in the Battle of Bennington in 1777, when Pittsfield's "Fighting Parson" Thomas Allen accompanied a contingent to the aid of the Vermont and New Hampshire militias.

During the 19th century the region saw industrial development as textile and paper mills flourished, iron foundries produced ore for industry, and marble was quarried for public buildings. The Hoosac Tunnel blasting eastward through the Hoosac Range from North Adams was begun in 1851 and completed in 1875, fostering the industry of that manufacturing town. At the same time the beauty and climate of the mountains attracted summer residents who built homes and estates.

Now the towns and villages abound with historic homes, museums, antiques shops, and fairs. And the whole region is touched with a rich heritage of art, literature, drama, dance, and music. The Sterling and Francine Clark Art Institute in Williamstown has a world-renowned collection of impressionists, and the Massachusetts Museum of Contemporary Art (MASS MoCA) in neighboring North Adams draws visitors to its renovated mill complex that houses contemporary art on a massive scale. The Berkshires come alive each summer with music at Tanglewood in Lenox, theater in Williamstown, Lenox, Pittsfield, and Stockbridge, opera in Great Barrington and Pittsfield, and dance at Jacob's Pillow in Becket. Gilded Age "cottages" such as Naumkeag in Stockbridge and Edith Wharton's Mount in Lenox also have colorful gardens.

WILLIAMSTOWN

West Hoosac was established in 1750 but was little more than a frontier outpost, in constant peril of attack, during the French and Indian War. Its name was changed to Williamstown in 1765 in honor of Ephraim Williams, who had been killed in an ambush prior to the Battle of Lake George in 1755 and had made a bequest to the town to establish a free school. Williams College, chartered in 1793, remains his legacy: The school's teams are nicknamed "Ephs." If you would like to look at a successful and aesthetically beautiful marriage of town and gown, come to Williamstown. The campus, set on rolling hills, merges seamlessly with the surrounding town in an idyllic setting. A walk through the campus will reward you with some stunning architecture.

MUSEUMS

The **Sterling and Francine Clark Art Institute** (413-458-2303); 225 South St. This renowned museum exhibits collections from the 15th through the 19th centuries, with a major focus on impressionism. It has a fine collection of colonial silverwork.

The Williams College Museum of Art (413-597-2429), Main St. With 11,000 holdings, the museum emphasizes American, modern, contemporary, and non-Western art.

PITTSFIELD

Named for William Pitt the Elder and settled after the French and Indian War made the New England frontier more secure, Pittsfield is the largest community and commercial hub of Berkshire County.

HISTORICAL SITES *and* MUSEUMS

At the western edge of the city, on US 20, lies **Hancock Shaker Village** (413-443-0188; www.hancockshakervillage.org). As its name would indicate, the village lies mostly in the town of Hancock, although it is actually considerably closer to down-

The Brick Dwelling at Hancock Shaker Village

Hancock Shaker Village's iconic Round Stone Barn

town Pittsfield than to the town center of Hancock. This is one of several extant Shaker communities founded by Mother Ann Lee, who came to America in 1774. By 1780 people were becoming attracted to the Shakers, and in 1783 Mother Ann Lee preached at Hancock in a house near the village's Trustees' House.

In 1790 Hancock was the third of the eighteen communities she established. Besides being pacifists, the Shakers believed in withdrawal from the world, holding property in common, confession of sin, celibacy, and separation but equality of the sexes. A Shaker motto was "Do all your work as though you had a thousand years to live and as you would if you knew you must die tomorrow." Today, visitors can walk through twenty-one buildings, many of them designed with elegant simplicity, and appreciate the utility and beauty of Shaker architecture and furniture. Interpreters demonstrate crafts, cooking, farming, and gardening.

In the southeast corner of Pittsfield near the Lenox town line is **Arrowhead** (413-442-1793), on Holmes Rd. Now owned by the Berkshire County Historical Society. Open Memorial Day–Columbus Day and by appointment during the rest of the year. Herman Melville lived and wrote in this 18th-century farmhouse for 13 of his most productive years. He finished *Moby Dick* while looking at the whalelike profile of Mount Greylock. Inside you'll find Melville manuscripts, first editions of his books, and memorabilia from his voyages. If you want to see more Melville material, visit the **Berkshire Athenaeum** (413-499-9486), at 1 Wendell Ave. just off Park Square in the center of Pittsfield.

In recent years, Pittsfield discovered another claim to historical fame: Town documents provided the earliest written source on record in North America for the game of "base ball." A 1791 town bylaw prohibited the playing of the apparently popular pastime in front of the town's new meetinghouse on Park Square, for fear that its windows might get broken.

LODGING

WHITE HORSE INN
378 South St.,
Pittsfield, MA 01201
413-442-2512;
www.whitehorsebb.com
This house built at the turn of the 20th century is comfortable, not pretentious. It has eight well-equipped rooms with many conveniences.

Not far away to the south you will find a number of historic accommodations in Lenox.

1897 HAMPTON TERRACE
91 Walker St., Lenox, MA 01240
800-203-0656, 413-637-1773;
www.hamptonterrace.com
This historic Gilded Age mansion has been an inn since 1937.

BIRCHWOOD INN
7 Hubbard St., Lenox, MA 01240
800-524-1646, 413-637-2600;
www.birchwood-inn.com
This 1767 mansion is a block away from the main street. Afternoon tea is served every day.

BLANTYRE
16 Blantyre Rd.,
Lenox, MA 01240; 413-637-3556;
www.blantyre.com
This country house hotel could have been transplanted from England, complete with gargoyles and turrets.

BROOK FARM INN
15 Hawthorne St.,
Lenox, MA 01240
800-285-POET, 413-637-3013;
www.brookfarm.com
This Victorian inn offers poetry readings, and a poem for each day is on display.

CORNELL INN
203 Main St., Lenox, MA 01240
800-637-0562, 413-637-0562
The Main House dates from 1888, the Carriage House from 1889, and the MacDonald House in 1777.

GATEWAYS INN AND RESTAURANT
51 Walker St., Lenox, MA 01240
888-492-9466, 413-637-2532;
www.gatewaysinn.com
Harley Proctor, of Proctor and Gamble, first owned the house. Arthur Fiedler reserved one of the suites when he came to conduct the Boston Pops.

VILLAGE INN
16 Church St., Lenox, MA 01240
800-253-0917, 413-637-0020;
www.villageinn-lenox.com
This inn dates from 1771 and has stenciled wallpapers and Oriental rugs. There is a full restaurant and tavern on the grounds.

WHEATLEIGH
Hawthorne Rd., Lenox, MA 01240
413-637-0610; www.wheatleigh.com
Wheatleigh looks like a European estate with a fountain near the front door. The cuisine is highly acclaimed.

Most of the inns listed above also have dining rooms.

EVENTS

September: Hancock Shaker Village County Fair, 413-443-0188
December: Hancock Shaker Village Christmas, 413-443-0188

INFORMATION

BERKSHIRE VISITORS BUREAU
3 Hoosac St., Adams, MA 01220
413-443-9186; www.berkshires.org

STOCKBRIDGE

Farther south (just off the Massachusetts Turnpike), Stockbridge was first an Indian mission in 1734. The Reverend John Sergeant decided that the Indians should live with the English settlers and perhaps become Christians. He taught them in their own language until he died prematurely in 1749.

HISTORICAL SITES *and* MUSEUMS

The **Mission House** (413-298-3239; www.thetrustees.org), Main St. This 1735 house was Sergeant's home. He ordered an elegantly carved wooden door that was brought over the mountains by oxcart from Connecticut. Jonathan Edwards lived and worked here after he left Northampton and before being appointed president of Princeton University. Colonial-revival gardens were designed by Fletcher Steele.

John and Abigail Sergeant are buried in the cemetery just down the road. Also in the cemetery is Theodore Sedgwick, who became well known after he defended a slave named Mum Bett. She wanted him to help her claim her liberty under the Bill of Rights of the new Massachusetts Constitution. He defended her against the claims of Colonel Ashley, who was forced to pay her 30 shillings. A free Mum Bett then chose to live with the Sedgwick family as their housekeeper. She is buried in the cemetery along with the Sedgwicks.

LODGING

THE INN AT STOCKBRIDGE
MA 7N, 30 East St.,
Stockbridge, MA 01262;
888-466-7865;
www.stockbridgeinn.com
The inn dates from 1906. Guest rooms are in the main house, the cottage house, and the barn.

THE RED LION INN
Main St.,
Stockbridge, MA 01262
413-298-5545;
www.redlioninn.com
The Red Lion was built in 1773 as a tavern and stagecoach stop, and now provides travelers with accommodations and both informal and formal dining.

RESTAURANTS

ONCE UPON A TABLE
36 Main St., Stockbridge, MA 01262
413-298-3870
Walk around into "The Mews" to find this restaurant, which is popular with its eclectic menu

THE RED LION INN
Main St., Stockbridge, MA 01262
413-298-5545; www.redlioninn.com
The inn includes a large dining room, a tavern, a courtyard, and a cellar pub.

INFORMATION

STOCKBRIDGE CHAMBER OF COMMERCE
6 Elm St., Stockbridge, MA 01262
413-298-5200

GREAT BARRINGTON

Seven miles south of Stockbridge, the town of Great Barrington was settled in 1726 as a farming community. It is now perhaps the most fashionable town in the Berkshires, filled with restaurants, galleries, and shops.

In 1774 the citizens captured the courthouse to prevent the King's Court from holding a session. A stone marker describes this feat as "the first act of open resistance to British rule in America." But another attempt at individual rebellion didn't pay. **Belcher Square** was named after Gill Belcher, a counterfeiter who made coins in a cave near his house in the 1770s. He was captured and hanged. Laura Secord, a War of 1812 heroine (for the other side) known to every Canadian schoolchild, was from Loyalist stock in Great Barrington.

LODGING

TURNING POINT INN
3 Lake Buel Rd.,
Great Barrington, MA 01230
413-528-4777;
www.turningpointinn.com
The 1800 brick building has wide-board floors. It was once a tavern on the Boston-Albany stagecoach run.

THE EGREMONT INN
Old Sheffield Rd.,
South Egremont, MA 01258
413-528-2111; www.egremontinn.com
This 1780 inn was built by Francis Haere, an Irishman who fought in three battles of the American Revolution. It has an 18th-century fireplace and wide porches.

THE WAINWRIGHT INN
518 S. Main St.,
Great Barrington, MA 01230
413-528-2062;
www.wainwrightinn.com
Captain Peter Ingersoll built the inn in 1766, naming it the Troy Tavern and Inn. David Wainwright, a statesman and state representative, bought the house in 1790.

RESTAURANTS

Great Barrington has more restaurants per capita than any community in the well-touristed Berkshires. But for a more colonial ambience, you may want to explore southwest of town in nearby South Egremont.

THE EGREMONT INN
Old Sheffield Rd.,
South Egremont, MA 01258
413-528-2111; www.egremontinn.com
Meals are served in the dining room and also the tavern.

JOHN ANDREWS RESTAURANT
MA 23/224 Hillsdale Rd.,
South Egremont, MA 01258
413-528-3469; www.jarestaurant.com
The chef-owner offers local produce and organic poultry and meat.

THE OLD MILL
MA 23, South Egremont, MA 01258
413-528-1421
The chef-owner provides a varied menu in a 1797 gristmill with a dining room and a tavern.

The *Knox Trail* is remembered as the route Colonel Henry Knox took from Fort Ticonderoga to Boston during the winter of 1775–76. He set out with 60 tons of artillery that had been seized by Ethan Allen and his Green Mountain Boys with Benedict Arnold. The route through Massachusetts begins in the Alford-Egremont area in the Berkshires across Routes 71, 23, 20, 67, 98, and 20. Knox and his men traveled more than 300 miles through deep snow in the mountains, over rivers, and through forests. Oxen pulled the heavy equipment on sleds, now and then crashing through frozen rivers. "Snow detain'd us some days and now a cruel thaw hinders," Knox wrote in his diary January 5, 1776. Either too much snow or too little ice disrupted this epic trek across part of New York and all of Massachusetts, all done in an amazing 40 days..

SHEFFIELD

Land that was to become the town of Sheffield was purchased from the Mohicans for three barrels of cider, 20 quarts of rum, and some cash. Settled in 1725, incorporated in 1733, it is the oldest town in Berkshire County. It was the site of a battle in Shays' Rebellion shortly after the Revolution. A granite post off Egremont Road marks the spot.

HISTORICAL SITES *and* MUSEUMS

The **Sheffield Historical Society** (413-229-2694; www.sheffieldhistory.org). The society's visitor center and exhibit space are in the 1834 Stone Store on 159 Main St.

The **Dan Raymond House**, 159 Main St., is owned by the historical society. Open Memorial Day–Oct. It dates from 1775, when Dan Raymond built the house from his own bricks. The house contains objects used during the 18th century.

In the Ashley Falls section of town is the oldest house in Berkshire County, the **Colonel John Ashley House** (413-229-8600), Cooper Hill Rd. Ashley and other townsmen drafted the Sheffield Declaration, a petition against British tyranny, in his home in 1773. His slave, Mum Bett, fought for and won her freedom after hearing talk in the house of individual rights. The house contains period furnishings and has a collection of early farm tools. A walking trail leading to a superb view of the Berkshire Hills is nearby.

Current Information

MASSACHUSETTS OFFICE OF TRAVEL AND TOURISM
10 Park Plaza, Suite 4510
Boston, MA 02116
617-973-8500, 800-447-6277
fax 617-973-8525
www.massvacation.com

Connecticut

Historical Introduction *to the* Connecticut Colony

The Dutch were the first Europeans to arrive in the Connecticut River valley. Adriaen Block (Block Island is named for him) sailed up the river in 1614, exploring as far as present-day Enfield, and in 1633 the Dutch built a fortified trading post at the site of present-day Hartford. Shortly afterward Pilgrims from Plymouth settled and built a trading post just upriver, at Windsor.

The Reverend Thomas Hooker, who had settled in Newtown (Cambridge) a few years earlier, left Massachusetts in May 1636 with a hundred followers. Motivated by theological differences with the leadership of Massachusetts Bay, Hooker and his congregation also sought better land for agriculture in the fertile Connecticut River valley. To reach it they struggled overland through the wilderness for 120 miles to found a settlement at the site of Hartford. Because the emigrants were traveling with all their possessions and cattle, they made only about ten miles a day. Within a few months others had come to settle in Windsor and Wethersfield.

Hooker, whose democratic leanings had caused him friction in Massachusetts, believed that a "general council, chosen by all, to transact business which concerns all, I conceive most suitable to rule and most safe for the relief of the whole people." His views were to lead to the adoption by Hartford, Windsor, and Wethersfield of the Fundamental Orders of Connecticut in January 1639. The nucleus of the future colony was now established.

Deacon John Grave House in Madison

The Pequot War

At the time Hooker settled in Hartford, sixteen Indian tribes in Connecticut were all under the loose Algonquian Confederation. These Indians were fearful of the Mohawks to the west and Pequots to the east and thus wished to live harmoniously with the newcomers. They sold land and helped the settlers learn more about hunting, fishing, and farming in the region.

But the Pequots, who were based in the vicinity of the Thames and Mystic Rivers, upset the short-lived equilibrium of peaceful coexistence. There was no doubt that the Pequots, who felt that the colonists were interlopers on their territory, were intent on getting rid of the white communities in Connecticut. Both the colonies of Massachusetts Bay and the settlements on the Connecticut wanted "rights of conquest" over the Pequot land. After several white traders were killed in 1634 and 1636, the Massachusetts colonists felt that the Pequots were guilty of treaty violations and tried to get them to surrender as tributaries to the colony. The Pequots refused and later attacked Saybrook and Wethersfield.

After the Wethersfield attack in April of 1637, during which nine settlers were slain, the three Connecticut River towns organized troops under Captains John Mason and John Underhill. With Mohegan and Narragansett Indians as allies, the settlers planned an offensive to decimate the Pequots. In a surprise night raid near Mystic, the colonists and their allies set fire to the Pequot compound, burned alive many of the hundreds trapped inside, including women and children, and killed those who tried to escape. Subsequently they hunted down the remnant of the tribe in a swamp in Fairfield and killed more of them. Those who surrendered were sold into slavery.

> Of the Mystic massacre, Plymouth's governor and historian William Bradford wrote: "It was conceived they thus destroyed about 400 at this time. It was a fearfull sight to see them thus . . . but the victory seemed a sweete sacrifice . . . thus to inclose their enimise in their hands, and give them so speedy a victory over so proud and insulting an enimie."

CONNECTICUT *Time Line*

1614	1623	1633	1633
Adriaen Block sails up coast, explores Connecticut River	Dutch settle Kievit's Hoeck (Old Saybrook), which is abandoned after a few months	Dutch establish trading post at site of present-day Hartford	Windsor founded as trading post by Pilgrims from Plymouth Colony

In 1638 the Puritans proceeded to write the "Articles of Agreement betweene Theophilus Eaton and John Davenport and others English Planters att Quinopiocke on the one party and Momaugin the Indian Sachem of Quinopiocke" which gave them the right to the land. In return, the Indians received "Twelve Coates of english trucking cloat[h], Twelve Alcumy spoones, Twelve Hatchetts, twelve hoes, two dozen of knives, twelve porengers and foure Cases of french knives and sizers." In addition, another Indian, Mantowese of Mattabezeck, offered a larger piece of land for "Eleven coates made of Trucking cloth, and one Coate for himselfe of English cloth, made up after the English maner."

Founding of Shore Towns

Well-known Puritan clergyman John Davenport reached Boston in 1637 with a group of followers, spent the winter there, then journeyed to the mouth of the Quinnipiac River and established a settlement at what is now New Haven. Although the area was thought to belong to the Dutch of New Netherland, the Earl of Warwick had granted the same land to friends of Davenport and Theophilus Eaton.

The members of the New Haven group established the colony on strict theocratic principles. They believed that "the word of God shall be the only rule" and allowed only church members to vote. Eaton, a London merchant, became the first governor, and he gave primacy to the laws of Moses as the model for the colony. New Haven did not allow trials by jury because this concept is not mentioned in the Bible. In 1639, when the Fundamental Orders of Connecticut were drafted to make Connecticut a self-governing colony, New Haven did not join the Connecticut River towns in that agreement. They objected to provisions that allowed freemen to elect the governor and his council.

During the colony's first years, other towns grew around it—Milford, Guilford, Stamford, Fairfield, Greenwich, and Branford, as well as settlements across the sound on Long Island. They were all part of the colony of New Haven and opposed to the politics of the river towns clustered around Hartford.

1634	1636	1637	1638
Wethersfield founded by Puritans from Massachusetts Bay	The Rev. Thomas Hooker from Newtown (Cambridge) in Massachusetts establishes Hartford	Pequots virtually wiped out in short Pequot War	New Haven founded by the Reverend John Davenport

When both the Connecticut and New Haven colonies accepted the end of Puritan rule in England and restoration of Charles II in 1661, the validity of their land claims needed to be established. John Winthrop Jr., who had helped found New London in 1646 and had later served as governor of the Connecticut colony, was sent to London in 1661 to try to get a charter for Connecticut from the newly restored Crown. The charter was ready on May 10, 1662, and the colony was authorized to govern itself. But the charter had granted to Connecticut control over New Haven and a tract of Rhode Island land, and leaders in both those areas protested. New Haven finally reluctantly accepted the charter and joined Connecticut a few years later.

A Unified Connecticut

With a valid charter in hand, a unified Connecticut was able to maintain the independence its founding colonies had always enjoyed. It had no royal governor imposed upon it, choosing its own governor and other public officials, and its General Assembly did not have to send legislation to London for approval. Connecticut inherited only a few strictures of royal or Parliamentary control, like the long-standing Navigation Acts. That independence was temporarily upset when James II took the throne and created the short-lived Dominion of New England in 1685. First imposed on Massachusetts, it gave the power of appointment and taxation to Sir Edmund Andros as governor in chief a year later and was extended to Rhode Island, with Connecticut included in 1687. This first serious attempt at royal control of the New England colonies collapsed with England's Glorious Revolution of 1688 and the ascension of William and Mary to the throne. In the aftermath Massachusetts lost its original charter and would henceforth have a royal governor to contend with, but Connecticut's charter was restored intact.

Connecticut's continuing independence through the colonial era was also fostered by patterns of settlement, culture, and religion. Unlike Massachusetts or New York, it had developed no single dominant city, with the river cities and Long Island Sound ports sharing trade. Much of its land was in agriculture, in spite of rocky soil beyond the river plains, and small towns and villages dominated the landscape and maintained their independence. Yet as in Massachusetts, the theo-

---

CONNECTICUT *Time Line*

1639	**1646**	**1662**	**1665**	**1675-76**
Fundamental Orders of Connecticut adopted by Hartford, Windsor, and Wethersfield	New London founded by John Winthrop Jr.	Royal charter recognizes Connecticut with authority vested in the governor and freemen	New Haven accepts charter	King Philip's War

---

cratic principles of the founders gave Puritan congregations and the ministers who led them extraordinary political and moral influence over the lives of townspeople, including chastisement for conduct and fines for not attending services. Generally there was no tolerance for Quakers and Baptists, who were branded as heretics and banished. Congregations resisted any attempts at outside control, even within the Puritan world, until a synod of twelve ministers met in 1708 and established voluntary ecclesiastical associations in each county to oversee individual congregations and approve candidates for the ministry.

By 1700 the General Assembly in Connecticut also made sure that all children were going to be literate enough to read the Bible. Money was made available to schools, and by 1717 an eleven-month school year was in place for the larger towns, with six months for smaller ones. Grammar schools were established in Hartford, New London, Fairfield, and New Haven to prepare students for higher education. John Davenport had urged establishing a Puritan college, but the idea was not seriously entertained until 1701, when the General Assembly chartered a college to "promote the power and Purity of Religion and Best Edification and peace of these New England Churches," with clergymen over forty years old as trustees. The infant college floated from place to place for nearly two decades until it settled in New Haven, established a library, appointed a rector, and took on the name Yale College in honor of a donor.

Compared with other New England colonies, Connecticut suffered less from internal and external armed conflicts during the colonial era. During King Philip's War (1675–76), Connecticut established a draft of able-bodied men and forbade them to emigrate to avoid it, and provided a major force in the climactic Great Swamp Fight. Connecticut militias were involved in the string of raids and expeditions during King William's War (1689–97) and Queen Anne's War (1702–13), the almost incessant though sporadic conflicts between England and France. These were the precursors to the major war for control of North America, the French and Indian War, in which Connecticut men and money were heavily involved. When that war ended 5,000 men had been in battle and nearly 260,000 pounds spent on the war effort; yet none of the battles in this wide-ranging conflict had been fought on Connecticut territory. That injury would wait until the Revolu-

1687	**1701**	**1777**	**1781**	**1788**
Hartford patriots hide charter in Charter Oak after Governor Edmund Andros declares all charters void	Yale College founded	British and Loyalists raid Danbury	British burn New London, massacre the garrison at Fort Griswold	Connecticut ratifies U.S. Constitution, becomes fifth state

tion and culminate when a native son who had earned praise as a hero turned traitor and led a devastating assault on a port just downriver from his birthplace.

When Britain passed revenue-raising acts such as the Sugar Act of 1764, the Stamp Act of 1765, and the Townshend Acts of 1767, Connecticut lost its peaceful equilibrium. On a number of issues—including the issuance of paper money, which coastal merchants needed for trade, and toleration or repudiation of the Great Awakening—citizens of eastern and western Connecticut were increasingly at odds. While those in the west tended to oppose but ultimately accept the repressive taxes, more radical easterners rejected that tepid response and began to take things into their own hands. In response to the Stamp Act, five prominent citizens and militia officers from the French and Indian War met to form the Sons of Liberty in eastern Connecticut. A large group of Sons met Jared Ingersoll, who had accepted the post of stamp collector, on his way to Hartford and forced him to resign. In 1766 William Pitken, a Hartford merchant, and Jonathan Trumbull, one of the founders of the Sons, were elected governor and deputy governor in an upset, shifting sentiment about British intrusions on Connecticut rights from reluctant acquiescence to aggressive protest. After the Townshend duties were imposed, the Sons of Liberty organized a campaign against importing or consuming British goods. After the Boston Tea Party, the Connecticut General Assembly continued to support vigorous opposition to the Coercive Acts laid on Massachusetts, formed a committee of correspondence, and began arming and training its militias.

Revolutionary War Attacks

During the Revolutionary War Connecticut was struck by several British raids. Danbury was the first in 1777, when Major General William Tryon, the royal governor of New York, led British and Loyalist troops on a raid against a Continental Army supply depot and burned tents and food. In 1779 Tryon arrived in Greenwich to destroy the saltworks, and in July of that year the British ravaged New Haven, Fairfield, and Norwalk.

The last British naval assaults, against New London and Groton in 1781, were led by the notorious turncoat Benedict Arnold, formerly of New Haven. (Ironically, Arnold, before he had turned traitor at West Point, had valiantly led some of the patriot resistance to the 1777 Danbury raid.) First Arnold attacked Fort Trumbull and then moved on to Fort Griswold. The British continued to kill soldiers after they had surrendered, including those who were wounded, and they torched New London. Connecticut patriots found this brutal attack by a native son particularly repugnant. The sentiment was shared in other colonies. John Brown of Pittsfield, Massachusetts, wrote that "money is this man's god, and to get enough of it he would sacrifice his country."

From the British point of view, the attack was not unwarranted. By 1779 New London had become a major privateering center. Merchant-ship owners applied for commissions from Governor Trumbull to legalize their raiding operations. These privateers continually harassed British ships and captured a number as prizes of war.

Regions *to* Explore

CONNECTICUT RIVER VALLEY

While living for nine years in the Connecticut River valley, we savored the beauty of its rolling hills and its streams and lakes. Those same streams contributed to the development of mills and factories. Today the lakes and rivers beckon people to enjoy leisurely water sports, or kayaking on spectacular white-water stretches.

Native Americans were growing tobacco here when the first settlers arrived. Later the area became known as Tobacco Valley. (Connecticut Valley tobacco leaves are especially prized for their use as cigar wrappers.) We wondered about the gauzy white sheets covering the fields and soon learned that they provided humidity for the growing tobacco and helped protect the delicate leaves. Although not a great deal of tobacco is grown now, farmers offer produce from their orchards and farms.

HARTFORD

In the Hartford area many people lived along the Connecticut River until construction of the interstate highway system put and end to that possibility. I-91 was laid out along the west bank, separating the city center from the river and destroying a lively Italian neighborhood. When Constantinos Doxiodus, a city planner from Greece, took a tour of the area near the river with a group from Trinity College, he observed that plazas were empty after working hours. Because the highway had sealed off the river and no one lived on or near it, there was no sense of community to support activity beyond the end of the workday.

Fort Good Hope was founded by Dutch fur traders from New Amsterdam in 1633. Three years later, the Reverend Thomas Hooker and the first group of English settlers arrived overland from Massachusetts Bay. Like the traders before them, these early settlers used the Connecticut River to transport furs, timber, fish, game, and tobacco.

One industry that eventually grew to dominate the town was the result of worry by shipowners over losses from storms, fire, and shipwreck. They had moved upriver to be less vulnerable to attacks from the sea and now set aside some of their profits to insure themselves against these other possible losses. Thus the insurance industry was born in Hartford, which today remains dominated by insurance companies and banking institutions, while the aircraft industry flourishes across the river in East Hartford. The city, which has struggled with the problems that have beset many urban areas since the middle of the 20th century, is nonetheless blessed with many educational and cultural institutions.

HISTORICAL SITES *and* MUSEUMS

Hartford's growth has obliterated all but a few traces of the 17th-century settlement, but you can still find remnants from the 18th century. The oldest surviving house in Hartford is the **Butler-McCook Homestead** (860-522-1806 or 860-247-8996; www.hartnet.org/als), 396 Main St. Open daily. It was home to four generations of the same family. The part dating from 1782 was built as a blacksmith shop and a butcher shop. Original furnishings, silver, and children's toys belonging to the family are on display.

The **Wadsworth Atheneum** (860-278-2670; www.wadsworthatheneum.org), 600 Main St. Open daily except Mon. and Tues. The Nutting Collection includes two restored colonial period rooms that were taken out of their original homes, and the 17th-century furniture is authentic. The Atheneum contains a fine collection of artworks from across the centuries. When it's time for lunch try the Atheneum café (203-278-2670).

Just across the corner, at Main and Gold Sts., stands **Center Church**, at the

---

The story of the Charter Oak in **Hartford** may be more legend than fact, but it does incorporate some real political events that took place where the Traveler's Tower stands today. On October 31, 1687, the Zachary Sanford Tavern stood there. Sir Edmund Andros, the governor appointed by King James II, had arrived in town and demanded the return of the liberal charter that had been given to the Hartford colony in 1662 by Charles II.

According to the legend, during a discussion of the charter the sun set, candles were lit, and then mysteriously blew out. The charter disappeared—one of the colonists had spirited it away and hidden it in the trunk of an old oak tree, thereafter known as the Charter Oak. The charter did not reappear until 1715.

Although the Charter Oak blew down during a hurricane in 1856, Mark Twain—never one to be reverential—listed some of the objects that were said to have been made from its wood: "A walking stick, dog collar, needle case, three-legged stool, bootjack, dinner table, tenpin alley, toothpick, and enough Charter Oak to build a plank road from Hartford to Salt Lake City."

Twain might be amused to know that the Charter Oak has continued currency, not in wood but on the Connecticut state quarter. Visitors can see the original charter in the Raymond E. Baldwin Museum of Connecticut History in the **State Library** (203-566-3056; www.eslib.org), 231 Capitol Ave. Open daily except Sun.

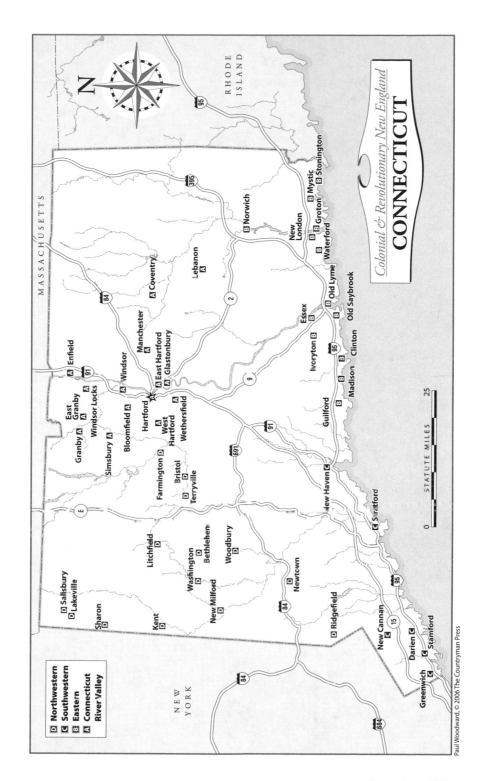

Colonial & Revolutionary New England

CONNECTICUT

Legend:
- D Northwestern
- C Southwestern
- B Eastern
- A Connecticut River Valley

MASSACHUSETTS

RHODE ISLAND

NEW YORK

Enfield A
East Granby A
Granby A
Simsbury A
Windsor Locks A
Windsor A
Bloomfield A
Hartford
West Hartford A
Wethersfield A
East Hartford A
Glastonbury A
Manchester
Coventry A
Lebanon A
Norwich B

Salisbury D
Lakeville D
Sharon
Kent D
Litchfield D
Washington D
New Milford D
Bethlehem D
Woodbury D
Bristol D
Terryville D
Farmington D
Newtown
Ridgefield D
New Canaan C
Greenwich C
Darien C
Stamford
New Haven C
Stratford C

Essex B
Ivoryton B
Old Lyme B
Old Saybrook
Clinton
Madison
Guilford B
Waterford
New London
Groton B
Mystic B
Stonington B

STATUTE MILES
0   25

Paul Woodward, © 2006 The Countryman Press

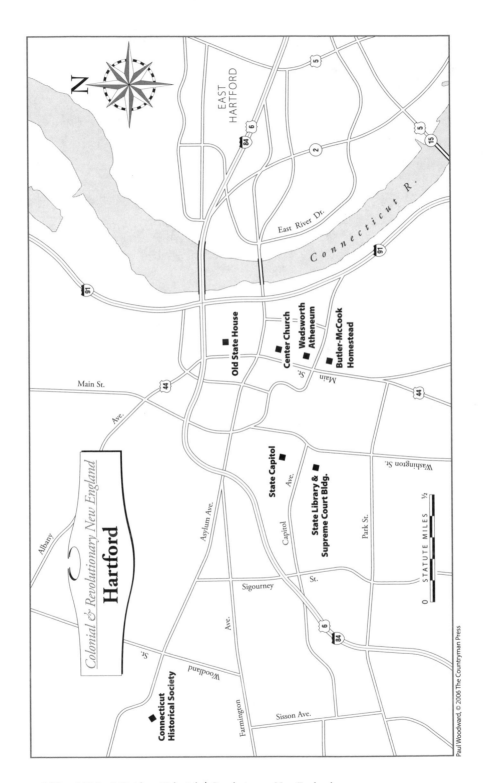

Colonial & Revolutionary New England

Hartford

Albany

Main St.

Ave.

Asylum Ave.

Sigourney

Ave.

St.

Woodland St.

Farmington

Sisson Ave.

■ Connecticut
Historical Society

■ State Capitol

Capitol

Ave.

St.

■ State Library &
Supreme Court Bldg.

Park St.

Washington St.

44

Main St.

44

Main St.

■ Old State House

■ Center Church
■ Wadsworth
Atheneum

■ Butler-McCook
Homestead

EAST
HARTFORD

84
6

2

5

5
15

91

91

East River Dr.

Connecticut R.

6
84

0   STATUTE MILES   ½

Paul Woodward, © 2006 The Countryman Press

site where Thomas Hooker preached more than 350 years ago. The present church dates from 1807 and has Tiffany windows for you to admire. Many of the first settlers in Hartford lie in the adjacent **Ancient Burying Ground**. If you can't pass by old cemeteries, plan to spend some time here searching for stones dating from the 1640s.

A portrait of George Washington by Gilbert Stuart hangs in the **Old State House** (860-522-6766; www.ctosh.org), 800 Main St. Open daily except Sun. This is one of the oldest statehouses in the country, and like Massachusetts' "new" State House, it was designed by Charles Bulfinch. Dating from 1796, the building is a National Historic Landmark. Tour the 1820 Senate Chamber, Victorian-era City Council Room, and the colonial revival–style Supreme Courtroom. A large interactive exhibit tells the story of Hartford.

The **Winthrop-Hutchinson Tree** was planted on the campus of Trinity College in November 2004. John Winthrop, a 12th-generation descendant of Governor John Winthrop, and Eve LaPlante, 13th-generation descendant of Anne Hutchinson, presented the tree. It was dedicated as "a symbolic reconciliation of a religious and ideological conflict between their ancestors that began in colonial Massachusetts more than 300 years ago." In 1637 Governor Winthrop, a founder of the Massachusetts Bay Colony, banished and excommunicated Anne Hutchinson, who then set up her own colony and became a co-founder of what is now Rhode Island.

If you're interested in genealogy, visit the **Connecticut Historical Society** (860-236-5621; www.chs.org), One Elizabeth St. Open daily except Mon. Here are over two million manuscripts on Connecticut history and genealogy, plus nine galleries of permanent and changing exhibits. You'll also find colonial furniture from the 17th century. Special events and programs are held during the year.

LODGING

GOODWIN HOTEL
1 Haynes St.,
Hartford, CT 06103
800-922-5006, 860-246-7500;
www.goodwinhotel.com
This historic hotel dates from 1881, and the Queen Anne facade remains.

RESTAURANTS

CARBONE'S
588 Franklin Ave.,
Hartford, CT 06114 , 860-296-9646
Since 1938 three generations of the Carbone family have run this Italian restaurant.

PIERPONT'S
At the Goodwin Hotel,
1 Haynes St., Hartford, CT 06103
860-246-7500; www.goodwinhotel.com
The restaurant was named for J. Pierpont Morgan.

WADSWORTH ATHENEUM CAFÉ
At the Atheneum,
600 Main St., Hartford, CT 06103
860-728-5989
The menu is varied and changes with the seasons.

EVENTS

July: Riverfest, 860-713-3131
December: Holiday Light Fantasia 860-343-1565

INFORMATION

GREATER HARTFORD CONVENTION AND VISITORS BUREAU
31 Pratt St., Hartford, CT 06103
800-446-7811, 860-728-6789;
www.enjoyhartford.com

GREATER HARTFORD WELCOME CENTER
45 Pratt St., Hartford, CT 06103
860-244-0253;
www.connectthedots.org/
hpb/wcenter.html

CENTRAL REGIONAL TOURISM DISTRICT, CONNECTICUT'S HERITAGE RIVER VALLEY
31 Pratt St., 4th Floor,
Hartford, CT 06103
800-793-4480, 860-244-8181;
www.enjoycentralct.com
For more information about the following sections on the Connecticut River Valley

WEST HARTFORD

West Hartford is now a pleasant semiurban area with lovely homes, large trees, and landscaped gardens, an unbroken continuation of Hartford's finest residential district. When we arrived forty-five years ago, we were told that it was "the" place to live and not to bother looking east of the river.

HISTORICAL SITES *and* MUSEUMS

Noah Webster wrote the *Blue Backed Speller* of 1783 in the **Noah Webster House** (860-521-5362; www.noahwebsterhouse.org), 227 S. Main St. Open daily. Webster was born in the house in 1758. Some of his possessions, including his desk, are in this 18th-century farmhouse.

After Ethan Allen and Benedict Arnold burst into Fort Ticonderoga and captured a number of sleeping British officers, some of them were held in the **Sarah Whitman Hooker House** (800-475-1233, 860-523-5887; www.sarahwhitman-hooker.org), 1237 New Britain Ave. Open Mon. and Wed. and by appointment. Built in 1720 as a saltbox, the house was remodeled into a Federal structure in 1807. Visitors can see the porcelain collection as well as original wallpapers, and the garden blooms with plants of the period.

LODGING

AVON OLD FARMS HOTEL
279 Avon Mountain Rd.,
Avon, CT 06001
800-836-4000, 860-677-1651;
www.avonoldfarmshotel.com
Head west over the mountain to this Georgian colonial decorated with antique furnishings.

RESTAURANTS

AVON OLD FARMS INN
CT 10 and US 44,
Avon, CT 0600i; 860-677-2818;
www.avonoldfarmsinn.com
The 1757 colonial building has several dining rooms and a popular Sunday brunch.

SEASONS RESTAURANT
In Avon Old Farms Hotel,
279 Avon Mountain Rd.,
Avon, CT 06001; 860-269-0240;
www.avonoldfarmshotel.com
Continental menu.

FARMINGTON

Now another satellite of Hartford, Farmington was once the largest town in area in the Connecticut colony. This attractive historic town is similar to West Hartford, with many lovely colonial homes. The Farmington River flows through town, and the main street follows the river. Dating from the 1830s, the Farmington Canal ran for eighty miles between New Haven and Northampton, Massachusetts, with fifty-six miles in Connecticut running through Hamden, Cheshire, Southington, Plainville, Farmington, Avon, Simsbury, and Granby. The Farmington Canal Trail is now being developed as part of Connecticut's Greenway System. Canoeists and tubers flock to the river during the summer. But don't go beyond the bridge at Satan's Kingdom on Route 44! The gorge is nicer to look at than be in.

HISTORICAL SITES and MUSEUMS

You may wonder why the **Stanley-Whitman House** (860-677-9222; www .stanleywhitman.org), 37 High St., has such an enormous overhang, making the second floor far larger than the first. Some speculate that it may have been to avoid high taxes, which were traditionally levied on the first floor of a home. This 1720 house has handsome diamond windowpanes. An 18th-century garden is a bonus. Open May–Oct., Wed.–Sun.; Nov.–Apr., Sat.–Sun., and by appointment.

Farmington was once the home of the Tunxis Indian tribe. If you have a passion for Indian lore, head for the **Day-Lewis Museum** (860-678-1645), 158 Main St. This archaeology museum displays artifacts that were found locally.

SIMSBURY

North of Farmington in the Farmington River valley, Simsbury was settled by British emigrants from Dorsetshire, England, in 1640. They had come by way of Windsor in the Connecticut River valley but had to abandon Simsbury and flee back to Windsor during King Philip's War. When they returned, nothing remained; the Indian warriors had burned the town to the ground.

Today Simsbury is a pleasant residential town with rolling hills and Talcott Mountain State Park, where hikers and picnickers enjoy outings. The Heublein Tower offers view of the surrounding countryside.

HISTORICAL SITES and MUSEUMS

Phelps Tavern Museum and Homestead, the Historical Society (860-658-2500), 800 Hopmeadow St., is a complex of buildings centering on an 18th-century house that contains period furnishings and a collection of costumes. Open Tue.–Sat. Don't miss the vaulted ceiling in the ballroom. **Phelps House** (1771) was a tavern when the canal trade was thriving in Simsbury. The Farmington Canal was active until the mid-1800s. A one-room schoolhouse dates from 1741. Weavers will be interested in the loom in the Hendricks Cottage.

LODGING

THE SIMSBURY 1820 HOUSE
731 Hopmeadow St.,
Simsbury, CT 06070
800-TRY-1820, 860-658-7658;
www.simsbury1820house.com
This historic inn is furnished with antiques
and enhanced with paintings.

THE SIMSBURY INN
397 Hopmeadow St.,
Simsbury, CT 06070
800-634-2719, 860-651-5700;
www.simsburyinn.com
A full-service hotel with a country-inn
ambience.

RESTAURANTS

EVERGREENS
At the Simsbury Inn,
397 Hopmeadow St.,
Simsbury, CT 06070
860-651-5700; www.simsburyinn.com
The Simsbury Inn also offers a café
and a lounge.

SIMSBURY 1820 HOUSE CAFÉ
731 Hopmeadow St., Simsbury, CT 06070
800-TRY-1820, 860-658-7658;
www.simsbury1820house.com
This café serves full dinners Mon.
through Thu.

GRANBY

A number of Simsbury residents moved out of town and settled farther north on
Salmon Brook Street in Granby.

By 1709 eleven families lived in the Salmon Brook settlement, but they were always concerned about Indian attacks. Daniel Hayes was out looking for his horse one day when he was spotted and captured by Indians, who then took him to Canada. During the thirty-day trip he was tied up at night, beaten, and starved.

When they reached a large Indian settlement he was forced to "run the gauntlet" between two rows of Indians with clubs. He ran into a wigwam where an old woman lived; she told the Indians that her house was "sacred" and saved his life. He lived with her until she died, then he was sold to a Frenchman who taught him to weave and shared the profits of their work. After seven years of captivity he bought his freedom and returned to his home in Granby.

Hayes's headstone in the Granby Cemetery is not visible, but there is a replica of it in the older part of the cemetery, in section 6. A man who has worked there for twenty years said you can't miss spotting the replica because all the stones around it are old. The inscription does not refer to Hayes's captivity: "Here lies ye body of Mr. Daniel Hayes who served his generation in steady course of Probity and Piety, and was a lover of Peace, and God's Public Worship: and was satisfied with long life, left this work with a comfortable Hope of Life Eternal—Sept. 3, 1756—in ye 71 year of his life."

HISTORICAL SITES *and* MUSEUMS

The oldest building left in the Salmon Brook settlement is the **Abijah Rowe House** (860-653-9713), 208 Salmon Brook St. Rowe built the house sometime around 1753; he was a blacksmith and a farmer. The paneling and corner cupboard in the south parlor are original. Look for the unusual front door with its carved trim, a frieze with triglyphs, and a cornice. The furniture comes from early Granby homes; two rare Connecticut spinning wheels stand in the house.

EAST GRANBY

The name of this area when it was settled in 1710 was Turkey Hills.

HISTORICAL SITES *and* MUSEUMS

In this town north of Hartford was located a notorious prison, **Old New-Gate Prison and Copper Mine** (860-566-3005; www.ehc.state.ct.us), Newgate Rd. Open mid-May–Oct. 31. In 1703 English settlers discovered a green rock and surmised that copper was present. The mine was developed, but the miners were required to send the ore to England to be smelted, which cut their profits considerably. Other illegal mines sprang up, sponsored by Dutch or New York companies. Doctor Samuel Higley even minted his own coins—with which (if the story can be believed) he paid his bar bills!

When the mine faltered, the colonial government of Connecticut bought it and turned it into a prison. Thus began one of the darker chapters in Revolutionary history. Officials thought that prisoners would not be able to escape from the deep pit, but actually they turned their spare time to profit, using mining tools, not unsurprisingly, to dig tunnels to the outside. Then they were brought above ground to work making nails, shoes, or wagons, but returned to the damp, crowded, rheumatic mine to sleep at night. Besides murderers, horse thieves, and counterfeiters, Tories or Loyalists were placed in the prison if they were considered too dangerous to the Revolution to be left free.

There are many stories of ingenious escapes in the lore of the prison. John Hinson was the first prisoner in New-Gate in 1773. Hinson spent eighteen days in the prison until his girlfriend tossed a rope down into a shaft near the entrance. He climbed up it and they both fled. In 1781 the wife of one of the imprisoned Tories arrived to see her husband. The sergeant escorted her to the entrance, then changed his colors to become British instead of American. The Tories were freed, two guards were killed, and the mass escape succeeded.

Visitors to the mine will see the room where the prisoners slept, the solitary confinement room where a bench is dug out of the rock, some carved initials, and a link of chain. One prisoner thought he was being clever when he pulled his leg irons over his knees to cause injury so they would remove him; his legs developed gangrene and had to be amputated in that room.

Above ground visitors can see the chapel, remains of some workshops, and a cell block. One can imagine how grim life must have been there. According to regulations but probably not in actuality, each prisoner was supposed to receive 1 pound of meat every day, 2 pounds of potatoes, and a dry measure of beans. (Sailors on board the fighting ships of either navy would have been delighted with those rations!) Three half-pints of hard cider were also supposed to be provided, plus a shot of rum for good behavior.

BLOOMFIELD

Although the Connecticut River remained the lifeblood of the region, eventually more settlers moved farther from it seeking land. Not far north of Hartford lies the town of Bloomfield, where early settlers arrived in 1661 to buy land from the Indians. Like West Hartford now an extension of Hartford, Bloomfield was originally separated but has now become a commuting suburb.

HISTORICAL SITES and MUSEUMS
The oldest house, the **Fuss House**, at 4 Park Ave., was built by the Goodwin family. It is privately owned and not open to the public.

St. Andrew's Church, in North Bloomfield, dates from the early 1740s. It is the oldest Episcopal Church in northern Connecticut. The parish was called Wintonbury, using parts of the names of the three towns the people came from—Windsor, Farmington, and Simsbury. Roger Viets, an early rector, was responsible for the establishment of many other Episcopal parishes in Connecticut and Massachusetts.

WINDSOR

Windsor was founded as a trading post by Plymouth Colony in 1633. With a location just upriver from the Dutch trading post at the site of Hartford, they got first crack at the fur trade coming downriver. But life on the frontier involved danger as well as profit: Three-quarters of a century later, the Windsor colony was still having a lot of trouble with the Indians, as this 1706 letter written by William Pitkins attests: "Since I cam home I am informed that Sollomon Andross having had his house broaken up by the Indians, and three Indians breaking in again this morning a little before day—hath killed one of them and the other two fled up this way, he pursued but they were too light of foot for him . . . probably they swam over the River, where they left the horse they tooke."

Today Windsor is home to Bradley International Airport, serving Hartford, Springfield, Massachusetts, and well beyond. The New England Air Museum is on the grounds of the airport. But Windsor isn't all commercial aviation, since it has a 473-acre park and nature center laced with trails and country roads.

HISTORICAL SITES
and MUSEUMS

Windsor was the most significant early settlement north of Hartford. One of the oldest frame houses in Connecticut is the **Walter Fyler House** (860-688-3813; www.windsorhistoricalsociety.org), 96 Palisado Ave. Fyler arrived in America aboard the *Mary and John* in 1630 and received land because of his devotion to the cause of fighting the Pequots. His house is the last surviving building within the "pallizado," the stockade fort designed to protect the settlers from Indians and wolves.

Nathaniel Howard, a sea captain in the West Indies and coastal trade, bought the

> Windsor account books indicate the abundance of game that was available to the colonists: "Between 1691 and 1702, 1,636 lbs of venison, 50 lbs moose, 60 lbs of bear, besides numberous Blak Duks, Rakoons, piegones, dear skins are charged and credited." The venison was prepared for family use by salting, and the business of dressing the skins of the wild animals entered largely into the occupations of the period.

property in 1772 and started a general store and post office. It is now the home of the Windsor Historical Society. The **Hezekia Chaffee House** dates from 1765 and adjoins the Fyler House. Dr. Chaffee practiced medicine here until his death in 1819. The house has been furnished with period pieces from the Windsor Historical Society collection. The **Wilson Museum** on the same property is a fine place to see colonial furnishings. Open Tues.–Sat. year-round.

The Old Burying Ground nearby was also inside the pallizado. The cemetery was later expanded to the west, where visitors can look for graves of Roger Wolcott, a Connecticut governor; Oliver Ellsworth, the third chief justice of the United States; and Ephraim Huit, who died in 1644. **The Founder's Monument** on Pallizado Green stands on the site of the 1639 meetinghouse. The monument was dedicated in honor of the early founding families of Windsor and their First Congregational Church, which had been founded in Plymouth, England, before the group left for America.

A famous Revolutionary patriot, Oliver Ellsworth, built his home here in 1781. The **Oliver Ellsworth Homestead** (860-688-8717), 778 Palisado Ave., remained home to Abigail and Oliver Ellsworth until his death in 1807. Open mid-May–mid-Oct., Mon. and Wed. Besides being a member of the Continental Congress and one of the framers of the United States Constitution, Ellsworth was one of Connecticut's first senators and the author of the Judiciary Act, now the key to our federal judicial system. Visitors will see Ellsworth possessions and documents, including a letter to him from George Washington, who visited in 1789.

RESTAURANTS

JONATHAN PASCO'S
31 S. Main St., East Windsor, CT 06088
860-627-7709

Pasco served under George Washington in the Revolution and the 18th-century brick house was named after him.

THE MILL ON THE RIVER
989 Ellington Rd.,
South Windsor, CT 06074, 860-289-7929
The building, once a gristmill, overlooks the river.

SOMERS INN
585 Main St., Somers, CT 06071; 860-749-2256
This inn dates from 1769. The menu offers a variety of American favorite dishes.

INFORMATION

WINDSOR CHAMBER OF COMMERCE AND TOURIST INFORMATION CENTER
261 Broad St.,
Windsor, CT 06095
www.windsorcc.org/visitors

WINDSOR LOCKS

The first mention of a Christmas tree in the colonies dates from the story of a Hessian soldier, Hendrick Roddemore. He put up a Christmas tree in his cabin in Windsor Locks after deserting the British forces and arriving in Windsor to work as a farmhand. He wanted to remember the Christmas traditions of his homeland. Every year a star is placed on the largest pine tree near the site of his cabin.

Henry Denslow, a founder of the Windsor Locks community, built a house on West Street. At one point the family fled to the Windsor palisade; Henry went back to his house on April 6, 1676, and was killed by Indians.

HISTORICAL SITES and MUSEUMS
Visitors can see an engraved memorial boulder honoring Henry Denslow on South Main Street. Later the **Noden-Reed House** (860-627-9212) was built on the site at 58 West St. Mrs. Reed was the last resident of the house; the furnishings were auctioned off, but some have returned to the house. Open May–Oct. on Sun. Visitors today will see period rooms with colonial furniture, clothing, shoes, muskets, and displays of Indian artifacts. The barn houses sleighs, surreys, and old farm equipment.

ENFIELD

Dutch explorer Adriaen Block got this far up the Connecticut River in 1614 before turning back. The town was settled in 1679. It was the site of a Shaker settlement in 1793.

HISTORICAL SITES and MUSEUMS
Land was set aside for the use of future church parsons in Enfield, and John Meacham built the **Parsons House** (860-745-6064), 1387 Enfield St., US 5, in 1782. It was called Sycamore Hall, because a row of sycamore trees once stood here. By coincidence, the last family to live in the house was named Parsons— John Ingraham, a retired sea captain from Saybrook, bought the house for his family in 1800, and his granddaughter married a Simeon Parsons. The furniture now in the house belonged to the families who lived there. The George Washington Memorial Wallpaper was advertised in patriotic terms: "It is hoped that all true-

born Americans will so encourage the Manufactories of their Country, that Manufactories of all kinds may flourish, and importation stop."

WETHERSFIELD

Wethersfield, on the west side of the Connecticut River just south of Hartford, is the second-oldest English settlement in the state. The town was founded in 1634, a year after Windsor, but its first decade was a bumpy one. In 1637 the Pequots sacked it, killing nine settlers, and in 1640 the townspeople defied British authority by holding an illegal election. The Royal Court fined them five pounds, which they chose not to pay. Before long Wethersfield became a commercial and shipbuilding center and even entered the West Indies trade with Connecticut Valley produce. The Cove Warehouse at the north end of Main Street dates from the 1600s.

Some remarkable colonial houses still stand in the center of Old Wethersfield. Like parts of Providence and Salem, Wethersfield's old homes survived over the years because the area was bypassed by industrial development.

HISTORICAL SITES and MUSEUMS
The **Wethersfield Historical Society** (860-529-7656; www.wethhist.org), 150 Main St., houses pieces of local historical interest, and the building contains a library with research archives. The historical society is active with events and exhibits. Open daily.

Look for the house with small casement windows that seem almost medieval and you've found the **Buttolph-Williams House** (860-529-0460, 860-247-8996; www.hartnet.org/als), Broad and Marsh Sts. Open mid-May–mid-Oct. Dating from the 18th century, this is the oldest restored house in Wethersfield. It is furnished with antique pieces of the period; you'll see 17th-century chairs and tables, pewter and Delft, a curved settee, and authentic implements in "Ye Great Kitchin."

Three 18th-century houses are grouped together as the **Webb-Deane-Stevens Museum** (860-529-0612; www.webb-deane-stevens.org), 211 Main St. Open May 1–Oct. 1, Wed.–Mon.; Nov. 1–Apr.30, Sat. and Sun. These houses were used during the 1781 strategy conference between George Washington and French general Rochambeau that resulted in the British defeat at Yorktown. Visitors today will become familiar with the different lives of the owners of the three houses—a merchant, a diplomat, and a tradesman.

The **Webb House** (1752) was built by a West Indies merchant, Joseph Webb.

> Colonial furniture included a settle or settee, which was designed with a high back to ward off drafts. Wainscot chairs look very stiff and square, and they pulled up to oak trestle tables. A combination bench-table could be converted easily with a flick of the wrist.

Mrs. Webb redecorated in a flurry with French red-flocked wallpaper just before Washington arrived; you can still see the paper on the walls of the room where he slept. A china closet glows with bright red, blue, and mustard paint and has a scallop-shell dome; bright colors were often used to enliven rooms that depended upon candlelight.

After Webb's death in 1761, his widow married Silas Deane, a diplomat and lawyer who played a prominent role in the Revolution. He was one of the commissioners, with Benjamin Franklin, who helped negotiate a treaty with France. The couple lived in the **Deane House**. A number of Deanes had tuberculosis, and one of the bedrooms contains a mahogany medicine chest. Copper wires were kept in one of the drawers and used to produce a chemical reaction after being dipped in vinegar. The resulting fluid, called verdigris, although actually poisonous, was thought to minimize chest pains.

The **Stevens House** was built by a leather worker, Isaac Stevens. Furniture and household pieces date from 1690 and later. Call 860-529-0612 for more information on all three houses.

LODGING

**CHESTER BULKLEY HOUSE
BED & BREAKFAST**
184 Main St., Wethersfield, CT 06109
860-563-4236;
www.choicebedandbreakfast.com/ct/bulkley
This 1830 Greek-revival home in the center of historic Old Wethersfield has the original beehive oven still in the house.

RESTAURANTS

**CARMEN ANTHONY
FISHHOUSE**
1770 Berlin Turnpike,
Wethersfield, CT 06109
860-529-7557
This seafood restaurant is famous for crab cakes.

GLASTONBURY

Across the river from Wethersfield, Glastonbury has a number of historic homes, most of them in private hands. We remember visiting several owned by Trinity College professors who took pride in maintaining the heritage of their homes. There is a green with a 1690 cemetery adjacent.

HISTORICAL SITES and MUSEUMS

In South Glastonbury you can visit the **Welles-Shipman-Ward House** (860-633-6890), 972 Main St. Captain Thomas Welles built it as a wedding present for his son in 1755. The U.S. Department of the Interior describes this house as having "exceptional architectural interest," and the woodwork is certainly worth a visit to see.

The **Museum on the Green** (860-633-6890), Main and Hubbard Sts., is the home of the Historical Society of Glastonbury. Exhibits include local Indian history, early farming artifacts, and folk art portraits. Open Mon. and Thu.

LODGING

BUTTERNUT FARM
1654 Main St.,
Glastonbury, CT 06033; 860-633-7197;
www.butternutfarmbandb.com
This B&B is in a jewel of an 18th-century colonial home, and is furnished with antiques.

RESTAURANTS

MAIN AND HOPEWELL
2 Hopewell Rd.,
South Glastonbury, CT 06073
860-633-8698
The restaurant is located in a 200-year-old building and features both a dining room and a pub.

EAST HARTFORD

During the Revolution General Rochambeau's soldiers set up their tents on Lawrence Street and Silver Lane in East Hartford. A marker identifies the spot. In later days, Pratt & Whitney, first part of United Aircraft and then of United Technologies, has been a prime industry producing aircraft engines in East Hartford. Connecticut's new sports and entertainment stadium and home of the University of Connecticut Huskies football team is a fairly new addition.

HISTORICAL SITES *and* MUSEUMS

Across the river from Hartford, a colonial saddle-maker built the **Huguenot House** (860-568-6178; www.hfeh.com), 307 Burnside Ave. Open by appointment. This gambrel-roof house has vaulted dormer windows. Don't forget to ask about the ghost!

MANCHESTER

Long a small manufacturing city east of Hartford, Manchester once produced gunpowder for the Continental Army and gained prosperity as the center of silk production in the 19th century, until the industry petered out after World War II. Now this pleasant town is a bedroom community for greater Hartford and a hub for shoppers in surrounding smaller towns.

HISTORICAL SITES *and* MUSEUMS

Manchester was home to the Cheney family, known around the world in the silk industry. The **Cheney Homestead** (860-643-5588; www.manchesterhistory.org), 106 Hartford Rd., is open year-round, Fri.–Sun. and by appointment. The house dates from 1785 when a clockmaker, Timothy Cheney, built it. His sons imported silkworms for their manufacturing business, and Cheney became a major silk-producing company. The museum offers displays of engravings, portraits, and even quilts made from Cheney silk. You'll also see grandfather clocks and antique furnishings. The **Keeney School House** on the grounds features early school supplies. The schoolhouse dates from 1751.

LODGING

THE MANSION INN BED & BREAKFAST
139 Hartford Rd.,
Manchester, CT 06040; 860-646-0453;
www.themansioninnct.com
This was once home to the Cheney family,
silk barons, and is listed on the National
Register of Historic Places.

RESTAURANTS

CAVEY'S
45 E. Center St.,
Manchester, CT 06040
860-643-2751
Cavey's serves Italian fare upstairs and
French downstairs.

COVENTRY

Farther east on CT 31 lies the town of **Coventry**, remembered in Revolutionary history as the birthplace of Nathan Hale, Connecticut's official state hero. Surrounded by rolling, wooded hills interspersed with lakes and ponds, Coventry brings to mind the peaceful countryside of England.

HISTORICAL SITES *and* MUSEUMS

The **Nathan Hale Homestead** (860-742-6917, 860-247-8996; www.hartnet .org/als), 2299 South St. Open mid-May–mid-Oct., Wed.–Sun. Unfortunately, Hale never lived in the house because he was captured and executed by the British before it was finished. A Yale graduate and schoolteacher, Hale would perhaps be pleased to know that his reported final words, "I only regret that I have but one life to lose for my country," have been taught to students ever since. Many Hale family pieces are here.

Nearby, the **Strong-Porter House Museum** (860-742-1419; www.coventry cthistoricalsociety.org), 2382 South St. Open the first and third weekends, mid-May–mid Oct. The eastern part of the house dates from 1730. It was built by Aaron Strong, a maternal great-uncle of Hale. Call 860-742-7847 for more information.

LODGING

BIRD IN HAND BED & BREAKFAST
2011 Main St., Coventry, CT 06238
860-742-0032; www.thebirdinhand.com
Built in 1731, this former tavern is now a
B&B.

RESTAURANTS

CAPRILANDS HERB FARM
534 Silver St., Coventry, CT 06238
860-742-7244; www.caprilands.com
 Lunch is still served today at this 18th-century farmhouse surrounded by 30 herb gardens.

BIDWELL TAVERN
1260 Main St., South Coventry, CT
06238; 860-742-6978
Dating from 1822, this restaurant has
several dining rooms.

EVENTS

July: Reenactments of Revolutionary War battles and musters with the Nathan Hale Ancient Fifes and Drums and Knowlton's Rangers. Coventry Colonial Days are an opportunity for students to immerse themselves in the era. Sponsored by the Antiquarian and Landmarks Society, 860-247-8996

EASTERN CONNECTICUT

Eastern Connecticut offers the "Quiet Corner" of the state with its meandering back roads and peaceful lifestyle. The northeastern quadrant is dotted with farms and villages with antiques shops, while the seacoast attracts boaters and those who love salt air and ships. The exception to quiet and calm is the development of gambling casinos on Indian lands. Ironically, the one run by the Pequots has brought great prosperity to the tribe that was almost completely wiped out in the brutal Pequot War more than three centuries earlier.

NEW LONDON

Leaving the Connecticut River towns of Hartford, Wethersfield, and Windsor does not mean leaving rivers as we explore the colonial history of Connecticut. The Thames River (pronounced "thaymes" not "tems") gives New London one of the best deepwater ports in New England. In the 17th century farmers used the river to ship their produce; a hundred years later whalers sailed home with fortunes to be made from the oil in their holds.

Although we are no longer as dependent upon rivers and ports for transportation as our colonial ancestors were, New London remains important in the 20th century as the home of a major naval submarine base as well as the Coast Guard Academy.

We always peer over the bridge when on the highway to see if the Coast Guard training bark *Eagle* is in. Once a German sail-training ship, she was confiscated as a war prize, restored, and then given her present name. She is America's official "tall ship" and represents the United States all over the world. To watch *Eagle* sail into New London or see her somewhere in Europe with all sails pulling brings a lump to the throat similar to the first sight of the Statue of Liberty after a voyage.

The New London colony was founded by John Winthrop Jr. in 1646. He became a major figure in the political history of Connecticut, and his statue stands where Masonic Street and Eugene O'Neill Drive meet— names themselves suggestive of the varied history of this corner of the New England seaboard. Luckily the coastal area, which includes Groton, Mystic, and Stonington, has long been concerned with preserving its colonial heritage, so there is much for a visitor to see.

During the Revolution, ships from this corner of Connecticut were active in harassing the British fleet; New London–based vessels, acting as privateers, raided and captured hundreds of British ships. The devastating attack on the town near the end of the war, on September 6, 1781, was retribution: Thirty-two British ships with 1,700 men on board, led by turncoat Benedict Arnold, destroyed the city. As a native of nearby Norwich, Arnold knew the area. According to some reports, he watched New London burning from the burial ground on Hempstead Street.

HISTORICAL SITES *and* MUSEUMS

The **Joshua Hempstead House** (860-443-7949, 860-247-8996; www.hartnet.org /als), 11 Hempstead St., dates from 1678. It is one of the few intact 17th-century houses in Connecticut. And there is an added attraction here: The diary of Joshua Hempstead, describing the daily life of his family, provides a window into the colonial mind and experience.

Another home to visit on the same grounds is the **Nathaniel Hempstead House**, built in 1759 for a rope-maker grandson of Joshua. It is one of two houses in the state representing the cut-stone architecture of the mid-18th century, and it also has a beehive oven. Both Hempstead houses contain a number of original pieces of furniture. Both are open May–Oct., Thu.–Sun.

During the Revolutionary War the **Shaw-Perkins Mansion** (860-443-1209; www.newlondonhistory.org), 11 Blinman St., was used as Connecticut's naval office; George Washington really did sleep here. Open July–Sep., Wed.–Sat. Captain Nathaniel Shaw Jr. was a shipowner. The house contains family portraits and collections of silver and china. Call 203-443-1209 for more information.

The **Nathan Hale Schoolhouse** (860-873-3399), Captain's Walk. Open Memorial Day–Labor Day, Wed.–Sun. Hale taught here before he enlisted in the army. After Lexington and Concord he felt inspired to join the patriots and gave a speech declaring his feelings.

LODGING

LIGHTHOUSE INN
6 Guthrie Place,
New London, CT 06320; 860-443-8411;
www.lighthouseinn-ct.com
Four-poster beds and antique furnishings are featured here, along with an elegant spiral staircase.

RESTAURANTS

THE BULKELEY HOUSE
111 Bank St., New London, CT 06320
860-444-7753
This restaurant is in a building dating from 1790.

CAPTAIN SCOTT'S LOBSTER DOCK
80 Hamilton St.,
New London, CT 06320; 860-439-1741
How many ways can you enjoy lobster? Find out here.

EVENTS

July: New London Sailfest featuring tall ships, fireworks, museums. 860-444-1879
September: Boats, Books & Brushes with Taste is a literary, art, maritime, and food festival. 888-766-2228

INFORMATION

CONNECTICUT EAST CONVENTION AND VISITORS BUREAU, NEW LONDON
800-863-6569, 860-444-2206;
www.mysticmore.com
For the following locations in this section contact the site listed above.

WATERFORD

Founded in 1646, Waterford was a part of New London until it became a separate town in 1801. Early wealth came from stone quarries. A number of estates remain today along the Niantic River.

HISTORICAL SITES and MUSEUMS

Colonial Village (860-442-2707), Jordan Green, CT 156, Avery Lane and Rope Ferry Rd., is a replica of a colonial village, including the 1740 Jordan Schoolhouse, a farmhouse, blacksmith shop, and barn. Open June 30–Sep. 30, Wed.–Fri.

GROTON

Directly across the Thames River from New London, Groton is the submariners' capital of New England, long the home of the Electric Boat Division of General Dynamics and the site of a major submarine base for the U.S. Navy. The USS *Nautilus*, the first atomic-powered submarine, was built here in 1954. She is on display, and tours are available. In town a Wall of Honor is inscribed with the names of the 3,600 American submariners who lost their lives in World War II.

HISTORICAL SITES and MUSEUMS

The Jabez Smith House (860-445-6689), 259 North Rd. This one-and-one-half-story home dating from 1783 has a central brick chimney. Antique furnishings belonging to the Smith family are still here. Open Apr.–Dec. 31.

Fort Griswold Battlefield State Park (860-449-6877), Monument St. and Park Ave. Open daily Memorial Day–Labor Day; Sat. and Sun., Labor Day–Columbus Day. Fort Griswold stands on Groton Heights, where it was crucial to the defense of New London, as well as coastal shipping. Groton men were active in the Revolutionary War, many of them on privateers. So it was no accident that the British attacked here in the retaliatory raid on New London on September 6, 1781. The British stormed the fort, and after fierce resistance, a massacre of the patriot defenders ensued.

The Groton Battle Monument was dedicated to those who died, and their names are inscribed on it. The museum contains mementos of the massacre, period furniture, and displays on whaling.

Also on the park grounds is the **Ebenezer Avery House**, where many American wounded were taken after the fighting. Open June–Aug., Sat.–Mon. and holidays. The house was moved from its original location nearby in 1971.

EVENTS

Labor Day Weekend: Annual commemoration of the Battle at Fort Griswold, with speeches and a wreath-laying ceremony, drawing large crowds; 225th anniversary reenactment in 2006. www.fortfriends.org

MYSTIC

First settled in 1654, the town derived its name from the Pequot Indians' Mistuket. Earlier, during the Pequot War in 1637, a force of colonial militia and their Indian allies surprised hundreds of their enemy at night on Pequot Hill and set fire to the Pequots' compound. In one of the bloodiest actions of the colonial era, those trapped inside, including women and children, were burned alive, and many of those who tried to escape were shot. Luckily, the later history of Mystic has been much more tranquil, as the town prospered both as a seaport and shipbuilding center, producing many fine old houses that you can see by walking through Old Mystic and along the Mystic River.

The town has been a major tourist destination for decades, largely because it is the site of the first and most extensive living-history museum dedicated to preserving New England's maritime heritage. A more recent addition is the Mystic Aquarium, headquarters for Robert Ballard's Institute for Underwater Exploration. For us, Mystic holds special memories, as we took houseguests as well as our young children to visit there many times. You can smell the fish and the pine tar used on sailing ships, and you can hear the gulls squawking and crying, a foghorn in the distance, someone singing sea chanteys. One half of this writing team also took Skidmore College students there to join others from Colgate and Williams for January terms at Mystic Seaport during the 1980s. In addition to academic study of maritime history and literature, each student chose a specialty and interned with staff in the various departments. An outgrowth of that activity is the Williams College–Mystic Seaport Program in American Maritime Studies.

HISTORICAL SITES and MUSEUMS
The **John Mason Monument**, named for the leader of the settlers' expedition against the Pequots, marks the spot on Pequot Hill where the Indian compound was attacked and burned.

The **Denison Homestead** (860-536-9248; www.denisonsociety.org), Pequot-sepos Rd. Open mid-May–mid-Oct. It was built in 1717. Eleven generations of the Denison family lived here, and some of their possessions are still in the house. Visitors take delight in the wooden Indian doll, period costumes, spinning wheels, silver, glass, and even George Denison's will from 1693. Captain George Denison first built here; his grandson George Denison III erected the house that stands today. Look for the rare "trimmer arch" over the kitchen fireplace—it holds up a hearthstone in the room above.

At **Mystic Seaport Museum** (888-973-2767, 860-572-5315; www.mysticseaport.org), 50 Greenmanville Ave., you will find boats and ships galore, in all sizes and from many eras, including a classic whaleship, a Grand Banks schooner, and a sail-training square-rigger, all from later times. You'll want to spend a full day at the Seaport. Most visitors start with a tour of the ships. The *Charles W. Morgan*, a 19th-century wooden whaler, is usually moored at Chubb's Wharf. You can climb all over her, learn how whales were caught, and feel what it must have been like to live on board: the captain sleeping in a gimballed bed—designed to remain level—the crew in the cramped, uncomfortable forecastle.

The *Joseph Conrad*, built in Copenhagen as a Danish sail-training ship, was rammed by a British freighter and sank, losing 22 cadets. She was later raised, and from 1934 to 1936 Alan Villiers and a group of students took her around the world on a 58,000-mile cruise. She is now a permanent floating dormitory for visiting students. When you visit look for demonstrations of sail setting and handling and chantey singing on board both ships.

Alas, there are no ships from the colonial era. Wooden vessels don't last that long, unless they are buried in sand or mud. Nevertheless, the Seaport is the best place to go if you want to sense what seafaring under sail or oar was like—the only power available to colonial seamen. Interpreters row classic craft on the river and set and furl sails on square-rigged ships; shipwrights repair the Seaport's vessels using traditional techniques, and boatbuilders produce authentic replicas of older types.

The Seaport also offers 17 acres of homes and buildings collected within a village setting, and some of these do represent ways of life that go back to the colonial era. It really is a living village—craftsmen ply their trades here and are more than willing to talk with visitors. Many of the displays and centers relate to maritime activities and occupations, but others demonstrate weaving, printing, and other land trades. Some interpreters might even be cooking colonial-style dishes on an open fireplace. **Buckingham House** (1695) is the place to be when they're cooking—the smells are wonderful.

LODGING

Since there are other attractions in Mystic, including cruises and the aquarium, you may want to stay the night.

THE ADAMS HOUSE
382 Cow Hill Rd.,
Mystic CT 06355; 860-572-9551;
www.adamshouseofmystic.com
This 1749 colonial has three fireplaces and is in a quiet country setting.

THE INN AT MYSTIC
US 1 and CT 27, Mystic, CT 06355
800-237-2415, 860-536-9604;
www.innaatmystic.com
The center of the complex is a Georgian colonial mansion. Lauren Bacall and Humphrey Bogart spent their honeymoon here.

THE OLD MYSTIC INN
58 Main St., Old Mystic, CT 06372
860-572-9422; www.oldmysticinn.com
The house dates from the early 1800s and is on the Mystic River.

RED BROOK INN
Wells Rd., P.O. Box 237,
Old Mystic, CT 06372; 860-572-0349;
www.redbrookinn.com
Two 18th-century buildings, the Haley Tavern and Crary Homestead, offer 10 guest rooms.

RESTAURANTS

CAPTAIN DANIEL PACKER INNE
32 Water St., Mystic, CT 06355
860-536-3555; www.danielpacker.com
This 1754 inn also has a pub.

DRAW BRIDGE INN
34 W. Main St., Mystic, CT 06355
860-536-9653
Seafood is high on the menu.

FLOOD TIDE
At the Inn at Mystic,
US 1 and CT 27, Mystic, CT 06355
860-536-8140;
www.innaatmystic.com
Besides meals all day long the Sunday
brunch is popular.

SEAMEN'S INNE
105 Greenmanville Ave.,
Mystic, CT 06355; 860-572-5303
Just outside of the north gate of the
Seaport, it was built as a replica of a sea cap-
tain's home.

EVENTS

December: Lantern Light Tours. Travel
back in time with theatrical scenes of
Christmas past. 888-973-2767

STONINGTON

East of Mystic, near the Rhode Island border, Stonington has both a sheltered deepwater harbor and a fine collection of captains' houses—both suggesting its primary activity in earlier eras. And that has not changed much: The harbor is now full of yachts, and the houses have been elegantly restored.

Most of the old houses are privately owned, but you can enjoy their facades and gardens by wandering around the quiet streets near the end of the peninsula. Some of the houses have cannonballs embedded in them, prized remnants not of the Revolution (although the town was attacked then) but the War of 1812, when Stonington successfully withstood three days of heavy bombardment from a British fleet and wreaked enough damage from its own cannons to drive the attackers away.

The town was not settled until after 1662, when the competing territorial claims of Massachusetts and Connecticut were resolved. As the name suggests, the land around Stonington was rocky, and settlers had a difficult time producing food.

Stonington's settlers found it hard to keep wolves from ravaging necessarily shallow graves. Eventually, they began to top each grave with a heavy stone slab. These "wolf stones" can still be seen in the cemetery near Wequetequock off Greenhaven Rd., south of US 1.

RESTAURANTS

RANDALL'S ORDINARY
CT 2, North Stonington, CT 06359
877-599-4540;
www.randallsordinary.com
This 1685 farmhouse is the scene of old-
fashioned cooking in a large fireplace,
when you're ready for an authentic
colonial meal.

EVENTS

**August: Schemitzun: Annual Feast of
Green Corn And Dance** is an intertribal
powwow gathering of Native American Nations with song, dance, bull riding, drum contests, traditional dance
contests, educational exhibits, arts and
crafts. 800-224-CORN

MASHANTUCKET

The Mashantucket Pequot Indian Reservation offers a large gaming and entertainment center. There are six casinos on the grounds.

HISTORICAL SITES and MUSEUMS
Mashantucket Pequot Museum (800-411-9671; www.pequotmuseum.org), 110 Pequot Trail. This is the largest Native American museum in the world. It offers multisensory experiences, including the chill of an ice age crevasse, the thrill of a caribou hunt, and the varieties of life in a 16th-century Indian village. Open year-round.

NORWICH

North of New London on the Thames River, Norwich was the birthplace of Benedict Arnold. He was an apothecary in New Haven before leaving to fight in the American Revolution. Today the town is known for its roses. The Memorial Rose Garden in Mohegan Park honors war veterans, and the blooms last from late June to mid-July. Nature trails attract walkers, and picnicking is popular.

HISTORICAL SITES and MUSEUMS
The **Leffingwell Inn** (860-889-9440), 348 Washington St. Open Apr.–Dec. and by appointment. This is actually two small saltbox houses joined together with an addition at the back. The older section dates from 1675, when it was owned by William Backus, one of the original settlers of Norwich. In 1701, owner Thomas Leffingwell received a license to "keep a publique house for the entertainment of strangers."

As his family grew, more additions were built. His descendant Christopher Leffingwell was an adventurous entrepreneur and patriot who became one of the chief financial backers of the Revolution. The Tavern Room was the site of many Revolutionary War meetings, which included major figures like George Washington, Governor Jonathan Trumbull, and Silas Deane.

Norwich is also known as the burial site of Chief Uncas in 1683. He was the most famous chieftain of the Mohegan Indians, and his monument stands in the **Royal Mohegan Burial Ground** on Sachem St.

Indian Leap, located off Yantic St. at Yantic Falls, was a watering hole of the Mohegans. It has been reported that as Narragansetts fled from the Mohegans during the 1643 Battle of the Great Plains, they suddenly came to the falls and had to leap into the chasm below. After the Narragansetts were defeated, the colonists, who were allied with the Mohegans, condemned to death the captured leader, Miantonomo. Chief Uncas believed that he would receive strength if he cut a bit from the dead Indian's shoulder and ate it—he did. The Miantonomo Monument stands on Elijah Street, where he was captured. Another marker, that of the **Battle of the Great Plains**, stands on the New London Turnpike in Norwich.

LEBANON

Heading northwest on CT 87 from Norwich will take you to Lebanon, a very pleasant small town with major historical sites from the Revolution. When it was first settled in the late 1600s by people who left Norwich, they were heading into real wilderness. Later it was the home of the Trumbull family, prominent in the West Indies trade and instrumental in the politics of the Revolution. Now Lebanon is known for its mile-long green surrounded by historic homes.

HISTORICAL SITES and MUSEUMS

The **Jonathan Trumbull House** (860-642-7558; www.lebanoncthistsoc.org), on W. Town St., dates from 1735. Trumbull was known as a "war governor" because of his staunch support for the Revolution. He was involved in the transfer of equipment from Connecticut to the Continental Army. George Washington wrote, "But for Jonathan Trumbull, the war could not have been carried to a successful conclusion."

After a price was set on his head, Trumbull retired to a room on the second floor that does not have windows, except for a shuttered opening 27 inches square. No one outside the house could observe him, and a sharpshooter wouldn't have a chance to kill him while he was seated—although he had to be careful about standing up.

Trumbull furnishings in the house include a Queen Anne chair used by the governor at church; a Duxbury chair brought by his bride, Faith; a Chinese lacquer dispatch box used by Trumbull; and a spectacular set of red china with the medallion of a bull indicating the family name. The **Wadsworth Stable** was moved from Hartford to the Trumbull property in 1954. George Washington kept his favorite horse, Nelson, there when he visited Hartford.

Trumbull's son, John, became famous as the painter of the Revolution. He created stirring scenes of the major events of the war and portraits of Revolutionary leaders. Many of his works are now in the Yale University Art Gallery in New Haven (see page 157). He also painted scenes in the U.S. Capitol rotunda, including the well-known "Signing of the Declaration of Independence" (it's also on the back of the U.S. two-dollar bill). The **Jonathan Trumbull Jr. House** (860-642-6100; jtrumbulljr.org), 780 Trumbull St., dates from 1769. This center-chimney farmhouse has eight corner fireplaces—count them. The Trumbull houses are open from May–Oct., Wed.–Sun.

The **Revolutionary War Office** (860-873-3399; www.connecticutsar.org), W. Town St., was built as the Trumbull family store in 1727. Ox-sleds of supplies, including arms, tents, food, and clothing, were sent from this store to Washington's army.

The "Father of the Physiology of Digestion" lived in the **Dr. William Beaumont House** (860-642-6579; www.lebanoncthistsoc.org), W. Town St., also part of the Trumbull complex. Displays include Beaumont's trunk and surgical instruments of the period. At a later time Beaumont lived at Fort Mackinac on the island in Lake Michigan. There he attended a man whose stomach wound never did heal; Beaumont was able to observe gastric secretion over an 11-year period. (One of the displays in the fort has two models of the stomach in graphic detail.)

OLD LYME

Old Lyme is filled with 18th- and 19th-century captains' houses spread along Lyme Street. In more recent times the town became a noted art colony associated with American impressionism. Most of the houses are still private homes.

HISTORICAL SITES *and* MUSEUMS
The **Thomas Lee House** (860-739-6070; www.eltownhall.com), CT 156, East Lyme. Open mid-May–Labor Day, daily except Mon. This house dates from 1660 and is the oldest wood-frame house in the state. Also on the grounds is the first district school, from 1734.

LODGING

THE BEE AND THISTLE INN
l00 Lyme St., Old Lyme, CT 06371
800-622-4946, 860-434-1667;
www.beeandthistleinn.com
Dating from 1756, the house contains many fireplaces, four-poster beds,quilts, and early American furnishings.

OLD LYME INN
85 Lyme St., Old Lyme, CT 06371
800-434-5352, 860-434-2600;
www.oldlymeinn.com Built in 1850, this country village inn was once a working farm on 300 acres.

RESTAURANTS

Both of the inns listed above have noted restaurants in elegant and historic surroundings, so dinner reservations are advised.

OLD SAYBROOK

The broad reaches of the lower Connecticut River invited maritime activity. At the river's mouth, Old Saybrook was first settled by Dutch traders during the early decades of the 17th century, but they were soon displaced by John Winthrop Jr., who brought English Puritans in 1635 and founded a colony.

HISTORICAL SITES *and* MUSEUMS
The **General William Hart House** (860-388-2622), 350 Main St., dates from 1767. Open Memorial Day weekend–Sep. It was the home of a colonial merchant who was proud to put in beautiful paneling. Count the eight fireplaces inside. One is especially interesting, with Sadler & Green transfer-print tiles that depict Aesop's fables. There is a colonial garden to explore and sniff.

    Fort Saybrook Monument Park (860-395-3152), Saybrook Point. This park has storyboards detailing the history of the Saybrook colony.

INFORMATION

OLD SAYBROOK CHAMBER OF COMMERCE
146 Main St., Box 625, Old Saybrook, CT 06475
860-388-3266; oldsaybrookchamber.com

ESSEX

Half a dozen miles upriver from Old Saybrook and Old Lyme is the lovely town of Essex, which has preserved the romance of its maritime and architectural past. Its sheltered riverside setting, now filled with yacht yards and yachts, first became a major shipbuilding center in the 1720s. The town gave the *Oliver Cromwell,* a twenty-four-gun vessel built in 1776, to the patriots during the Revolutionary War.

A local inventor, David Bushnell, was far ahead of his time when in 1775 he designed a compact submarine vessel that could theoretically submerge long enough to travel to an enemy vessel and attach a mine to it. Benjamin Franklin was on hand to watch the sea trials of Bushnell's *American Turtle* off Ayer's Point in the Connecticut River.

Bushnell's invention was greatly admired, even though its pilot couldn't make the mine adhere to a British ship. Later Bushnell made a "drift" mine that worked, in a way: The crew of an enemy frigate pulled the drifting object onto the deck and it exploded, killing three British soldiers.

> The "Battle of the Kegs" was set off by David Bushnell, who produced forty buoyant wooden kegs housing his mines. In Pennsylvania he set them adrift to float down the Delaware River and into the British fleet. However, the British fired on the mines before they reached their ships. There's a song that mentions the fears of the British, including their idea that the kegs contained rebels "packed up like pickled herring."

HISTORICAL SITES *and* MUSEUMS

A replica of the *American Turtle* can be seen at the **Connecticut River Museum** (860-767-8269; www.ctrivermuseum.org), 67 Main St., which tells David Bushnell's story and much more related to the rich maritime history of the area. Open year-round except for Mon. Archaeological exploration has produced artifacts from the foundation's home at Lay's Wharf, a site that has been in use since prehistoric times. Other exhibits include a display on shipbuilding, a collection of traditional boats from the region, models, and paintings.

Like the other towns in this region, Essex has many fine old houses. The **William Pratt House** (860-767-1249), 20 West Ave., dates from 1725 when it began life with only one room. It later expanded to four rooms with a gambrel roof. The house is filled with early period furniture. Open June–Sep.

If you would like to see more of the lower Connecticut Valley and the river by land and water, you can take a combined steam train ride and river cruise. Start out on the **Valley Railroad** (860-767-0103; www.essexsteamtrain.com), Railroad Ave., and connect with a boat, or finish the round trip on the train.

LODGING

THE GRISWOLD INN
36 Main St., Essex, CT 06426
860-767-1776; www.griswoldinn.com
This popular inn, in business since 1776, has the charm of the past with modern conveniences.

RESTAURANTS

THE GRISWOLD INN
36 Main St., Essex, CT 06426
860-767-1776;
www.griswoldinn.com
Dinners are memorable in this authentic colonial setting, with several dining rooms.

IVORYTON

As you might imagine, ivory piano keys were made here.

HISTORICAL SITES and MUSEUMS

Museum of Fife & Drum (860-767-2237, 860-399-6519), 62 N. Main St. Open weekends June–Sep. or by appointment. This is the only museum in the country showing America on parade from the Revolutionary War to today. You can learn about the development of music and see uniforms and instruments from 18th-century bands. Concerts are given in July and Aug.

LODGING

COPPER BEECH INN
46 Main St., Ivoryton, CT 06442
888-809-2056, 860-767-0330;
www.copperbeechinn.com
An ivory importer once lived in this 1890 home.

RESTAURANTS

COPPER BEECH INN
46 Main St., Ivoryton, CT 06442
888-809-2056, 860-767-0330;
www.copperbeechinn.com
Three different rooms offer elegant dining.

CLINTON

Clinton traces its settlement to 1663, when it was called Kenilworth, which later became Killingworth. It was the home of Abraham Pierson, the first rector of Yale College, who taught the students in his home. The university was known as Collegiate School until 1707; there is a monument on the green for this institution. Clinton is now a pretty beach town that is very popular all summer and especially in mid-August during the Bluefish Festival.

HISTORICAL SITES and MUSEUMS

The **Stanton House** (860-669-6364), 63 E. Main St. Open on weekend afternoons. The house dates from 1790 and is furnished with 18th- and early 19th-century pieces. There is a collection of Staffordshire dinnerware on display.

MADISON

Madison, originally part of neighboring Guilford, the easternmost outpost of the New Haven colony, was named for the fourth president of the United States. Shipbuilders and captains built their homes around the green.

HISTORICAL SITES *and* MUSEUMS

The **Allis-Bushnell House** (203-245-4567), 853 Boston Post Rd. Open May–Sep. This house is headquarters of the Madison Historical Society and offers displays of local history. It has handsome corner fireplaces and cupboards filled with china and glassware. Cornelius Scranton Bushnell, sponsor of the *Monitor*, once lived here, and a model of the ship stands in the house.

The **Deacon John Grave House** (203-245-4798), 581 Boston Post Rd. Open during the summer through Columbus Day and then by appointment. Grave's descendants lived here for over 300 years. The house dates from 1675.

The Allis-Bushnell House

GUILFORD

In 1639, a year after the New Haven colony was established, Henry Whitfield led another Puritan congregation from England to Connecticut. They settled just east of New Haven in Guilford, probably named after Guildford in Surrey. The town has been spared the industrial development of its neighboring city and thus has been able to preserve a remarkable number of houses from the colonial era.

HISTORICAL SITES and MUSEUMS

The **Henry Whitfield State Historical Museum** (203-453-2457; www.whitfieldmuseum.org), Old Whitfield St. Open Apr.–Dec. 14, Wed.–Sun.; Dec. 15–Mar. by appointment. It is the oldest house in Connecticut, dating from 1639, as well as the oldest stone house in New England. Henry Whitfield was rector of St. Margaret's Church in Ockley, Surrey, beginning in 1618. (We lived in Ockley in 1960 and remember the beautiful village with fondness.) When Whitfield and his wife, Dorothy, left England for the New World, the men on board ship signed the Guilford Covenant, an agreement of mutual support.

Whitfield's stone house—also intended as a secure fortress for the colony, if needed—rose with a large north chimney stack; the original masonry has held up remarkably well over the centuries. Diamond-paned leaded casement windows give charm to the front of the house. Inside, the Great Hall is 33 feet long with a fireplace at each end. The Whitfields and seven of their nine children lived in the house, along with servants and maids.

The Whitfield group landed in New Haven to a warm welcome from the settlers who had come there two years earlier, since the new arrivals had brought news of friends and relatives. The new settlers agreed to buy land from the Menuncatuck Indians and paid "12 coates, 12 fathom of Wompom, 12 glasses, 12 payer of shooes, 12 Hatchetts, 12 paire of stockings, 12 hooes, 4 kettles, 12 knives, 12 hatts, 12 porringers, 12 spoons and 2 English coates." Henry Whitfield signed the Indian deed.

Today the house contains a collection of 17th- and 18th-century furnishings, including the Governor William Leete wainscot chair, a 1685 Phinney chest with carved front and sides, a Jacobean press cupboard, and a large 17th-century loom. The Whitfields owned pieces still in the house—a bedstead, a table and chairs, and books. Outside, visitors may stroll in the formal herb garden.

More houses to see? Scores of them from the 17th and 18th centuries are very much alive today as private homes, but visitors can get inside two more. The **Hyland House** (203-453-9477), 84 Boston St., is a 1660 colonial saltbox with striking woodwork inside. Three fireplaces big enough to walk into display 17th-century cookware.

Another saltbox in town is the **Thomas Griswold House Museum** (203-453-3176), 171 Boston St., dating from 1774. Open mid-June–Oct. 1, Tue.– Sun.; Oct., Sat. and Sun. Displays detail local history, and there is a collection of costumes and furniture. The museum includes a restored blacksmith shop and a colonial garden.

INFORMATION

GREATER NEW HAVEN CONVENTION AND VISITORS BUREAU
169 Orange St., New Haven, CT 06510
800-332-7829, 203-777-8550; www.newhavencvb.org

SOUTHWESTERN CONNECTICUT

E arly English settlements in this region came in the wake of the 1637 Pequot War, which removed the major threat. Today, the Gold Coast from the New York border eastward to New Haven forms an almost unbroken line of residential suburbs on Long Island Sound. Wealthy residents have brought arts and culture to the scene, and in recent decades many corporations have moved their headquarters from New York City to sites along this bustling shore. Yet there is still some open space in gardens and nature sanctuaries, as well as remnants of the colonial era. Early 18th-century settlers built homes and stone walls that are still there, and Yale University still spreads out from the New Haven Green.

NEW HAVEN

The **New Haven colony,** one of the most powerful in Connecticut, began with a strong Puritan bias. In 1638, the Reverend John Davenport and Theophilus Eaton came from England to settle here after a brief stay in what they felt was a too liberal Boston. They framed a code of laws to govern the settlement through the church. They interpreted the Bible strictly and enforced its edicts rigidly. With good financial backing and a fine deepwater harbor at the mouth of the Quinnipiac River, the colony prospered and soon spread out to additional settlements along the sound, including outposts to the south on Long Island.

Today New Haven offers a conglomeration of restaurants, bistros, and bookstores around the Yale campus. Theater, concerts, fairs, and festivals enliven the scene. The Shubert Theatre, where many musicians and actors made their debuts, has been called the "Birthplace of the Nation's Hits." Yale University is famous for its libraries and art galleries, including collections of rare books and British art.

HISTORICAL SITES and MUSEUMS
Yale University was founded in 1701 in Branford, just east of the city; classes were held in Killingworth (now Clinton) and Old Saybrook, until the school finally

moved to New Haven in 1716. Two years later the school was renamed for Elihu Yale, in appreciation of his gift to the college of 562 pounds. The oldest building is the 1752 Connecticut Hall. Tours of the University are available from **Yale University Visitor Center** (203-432-2300), 149 Elm St., at the green. The Yale information office located there provides maps and schedules. Open daily, tours Mon.–Fri. at 10:30 and 2, Sat. and Sun. at 1:30.

The campus, with its separate enclosed colleges sealed off from busy streets, is laid out very much like Oxford University. A carillon in Gothic-style Harkness Tower fills the air with melody throughout the day. Inside, in the Memorial Room, you can follow the history of the college through a series of woodcarvings. Call 203-432-2300 for more information.

Yale University Art Gallery (203-432-0600; www.yale.edu/artgallery), 1111 Chapel St. Open Tue.– Sat. 10–5, Sun. 1–6, closed major holidays. Founded in 1832 with a gift from patriot and artist John Trumbull, this is the oldest university art gallery in the country. It contains more than 185,000 objects, dating from ancient Egypt to the present. The outstanding American collection includes a trove of historical paintings and miniature portraits by Trumbull, the premier artist of the Revolution, who willed 100 of his works to the college. The museum's collections also include paintings by Benjamin West and John Singleton Copley, as well as Van Gogh, Manet, Monet, Homer, Hopper, Matisse, and Picasso.

Just across the street is the **Yale Center for British Art** (203-432-2800; www.yale.edu/ycba), 1080 Chapel St. Open Tue.– Sat. 10–5, Sun. 12–5, closed major holidays. It was designed by Louis Kahn and opened in 1977. It houses the largest and most comprehensive collection of British art outside Britain. Paul Mellon (Yale class of 1929) donated paintings, drawings, prints, rare books, manuscripts, and sculpture. You can trace the development of British art, life, and thought from the Elizabethan period onward.

Beinecke Rare Book and Manuscript Library at Yale (203-432-2966), 121 Wall St. Open Mon.–Thu. 8:30–8, Fri. 8:30–5, Sat. 10–5, closed Sun. One of the largest and most famous rare book and manuscript libraries in the country, the Beinecke has collections in literature, theology, history, and the natural sciences. It houses several million manuscripts and 600,000 rare books, including a copy of the Gutenberg Bible.

The **New Haven Green**, one of nine laid out by the founders of the colony, is like a European park, filled with people doing business, relaxing, or talking with friends. It is also the site of local celebrations. In late April or early May there is a historical reenactment of Powder House Day, the day Captain Benedict Arnold asked for the keys to the powder house before he took his troops off to Boston to join the rebellion. The ceremony is complete in detail, with the Governor's Footguard wearing Revolutionary War uniforms.

Another relic of the Revolutionary era is the 1780 **Pardee-Morris House** (203-562-4183), 325 Lighthouse Rd. Amos Morris had built the house earlier, but it was burned when the British invaded the city in July of 1779; he rebuilt it in 1780 with the help of his son. The house contains furnishings from the 17th through the 19th century.

West Rock Nature Center (203-946-8016) in West Rock Ridge State Park on Wintergreen St. is a place many visitors want to explore. There's a trail along the ridge that offers views of cliffs and harbors, tracks of prehistoric animals, and marks of glacial movement in the sedimentary rocks. Along the trail visitors will come to **Judges' Cave**, which was home for three months to two British regicides. In 1661 Edward Whalley and William Goffe, who 14 years earlier had signed a warrant for the arrest and execution of King Charles I, fled for their lives when Charles II, the son of the beheaded king, offered a 100-pound reward for their capture. A plaque bolted to a nearby boulder tells the story: "Here, May 15th 1661, and for some weeks thereafter, Edward Whalley and his son-in-law William Goffe, Members of Parliament, General Officers in the Army of the Commonwealth and signers of the death warrant of King Charles I, found shelter and concealment from the officers of the Crown after the Restoration. Opposition to tyrants is Obedience to God!"

Black Rock Fort and Fort Nathan Hale (203-946-8790), 36 Woodward Ave. Open daily Memorial Day–Labor Day. They are reconstructed forts from the Revolutionary War and the Civil War respectively. British troops under General Tryon captured and burned Black Rock Fort during the invasion of 1779, but it was later rebuilt. Both forts are currently being restored; they also offer views of the harbor.

The **New Haven Colony Historical Society** (203-562-4182), 114 Whitney Ave., has historical and industrial exhibits, a research library, and a permanent decorative arts gallery displaying tablewares of New Haven. It offers both permanent and changing exhibits of maritime artifacts, furniture, and paintings.

LODGING

HISTORIC MANSION INN
600 Chapel St.,
New Haven, CT 06511; 203-865-8324;
www.the historicmansioninn.com
This 1844 Greek-revival mansion is close to Yale University.

THE INN AT OYSTER POINT
104 Howard Ave.,
New Haven, CT 06519; 203-773-3334;
www.oysterpointinn.com
This 1903 Victorian home was once home to an oysterman.

THE THREE CHIMNEYS INN
1201 Chapel St.,
New Haven, CT 06511; 203-789-1201;
www.threechimneysinn.com
This Victorian mansion dates from 1870.

RESTAURANTS

New Haven has an abundance of restaurants, offering almost every kind of cuisine imaginable. Following are a handful of places offering unusual local color.

ATHENIAN DINER
1426 Whaley Ave,
New Haven, CT 06515; 203-397-1556
This is one of the most popular diners in town.

ATTICUS BOOKSTORE CAFÉ
1082 Chapel St., New Haven, CT 06510
203-776-4040
This café is located southwest of Yale Green. Just the place to read a few books.

LOUIS' LUNCH
261-263 Crown St.,
New Haven, CT 06510; 203-562-5507;
www.louislunch.com
The building is on the National Register of Historic Places. Those who donated funds to keep the restaurant there have their names on bricks.

PEPE'S PIZZERIA NAPOLETANA
157 Wooster St.,
New Haven, CT 06511; 203-865-5762
The perennially popular pizza place in New Haven's Little Italy.

RUSTY SCUPPER
501 Long Wharf Dr.,
New Haven, CT 06511; 203-777-5711
The restaurant is right on the water and serves Sunday brunch.

INFORMATION

GREATER NEW HAVEN CONVENTION AND VISITORS BUREAU
169 Orange St., New Haven, CT 06510
800-332-7829, 203-777-8550;
www.newhavencvb.org

STRATFORD

Stratford, settled in 1639, is at the mouth of the Housatonic River, the longest and most important river in western Connecticut. The early town included neighboring Shelton, Trumbull, and parts of Bridgeport.

HISTORICAL SITES *and* MUSEUMS

Most of the old houses in town remain in private hands. An exception is the **Captain David Judson House** (203-378-0630), 967 Academy Hill. Judson built his home in 1750 on the site of his grandfather's 1639 stone house; Academy Hill was the site of the town stockade. The house contains a collection of Chinese porcelain and a 1750 crown great chair. A large fireplace in the kitchen has period utensils. A clothes press, which was rare in the 18th century, is in the west chamber. The basement has displays on fishing, oystering, and farming, as well as slave quarters. Open mid-May–Oct.

INFORMATION

COASTAL FAIRFIELD COUNTY CONVENTION AND VISITORS BUREAU
297 West Ave., Norwalk, CT 06850
800-866-7925, 203-853-7770; www.coastalct.com
For more about the following locations in this section contact the site listed above.

DARIEN

One of the most affluent of Connecticut's New York commuting suburbs, Darien, like many towns in this region, has a scenic shoreline and a backcountry filled with large homes and estates.

HISTORICAL SITES *and* MUSEUMS

The Bates-Scofield House (203-655-9233), 45 Old Kings Highway North. Open year-round by appointment. This saltbox-style house dates from 1736. The Bates family built the house and the Scofields later lived there. The central chimney above the huge fireplace and beehive oven are original. Period furnishings are on display. The garden has over 30 varieties of culinary, medicinal, and strewing herbs known to have been used in Connecticut in the 18th century.

NEW CANAAN

Another affluent suburb of New York, New Canaan is known for its bird sanctuary and wildlife preserve at the New Canaan Nature Center, where birders and walkers enjoy the nature trails.

HISTORICAL SITES and MUSEUMS
The Hanford-Silliman House (203-966-1776), 13 Oenoke Ridge. Open Sep.–June. Stephen Hanford, a weaver and early licensed tavern keeper, built his home in 1764. When he died the house was sold to Elisha Leeds, who gave it to his daughter and her husband, Joseph Silliman. Displays include many of the original furnishings and other colonial items.

INFORMATION
COASTAL FAIRFIELD COUNTY
CONVENTION AND VISITORS BUREAU
297 West Ave., Norwalk, CT 06850
800-866-7925, 203-853-7770; www.coastalct.com

STAMFORD

Nathaniel Turner, an agent for the New Haven colony, bought land in 1640 from the Siwanoys Indians. Settlers arrived the next year. Stamford is located on a wide bay crossed by two tidal inlets, and its proximity to New York City has filled its center with high-rise corporate headquarters.

HISTORICAL SITES and MUSEUMS
Fort Stamford, 900 Westover Rd., overlooking Long Island Sound, is being restored by volunteers. It was originally manned by 300 men under the command of General David Waterbury. The fort was used in the waning years of the Revolution, from 1781 to 1783, when British naval raids were still a real danger.

INFORMATION
COASTAL FAIRFIELD COUNTY
CONVENTION AND VISITORS BUREAU
297 West Ave., Norwalk, CT 06850
800-866-7925, 203-853-7770;
www.coastalct.com

GREENWICH

At the western edge of the New Haven colony's influence lies Greenwich, first settled in 1640 when the Indians sold the land for twenty-five coats. Try that for a
down payment on property here today! Buried in the modern, fashionable suburb are two colonial houses.

HISTORICAL SITES and MUSEUMS

You can't miss seeing the scalloped-shingled house known as the **Putnam Cottage** (203-869-9697; www.putnamcottage.org), 243 Putnam Ave., which dates
from 1690. Open Apr.– Dec., Sun. and by appointment. During the Revolution
it was called Knapp's Tavern, and General Israel Putnam entertained leaders here.
When the British arrived to destroy the saltworks in February 1799, "Old Put"
reportedly escaped by riding his horse over a cliff. The house has handsome field-
stone fireplaces.

The 1732 **Bush-Holley House** (203-869-6899; www.hstg.org), 39 Strick-
land Rd., was the home of David Bush, a mill owner and farmer. Open year-round.
The house contains interesting collections of 18th-century Connecticut furniture,
as well as paintings, sculpture, and pottery.

LODGING

HOMESTEAD INN
420 Field Point Rd.,
Greenwich, CT 06830; 203-869-7500;
www.homesteadinn.com
This attractive inn dates from 1799 and
has Italianate Gothic styling and individually decorated rooms.

THE STANTON HOUSE
INN BED & BREAKFAST
76 Maple Ave.,
Greenwich, CT 06830; 203-869-2110;
www.shinngreenwich.com
Stanford White designed this inn
around 1900.

RESTAURANTS

L'ESCALE
At the Delamar on
Greenwich Harbor Hotel,
500 Steamboat Rd.,
Greenwich, CT 06830; 203-661-4600;
www.thedelamar.com
The hotel may be new but the dining room
is decorated with antique tiles and an
18th-century French fireplace.

THOMAS HENKELMANN RESTAURANT
At the Homestead Inn,
420 Field Point Rd.,
Greenwich, CT 06830; 203-869-7500;
www.thomashenkelmann.com
Contemporary French cuisine is served in
well-appointed dining rooms.

*If you're heading east and need a meal
or an overnight stay, try the following
establishment:*

SILVERMINE TAVERN
194 Perry Ave.,
Norwalk, CT 06850; 203-847-4558;
www.silverminetavern.com
The Coach House, the Old Mill, the
Gatehouse, and the Tavern are all within
earshot of a waterfall.

INFORMATION

COASTAL FAIRFIELD COUNTY
CONVENTION AND VISITORS BUREAU
297 West Ave., Norwalk, CT 06850
800-866-7925, 203-853-7770;
www.coastalct.com

NORTHWESTERN CONNECTICUT

The landscape of northwestern Connecticut, where the Taconic Range tails off into hills, reminds us of the Cotswolds in England, and it has the same kind of charm today. But remote from the navigable water that was so essential in the colonial era, the region was settled relatively late and only then for its industrial potential. Like much of rural Connecticut in the 18th century, it was largely deforested for farms and to produce charcoal to feed its early manufacturing, and its factories built the towns that are now so attractive to residents and visitors. Gone now are the noise, stench, and confusion that produced the affluence so evident in the beautiful colonial houses that remain.

Today this quadrant of the state is always a treat to visit, offering quiet for the ears and pleasure for the eyes. You can ramble through it on winding roads over rolling hills and by the clear water of lakes. It is loaded with state parks and forests for hiking and streams and rivers for canoeing and kayaking. Many artists, writers, musicians, and playwrights choose to live here, and innovative restaurants have opened to serve them. Years ago friends in residence cautioned us not to write too much about this area—they like it as it is.

LITCHFIELD

If you would like to visit a living museum of 18th-century life, without any 18th-century grime, head for Litchfield, one of the earliest spontaneous restoration projects in America. Its residents, through amazing foresight, began preparing for the 20th century in the 19th by restoring older buildings to their original state and converting newer ones to colonial styles. And there were plenty of buildings to work on.

In 1715 John Marsh left Hartford to explore the "Western Lands" and give a report on how the area would be suited for a settlement. Early settlers, led by Marsh and John Buell in 1719, built churches, gristmills, houses, and a school on the rolling hills of the town.

During the Revolution the town's Oliver Wolcott served as delegate to the Continental Congress, signed the Declaration of Independence, and was appointed to command a regiment of Connecticut militia. The legendary leader of Vermont's Green Mountain

At the beginning of the Revolution, a lead statue of King George III was toppled from its base on Bowling Green in New York by a raucous crowd, transported to Norwalk and taken inland from there, to end up in the woodshed behind Oliver Wolcott's house in Litchfield. There it was melted down, and the women and girls in town helped cast the lead into bullets. Many pieces of the statue disappeared, to turn up in later years. King George's head was saved by Tories and ended up in England.

Boys, Ethan Allen, who was instrumental in obtaining the surrender of Fort Ticonderoga in May 1775, was a Litchfield native. The town was in a good position to be a communication and supply link for the patriots.

HISTORICAL SITES *and* MUSEUMS

The **Litchfield Historical Society** and **Litchfield History Museum** (860-567-4501; www.litchfieldhistoricalsociety.com), 7 South St. Open Apr.–Nov. Visitors are offered an 18-page booklet for a walking tour; it includes information on the date, style, and original owners of the houses on North and South Streets. Although most of the homes are private, some of them welcome visitors on each Open House Day in July. The museum houses a fine collection of early American paintings, furniture, decorative arts, galleries of special exhibits, and a research library.

South Street takes you by the historical society's **Tapping Reeve House and Law School** (860-567-4501), 82 South St. In the house you'll find hand-stenciled walls in the front hall, a lovely paneled dining room, and fine period furnishings, many of which belonged to the Reeve family. Tapping Reeve graduated first in his class from Princeton University in 1763. While working as a tutor he taught Sally and Aaron Burr, the children of the late president of the college. He and Sally fell in love but were not allowed to marry because she was too young. Finally, in 1773, Tapping and Sally were wed and set up housekeeping in Litch-

Tapping Reeve House and Law School

field. The school, 100 feet from the house, is a one-room building where legal education in this country began in 1784. Among its illustrious graduates were Aaron Burr, John C. Calhoun, Horace Mann (often considered the father of public school education), and many members of Congress.

LODGING

THE LITCHFIELD INN
432 Bantam Rd., Litchfield, CT 06759
800-499-3444, 860-567-4503;
www.litchfieldinnct.com
The building is colonial in decor and
the guest rooms have individual themes.

THE TOLL GATE HILL INN
CT 202, Litchfield, CT 06759
860-567-1233; www.tollgatehill.com
This was once a way station on the
stagecoach line between Litchfield and
Hartford in the late 18th and early 19th
centuries. Dating from 1745, the building
is also called the Captain William
Bull Tavern.

RESTAURANTS

BISTRO EAST RESTAURANT
At the Litchfield Inn,
432 Bantam Rd., Litchfield, CT 06759
860-567-4503; www.litchfieldinnct.com
The restaurant is in the Joseph Harris room;
he was among the first Litchfield settlers
and was killed by Indians.

TOLL GATE HILL RESTAURANT
At the Toll Gate Hill Inn,
CT 202, Litchfield, CT 06759
860-567-4503; www.tollgatehill.com
Also called the Captain William Bull
Tavern, the restaurant's menu is
"American with a flair."

THE VILLAGE PUB AND RESTAURANT
25 West St., Litchfield, CT 06759
860-567-8307
Overlooking the Litchfield Green,
for lunch and dinner.

EVENTS

July: Open House Day Tour of
Litchfield visits historic homes and
other sites (860-567-9423).

INFORMATION

LITCHFIELD HILLS/NORTHWEST CONNECTICUT CONVENTION AND VISITORS BUREAU
P.O. Box 968, Litchfield, CT 06759
800-663-1273, 860-567-4506;
www.litchfieldhills.com

SHARON

Sharon was founded in 1738, and settlers had to clear six acres, build a house, and live there for three years. By 1739 the proprietors had decided to create a town green. Grazing was permitted—a good way to keep the grass in shape. Today historic houses line both Main Street and Upper Main Street in the very pleasant town center.

HISTORICAL SITES *and* MUSEUMS
Gay-Hoyt House Museum (860-364-5688; sharonhist.org), 18 Main St. Open Tue.–Fri. and by appointment. Ebenezer Gay built the house in 1775. He was a prosperous merchant who spent a lot of his wealth supporting the Revolutionary effort. He served in the war with the rank of lieutenant colonel. His brick house was built in Flemish bond and has a central-hall plan with chimneys at the sides. There's a hands-on history room for children.

SALISBURY

Apart from Litchfield, most of the prosperous 18th-century industrial towns of northwestern Connecticut were located on or near the upper Housatonic River, hardly navigable (although good for canoeing) but nevertheless a source of water power. Salisbury, on a tributary of the Housatonic, benefited from very rich iron ore beds and soon became an iron manufacturing center. It was first settled in the 1720s by Dutch families from New York.

The earliest forge dates from 1734 and was located in the Lime Rock area on Salmon Creek.

LODGING

THE WHITE HART INN
CT 41 and US 44, Salisbury, CT 06068
800-832-0041, 860-435-0030;
www.whitehartinn.com
This 19th-century inn has a very wide porch, just made for rocking and watching the world go by.

RESTAURANTS

THE WHITE HART INN
CT 41 and US 44, Salisbury, CT 06068
800-832-0041, 860-435-0030;
www.whitehartinn.com
The Riga Room and Garden Room are both restaurants in the White Hart Inn, along with a tap room.

LAKEVILLE

The nearby village of Lakeville was the site of the most important blast furnace in the colony. In the Salisbury area three blast furnaces were in full swing during the Revolution: the **Lakeville, Mount Riga, and Lime Rock blast furnaces.** Ethan Allen was one of three partners in the Lakeville furnace. He came to Salisbury in 1761, heard about an iron deposit called "Ore Hill," and was determined to build a charcoal blast furnace to smelt the ore. But he needed to find financial backers and persuaded John Hazelton to become his partner, along with Samuel and Elisha Forbes. The blast furnace was finished in 1762 and continued to operate until 1844. During the Revolution it produced more than 800 iron cannon. It also produced cannonballs, grapeshot, and huge cast-iron kettles used to help feed the Continental Army. Today visitors can see the remains of a furnace on Mount Riga.

HISTORICAL SITES *and* MUSEUMS
The Holley-Williams House Museum (860-435-0566; www.salisburycannon-museum.org), 15 Millerton Rd. This classical-revival house dates from 1808. Open Memorial Day–Columbus Day, Sat. and Sun. The grounds are open year-round. This family museum has 173 years of the Holley family possessions. There is also a model of an iron furnace. Don't miss the maze.

The **Cannon Museum** is on the same grounds. It is on the site of the first iron blast furnace built in 1762 by Ethan Allen. Exhibits feature seven people and how they responded to the events of 1775. Activities for children include dress-up uniforms and secret messages.

The Mount Riga Furnace in Lakeville

LODGING

THE INN AT IRON MASTERS
229 Main St., Lakeville, CT 06039; 860-435-9844; www.innatironmasters.com
This inn is named for the area's early iron manufacturing industry.

KENT

On the upper Housatonic, Kent was incorporated in 1739 and had become a busy industrial center by 1758, with three iron furnaces roaring in the area. Just downstream, Bulls's Bridge was built during the Revolution so iron ore could be brought to a forge.

HISTORICAL SITES *and* MUSEUMS

Just north of Kent, in a rustic barn on US 7, is the **Sloane-Stanley Museum** (860-927-3849). Open mid-May–Oct. 31, Wed.–Sun. It contains a replica of Eric Sloane's studio, exhibits of his work, and an extensive collection of wooden tools, some dating to the 17th century. If you love old barns, this is the place for you. The ruins of a Kent iron blast furnace on the grounds help to complete the picture of work in early Kent.

Bulls' Bridge achieved a bit of notoriety in 1781 when a horse, perhaps one of George Washington's favorites, fell into the tumultuous Housatonic River. Washington's travel expense account detailed: "Getting a horse out of Bull's Falls, $215.00." From the size of the bill—a considerable sum at the time—the rescue must have been difficult. Washington, as always, was under time pressure to get on his way—perhaps to the next place that might claim he slept there.

LODGING

FIFE 'N DRUM INN
53 N. Main St., Kent, CT 06757
860-927-3509; www.fifendrum.com
This B&B is across the road from the restaurant
with the same name, described below.

THE INN AT KENT FALLS
860-927-3197; www.theinnatkentfalls.com
107 Kent Cornwall Rd., Kent, CT 06757
The building dates from 1741 and is on 2.5 acres.

RESTAURANTS

FIFE 'N DRUM RESTAURANT
53 N. Main St.,
Kent, CT 06757
860-927-3509;
www.fifendrum.com
A handy place for lunch after
touring the Sloane-Stanley
Museum. Eric Sloane prints hang
on the walls of the Tap Room.

WASHINGTON

This is the first town named after George Washington. A number of houses on
the green date from colonial times. Cogswell Tavern was built in 1756–57 by
William Cogswell, the youngest son of Edward Cogswell, who was the first settler in 1746. William was active in military affairs, attaining the rank of major. On
May 25, 1781, George Washington and his staff stopped at Cogswell Tavern, now
a private home. Today some visitors come to Washington for its peaceful setting
or to enjoy its wonderful inn, others for the spectacular scenery in the gorge of the
Shepaug River.

HISTORICAL SITES and MUSEUMS
The **Institute for American Indian Studies** (860-868-0518; www.birdstone.org),
38 Curtis Rd., is a wonderful place to learn about Indians—not only of the colonial period but all the way back to prehistory. Open year-round. Visitors can explore
a simulated archaeological site, a reconstructed 17th-century Algonquian village
that contains a longhouse furnished with sapling-supported bunks covered with
skins, and then walk along the Quinnetukut habitat trail through the woods.

A reconstructed shelter at the Institute for American Indian Studies

The **Gunn Historical Museum** (860-868-7756; www.bblio.org/gunn), Wyke-ham Rd., is located in a 1781 house. The house originally had a gambrel roof and two chimneys instead of the one remaining. Today visitors will see dolls, doll-houses, period furnishings, needlework, and spinning wheels. Open year-round.

LODGING

MAYFLOWER INN
118 Woodbury Rd.,
Washington, CT 06793; 860-868-9466;
www.mayflowerinn.com
This country inn is decorated with 19th-century art and antiques. Maple trees and landscaped gardens enhance the 28-acre site.

RESTAURANTS

MAYFLOWER INN
118 Woodbury Rd.,
Washington, CT 06793
860-868-9466;www.mayflowerinn.com
The dining rooms include the Terrace, where you can look out over the Shake-speare garden.

BETHLEHEM

South of Litchfield, Bethlehem was settled during the 18th century and incorpo-rated in 1787. Now it is famous for its special Christmas postmark and Christmas Festival.

For a very unusual and moving experience visit **Regina Laudis Abbey** (860-266-5702), Flanders Rd. An 18th-century Neapolitan nativity scene is on display here. It's the sort of exhibit you can look at for a long time without seeing every figure.

HISTORICAL SITES *and* MUSEUMS

Bellamy-Ferriday House & Garden (203-266-7596; www.hartnet.org/als), 9 Main St. Open May–Oct. The house dates from the mid-1700s when it was built for the town's first minister, the Reverend Joseph Bellamy. The house was later bought by Henry Ferriday of New York. Family furnishings with a French influ-ence are on display, as well as a formal garden.

TERRYVILLE

Southeast of Litchfield and west of Bristol, Terryville was known as the site of the Pequabuck railroad tunnel in the early 20th century and now is noted for its lock museum, representing one of the oldest manufacturing industries in Connecticut.

HISTORICAL SITES *and* MUSEUMS

The Lock Museum of America (860-589-6359; www.lockmuseum.com), 230 Main St. Open May 1–Oct. 31, Tue.– Sun. The largest collection of locks, keys, and hardware in the country is housed in this museum. You will see American locks and keys from the colonial era and later. There are also British locks, locks from banks and prisons, and ornate Victorian hardware. Don't miss the cannonball safe.

BRISTOL

Bristol, important for its role in clock and watch manufacturing, is another showcase of Yankee ingenuity. The town is now known for it recreation areas such as Page Park in the Federal Hill section and Rockwell Park.

HISTORICAL SITES and MUSEUMS

The American Clock & Watch Museum (860-583-6070; www.clockmuseum .org), 100 Maple St. Open Mar.–Nov. This is the largest collection of American production clocks. It is in the 1801 Miles Lewis House and includes more than 3,000 clocks and watches dating from the 1590s. One of the additions was built with trusses and paneling from the 1728 Ebenezer Barnes house. Many of the clocks were made in Bristol.

INFORMATION

BRISTOL CHAMBER OF COMMERCE
200 Main Street, Bristol, CT 06010; 860-584-4718; www.bristol-chamber.org

NEW MILFORD

The earliest settler, Zachariah Ferriss, came in 1706. In 1712 the area was incorporated with the first twelve families as the forty-seventh Connecticut town. After Lexington and Concord in 1775, 285 men enlisted in the Continental Army. Some of them crossed the Delaware River with General Washington on December 25, 1776.

HISTORICAL SITES and MUSEUMS

New Milford Historical Society Museum (860-354-3069; www.nmhistorical.org), 6 Aspetuck Ave. Open May–Oct. The main gallery building connects to the Knapp House, built in 1770 by Daniel Burritt. The house has a large open hearth with a display of period cooking and other utensils.

LODGING

HERITAGE INN
34 Bridge St., New Milford, CT 06776
800-311-6294, 860-354-8883;
www.heritageinnct.com
Dating from the 1800s, this was once a tobacco warehouse.

THE HOMESTEAD INN
5 Elm St., New Milford, CT 06776
860-354-3080; www.homesteadin-nct.com
The 1850s Victorian inn is next to the village green.

WOODBURY

Chief Pomperaug of the Pootatuck Indians sold land for "ancient Woodbury" in 1659. A marker for him stands in the middle of town. The first settlers built stone walls to keep in their sheep. By the time of the Revolutionary War they were exporting woolen products, including shipments to the army.

HISTORICAL SITES and MUSEUMS
Glebe House (203-263-2855; www.theglebehouse.org), Hollow Rd., was built as a minister's farm in 1771. Open May–Oct., Wed.– Sun.; Nov., Sat. and Sun. A "glebe" is a plot of land given to a clergyman as part of his salary. Woodbury's first Episcopal priest, John Rutgers Marshall, lived in the house with his wife, Sarah, and their children. The garden was designed by Gertrude Jekyll and is the only one of her gardens left in the country.

A very important meeting was held in the house just after the declaration of American independence. Samuel Seabury was elected by a group of Episcopalians as the first bishop in America. This group proclaimed both the separation of church and state and religious tolerance in the newly independent colonies.

The oldest house in town, dating from about 1680, is the **Hurd House** (203-263-2446), Hollow Rd. Open June–Oct. It is actually two houses joined together; visitors can see the joint in the upstairs hall, to the left of the window. John Hurd built the first gristmill in Woodbury 300 yards away from his house, on the Pomperaug River. Period furniture embellishes the house, which also has colonial-style gardens. The property is owned by the Old Woodbury Historical Society.

LODGING
CURTIS HOUSE
506 Main St., Woodbury, CT 06798; 203-263-2101
First opened as the Orenaug Inn in 1754, it was later called Kelly's Tavern.

RESTAURANTS
CURTIS HOUSE
506 Main St., Woodbury, CT 06798; 203-263-2101
The dining room offers regional American cuisine.

GOOD NEWS CAFÉ
694 Main St. South, Woodbury, CT 06798; 203-266-4663; www.good-news-cafe.com
Art lines the walls and statuary accents the space.

NEWTOWN

Newtown, holding on to a temporary name used at one time or another by many New England towns, is noted for its restored 18th-century homes.

HISTORICAL SITES and MUSEUMS
Mathew Curtiss House (203-426-5937), 44 Main St. This 18th-century saltbox displays 300 years of Newtown history. Furniture, paintings, and decorative objects are on display. Open house and living-history demonstrations are held one Sunday per month Mar.–June and Sep.– Dec.

RIDGEFIELD

Connecticut's only inland battle of the Revolution took place in Ridgefield. On April 27, 1777, American generals Benedict Arnold, Gold Silliman, and David Wooster tried to confront British troops as they withdrew from a raid against the Continental supply depot in Danbury. The patriots were outnumbered three to one and had to retreat after fighting all day. Wooster was killed, and Arnold barely escaped after his horse was shot from under him. Today, the town's streets, lined with many restored colonial homes, are comparatively quiet.

HISTORICAL SITES *and* MUSEUMS

Keeler Tavern Museum (203-431-0815; www.keelertavernmuseum.org), 132 Main St. Open year-round. A British cannonball is embedded in the building from the 1777 battle. Guides are in colonial dress, and the house has 18th-century furnishings. The garden has a reflecting pool. Cass Gilbert, a famous architect, bought the property in 1907.

Current Information

STATE OF CONNECTICUT DEPARTMENT OF ECONOMIC DEVELOPMENT
505 Hudson St.
Hartford, CT 06106
800-282-6863; 860-270-8080; www.ctbound.org

CENTRAL REGIONAL TOURISM DISTRICT, CONNECTICUT'S HERITAGE RIVER VALLEY
31 Pratt St., 4th Floor, Hartford, CT 06103
800-793-4480, 860-244-8181; www.enjoycentralct.com.

EASTERN CONNECTICUT TOURISM DISTRICT
470 Bank St., New London, CT 06320
800-TOENJOY, 860-444-2206; www.mysticmore.com

SOUTHWESTERN CONNECTICUT TOURISM DISTRICT
297 West Ave., Norwalk, CT 06850
800-866-7925, 203-853-7770; www.coastalct.com

NORTHWESTERN CONNECTICUT TOURISM DISTRICT
21 Church St., Waterbury, CT 06702
888-588-7880, 203-597-9527; www.northwestct.com

Rhode Island

Historical Introduction *to the* Rhode Island Colony

W hile on a journey of exploration sponsored by the king of France, Giovanni da Verrazano recorded in his journal his impression of beautiful Narragansett Bay and declared, "I've decided to linger for a fortnight." His happy encounter, perhaps the first arrival by a European in these waters, set the tone for the place that was to become a refuge for the unwanted and expelled, a model for cooperation between religious denominations, and a puzzle for historians trying to explain why an unusual degree of tolerance emerged at this time in this place.

The Colony of Rhode Island and Providence Plantations, as it was to become known, was truly a godsend for its early settlers. Here was not only a marvelous harbor near the sea (which was to become Newport), but also a string of protected harbors reaching far inland on both sides of the bay. In an era when transport by sea was far more efficient than rudimentary land conveyance, this was indeed a magnificent find, a region that invited settlement.

Roger Williams, the founder and guiding light of the colony, arrived as an exile from Massachusetts Bay and spent his first winter among the Narragansett Indians. He established the first settlement in Providence in the same year, 1636. Williams could not tolerate the conduct of the strict Puritans. He wrote, "Yourselves pretend liberty of conscience, but alas! it is but self, the great god self, only

The First Baptist Church in Providence

to yourselves." Williams felt that church and state should be separate; the magistrates could deal with civil offenses but leave religious matters to the church. He advocated respecting all religions, instead of persecuting them, and that other sects should not be forced to attend Puritan services. Forced worship he said, "stinks in God's nostrils."

Williams also held an extraordinary and dangerous conviction that would not be taken seriously for most of three centuries: He believed that the king could not grant land to his subjects unless the Indian inhabitants were paid for it. He wrote, "James has no more right to give away or sell Massasoit's lands . . . than Massasoit has to sell King James' kingdom."

Williams opened a trading post and proceeded to make friends with the Indians. He was fascinated with the Narragansetts who had befriended him, and he kept records on their language, crops such as corn, squash, beans, and tobacco, recipes including the strawberry bread that became a favorite in colonial kitchens, and work, like their method of building stone walls. He also noted their ball games, somewhat similar to modern football. Their sports events included tomahawk throwing, bow-and-arrow competition, and races on horseback. Williams was upset to learn that the Indians gambled and frequently lost everything they had.

Like Williams, Anne Hutchinson, intelligent, energetic, and charismatic, had posed a danger to theocratic order in the Massachusetts Bay Colony. She had used her front parlor for discussions of the local ministers' sermons, which she thought extended beyond the intent of Christianity. Hutchinson felt that devout Christians could commune with God instead of believing that God had spoken only once through the scriptures. To add to this discomfort with theocratic rule, the merchants in the Massachusetts Bay Colony were upset with governmental restrictions and eager to side with her rational approach to civil government.

She was arrested, brought to trial, and stood her ground against the strict interpretation of the Bible advocated by the Puritan magistrates. John Winthrop wrote that she had a "nimble wit and active spirit and a very voluble tongue." Hutchinson was convicted of heresy, sedition, and contempt in the Massachusetts Bay Colony and subsequently left there for Portsmouth with her husband, William, John Clarke, and William Coddington.

RHODE ISLAND *Time Line*

1524	1636	1638	1639	1640
Giovanni da Verrazano explores Narragansett Bay	Roger Williams settles at site of Providence	Anne Hutchinson founds Portsmouth	William Coddington and John Clarke found Newport	The first public school in the colony established in Newport

Williams actually was not the first white man to settle in what is now Rhode Island. That distinction belonged to William Blackstone, the bookish, Anglican minister-turned-hermit who left the Massachusetts colony a year before Williams. He had settled on the site of Boston before the Puritans arrived, and when the Massachusetts Bay Colony had trouble getting good water he invited them to his land. But Blackstone soon had more company than he wanted and moved on. He developed a 200-acre estate on the Blackstone River north of Providence, where he planted the first apple orchard in the colony. He introduced the first dairy cattle and also kept hogs. His wandering hogs were often swept up by Indians, and an Indian named Nahanton had to give him two beaver skins "for damage done him in his swine, by setting of traps."

Richard Smith of Cocumscussoc (near Wickford) used to invite Blackstone to conduct monthly Church of England services at his home, known as "Smith's Castle." The minister would ride his beige-colored bull from his home along the Pequot path to Cocumscussoc.

Roger Williams was instrumental in negotiating a contract for the island of Aquidneck as a home for these exiles from Massachusetts. The settlement was named Portsmouth, and later some of the group settled Newport. There was also a newcomer: After being ejected from Portsmouth and not fully welcome in Providence, Samuel Gorton and his group of followers in 1643 bought from the Narragansetts the Shawomet Purchase, running twenty miles west from the bay south of Providence. To protect this purchase from rival claims by Roger Williams and Massachusetts, Gorton sailed to England to get a royal patent. In 1646 the Earl of Warwick granted him the land he had already bought (including the site of modern Warwick) on the western side of Narragansett Bay, roughly equivalent to modern Kent County. Narragansett land was defined as everything south of Shawomet, now Washington County, usually called South County. With this success

1642	1663	1664	1675	1676
Samuel Gorton founds Warwick	Colony of Rhode Island and Providence Plantations granted charter by Charles II	Block Island included in the colony	King Philip's War begins; Great Swamp Fight	King Philip (Metacomet) killed near Mount Hope

Gorton changed the name of Shawomet to Warwick. Although the four settlements had their differences, Roger Williams acted as a mediator, and finally in 1647 they united, which eventually led to a charter by Charles II in 1663 as the Colony of Rhode Island and Providence Plantations.

The Heritage of Religious Tolerance

Settlers in the four Rhode Island communities were learning a fundamental lesson: Playing the role of dissenter in a Puritan community and creating a colony that tolerated a wide range of dissent were two different matters. Yet the unified Colony of Rhode Island and Providence Plantations did become a refuge for Quakers, Jews, and other nonconformists. It is difficult to summarize the many shades of theological opinion that flourished among varied segments of Rhode Island communities, but there was a general divide between those who continued to regard the Bible as the primary religious authority, the heritage of Roger Williams,

Like William Blackstone, Samuel Gorton was an eccentric, but of a different stripe altogether. Although technically a Puritan, his beliefs radically contradicted most of Puritan theology and practice. For example, he held that the meaning of the Bible was not fixed forever but needed human interpretation, and that that was bound to be imperfect in each age; moreover it should not be turned into a theological system. Church attendance should not be required and ministers should not hold sway over territorial parishes or be paid through taxes. Government should be based on English common law, not church edicts. With such beliefs it is not surprising that Gorton was a thorn in the side of the Puritan community, and his pugnacious temperament disturbed the peace of the more liberal Rhode Island settlements as well. He quarreled with settlers in Newport, was whipped and banished from Portsmouth, and tried and put in irons in Massachusetts, which also claimed the land he had settled. Ultimately, after some years spent in England to secure his patent, he returned to Warwick Cove, and the settlement slowly grew.

RHODE ISLAND *Time Line*

1687	**1765**	**1769**	**1772**
Sir Edmund Andros assumes government of Rhode Island	Stamp Act Riot in Newport	British sloop *Liberty* destroyed at Newport, in first overt act of violence against British authority by colonists	American patriots burn the British revenue schooner *Gaspee*

and others who believed in the fundamental importance of the "inner light," the heritage of Anne Hutchinson—with many crossing that divide in specific beliefs. Following Williams, who noted no reference to infant baptism in the scriptures, many in Providence became Baptists, while those in Portsmouth and Newport became Quakers. After a visit by Quaker founder George Fox to Newport in 1672, Williams, then elderly, rowed eighteen miles down Narragansett Bay to debate his views with three Quakers. Yet he regarded himself as a lifelong seeker, never settling into one church or stable doctrinal position, no matter how much he thought the Quakers wrongheaded.

In that sense Williams represents the unintended genius of Rhode Island that led to tolerance. The colony's diversity of belief—regarded by Massachusetts Puritans as heresy and iniquity—led not to legal action and expulsion in most cases, because there never was a monolithic structure of unified church and state. Even church buildings were late in coming and generally unpretentious, with worship often conducted in homes or even in fields, and there was little ceremony and no hierarchy or required church attendance. In the neighboring Massachusetts Bay and New Haven colonies, Quakers were persecuted vigorously for their heresies and were especially vulnerable because of their refusal to swear oaths of allegiance. Those who landed in Boston were quickly deported, and when the first Quaker missionaries from England landed in Newport in 1657 and some fanned out into the Bay colony, they faced not only fines and imprisonment but physical abuse like whipping and branding. If they returned to Massachusetts a third time after being banished they could be hanged. Mary Dyer, one of Anne Hutchinson's followers, barely escaped that fate once but suffered it on her fourth return in 1660. When urged by Massachusetts to pass similar laws against the Quakers, Rhode Island legislators effectively shrugged their shoulders and refused.

This willingness to let religious belief remain a private matter rather than a public trust carried over to non-Christian groups. Some Jews had reached Newport in the late 17th century from Brazil, forming a congregation and buying land for a cemetery, but this group dispersed. Later immigrants formed a new congregation in the 1750s and raised money to build a synagogue. Peter Harrison, an Anglican, provided plans for the elegant Georgian-style Touro Synagogue in New-

1776	**1776**	**1778**	**1779**	**1780**
General Assembly approves Declaration of Independence	British occupy Newport	Battle of Rhode Island on Aquidneck	British evacuate Newport	Comte de Rochambeau arrives in Newport with French troops

port, dedicated in 1763. The first Jewish sermon to be printed in America was preached in 1773 in Newport by Haym Carregal, an itinerant rabbi who also went to a service in Ezra Stiles's Congregational church. Stiles, who later became president of Yale, spoke of the friendship between Jews and Christians at that service and later studied many tenets of the Jewish faith.

Rhode Island's Response to Wars

The first and most serious threat to Rhode Island settlers was King Philip's War (1675–76), during which attacks or battles occurred in Tiverton, Smithfield, South Kingstown, Central Falls, Warwick, Providence, and Old Rehoboth (East Providence). It was by far the bloodiest confrontation between Indians and New England colonists, brutal on both sides. The Wampanoags and their allies attacked fifty-two of ninety settlements throughout New England, destroyed thirteen entirely, burned houses, and killed more than six hundred colonists, including women and children. The peaceful relations between settlers and tribes that had persisted through Massasoit's life had deteriorated after his death in 1662. This war resulted in the death of Massasoit's son, Metacomet (called King Philip), near Mount Hope (later Bristol), where Metacomet had his base. The neighboring Narragansett Indians had their stronghold on an island in the Great Swamp north of what is now Worden Pond in South Kingstown. In the Great Swamp Fight, the first major battle in the war, a force of 1,100 colonists attacked the Narragansett stronghold, broke through at a weak point in the defenses, and set fire to the wigwams. Hundreds of Narragansetts were killed, including women, children, and old people, and many others fled, but they were now committed to joining the Wampanoags and other allies in a destructive war against the colonists.

King Philip's War resulted from continued pressure on the native peoples, including not only the Wampanoags and Narragansetts, but the Poducks, Mohegans, and Nipmucs as well. Although there were minor problems with adjacent settlements as hogs and cattle strayed into Indian fields, the major cause was loss of land, a problem that continued for two more centuries as white settlers pushed relentlessly westward. Even though Rhode Island settlers were reluctant participants in the extermination of Indians pursued by Massachusetts and Connecticut forces, the coexistence on friendly terms advocated and practiced by Roger Williams did not survive the war. When Providence was attacked, he was spared for his long friendship with Indians, but the settlement was burned, including his own house.

Perhaps because of its heritage, Rhode Island was also a reluctant participant in some of the European wars that spilled over into North America at the end of the 17th and first half of the 18th centuries. In King William's War (1689–97), Rhode Island hung back in providing men and supplies to joint colonial efforts demanded by the Crown, in spite of attacks on Block Island. Again in Queen Anne's War (1703–13), after censure from the Crown for its recalcitrance, and threats to its charter, Rhode Island provided some militia and ships to support expeditions against the French, including the successful attack on Port Royal. In King George's War (1744–48), Rhode Island fitted out a sloop to take part in the siege of Louisbourg, a stunning colonial success. The culmination of these wars between England and France for the control of North America was the French and Indian War (1754–60), officially terminated by the Treaty of Paris in 1763. In this conflict Rhode Island participation was more substantial, with militias participating in the crucial battles to control the Champlain-Hudson waterway. Merchant shipping from Newport had been harassed for years by French ships, so a number of privateers set out to settle that score and make a profit by taking prizes at the same time.

Trade and Enterprise

With so much area within Rhode Island's borders water rather than land, it was perhaps inevitable that the colony would turn to trade as its principal economic activity, and so it did during the first half of the 18th century. Narragansett Bay was ideal to sustain seafaring activity, with sheltered coves on both shores all the way from Newport to Providence. The issuing of paper money began in 1710, ostensibly to pay off debt incurred in supporting Queen Anne's War. It made wider trade possible by giving merchants a means of exchange. The paper money was backed by land, making it less attractive to merchants in Boston and England, but it worked well for Newport merchants through four decades until depreciation destroyed its value. The focus on trade had many side effects that stimulated the economy. Shipbuilding grew, farmers had wider markets for their produce, and some invested in shares of ships. Industries like distilleries and candle-making thrived.

Newport was the prime center of commercial activity for the first half of the century, when challenges from Providence increased. Newport citizens' spirit of enterprise led them into lucrative ventures like privateering and the slave trade. Merchants exported what they had—cattle, barrels, cider, rum, cheese, mutton, salt fish, leather hides. Ships carried these goods to the southern colonies, the West Indies, and West Africa, exchanging them for tobacco, sugar, and slaves. The slave trade was especially lucrative when rum was the medium of exchange, but the trade's moral implications began to trouble Newport's Quaker merchants. Yet black servants outnumbered white servants in Newport and Jamestown, and major entrepreneurs like John, Nicholas, and Moses Brown of Providence gained substantial wealth from trafficking in slaves.

After midcentury, in the decades leading up to the Revolution, British restrictions on trade became increasingly irksome to Rhode Island merchants and all others affected by the health of this economic engine. The Molasses Act of 1733 had given British colonies in the West Indies a monopoly, cutting off other sources of supply for Newport's many distilleries, but enforcement was lax, and smuggling thrived. Some ruses like flying the flag of truce to exchange prisoners got ships into French ports and also lessened the effect of the act. Those evasions were no longer available after the French and Indian War, when British goals changed from regulating trade to raising revenue to pay for the war. The new Sugar Act of 1764 was backed by British revenue ships patrolling Narragansett Bay, and an admiralty court without jury was set up in Halifax, Nova Scotia, to punish violators. Protests from Governor Stephen Hopkins before the act took effect were ignored, and his "Remonstrance" to the Board of Trade raised one of the rallying cries of the pre-Revolutionary period—"No taxation without representation."

Although some Loyalists in Newport supported Parliament's authority, the succeeding acts that stifled trade were vigorously opposed by Rhode Island officials, legislators, and the public at large. The General Assembly asserted its sole right to impose taxation and declared the 1765 Stamp Act null and void. A mob forced the distributor to resign, and the cargo of stamps was never unloaded. After the Townshend duties were imposed in 1767, Rhode Island merchants balked at signing the nonimportation agreement endorsed by other major colonial ports but finally gave in. Before and after the repeal of those duties three years later, the presence of British ships in the bay enforcing regulations inevitably led to incidents where colonials took to violence, like the destruction of the sloop *Liberty* in 1769 and the burning of the schooner *Gaspee* in 1772. After the Coercive Acts of 1773 closed down the port of Boston, Rhode Island sent immediate aid, and the General Assembly was the first in the colonies to call for a Continental Congress, in 1774.

The Occupation of Newport

From the siege of Boston to the surrender at Yorktown and beyond, a substantial number of Rhode Island troops fought in the major battles of the Revolution and many minor ones as well. Rhode Island's Nathanael Greene became one of Washington's most important generals and effective aides, eventually leading a brilliant campaign to weaken British forces in the South. Yet only one major battle was fought on Rhode Island soil, and the major effect of the war was a long occupation of Newport by the British forces. The occupation began in December 1776 and lasted for nearly three years, until October 1779, by which time the British had turned their attention to the southern colonies.

During the long occupation, Newport's prosperity based on shipping vanished, and many of its residents fled Aquidneck for Providence and other mainland towns. Of course the occupying troops took the best of scarce supplies from the remaining residents, including food. During shortages they stripped the insides of buildings for fuel and scavenged throughout the island for whatever they needed. And they continued to harass those who lived inland as well as those on the shores of Narragansett Bay.

Relieving Newport was not a high priority for the Continental Congress, and only one attempt to do so was made, in August 1778. According to the plan for the Battle of Rhode Island, French admiral d'Estaing was to approach Newport from the sea with a fleet and marines while General John Sullivan invaded Aquidneck from Tiverton. Sullivan's forces were to be reinforced by Continental troops led by the Marquis de Lafayette. Like many battle plans requiring coordination of timing, this one went askew when the French fleet arrived before Sullivan was ready to attack, then engaged a new British fleet, suffered damage in a hurricane, and withdrew to Boston for repairs, while the expected reinforcements were late. Nevertheless Sullivan had pushed the British troops back to barricades around Newport in eleven days of attacks, but he did not have enough forces to capture the city and withdrew in an orderly retreat, beating off British attempts to press their advantage.

In July of 1780 Newport was occupied again, this time by the French allies, who stayed through the winter. The Comte de Rochambeau landed with six thousand men and a fleet of warships to help Washington. British ships blockaded the mouth of Narragansett Bay in the spring, so Rochambeau marched across Connecticut with his troops to join the Continental Army in June. Their ultimate destination was Yorktown. The war in Rhode Island territory was over.

Regions *to* Explore

All these regions are within easy reach of one another, so you can use any one of them as a base for day trips throughout the original colony.

PROVIDENCE AND WEST BAY

The colony was earlier referred to simply as Providence Plantations by Roger Williams, who somewhat curiously placed its name after "Rhode Island" in the 1663 charter. Because of Newport's immediate access to the sea, it overshadowed Providence in commercial development until the middle of the 18th century. Thereafter Providence began to challenge that priority, and it assumed dominance after the British occupation during the Revolution left Newport partly in shambles and deprived of its customary commerce. Providence entrepreneurs began to develop water power for industrialization and enter expanded worldwide trade.

PROVIDENCE

The "mile of history" advertised in brochures about Providence is more than mere tourist boosterism. Benefit Street backs it up, offering a treasure in its almost unbroken string of colonial and early Federal buildings. How lucky it seems now that the area had been neglected and almost forgotten during the years when other cities were tearing down decaying historic landmarks to make room for "urban renewal" projects. Benefit Street sat undisturbed and waiting.

Not only Benefit Street but the whole hill above it in the eastern section of Providence is loaded with colonial, Federal, and later pre–Civil War houses, most of them marked with dates. You can walk all the streets intersecting Benefit Street to enjoy this splendid last quarter of the 18th and the first half of the 19th century.

Originally, the street developed in the 1760s to house the overflow from Town Street, now called Main Street. Benefit Street, once called Back Street, provided a pathway "for the benefit of all," as people walked to family burial sites, orchards, and gardens along the back of town. Shipowners, sea captains, merchants, and persons skilled in marine trades built their homes all along the street.

During the era of Providence's preeminence as a seaport, the street glowed with the evidence of prosperity. Comparable to Chestnut Street in Salem, it saw the construction of elegant mansions like the John Brown House and the Nightingale Brown House. But as the source of this prosperity—world trade—moved to other deepwater ports and was not replaced by other economic bonanzas, the port section of Providence gradually slid into decline. By the end of the First World War, Benefit Street was full of decaying buildings split up into small apartments for low-cost housing.

The transformation we see now was the first large-scale historic restoration project in America, a model for other major efforts in the heart of cities like Philadelphia, Charleston, and Savannah.

Before the wrecking ball could swing in the resurgence of building after World War II, local citizens became interested in preservation. The Providence Preservation Society had already begun its work in the 1930s, rescuing almost-doomed historic buildings along this street that had fallen into disrepute; as late as the 1950s Pembroke girls were warned never to go there.

As the Preservation Society bought, restored, and sold house after house, the dilapidated street began to blossom. House tours were designed to show off miraculous changes, as residents told their horror stories of the "before" turned into a pleasant "after." The best part is that people now actually live and work here every day—it's not just a museum to visit on Sundays.

Another anchor of Providence's redevelopment has been Brown University. Like most colleges in New England, Brown, founded in 1764, grew out of the desire to have a college with religious affiliation to a powerful denomination, in this case the Baptists of Providence. The college's charter required that the presi-

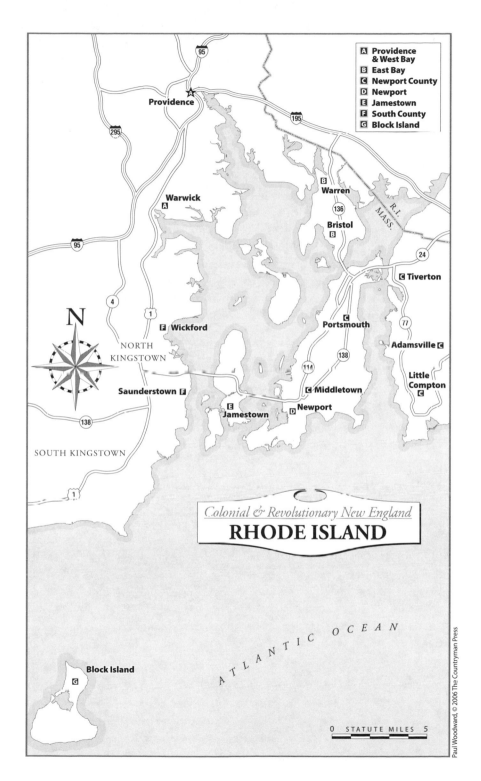

Colonial & Revolutionary New England
RHODE ISLAND

A Providence & West Bay
B East Bay
C Newport County
D Newport
E Jamestown
F South County
G Block Island

Providence

Warwick A

Warren B

Bristol B

Tiverton C

Wickford F

Portsmouth C

Adamsville C

NORTH KINGSTOWN

Saunderstown F

Middletown C

Little Compton C

Jamestown E

Newport D

SOUTH KINGSTOWN

ATLANTIC OCEAN

Block Island
G

R.I.
MASS.

0 STATUTE MILES 5

Paul Woodward, © 2006 The Countryman Press

dent and a majority of the board be Baptists, but in characteristic Rhode Island fashion, Anglicans, Congregationalists, and Quakers were also included. Today this flourishing university dominates the hill opposite the city center, surrounded by a marvelous residential district of colonial and Federal homes.

HISTORICAL SITES *and* MUSEUMS

As you walk **Benefit Street**—and walking is the only way to appreciate it properly—you will want to allow time for poking up and down interesting side streets, like Thomas Street, for an architectural feast.

You might begin at the **Providence Preservation Society** (401-831-7440; www.ppsri.org), at 21 Meeting St. Open Mon.–Fri. A guide to Benefit Street, as well as other tourist information, is available here. The building was built by John Carter, a former apprentice of Benjamin Franklin.

Both Washington and Lafayette were entertained in the 1762 **Old State House** (401-222-3103), 150 Benefit St. Open Mon.–Fri. On May 4, 1776, the colony renounced its allegiance to King George III—two months before the Declaration of Independence was signed.

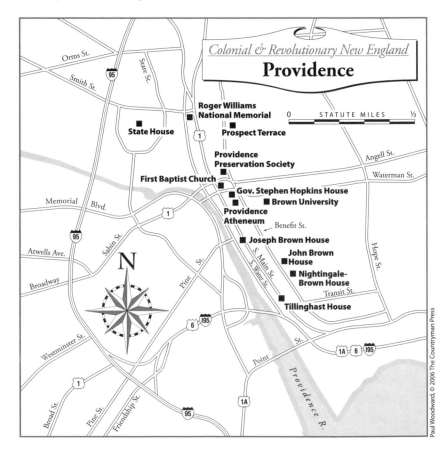

Colonial homes along north Benefit Street, not open except during house tours, include the 1774 Joseph Jenckes House, 43 Benefit St., which has a gambrel roof and pedimented entrance. The 1783–1792 John Reynolds House, 88 Benefit St., has paired interior chimneys. It was also the home of Sarah Helen Whitman, who was courted by Edgar Allen Poe. The 1784 John Howland House, 102 Benefit St., was the home of the father of the free-school system in Rhode Island.

From the middle of Benefit Street walk down to the 1775 **First Baptist Church**, 75 N. Main St., where the first congregation was formed by Roger Williams. James Manning was the minister and also the president of Brown College. He stated that the building was created for two purposes, "for the publick worship of Almighty God; and also for holding Commencement in."

A plaque on the Preservation Society building identifies the name of the building at 21 Meeting Street as "Shakespear's Head, 1772" That unusual name came from the sign that stood in front of the building during colonial days, a carved bust of William Shakespeare. The house, one of the oldest three-story structures in the city, was built by publisher John Carter in 1772 to accommodate the printing press of the Providence *Gazette*, the post office, and a bookshop, as well as Carter's growing family. In the 1930s, as residents of Providence began serious efforts to preserve their heritage, the building was saved from demolition by the Shakespeare's Head Association.

For more Roger Williams sites walk to the **Roger Williams National Memorial** (401-521-7266; www.nps.gov/rowi), 282 N. Main St. Open daily except Jan. 1, Thanksgiving, and Dec. 25. The original settlement in Providence took place here in 1636. The Roger Williams Spring is now a well. The visitor center exhibits include a three-minute slide show about Williams's life and the history of the area plus several videos, one of them narrated by Charles Kuralt.

If you're ready for a skyline view, head for **Prospect Terrace**, Congdon St. at Cushing St., which contains a Roger Williams Memorial statue; his remains are also buried here. From this park you can see the State Capitol with a statue of the "Independent Man" on top.

For a dollar a week during colonial days, 25 students were served "three good meals per day" in **University Hall** (1771), Prospect St. at College St. It was created for **Brown College**, chartered in 1764 as Rhode Island College. During the Revolution, University Hall was used as a barracks and hospital by the American army until 1780, then by the French until 1782, when it was returned to the college. The Admission Office (401-863-1000), 45 Prospect St., is open Mon.–Fri.

When you are on Brown's central quadrangle, you may want to visit the **John Carter Brown Library** (401-863-2725; www.jcbl.org), an elegant, monumental building that houses the collection of its founder, who was born at the end of the 18th century and began gathering Americana in the 19th century. With a focus

The John Carter Brown Libray in Providence

on the discovery and later development of the Americas during the colonial period, the library has an extensive collection of books that draws scholars from all over the world. Originally kept in the Nightingale-Brown House, which it outgrew, the collection was moved to the Brown campus in 1904. Exhibits, as well as public lectures and other events, are open to the public.

Down the hill, at the foot of College Street, stood Market Square, where the Wampanoag trail from the east and the Pequot trail from the west joined at a ford in the river. On March 2, 1775, "all true friends of their country, lovers of freedom, and haters of shackles" came together "to testify their good disposition, by bringing in and casting into the fire" about 300 pounds of British tea. The Market House was built in 1774 and is now part of Rhode Island School of Design.

A copy of the Declaration of Independence that Stephen Hopkins signed with a shaky, palsied hand still exists in Providence. On that occasion he said, "My hand trembles, but my heart does not." Visitors can see that copy in the 1707 **Governor Stephen Hopkins House** (401-421-0694), 15 Hopkins St. on the corner of Benefit. Open Apr.–Dec. 1, Wed. and Sat. afternoons. Hopkins was a member of the Continental Congress, signer of the Declaration of Independence, ten-time governor of Rhode Island, a chief justice of the Superior Court, and first chancellor of Brown University. This house was moved up the hill, and the two-story gable-roof section was added by Hopkins after 1743.

The house is open and guided tours are given by docents. Inside, the keeping room contains a revolving toaster, a foot stove that was taken to church with hot coals in it, a waffle iron, a pastry roller, and other household items. Colonial homes contained an assortment of cooking necessities, including pot hooks (iron rod bent into an "S" shape to hang pots from) and a trammel (a long rod with teeth for a choice of heights above the pot). A decanter set was given to Hopkins by George Washington, who visited in 1776, 1781, and 1791. The study contains a fireplace with Dutch maroon-colored tiles with biblical scenes, covered with a manganese glaze.

Governor Stephen Hopkins House in Providence

Climb upstairs to see the Washington room, where the general and later president stayed overnight. We were touched by the inscription in a book on the bedside table: "Sarah Wells her book given to her by her Mama January of 1700." Tabatha Hopkins's sampler was stitched when she was five years old. Stephen Hopkins's baby cap, baby shoes, porringer, and a buckle are on display in a case.

Outside, the 18th-century colonial garden is open to the public; it's a welcome respite after climbing up and down the hills of Providence. A sundial rises from the middle of symmetrical plantings. Hopkins proclaimed the site "a garden that might comfort yield," which indeed it does.

Across the street is the 1753 **Providence Athenaeum** (401-421-6970; www.providenceathenaeum.org), 251 Benefit St. Open daily. It was founded as one of the first libraries in America. Rare books and paintings are collected inside.

In the southern half of Benefit Street, restoration fever has spread all the way up the hill to Brown and beyond. If you have time to walk streets like Charlesfield, Power, Williams, John, Arnold, and Transit, and the lanes connecting them, you will find yourself wandering back into the 19th century.

John Brown House in Providence

The first house built on the hill above Benefit Street was the 1786 **John Brown House** (401-273-7507; www.rihs.org), 52 Power St. at Benefit St. Open varied hours and days. John Brown had a magnificent view of the sea and his own ships in the harbor. His three-story brick mansion has a balustrade around the roof and a Palladian window on the second floor. John Quincy Adams wrote that the house was "the most beautiful and elegant private mansion that I have ever seen on this continent."

John Brown, along with his family, created a dynasty in the China trade. The Browns were astute enough to shift their activities as old industries declined and new ones emerged. Thus as shipping became less lucrative in the middle of the 19th century, they also spurred on the growth of textile manufacturing in the state. Some of their wealth went toward Brown University

The house contains a collection of colonial furniture, much of it made by Rhode Island craftsmen. One of the finest pieces is a Rhode Island nine-shell, blockfront desk. Squirrels as a motif in the study indicate industriousness. The hall contains lithographs from England dating from 1740, marble busts, portraits of John Brown, and vases and urns from the China trade.

Upstairs, you will see John Brown's walking stick, made from wood taken from the *Gaspee.* Brown, a staunch American patriot, was involved in the burning of the ship on Namquid Point in 1772. (For an account of the *Gaspee* affair, see Warwick, pages 190–191.)

On the third floor there is a collection of family silver, including a fish server, caster and cruet set, and a 1755 tankard. A goblet taken from the *Gaspee* by Commander Abraham Whipple was considered a spoils-of-war gift.

The carriage house contains a 1782 American-made carriage. It is handsome in turquoise and gold, with gigantic wheels.

The elegant yellow mansion next down the street, one of the largest wooden houses in America, also was part of the Brown family domain. It is the 1792 **Nightingale-Brown House** (401-863-1177), 357 Benefit St. Open Thu. and Fri. afternoons as of press time. The house was built by merchant Joseph Nightingale just after the Revolutionary War. Nicholas Brown bought it in 1814, and it was home to the family until deeded to the John Nicholas Brown Center in 1985. The renovated house is also home for visiting scholars at the center.

Nearby, Planet Street was the site of **Sabin Tavern**, where a group met on June 9, 1772, to organize the burning of the *Gaspee*. **Transit Street** was named for the transit of Venus in 1769, which was observed by Joseph Brown, Stephen Hopkins, and Jabez Bowen through a telescope. They were standing on the corner of Transit and Benefit Streets, near the present location of a 1781 house at number 53 Transit. It was converted to a steeply pitched, gabled "lightning splitter house" in 1850.

Just a block downhill toward the river, parallel to Benefit Street, runs South Main Street, where some buildings of historic interest still stand. **Joseph Tillinghast's House**, dating from 1770, at 403 S. Main, was built by a sea captain, then used as a tavern for sailors during the China trade era.

Axel de Fersen, an aide-de-camp of Rochambeau, stayed at 312 S. Main St. A Swedish nobleman, he was also a lover of Marie Antoinette and drove the carriage in which she tried to escape from France in 1791. These houses are not open to the public.

The 1774 **Joseph Brown House**, 50 S. Main St., was used by Rochambeau's officers when the French were in residence. The house was the scene of unusual goings-on when one officer "rode his spirited charger up the flight of steps." When the horse refused to turn and head down the steps, the officer rode it through the house and out the rear door.

LODGING

**CHRISTOPHER DODGE HOUSE
BED & BREAKFAST**
11 W. Park St., Providence, RI 02908
401-351-6111; www.providence-inn.com

The house dates from 1858 and was home to the Dodge family until 1901. The three-story red brick Italianate mansion is now one of three bed & breakfast hotels in a group.

**EDGEWOOD MANOR
BED & BREAKFAST**
232 Norwood Ave., Providence, RI 02905
800-882-3285, 401-781-0099;
www.edgemanor@aol.com
This 1905 Greek-revival home is decorated with antiques and artwork.

**HISTORIC JACOB HILL INN
BED & BREAKFAST**
120 Jacob St., Providence, RI 02940
888-336-9165, 508-336-9165;
www.jacobhill.com
This historic inn dates from 1722. Guest rooms have canopied beds and antique furnishings.

**MOWRY-NICHOLSON HOUSE
BED & BREAKFAST**
57 Brownell St., Providence, RI 02908;
401-351-6111;

www.providence-inn.com
This 1865 Victorian home is named for its first two owners.

OLD COURT BED & BREAKFAST
144 Benefit St., Providence, RI 02903
401-751-2002; www.oldcourt.com
Designed in 1863 as a rectory for St. John's Episcopal Church, the house features ornate Italian mantelpieces, plaster moldings, and 12-foot ceilings.

STATE HOUSE INN BED & BREAKFAST
43 Jewett St., Providence, RI 02908;
401-351-6111;
www.providence-inn.com
This Colonial-revival bed & breakfast inn is decorated with Shaker pieces, American folk art, and primitive-style paintings.

RESTAURANTS

HEMENWAY'S SEA FOOD GRILLE
1 Old Stone Square at S. Main St.,
Providence, RI 02903; 401-351-8570

Fish is a specialty and there's a view of the Providence River.

POT AU FEU
44 Custom House St.,
Providence, RI 02903; 401-273-8953
The restaurant on the second floor offers French cuisine. The bistro downstairs is casual.

EVENTS

June: Providence Preservation Society Tours offer visits to private historic homes. 401-831-7440; www.ppsri.org

INFORMATION

PROVIDENCE WARWICK CONVENTION AND VISITORS BUREAU
1 W. Exchange Street, 3rd Floor,
Providence, RI 02903
800-233-1636, 401-456-0200;
www.pwcvb.com

WARWICK

Warwick, just south of Providence on the western shore of the bay, is now a sprawling bedroom community. But its old center had an important role in the colonial era, and the city is still well known for its "*Gaspee* Days" in June. This festival celebrates the prewar capture and destruction of the *Gaspee*, a British schooner that had been harassing the patriots, in June 1772. Beginning with the 1993 celebration, the Rhode Island Mace, which contains a piece of wood from the *Gaspee*, was carried in the parade. A colonial muster of fife and drums follows the parade. A Revolutionary War battle reenactment and the burning of the *Gaspee* take place the next day at Salter Grove State Park.

HISTORICAL SITES *and* MUSEUMS
Samuel Gorton, who founded Warwick in 1642, was regarded as extremely outspoken, a troublemaker who had been banished from Boston and Plymouth, as well as Anne Hutchinson's Portsmouth. The site of the Samuel Gorton House, at 190 Warwick Neck Ave., Warwick Neck, is marked by a bronze plaque. A new home built by the Gorton family now stands there.

During the Revolutionary War Israel Arnold supplied Continental troops with cattle, wood, and tobacco. The **John Waterman Arnold House** (401-467-7647), 11 Roger Williams Circle, dates from 1770. (The family was related to Benedict Arnold, whose grandfather was an early Rhode Island governor.) The Arnold house

BAITING *the* BRITISH

The *Gaspee* affair occurred off Namquid Point (now called Gaspee Point) in Warwick in 1772. It has been compared to the Boston Tea Party by some historians because it represents the response of a maritime community to British interference with trade. The incident started when Captain Thomas Lindsay of the packet sloop *Hannah,* one of the vessels harassed by the *Gaspee,* purposely led the deeper-draft revenue schooner aground on a sand spit during the afternoon of June 9. Lindsay got the news to John Brown, who gathered a group of leading Providence merchants in the Sabin Tavern that evening to organize the burning of the stranded *Gaspee* before the next high tide could get her off.

Captain Abraham Whipple led sixty-four men in a successful attack that captured and burned the ship. So much secrecy surrounded the plot that none of the patriot suspects were ever found, in spite of the obligatory proclamations of Governor Wanton and the arrest of Brown. How could a band of prominent citizens steal through the night unobserved? The investigating commission reported that not a soul in Rhode Island knew anything about the mysterious conflagration.

is a typical colonial farmhouse, with six-over-six windowpanes, and thumb latches on the paneled doors, as well as a beehive oven. Look for the niche in the stairway that allowed the inhabitants to move large pieces upstairs, such as coffins.

The Arnolds owned nearly 10,000 acres and paid the highest taxes in the colony. The house is now the home of the Warwick Historical Society, which rescued it from destruction.

EVENTS

June: Gaspee Days Parade and Reenactment, with colonial fife and drum corps plus modern-day drum and bugle corps. 401-781-1772; www.gaspee.com

INFORMATION

WARWICK TOURISM OFFICE
Warwick City Hall, 3275 Post Rd., Warwick, RI 02886
800-492-7942, 401-738-2000 x 6402; www.visitwarwickri.com

EAST BAY

Roger Williams canoed the Narragansett Bay from Providence to various sites along the way south to Portsmouth and Newport. The East Bay towns of Warren, Bristol, and Barrington are among the finest residential areas in greater Providence. Proud of their past and assiduous in preserving it, these attractive towns provide a feast for those interested in colonial architecture.

WARREN

Water Street in Warren, a National Register Waterfront District, runs along the eastern bank of the Warren River. Once the site of an Indian village, **Burr's Hill Park** contains Indian burial mounds. The Wampanoag chief Massasoit ruled the whole region, including southeastern Massachusetts and the lands bordering Narragansett Bay, when the *Mayflower* arrived in 1620. Massasoit's Spring is located on Baker Street near the water.

Some artifacts are in the **Charles Whipple Greene Museum** in the George Hail Library (401-245-7686), 530 Main St. It is open Wed. afternoons.

Warren is now restoring historic buildings where its residents were once involved in whaling and the sea trade. It was the fifth-largest whaling port in the country during the early 18th century.

HISTORICAL SITES *and* MUSEUMS

Maxwell House (401-245-0392; www.massasoithistoricalassociation.org), 59 Church St., was built by Samuel Maxwell in 1755 as a brick gable house. Open Sat. and by appointment. Inside, there are two beehive bake ovens that still produce colonial-style fare periodically. The house is owned by the Massasoit Historical Association. The association has conducted a tour of historical buildings in Warren's historic district, usually in October.

The **Nicholas Campbell House**, 23 Broad St. North, was the home of a rebellious patriot who joined the Boston Tea Party.

Peleg Rogers built the **Rogers-Hicks House** (1765) on School St. Josias Lyndon, the governor of Rhode Island from 1768 to 1769, escaped British troops during the Revolution and fled to this house. In 1778 he died of smallpox in Warren and is buried in Kickemuit Cemetery. The house has been the rectory of St. Mark's Church since 1921.

Carr Tavern, Washington and Water Sts., was owned by the family who also operated a ferry to Barrington. It dates from 1750. The 1752 **John Davol House**, 41 State St., is a two-and-a-half story gambrel-roof residence.

The 1753 **Jesse Baker House**, 421 Main St., is known for the courage of its owner, Mrs. Jesse Baker, who used blankets to fight the flames as the British were burning the nearby Baptist meetinghouse.

RESTAURANTS

THE NATHANIEL PORTER HOUSE,
401-289-0373; www.natporter.com,
125 Water St., was built by a whaling captain
in 1795 and has been meticulously restored.
Noted for its cuisine, the restaurant serves
dinner amid original murals and period antiques
in separate dining rooms, including two formal
parlors, a tavern room, and the courtyard.

INFORMATION

EAST BAY TOURISM COUNCIL
15 Cutler St., Warren, RI 02885
1-888-278-9948, 401-245-0750;
www.eastbayritourism.com

BRISTOL

Visitors know they are in Bristol when they spot the red, white, and blue stripe down the center of the principal through street (Highway 114). Bristol claims to be the first town to have held a Fourth of July parade, in 1785, and today the red, white, and blue centerline is a proud reminder of that tradition. The whole town looks like a Norman Rockwell painting, brimful of restored homes that are really lived in.

Bristol was a focal point of both peace and war as settlers and Indians lived side by side during much of the 17th century. The Wampanoag chief Massasoit had his headquarters in the Mount Hope lands that included Bristol. Although he sold much of his land, the Mount Hope Neck was not for sale.

Each of three colonies—Rhode Island, Massachusetts Bay, and Plymouth—wanted Bristol because of its fine harbor and ideal location on Narragansett Bay. Plymouth was granted the lands in 1680 by King Charles II, and people began to buy parcels as householders. By 1690 fifteen ships called Bristol home port.

By 1747 Rhode Island had won back Bristol as well as Cumberland, Tiverton, Little Compton, Warren, and part of Barrington. About fifty 18th-century homes are still standing in Bristol. Most of them were built in typical Rhode Island style as wood-frame structures with gable or gambrel roofs. The chimney was usually in the center of the house, with five rooms around it. Others were built as one-room-deep houses with a single room on each side of the chimney.

During the Revolution Bristol supported the independence movement. After fifteen British ships came into the harbor in 1775, demanded provisions, and fired upon the town, fortifications were constructed. In May 1778, 500 British soldiers landed on Bristol Neck and proceeded to burn and destroy buildings in both Warren and Bristol.

Those readers who are especially interested in colonial architecture will find a tour of Bristol illuminating. A good place to start is the **Bristol Historical and Preservation Society Museum and Library** (401-253-7223), 48 Court St., built from stone ballast brought over on Bristol sailing ships. Group walking tours are offered by appointment, and the society sells a book with detailed descriptions of the town's restored homes, many of which are opened up during special tour days. A house and garden tour is held in September.

Bristol is a perfect place to take a long walk, either with or without a camera in hand, and you can enjoy the exteriors of these fine houses at any time. Use a town map to locate the colonial buildings you are particularly interested in. Hope Street, stretching from end to end of town, is lined with a panoply of fine restored houses; if your time is limited, walk this street to get an overview of colonial Bristol. At 675 Hope is the John Liscomb–Isaac Camm House (1787, with a later Greek-revival section); at number 256 is the Jeremiah Wilson House (1750); at 693 is the hip-roof Dr. Chillingsworth Foster House (1780). Foster was ship's surgeon on the *Hiram*.

Bradford Street has two restored 18th-century houses: At 21 is the Samuel Royal Paine House (before 1775); at 98 is the Captain Allen Wardwell House (1760), built as a gambrel-roof cottage. At 22 Burton Street is a colonial-era cottage (1750). At 75 Constitution Street is the gambrel-roof Francis Bourne Cottage (1779). At 70 Griswold Avenue is the John Dewolf House (1787), a two-story farmhouse.

A visitor who has taken the time to sample even a part of this array of fine old houses may well ask why they were built and why they remain. The answer to the first question involves Bristol's fine harbor and enterprising merchants and shipmasters who quickly took advantage of pursuits that were immensely profitable—including privateering and slaving. The fact that so many fine houses are still standing is partly accidental—the shift of profitable trades to larger ports and the subsequent lack of further development and growth—and partly the result of local efforts to preserve a bountiful heritage as Bristol became a desirable residential community within easy commuting distance of Providence.

Coggeshall Farm (401-253-9062) in Colt State Park was first bought by Samuel Viall in 1723. Open daily. The Coggeshall family worked the land in the 1830s. Today the Coggeshall Farm Museum portrays rural life in the late 18th century. This salt-marsh farm includes a saltbox house, barns, a weaving shed, a blacksmith shop, and exhibits of agricultural implements and tools. The farm animals are the species living on farms during the 1700s.

Elizabeth and Isaac Royall lost their home because they had to flee as staunch Loyalists. **Mount Hope Farm** (401-254-1745), 250 Metacom Ave., was built in 1745 as a two-and-a-half-story, gambrel-roof house and added on to later. In 1776 the farm was confiscated by the state, after Royall had left for Nova Scotia. William Bradford bought it in 1783, and George Washington visited him there in 1789. The property was given to Brown University in the 1950s. **The Haffenreffer Museum of Anthropology** (401-253-8388) is now on the property. Open June–Aug., Tue.–Sun., and Sat.–Sun. the rest of the year. Visitors can see artifacts and displays of Native cultures of the area as well as other locations in the world, including South America, Central America, Africa, Asia, the Middle East, and Oceania.

> Coggeshall Farm is a "saltbox" type of construction, two stories in front and one in back, with a steeper and shorter roof pitch at the front than the back. Sometimes the back section was added later as a "lean-to." This design was familiar to colonists from East Anglia and Kent in England. It was an efficient way of rebuilding small houses to add sleeping space above and a kitchen behind. It was also economical, with two rooms for living on the ground floor and small bedrooms above, all drawing heat from a single central chimney stack.

LODGING

BRADFORD-DIMOND-NORRIS HOUSE
474 Hope St., Bristol, RI 02809
888-329-6338, 401-253-6338;
www.bdnhouse.com
William Bradford built his mansion in 1792 after the British demolished his home in 1778. Governor Francis Dimond owned the house in the 1840s; his daughter married Samuel Norris.

THE GOVERNOR BRADFORD HOUSE, A COUNTRY INN AT MOUNT HOPE FARM
250 Metacom Ave., Bristol, RI 02809
877-254-9300, 401-254-9300;
www.mounthopefarm.com
Mount Hope Farm dates from the 1680s.

POINT PLEASANT INN
333 Poppasquash Rd.,
Bristol, RI 02809
800-503-0627, 401-253-0627;
www.pointpleasantinn.com
The inn is open May–Nov. 1. Point Pleasant was the mooring for the *Belisarius*, the last yacht designed by Nathaniel Greene Herreshoff.

ROCKWELL HOUSE INN BED & BREAKFAST
610 Hope St.,
Bristol, RI 02809
800-825-0040, 401-253-0040;
www.rockwellhouseinn.com
The Federal-style inn was built in 1809.

WILLIAMS GRANT INN
154 High St., Bristol, RI 02809
800-596-4222, 401-253-4222;
www.wmgrantinn.com
This Federal-style inn dates from 1808, and was given to the grandson of Deputy Governor William Bradford.

RESTAURANTS

THE LOBSTER POT
119-121 Hope St., Bristol, RI 02809
401-253-9100
Dating from the 1920s, this seafood restaurant has a nice view of Narragansett Bay. Local artisans display their work on the walls.

REDLEFSEN'S
444 Thames St., Bristol, RI 02809
401-254-1188
Dishes are inspired by cuisine from Germany, France, and Sweden.

EVENTS

July 4: Independence Day Parade:
The oldest continuous Fourth of July celebration in the country marches along Hope and High Sts.
www.july4thbristolri.com

INFORMATION

**EAST BAY CHAMBER OF COMMERCE
16 CUTLER ST., WARREN, RI 02885**
888-278-9948, 401-245-0750;
www.eastbaychamber.org

NEWPORT COUNTY

Newport County boundary lines cross as much water as land—perhaps more—as they carve out islands in Narragansett Bay. The county includes the towns of Portsmouth, Middletown, and Newport on Rhode Island (Aquidneck); Tiverton and Little Compton on the eastern shore of the Sakonnet River; and Prudence Island and Jamestown Island. The quickest route today to Newport County from Providence is through a good piece of Massachusetts, including Fall River. Indeed, Rhode Island and Massachusetts cannot be divorced in this region—an interesting reflection of history, since control of this region was hotly disputed by Plymouth and Rhode Island during the early colonial era.

Before heading down to Newport, you may want to pause for a side trip across the Sakonnet River to Tiverton and Little Compton. This is great territory for wandering in unspoiled land. It is curious that this pocket of almost timeless rural New England, both in Rhode Island and in southern Massachusetts, remains largely untouched by suburbia and shopping malls in an area less than an hour's drive from Providence, Fall River, and New Bedford.

The lovely, quiet roads of the east shore area resemble English lanes—many of them unsigned. When driving through this undisturbed landscape we have followed our instincts and our noses to get from one place to another; a good map and a compass would make it easier. This is also a superb area for cycling, with many almost-deserted country roads to explore.

TIVERTON

Sitting in the middle of the old boundary dispute between Plymouth Colony and the Rhode Island colony, Tiverton was incorporated in 1694 as part of the Massachusetts colony, which by this time included Plymouth. In 1746 a royal decree reversed that, placing Tiverton within the boundaries of Rhode Island. But the dispute was not over, and Massachusetts reclaimed part of the town in 1862.

Today Tiverton is a resort town located at the narrowest and most accessible part of the Sakonnet River, with a waterfront now filled with marinas and boatyards.

HISTORICAL SITES and MUSEUMS

Fort Barton (401-625-6700), Highland Rd., was the troop staging place for the invasion of Aquidneck Island and Newport, leading to the Battle of Rhode Island in 1778. An observation tower and 3 miles of walking trails await visitors.

Nearby is the **Chase Cory House** (401-624-2096), at 3908 Main Rd., Tiverton Four Corners. Open June–Sep., Sun. This gambrel-roof building offers exhibits of paintings, clothing, and model ships.

LITTLE COMPTON

A monument to Elizabeth Pabodie stands in the Commons Burial Ground here. Elizabeth was the first girl of European ancestry born in New England, a daughter of Pilgrims John and Priscilla Alden.

A set of inscriptions on gravestones in the same burial ground gives a curious sense of feeling of the time: "Lydia, wife of Mr. Simeon Palmer" is one, and the other: "Elizabeth, Who Should Have Been the Wife of Mr. Simeon Palmer."

HISTORICAL SITES and MUSEUMS

The **Wilbur House, Barn, and Quaker Meeting House** (401-635-4035; www .littlecompton.org), on West Rd., was begun in the 17th century and completed in the 19th century. Open mid-June–mid-Sep. It is the home of the Little Compton Historical Society. The house contains period furnishings, and the barn houses New England farm tools and vehicles.

ADAMSVILLE

In Adamsville, on the Massachusetts border, Gray's Store (401-635-4566) at 4 Main St. was built in 1788 by Samuel Church. It is one of the oldest operating stores in the country. Visitors and shoppers will find the original soda fountain, aged cheddar cheese, penny candy, antiques, vintage clothing, and collectibles.

PORTSMOUTH

Visitors driving onto Aquidneck—the island of Rhode Island that gave the colony and the state their name—usually head toward Newport and fly right by some other sites of colonial significance in Portsmouth and Middletown. Entering Portsmouth and Middletown on RI 114, 138, or 24 gives you little sense of the older towns that have been cut into pieces by the new roads, portions of which are cluttered with shopping malls and other supporting services for the Newport Naval Station. But you can still find remnants of the first settlement on the island, now commonly called by its Indian name, Aquidneck. The two highways, 114 and 138, known locally as East and West Main Roads, follow roughly the Indian trails that the colonists made into roads.

Anne Hutchinson and her followers, after being banished from Boston, came overland in 1638 and established their settlement at **Founder's Brook**, off Boyd's Lane. A bronze and stone marker holds the inscription of the Portsmouth Compact, which outlined the first democratic form of government in the colony and the names of its twenty-three signers.

Butts Hill Fort, off Sprague St., contains redoubts left over from the only major Revolutionary battle in the state, the Battle of Rhode Island on August 29, 1778. Originally built by the British, then controlling Newport, the fort was later held by the patriots. Generals Lafayette, Hancock, Greene, and Sullivan were all here. A memorial to soldiers of the first black regiment to fight, valiantly, for the American flag on that day stands at the junction of 114 and 24.

The battle was the culmination of a campaign to relieve occupied Newport. General John Sullivan of Massachusetts was to prepare 8,000 soldiers for the attack, while the French were to send a fleet under Comte Jean Baptiste d'Estaing to attack the British. However, when all was ready, a surprise British fleet arrived off Point Judith. When a hurricane wreaked havoc with both fleets, the British retreated to New York City for repairs and d'Estaing to Boston. Sullivan did not have enough men to overcome the British force in Newport, and the plan failed.

"Hessians Hole," where many German mercenaries were buried after the 1778 battle, is now a depression in the earth just west of Route 114 where it joins Route

24, between Freeborn and Baker Streets. Appropriately, it is just north of the memorial to black soldiers; the Hessians had been killed in action against the black regiment. According to legend, on foggy nights some tall Hessian ghosts continue their march.

The **Portsmouth Historical Society** (401-683-9178), on the corner of East Main Rd. and Union St., has several historic buildings. Open Memorial Day–Columbus Day on Sun. The Old Stone Schoolhouse dates from 1716 and contains antique desks, school bells, and textbooks. The Old Union Church and the Portsmouth Town Hall are on the grounds.

MIDDLETOWN

Squeezed in between Portsmouth and Newport on Aquidneck Island is Middletown, which split off from Newport in the 1750s. The eastern end of the British defenses of Newport, 1776–79, was marked by **Green End Fort** (401-847-1993). The site is located on the north side of Vernon Avenue, off Miantonomi Avenue. The redoubt is still visible and is marked with a plaque.

Prescott Farm (401-847-6230; www.newportrestoration.org), 2009 W. Main Rd. Open Mon.–Fri., May–Oct. The farm has buildings from 1730 and 1790, restored by the Doris Duke Restoration Foundation, as well as woodland paths and a pond to explore. It was also the site of a significant raid during the British occupation of Newport. On July 7, 1777, a group of colonists led by Major William Barton landed their boats on Aquidneck Island, burst into the farmhouse where they knew a high-ranking British officer was staying, and grabbed General William Prescott, commander of the British troops. Totally surprised, he was taken in his nightclothes, rowed back to the mainland, and kept in Providence until he was exchanged for captured American general Charles Lee.

The town also contains a site associated with the mainstream of European intellectual life in the 18th century. Dean George Berkeley, philosopher, educator, and later an Anglican bishop in Ireland, lived in town from 1729 to 1731. He built a home, which he named Whitehall. **Whitehall Museum House** (401-846-3116) is at 3ll Berkeley Ave. Open July–Aug., Tue.–Sun. When Berkeley returned to Ireland, his library and the house were given to Yale College, where he is remembered in Berkeley College. The house contains period furnishings. It is owned by the Rhode Island chapter of the National Society of Colonial Dames.

NEWPORT

Although Newport was the fifth-largest city in colonial America, its early history is often overshadowed in a visitor's imagination by more recent eras—the grand showplace "cottages" of industrial magnates newly minted in the boom after the Civil War. Newport remains an active naval educational center and is the acknowledged yachting capital of the eastern seaboard, former home of the America's Cup and starting point for the Bermuda Race, and the site of such extravaganzas as the Newport Jazz Festival.

And there is more—a string of regattas, concerts, parties, and special tours in the cottages, conferences throughout the year—enough to justify construction of new hotels and a large visitor center. Almost everyone can find a good excuse to come to Newport.

Still a popular place to "summer," Newport was enjoyed for that purpose as early as the 1720s, as South Carolina plantation families came here to escape the heat. But even more remarkable than Newport's longevity as a summer resort is the fact that hundreds of its colonial-era houses are still standing and lived in today. Clustered along its two main original thoroughfares, Thames and Spring Streets, the historical district encompasses one of the finest collections of 17th- and 18th-century houses in America.

From the beginning Newport and the bay beyond attracted visitors who wished to stay. Giovanni da Verrazano, the first recorded European explorer on this coast, reported in his journal his impression of beautiful Narragansett Bay as he lingered

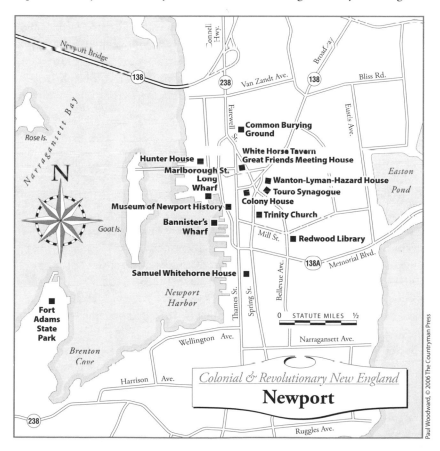

here in 1524. In 1639, a group of people split off from Anne Hutchinson's settlement at Portsmouth and moved to Newport, and as any visitor can see, their choice of site was fortunate. With a marvelous harbor near the open sea, Newport prospered. Ships from Newport engaged in a "triangular trade" to Africa with rum, from there to the West Indies with slaves, and back to Newport with spermaceti for candles, mahogany for furniture, and molasses to distill into more rum.

Easy access to and from the sea had its dangers, too, and the city was vulnerable during the Revolution. With most of its leading merchants Loyalists, Newport was occupied by the British from 1776 to 1779. It was a harsh time for many, as British soldiers were quartered in colonists' homes and even dismantled some houses to procure firewood. In 1780, following the British evacuation as their war effort shifted to the South, French admiral de Ternay and Comte de Rochambeau arrived with four thousand French soldiers. Rochambeau stayed in Newport for a year before departing overland, also for the South, where his forces became a critical element in the victory at Yorktown in 1781.

> Like mysteries? Sea lore is full of wrecks, collisions, and a variety of disasters, but the most enigmatic stories deal with ships that have been abandoned for no apparent reason. In 1750 local fishermen noticed a ship that headed for shore and beached itself without a crew in sight. The fishermen went on board and found a dog on deck, a cat in the cabin, and coffee boiling on the stove. Not a soul was on board the Newport-bound vessel *Sea Bird*.

HISTORICAL SITES *and* MUSEUMS

Because the old historic section of Newport is compact, taking a walking tour is one of the best ways to appreciate its beauty and value.

Newport on Foot walking tours, conducted by Anita Rafael, (401-846-5391) begin at Gateway Center and lead visitors through a "window-peeping" historical exploration, since colonial Newport is still very much lived in. You will hear stories of the earliest settlers who arrived in 1639, and of Newport captains who prospered and built these handsome houses. Some were privateers or smugglers, with secret tunnels from their homes to the water; others ran the slave trade from Africa; and still others ferried summer vacationers to Newport from the Carolinas and the West Indies. The captains' feet trod the walks you will wander, and their families peered out of the windows you will see.

Newport Historical Society walking tours begin at Gateway Center, the Museum of Newport History, and Colony House. At press time the dates of the tours are not final, so please phone the Newport Historical Society at 401-846-0813 or consult their Web site, www.newporthistorical.org/guided.htm. The Historical Society has also created a self-guided walking tour based on markers located through "Historic Hill." A free map is available at the Historical Society headquarters.

The Newport Historical Society headquarters, at 82 Touro St., contains the Seventh Day Baptist Meeting House built in 1730 by local builder Richard Munday, who was responsible for two other famous structures in town, Trinity Church and the Colony House.

The oldest restored house in Newport is the 1675 **Wanton-Lyman-Hazard House** (401-846-0813; www.newporthistorical.org), 17 Broadway. Open Thu.–Sat. This dark red house has a steeply pitched roof, typical of the time when roofers built them steep so the water would run off easily when they were thatched. Colonial governors lived here, and it was the site of the Stamp Act Riot in 1765 when its tenant, a Scottish physician, was run out of town with other royalists who had supported the Stamp Act.

Across the street from the White Horse Tavern is the **Great Friends Meeting House**, built in 1699, the oldest surviving house of worship in Newport. It is owned by the Newport Historical Society and open to the public on occasion.

The **Colony House** (401-846-0813; www.newporthistorical.org), Washington Square, dates from 1739 and is the fourth-oldest government building in the country. Open by appointment June 15–Aug. 30, Thu.–Sat. It was used by the General Assembly from 1739 to 1776 and then as a statehouse from 1779 to 1900. During the Revolutionary War the British used the building as a barracks, hospital, and stable. During the friendly French occupation beginning in 1780, the first Roman Catholic masses in Rhode Island took place in the building.

The **Second Congregational Church**, Clarke St., dates from 1735. It was known as "Dr. Stiles's Meeting House," after Ezra Stiles, who served as minister from 1755 to 1771. Stiles was a philosopher, diarist, and the president of Yale from 1778 to 1795. During the British occupation the British burned the pews for firewood and used the church as a riding ring.

The Artillery Company of Newport, headquartered in the **Military Museum** (401-846-8488; www.newportartillery.org), 23 Clarke St., was chartered in 1741 to protect Newport from invasion. Open Sat. and by appointment. John Malbone was elected captain of the company and conducted drills of his men in full uniform with gun, pouch, ball, and cartridge. These men were trained to take command of other units should the need arise in the colony. The museum, in an 1836 building, contains uniforms and memorabilia from 1741 to the present. Guns on carriages are stored here ready for colonial-era reenactments.

If you like Christopher Wren's churches, Newport has one that was designed by a local builder as an adaptation of Wren's work. **Trinity Church** (401-846-0660; www.trinitynewport.org), Queen Anne Square, Spring and Church Sts., is the home of a congregation assembled in 1698; the first church was built in 1702 and the present one in 1726. An addition was completed in 1762. During the occupation, the British did not damage the building, as it was used for the army's church services. It contains the only three-tiered, wineglass pulpit in the country that is still in its original location in front of the altar. Bishop Berkeley, whose infant daughter is buried in the churchyard, donated the original organ in 1733, of which the casework and original pipes remain in place. The original keyboard is in the Museum of Newport History. It is said that Handel may have tested the organ before it left England, and the first organist was Charles Pachelbel, son of the famous German composer. French admiral de Ternay was buried in the churchyard in December 1780. Oral tradition has it that George Washington worshipped in pew 81 in March 1781.

The **First Congregational Church** (1729), Mill St., has been converted into condominiums. The Reverend Samuel Hopkins, who was minister here, was instrumental in Rhode Island's pioneer move to ban slavery in 1774. Hopkins' character is reflected in an anecdote: Two slaves bought a lottery ticket and won enough money to buy freedom for only one of them—so the Reverend Hopkins paid for the other.

Redwood Library (401-847-0292; www.redwoodlibrary.org), 50 Bellevue Ave. Open daily. It is the oldest continuously used library building in the country. Local merchant Abraham Redwood gave 500 pounds sterling toward the purchase of the original books, all of which came together from London as the model of what a colonial library needed. The building was constructed in 1750 by Peter Harrison and is said to be one of the earliest classical-style buildings in the colonies. The Houdon statue in front somewhat anachronistically represents George Washington, who did visit Newport in the 1750s. Inside the recently restored building is a grandfather clock made by William Claggett of Newport in 1723.

The Old Stone Mill in **Touro Park** has attracted controversy for decades. No one knows the origin and date of the mill for sure. Some wildly speculate that it was built by Norsemen before Columbus arrived, while others more modestly claim that it was built in the 1670s by Governor Benedict Arnold (ancestor of his infamous namesake), who mentioned it in his will as his "stone-built windmill." It was used as a watchtower and a munitions storage depot by the British during the Revolution.

Henry Wadsworth Longfellow's "Skeleton in Armor," a ballad in which a Viking's ghost tells his story to the poet, is partly responsible for the legend. We now know that Vikings did sail from Iceland to Greenland, and from there to Newfoundland around A.D. l000, but did they reach farther southwest to what is now New England? And if so, did they leave behind a stone tower in Newport? The Viking tradition persists but has recently been deflated. In September 1993 a Danish researcher, Jorgen Siemonsen, reported that the tower was built "sometime between Christopher Columbus's first trip to the New World, in 1492, and the Pilgrims' landing aboard the *Mayflower,* in 1620," but that leaves a lot of questions unanswered. For the extensive controversial literature on the topic, seewww.redwoodlibrary.org/tower/millmenu.htm.

The oldest synagogue on the North American continent is **Touro Synagogue** (401-847-4794; www.tourosynagogue.org), 85 Touro St. Open Sun.–Fri., July 1 to the day before Labor Day. It was founded in 1758 by Rabbi Isaac Touro to serve Sephardic Jews arriving from the Caribbean, an extension of the diaspora to the Americas. Historians have not agreed on their origins, but many believe they came from Curaçao in the West Indies, where Rhode Islanders traded, and were attracted by Rhode Island's unique charter that provided for religious liberty. The building, designed by local architect Captain Peter Harrison, was dedicated in 1763.

Inside, the ark of the covenant, the cabinet that contains the tablets of the Ten Commandments, faces east, toward Jerusalem, as does the entire building, which is angled from the street to do this. The interior arrangement is similar to Amsterdam's synagogue and contains five 18th-century candelabra. A secret passage leads out to Barney Street to be used by anyone who needed to leave in a hurry. The General Assembly and the Supreme Court met in this building until the Old Colony House was repaired after the Revolution.

The romance of dining in a colonial setting is topped only by delectable tastes at the **White Horse Tavern** (401-849-3600; www.whitehorsetavern.com), corner of Marlborough and Farewell Sts., which claims to be the oldest operating tavern in the country. Built before 1673, it was called the William Mayes House and also the Nichols House. In 1708 the Newport Town Council began to meet there, also the General Assembly and the Criminal Court. By 1730 Jonathan Nichols had purchased the tavern and placed a "white horse" sign in front.

The Common Burying Ground on Farewell Street is one of several colonial-era cemeteries in Newport. It is just down from the White Horse Tavern. The cemetery has a fascinating array of carved headstones and contains gravestones from the 1670s of settlers born as early as the 1590s. A section of it recently marked with a modern sign, GOD'S LITTLE ACRE, is among the oldest known African American burial grounds in the country and contains what may be the first African artwork in the New World: headstones carved by Zingo Stevens, a slave, later freed, who worked in the shop of local stone carver John Stevens. In the more modern section one can find the grave of a signer of the Declaration of Independence, William Ellery, as well as that of one of the first captains in the U.S. Navy, Christopher Raymond Perry, and his two more famous sons, Oliver Hazard and Matthew Galbraith Perry.

The Revolutionary War headquarters of the French naval squadron under Admiral de Ternay was in **Hunter House,** and it is the place where the admiral died in December 1781. (401- 847-1000; www.newportmansions.org), 54 Washington St., near the Goat Island Causeway and Gladys Bolhouse Way. Open daily mid-June–mid-Sep. The house dates from 1746 and was built by Jonathan Nichols Jr., who was a merchant, privateer, and deputy governor. In 1756 Colonel Joseph Wanton Jr. purchased the house and built an addition. Wanton, a Loyalist, left when British forces evacuated Newport, and the colonists seized the house. The house is named for William R. Hunter, a U.S. senator who bought it in 1805.

Inside are collections of Newport-made Townsend-Goddard furniture, silver, and portraits. The keeping room contains 17th-century furniture, including a William and Mary table, a Jacobean chest, and a Carver chair. The staircase is made of mahogany, with a Jacobean balustrade. The master bedroom upstairs contains a Goddard chest, and 18th-century maps of Newport and Narragansett Bay line the hall walls.

Most visitors to Newport spend a good bit of time on the waterfront, which was of course the center of economic activity for the growing settlement, just as it is today for sailors and shoppers. Buildings in such districts are notoriously subject to change and demolition as one enterprise succeeds another, but some old harbor installations remain in different forms. **Bannisters Wharf** and **Long Wharf,** leading to present-day Washington Square (formerly the Parade), have long histories, the latter stretching back to 1685, when it was called Queenhithe and bounded by Queen and Anne Streets, later King and George Streets. During the Revolution Washington and Rochambeau reviewed the French troops here, and it was also the site of Admiral de Ternay's funeral procession to Trinity churchyard.

At the foot of Washington Square, the **Museum of Newport History** (401-841-8770 or 401-846-0813; www.newporthistorical.org) is located in the Brick Market, a structure designed by Peter Harrison and built in the 1770s, inspired by the work of Inigo Jones. The museum is operated by the Newport Historical Society and is a perfect place for visitors to orient themselves. Admission is free. Exhibits include displays on Newport's early maritime and religious history and furniture making. You can also see James Franklin's original printing press, for which his younger brother Ben learned to set type before the Franklins left Boston and James became Rhode Island's first printer.

Around Washington Square are several important colonial buildings, including the home of the deputy governor, now a bank, where the future Brown University was established in 1764, and, across the square, the house once owned by the War of 1812 naval hero Oliver Hazard Perry.

Farther to the south is the **Samuel Whitehorne House** (401-847-2448 or

---

 While you are on the waterfront, you may want to try another colonial-era restaurant, the **Clarke Cooke House** (401-849-2900), at Bannister's Wharf. Here is one of their popular recipes:

Indian Pudding

6 cups half and half	¼ teaspoon ginger	2½ cups molasses
13⅓ ounces corn meal	¼ teaspoon cinnamon	4 ounces sugar
5 ounces white rum	5⅓ cups milk	¼ teaspoon nutmeg

Heat 1 cup of the half and half and 1 cup of milk. Stir in corn meal and spices. In another pot, place butter, remaining milk, half and half, sugar, and rum. Bring to boil. Add first pot to second. Add molasses and boil until thick. *Yield: 2 gallons*

401-849-7300; www.newportrestoration.org), 416 Thames St. Open May–Oct. One of only two Federal-style homes in Newport, it is operated by the Newport Restoration Foundation and contains the collection of colonial Newport furniture from the period 1725 to 1790 gathered by Doris Duke. She was instrumental in saving much of Newport's colonial fabric from the developers in the 1960s and 1970s.

Along the southern shore of Newport Harbor is a statue honoring the Comte de Rochambeau, and at **Fort Adams State Park** (401-841-0707) the Fort Adams Trust maintains the fort, which is from the 1820s. A loan exhibit from the nearby Naval War College Museum provides information on local naval history, including the French military and naval activities in 1778 and 1780–81.

LODGING

ADELE TURNER INN
93 Pelham St., Newport, RI 02840
800-845-1811, 401-847-1811;
www.adeleturnerinn.com
Listed on the National Historic Register, this home dates from 1855 and is known for its 27 arched windows.

ADMIRAL FARRAGUT INN
3l Clarke St., Newport, RI 02840
800-524-1386, 401-848-5300;
www.innsofnewport.com
The inn is located in the 1750 Robert Stevens House. During the Revolution some of General Rochambeau's aides lived there, including Swedish count Axel von Fersen, who was romantically linked with Marie Antoinette and later drove the coach for Louis XVI's flight from Paris to Varennes in 1791.

ADMIRAL FITZROY INN
398 Thames St., Newport, RI 02840
866-848-8780, 401-848-8000;
www.admiralfitzroy.com
The inn was built in 1854 by architect Dudley Newton. Fitzroy was skipper of Charles Darwin's *Beagle*.

CASTLE HILL INN
590 Ocean Dr., Newport, RI 02840
888-466-1355, 401-849-3800;
www.castlehillinn.com
The mansion was built by Alexander Agassiz in 1877, who established his marine laboratory on the point. Guest rooms are in the main house as well as on the shore.

THE CHANLER HOTEL
117 Memorial Blvd.,
Newport, RI 02840
866-793-5664, 401-847-1300;
www.thechanler.com
This brick and stucco mansion was built in the 1870s. It overlooks First Beach and the ocean.

CLIFFSIDE INN
2 Seaview Ave., Newport, RI 02840
800-845-1811, 401-847-1811;
www.cliffsideinn.com
The house was built in 1880 by Governor Swann of Maryland as a summer residence. The artist Beatrice Turner, who specialized in painting self-portraits, lived there later.

FRANCIS MALBONE HOUSE
392 Thames St., Newport, RI 02840
800-846-0392, 401-846-0392;
www.malbone.com
Colonel Francis Malbone, who built this home in 1760, made his fortune as a shipping merchant.

HOTEL VIKING
1 Bellevue Ave., Newport, RI 02840
800-556-7126, 401-847-3300;
www.hotelviking.com
This hotel in the historic area originally opened in 1926 to house an overflow of "cottage" guests.

THE JAILHOUSE INN
13 Marlborough St., Newport, RI 02840
800-427-9444, 401-847-4638;
www.historicinnsofnewport.com
The inn is a renovated 1722 Newport jail.

THE MELVILLE HOUSE
39 Clarke St., Newport, RI 02840
800-711-7184, 401-847-0640;
www.melvillehouse.com
Owner John Odlin hosted soldiers of
Rochambeau's French army here in 1780.
It is right around the corner from Brick
Marketplace St.

THE PILGRIM HOUSE
123 Spring St., Newport, RI 02840
800-525-8373, 401-846-0040;
www.pilgrimhouseinn.com
This house dates from 1809 and is
in the Historic Hill district.

VANDERBILT HALL
41 Mary St., Newport, RI 02840
888-VAN-HALL, 401-846-6200;
www.vanderbilthall.com
This hotel dates from 1909 and is in the
Historic Hill district.

RESTAURANTS

THE BLACK PEARL
Bannister's Wharf,
Newport, RI 02840; 401-846-5264;
www.blackpearlnewport.com

In a sail loft right on the dock; a formal dining room is on one side and a tavern on the
other. The owner had a brig named
the *Pearl*.

CLARKE COOKE HOUSE
Bannister's Wharf,
Newport, RI 02840; 401-849-2900;
www.clarkecooke.com
The building dates from the 1790s when it
stood on Thames St.

CASTLE HILL INN
590 Ocean Dr.,
Newport, RI 02840
888-466-1355, 401-849-3800;
www.castlehillinn.com/Dining
Fine dining at the 1874 summer home of
Alexander Agassiz.

WHITE HORSE TAVERN
26 Marlborough St.,
Newport, RI 02840, 401-849-3600;
www.whitehorsetavern.com
This is the oldest tavern in the country, built
before 1673. Patriots used to meet there.

INFORMATION

**NEWPORT COUNTY
CONVENTION AND VISITORS BUREAU**
Newport Gateway Center,
23 America's Cup Ave.,
Newport, RI 02840
800-976-5122, 401-845-9123;
www.gonewport.com

JAMESTOWN

J ust across the Newport toll bridge, which offers magnificent views of Narragansett Bay and Rhode Island Sound, lies Jamestown, also known as Conan-
icut Island. It was settled in the 1650s by Quakers who made a living raising
sheep and farming. During the Revolution the British had an encampment on
the island.

Today Jamestown is a popular place for vacationers and summer residents; it
still retains a rural flavor, yet is close to all the activity of Newport. Restaurants
abound in the harbor area. One of our favorite places in the state is Beavertail
Lighthouse. Terraced rock faces shot through with quartz receive the brunt of
ocean waves, which crash on the rocks, then swirl down and back to sea. You can
actually see the wind as the fog blows in.

HISTORICAL SITES *and* MUSEUMS

Captain Kidd reputedly buried some of his treasure in Pirate Cave, but we know for certain that the Anglican clergyman who ministered to him on his passage from New York to London for his trial was the Reverend James Honeyman, who for half a century was the minister at Newport's Trinity Church. Kidd may have often visited Jamestown to see his friend, Thomas Paine, whose house still stands on the north end of the island. Pirate Cave is located in Fort Wetherill State Park (401-423-1771), across the channel from Fort Adams State Park in Newport.

Fort Getty State Park, across the channel from the Narragansett mainland, still has earthworks left over from the Revolutionary War, visible on Prospect Hill.

The striking rock formations at the southernmost tip of Jamestown have always been a landfall for seamen and the site of a lighthouse since the 18th century. At **Beavertail State Park** (401-423-9941 or 401-884-2010), the present Beavertail Lighthouse was built in 1856; the foundations of a 1749 lighthouse were exposed to view by the 1938 hurricane.

In the middle of the island, the **Jamestown Windmill** (800-976-5122), on North Rd. off RI 138, dates from 1787. Open Sat.–Sun. afternoons. The windmill was in use until the end of the 19th century. Also on North Rd., the **Sydney L. Wright Museum** (401-423-7280; www.jamestownri.com/library) contains collections of Indian and colonial artifacts.

Watson Farm (401-423-0005) is at 455 North Rd. in the middle of the island. Historic New England (formerly SPNEA) maintains it as a working farm that fosters the revival of heritage breeds.

Out in the harbor on Rose Island, the **Rose Island Lighthouse Foundation** (www.roseisland.org) maintains a 1912 lighthouse on an island that includes surviving buildings from Fort Hamilton, built in 1798–1800, and Revolutionary War fortifications. Access to the island is by the Jamestown ferry, but parts of the island are closed for periods of the year as a wildlife refuge.

SOUTH COUNTY

The communities in the lower third of Rhode Island west of Narragansett Bay make up Washington County, locally referred to as South County. Inland it includes the Great Swamp and the beautiful campus of the University of Rhode Island, but its most notable features are old lower bay settlements and an almost unbroken coast of superb ocean beaches backed by salt ponds. There are many traces of colonial America in the region, including historic homes, museums, and trails to explore.

The Great Swamp Fight of 1675 was the major battle in King Philip's War. On December 19 the united colonies sent eleven hundred men under Governor Josiah Winslow of Plymouth to attack the Indians. A Narragansett traitor led them over Tower Hill to the Indian fort north of Worden's Pond. The swamp was frozen enough for the men to cross, but they encountered a barrier of a wall of stakes, brush, and tree limbs. They found the one hole in the wall and attacked, then set fire to the village, where many of the women, children, and old people inside were burned alive.

WICKFORD

Dating from 1663, Wickford, the main village in the town of North Kingstown, retains an unusually large concentration of colonial and Federal-era homes. The village was named for the birthplace in Wickford, England, of Elizabeth Winthrop, the wife of the governor of Connecticut.

HISTORICAL SITES *and* MUSEUMS

Smith's Castle (401-294-3521), also called Cocumscussoc, 55 Richard Smith Dr., is the oldest building in South County. Open for guided tours; call for times.

As a friend of Richard Smith, Roger Williams spent time with him in Cocumscussoc and also preached in Smith's home. Both Williams and Smith established trading posts in 1637. The plantation house was built on an estate covering 27 square miles of coastal land. The first house was burnt by the Indians in 1676 at the end of King Philip's War; Richard Smith Jr. rebuilt it in 1678.

The wood-frame "castle" became the military headquarters for Massachusetts, Plymouth, and Connecticut troops in 1675. The Great Swamp Fight, fought at the Indian encampment on Great Swamp near Kingston, saw the colonists victorious and the Narragansetts almost eliminated.

The common grave for 40 of the dead colonists from that battle is on the grounds of Smith's Castle. The grave was once under an apple tree, which blew down during a gale in 1815. Now it is marked by a large stone with a bronze tablet, inscribed "Here were buried in one grave forty men who died in the Swamp Fight or on the return march to Richard Smith's Block House, December, 1675."

Not far from the grave site there is a green box with a lid you can lift to reveal an ongoing archaeological dig. On our last visit part of a wall had been excavated.

Inside, Smith's Castle is furnished with 17th- and 18th-century antiques, china, and utensils. The keeping room has a large fireplace complete with a recipe for Rhode Island johnnycakes on the hearth. Upstairs is a ballroom used for line dancing. Roger Williams owned a chair that is now in the house.

Lodowick Updike, a nephew of Richard Smith, inherited the castle when Smith died in 1692. The property continued down the Updike line through a number of generations (the writer John Updike is a descendant and also a native of Wickford). Over the years the family entertained the Marquis de Lafayette, Benjamin Franklin, and General Nathaniel Greene, among others, in the castle.

Old Narragansett Church (401-294-4357), Church Lane off Main St., is one of the oldest Episcopal churches in the country. It was built in 1707 and was moved to its present location in 1800. Inside, the church organ dates from 1660;

the wineglass pulpit looks out onto square box pews. Queen Anne sent a silver baptismal basin and communion service inscribed with the royal insignia and "Anna Regina"—it was melted down and made into a number of plates, by order of the vestry, after the Revolution. James MacSparren baptized Gilbert Stuart here on April 11, 1756.

SAUNDERSTOWN

The first snuff mill in the colonies was started by a Scottish emigrant and his wife on the Mettatuxet River, and it grew into Saunderstown. During the spring, herring swim up to the pond above the mill dam.

HISTORICAL SITES and MUSEUMS

If you're curious about snuff, visit the **Gilbert Stuart Birthplace** (401-294-3001), 815 Gilbert Stuart Rd. Open Apr.–Oct., Thu.–Mon. This was his father's snuff mill, where Gilbert was born in 1755. The gambrel-roof mill is located on the bank of the Mettatuxet in a picturesque setting and is equipped with a waterwheel and a fish ladder.

The lower floor of the mill is alive with large wooden gears and meshing teeth to supply the power for grinding tobacco into snuff. A heavy, pewter-covered iron ball roller does the job. In colonial days women took snuff as well as men, but behind closed doors.

In addition to the snuff mill downstairs you'll see household pieces, including a 1680 spinning wheel, a cooper's bench and draw knife, a butter skimmer, a cottage cheese press, a weasel to measure yarn, a butter churn, and more.

Upstairs are several paintings of George Washington, including one from the first sitting, and another unfinished portrait. Stuart painted six presidents and their wives. The house includes period furnishings such as a rope bed, a 1740 cradle, a tripod candle holder, a bed warmer, and a trundle bed.

Casey Farm (401-295-1030), on MA 1A, is an 18th-century farm on Narragansett Bay. Open Sat. The area was included in the Boston Neck Purchase of 1636 but not settled until 1702 because of Indian wars and disputes with Connecticut. The current house was built in the 1740s by Daniel and Mary Coggeshall of Newport as the country seat of a well-to-do merchant. It contains the original 300 acres and is large enough to be considered one of the South County plantations. In 1789 the Coggeshalls' daughter Abigail moved into the house with her husband, Silas Casey, and the house was kept in the family until 1955, when it was bequeathed to the Society for the Preservation of New England Antiquities.

SOUTH KINGSTOWN

The town of South Kingstown comprises nearly a quarter of the area of South County, covering most of the southeastern quadrant with the exception of the coastal area east of the Saugatucket River and around Narragansett. This is the place to drive on slow winding roads past 18th- and 19th-century homes. Worden's Pond is the largest lake in Rhode Island. Beaches include Sand Hill Cove and the Galilee State Beach.

HISTORICAL SITES
and MUSEUMS

Hannah Robinson's Rock is located at the intersection of US 1 and MA 138. There's an observation tower here for the view. Hannah Robinson fell in love with a French dancing teacher, Peter Simon, who serenaded her from the lilac bushes below her window. Her father was not pleased with the match, so she eloped after telling him that she was going to a dance given by her uncle, Lodowick Updike, at Smith's Castle. Later she fell upon hard times, returned home ill, and paused on her litter at that spot for a final view of the countryside she loved. After reaching her childhood home, Hannah died the same night.

At the foot of **Tower Hill,** near the Pettaquamscutt River, Thomas Carter, a convicted murderer, was hanged in chains in 1751. His body, then his bones,

Do the Norse sagas describe the landing of Leif Eriksson in Narragansett Bay? Researchers have followed the routes of the Viking exploration and uncovered a number of clues that point to this area. The configuration of the land, with a large bay (geologically a fjord), and the mouth of the Narrow River with a sandbar across match the place where Leif Ericksson went aground, since it is navigable only at high tide. The lake mentioned in the sagas could be Pettaquamscutt Cove, and the cliffs are in the right place. The native people could have been the Narragansetts, and Block Island fits the description of the offshore island.

swung there for many years, a grisly reminder of colonial justice. After the gallows rotted, the irons containing his bones were taken to the blacksmith shop of Joseph Hull, who had made the irons; he removed the bones and salvaged the irons.

Apparently Thomas Carter had met William Jackson on the road, pretended to be ill, and played on Jackson's sympathy enough to ride his horse while Jackson walked. They stopped for the night at a Mrs. Nash's house, and she noticed a round spot on Jackson's hair. During another stop a Mrs. Combs noticed a mismatched button on Jackson's vest. Near Tower Hill Carter hit Jackson on the head with a stone and Jackson ran, but Carter caught him and beat him to death. He dragged the body down the hill and pushed it under the ice. After a fisherman found the body, Mrs. Nash

Mysterious sightings were passed down through New England lore, including this one: Someone reported a mysterious happening on a foggy night near Kingston. As he rode home on horseback, his horse stopped and three pair of legs marched by . . . without bodies attached.

identified Jackson by the spot on his head and Mrs. Combs by the button. Carter was convicted of killing Jackson and robbing him of 1,080 pounds.

Call ahead to see when **Carpenter's Grist Mill** (401-783-5483) is grinding. Samuel E. Perry built the mill in 1703 on Moonstone Beach Rd., and it is still a working mill where Whitecap Flint Corn is stone ground by water power. Jonny-cake meal can be used in any recipe calling for cornmeal.

INFORMATION

SOUTH COUNTY TOURISM COUNCIL
4808 Tower Hill Rd., Wakefield, RI 02879
800-548-4662, 401-789-4422; www.southcountryri.com

BLOCK ISLAND

A lthough Block Island is nearly ten miles offshore and reachable only by sea or air, it is technically a part of South County. The island has something for everyone and has long been a mecca for those who want to relax at an island pace and enjoy its recreational offerings. For fishermen there are giant bluefin tuna, school tuna, swordfish, marlin, striped bass, and flounder in the waters off the island. For cyclists there are uncluttered roads with gradual inclines and beautiful views. For sailors who flock to Block Island Race Week it provides competition with a stunning collection of ocean-racing yachts. And for swimmers there are superb beaches everywhere. The ones on the east side are better for swimming when the afternoon southwesterly is blowing hard.

The island also has a history that stretches back into the early colonial era. Adrian Block discovered the island in 1614 and named it for himself, and the first settlers landed in Cow Cove in 1661. They were from Massachusetts Bay Colony and had each paid 25 pounds for a share in the island. Settlers' Rock is inscribed with a memorial to the brave people who set foot upon the island to stay.

In 1662 Block Island became part of Rhode Island at the settlers' wishes, but that did not protect them from continued depredations by pirates. One of the most notorious incidents was the raid by the Frenchman William Trimming, who tricked the islanders, imprisoned them, and plundered their houses in 1689. Privateer and piratical raids lasted throughout most of the 18th century, and even the Revolution brought little relief, since deserters from both armies flocked to the island.

Shipwrecks were frequent on an island that then had no sheltered deepwater harbor, and one of them became infamous. In 1732 the *Palatine* left Rotterdam laden with Dutch families who were on their way to Philadelphia. Most of them were poisoned by polluted drinking water, and even the captain died. Then they encountered a blizzard off Block Island, ran aground, and the crew abandoned ship. There is a legend that local Block Islanders lured the ship onto rocks just after

Christmas and then set her on fire when it looked as if she might be heading out to sea. The passengers dove into the water, and most of them did not survive. One woman, according to the legend, refused to leave the ship, and her screams were heard as the ship headed to sea. Some islanders say that during a storm her voice can still be heard. Palatine Graves, one and a half miles southwest of Cooneymus Road near Dickens Point, mark the spot of those who died. But there is evidence against this version of the story, some of which surfaced in response to John Greenleaf Whittier's poem "The Palatine."

HISTORICAL SITES *and* MUSEUMS

The **Block Island Historical Cemetery** overlooks New Harbor. Many 17th-century settlers are buried here.

The **Block Island Historical Society** (401-466-2481) is at Bridgegate Square. Open daily during the summer season. The museum has both permanent and special exhibits on the history of the island. Pottery made by the Manisses tribe is also displayed.

LODGING

THE ATLANTIC INN
High St., Block Island, RI 02807
800-224-7422, 401-466-5883;
www.atlanticinn.com
This 1879 inn has a wraparound veranda where guests can catch summer breezes and the beautiful view. The hotel is open seasonally.

THE 1661 INN AND HOTEL MANISSES
Spring St., Block Island, RI 02807
800-626-4773, 401-466-2421;
www.blockislandresorts.com
Although the 1661 Inn takes its name from the year Block Island was settled, it was built in 1890. Walk across the street to the Hotel Manisses for meals; guest rooms at the hotel are named for ships wrecked on the shores of the island. The Nicholas Ball Cottage is also part of the complex.

SPRING HOUSE HOTEL
Spring St., Old Harbor, RI,
Block Island 02807
800-234-9263, 401-466-5844;
www.springhousehotel.com
The inn dates from 1854. It sits up on a hill overlooking Block Island Sound. The hotel is open seasonally.

RESTAURANTS

THE ATLANTIC INN
High St., Old Harbor,
Block Island, RI 02807
800-224-7422, 401-466-5883;
www.atlanticinn.com
The restaurant offers a full range of cuisine.

HARBORSIDE INN
Water St., Old Harbor,
Block Island, RI 02807
401-466-5504
Diners can watch boating activity in the harbor.

HOTEL MANISSES
Spring St., Old Harbor,
Block Island, RI 02807
800-626-4773, 401-466-2421;
www.blockislandresorts.com
A varied menu is offered.

SPRING HOUSE
Spring St., Old Harbor,
Block Island, RI 02807
800-234-9263, 401-466-5844;
www.springhousehotel.com
The dining room overlooks the water.

INFORMATION

**BLOCK ISLAND CHAMBER
OF COMMERCE**
Drawer D,
Block Island, RI 02807
401-466-2982

BLOCK ISLAND TOURISM COUNCIL
PO Box 356, Block Island, RI 02807
800-383-BIRI, 401-466-5200;
www.blockislandinfo.com
The **visitor center** is on Water Street in
the center of town.

Current Information

RHODE ISLAND TOURISM DIVISION
1 W. Exchange St., Providence RI 02903
800-556-2484, 40l-222-2601
www.visitrhodeisland.com

New Hampshire

Historical
Introduction *to the*
New Hampshire
Colony

C aptain Martin Pring reported "goodly groves and woods and sundry sorts of beasts, but no people" when he sailed up the Piscataqua River— the present-day border between New Hampshire and southern Maine—in 1603. Explorer Samuel de Champlain may have paused at Odiorne Point at the mouth of the Piscataqua in 1605. During his cruise along the New England coast in 1614, Captain John Smith noticed the Piscataqua River as "a safe harbor with a rocky shore."

In 1620, the same year the *Mayflower* brought the Pilgrims to the New World, the Plymouth Company, reincorporated as the Council of New England, had provided grants to John Mason and Ferdinando Gorges for Maine, David Thomson for Odiorne Point, and Edward Hilton for Hilton's Point, Dover. Three years later, Thomson established the first settlement in New Hampshire on Odiorne Point.

Then, in 1629, John Mason received an additional grant for coastal land south of the Piscataqua River all the way to the Merrimack and named it after his home county of Hampshire. Like many venture capitalists who obtained similar land grants in England, Mason was more interested in profit than settlement and never came to inspect the land. But others did, and although the early enticements were sometimes illusory, the settlement of New Hampshire had begun.

Strawbery Banke in Portsmouth

New Hampshire under Massachusetts Rule

By 1641 New Hampshire's four towns—Portsmouth, Dover, Exeter, and Hampton—chose to place themselves under the jurisdiction of Massachusetts. The decision began a political seesaw that lasted until New Hampshire finally became an independent colony in 1692. While their colony was joined to Massachusetts, townspeople conducted democratic town meetings but did not necessarily adhere to the religious practices of the Puritans. However, families were required to attend church on Sunday, and they paid the salary of the minister.

People who chose to settle in New Hampshire had to be persistent in their struggle to tame the rocky soil, clear the forests, and cope with long winters and sometimes hostile Indians. Although farming was difficult, there were other economic opportunities. New Hampshire had produced ten cargoes of masts by 1671, highly valued by the expanding British navy, in addition to other lumber products. Shipbuilding and fishing were also profitable.

A SCHOOL *for* YANKEE INDIVIDUALISM

Jeremy Belknap assessed the character of colonists and the nature of their daily life in his History of New Hampshire, published in 1784:

> The inhabitants of New-Hampshire . . . have long possessed other valuable qualities which have rendered them an important branch of the American union. Firmness of nerve, patience in fatigue, intrepidity in danger and alertness in action, are to be numbered among their native and essential characteristics . . . Men who are concerned in travelling, hunting, cutting timber, making roads and other employments in the forest, are inured to hardships . . . their children are early used to coarse food and hard lodging; and to be without shoes in all seasons of the year is scarcely accounted a want. By such hard fare, and the labour which accompanies it, many young men have raised up families, and in a few years have acquired property sufficient to render themselves independent freeholders; and they feel all the pride and importance which arises from a consciousness of having well earned their estates . . . New-Hampshire may therefore be considered as a nursery of stern heroism; producing men of firmness and valor.

NEW HAMPSHIRE *Time Line*

1603	1604	1614	1623
Martin Pring sails up the Piscataqua River	Samuel de Champlain reaches the Piscataqua	John Smith arrives at the Piscataqua	Settlement by David Thomson on Odiorne Point in Rye near Portsmouth

Endless Indian Wars

Major Richard Waldron emigrated from England in 1635 and became the leader of the colonists at Cochecho (present-day Dover). He opened a trading post and was friendly with the Penacook Indians, holding conferences and signing agreements with them in his home. Chief Wonalancet was a peaceful man, and Waldron knew that.

During King Philip's War, which began in 1675, other Indians fled Massachusetts for the Cochecho village. As they stayed, relationships between the Penacooks and the colonists deteriorated. When Massachusetts troops came to retrieve the escaping Indians, Waldron decided to save the peaceful local Indians by staging a day of war games. As the Indians were surrounded by militias, the local Indians were sorted out and the rest taken to Boston for punishment.

Eventually, Wonalancet was replaced as sachem by his nephew, Kancamagus. Relations with the settlers deteriorated. The settlers took land from the Indians in response to minor problems, and Indians were not allowed to walk in certain areas without permission from Waldron. As many hostile Indians gathered in the area, they planned a massacre. A brave warned Waldron of "strange" Indians who might cause trouble, but that was cover for an attack that had already been planned. During the night the gates were opened by squaws who slept within the garrison. Waldron was among twenty-three colonists killed, while twenty-nine others were taken as prisoners to Canada. The Cochecho Massacre, as it became known, occurred at the start of King William's War (1689–97), which stirred up more trouble between colonists and French-backed Indians, who attacked settlements in Salmon Falls, Exeter, Durham, and Portsmouth.

The depressing pattern of Indian relations continued with Lovewell's War (1721–25), also known as Father Rasle's War for the French Jesuit missionary accused by the English of instigating raids by the Abenaki Indians. The war amounted to a series of bloody guerrilla skirmishes and raids, during one of which Father Rasle was killed. In 1724, a group of scalp bounty hunters led by Captain John Lovewell headed for an Indian village on the upper Saco River. He misjudged the number of Indians and was killed in the encounter. The Indians promptly moved away, and by 1730 a New Hampshire official wrote: "There are no Indians in this province that we know of."

1629	1631	1633	1638	1639
New Hampshire founded and named as a proprietary grant by John Mason	Edward Hilton settles Hilton's Point, now Dover	First town government in New Hampshire in Dover	Settlement of Exeter	Settlement of Hampton

The Wentworth Dynasty

Given the long history of overlapping or vague boundaries from multiple land grants, it is surprising that New Hampshire became the first colony to create an independent government during the Revolution. The situation had become so confused by 1641 that residents asked to become part of Massachusetts Bay, an uneasy relationship that lasted for thirty-eight years.

John Cutt was appointed president of the New Hampshire Province, separated from Massachusetts by command of Charles II in 1679, and reported to the king; New Hampshire was the only colony to have this type of royal government. By 1741 there was an independent governor, Benning Wentworth, who, following his father and succeeded by his nephew, maintained a political dynasty that endured until the Revolution cut it off in 1775.

John Wentworth had been appointed lieutenant governor in 1717 and died in office in 1730. His son Benning later served as governor for a quarter century, until 1766, when he began to lose influence and resigned. Benning's nephew John Wentworth II was appointed the following year and served until revolutionary ferment robbed him of effective power. Thus, in contrast to any other colony, a single family had provided leadership through nearly six decades of the 18th century, leaving a heritage of accomplishments and serious problems. John had negotiated a peace treaty with Indians in 1725 and fostered commerce. Benning's political skills managed to keep some minimal balance

In 1697 Penacook Indians abducted Hannah Dustin from her bed in Haverhill, Massachusetts, just one week after she had given birth to a child. With two other women, she was taken as a captive to the Concord area. On the journey, while the Indians were asleep, the three women split their captors' heads open with hatchets and escaped in a canoe. They carried ten scalps back to Haverhill and received a bounty of fifty pounds. There is a marker describing this ordeal in Boscawen on the US 3 and 4 bypass north of Concord.

between established coastal interests and burgeoning inland growth, and in the process he acquired great wealth, lived lavishly, and used his connections in England, patronage, and nepotism to maintain his influence until a backlash finally

NEW HAMPSHIRE *Time Line*

1641	**1679**	**1689**	**1725**	**1727**
New Hampshire under jurisdiction of Massachusetts	New Hampshire becomes a separate royal province	Cochecho Massacre in Dover	Lovewell's War with the Pequawket Abenakis	Settlement of Penacook (Concord)

destroyed it. His young nephew John tackled some of New Hampshire's problems—especially the long-suppressed rights of inland towns—and improved the financial stability of the colony before the events of 1775 ended his role.

Many of New Hampshire's problems emerged from Benning Wentworth's unusual method of granting townships. With each grant he kept a tract for himself, usually 350 acres or more; he also took a fee for each transaction. Seventy-five townships were either granted or incorporated in the colony during his long tenure. He also took to granting land west of the Connecticut River (later Vermont). New York, which also claimed the territory, followed suit. The result was a jurisdictional dispute between the so-called New Hampshire Grants and New York that lasted a full twenty years, until Vermont became the fourteenth state in 1791. The "Green Mountain Boys" of Vermont, a group that became legendary during the initial stages of the Revolution, initially gathered to resist New York claims against Benning Wentworth's land grants. Throughout these contentious years the "Boys" were not averse to using force and political chicanery—including overtures to bring the grants back under British rule as a province of Canada. (But that is a story told more fully in the chapter on Vermont.)

The Wentworth family was also involved in the founding of Dartmouth College when Eleazar Wheelock moved his school for Indians from Lebanon, Connecticut, to Hanover, on the eastern bank of the Connecticut River, in 1769. Wheelock, an ambitious Congregational minister and missionary, had political as well as religious aims in converting powerful Indians to control the frontier. John Wentworth II granted the college a royal charter and endowed it with forty thousand acres. During his tenure as governor, the legislature also agreed to a lottery for the benefit of the college in 1773. So the 20th-century New Hampshire lottery—a famous device for sidestepping state taxation—has historical precedent.

Revolutionary Warriors

Although there were Loyalists among the wealthier citizens of Portsmouth and the colony's other coastal towns, as well as among the scattering of prosperous farmers inland, support for independence gained rapidly from 1773 onward. In response to the Tea Act of that year a public meeting in Portsmouth suggested a

1741	**1751**	**1776**	**1788**
Benning Wentworth becomesfirst New Hampshire governor	Settlement of Derryfield (Manchester)	New Hampshire establishes the first independent government in the colonies	New Hampshire becomes the ninth state to ratify the U.S. Constitution

union of the colonies, and the Intolerable Acts in 1774 produced both outrage in many New Hampshire towns and help for Boston.

In 1774 the "Portsmouth Alarm," as historian David Hackett Fischer terms it, could indeed be called the first battle of the Revolution. On December 13 Paul Revere rode from Boston to Portsmouth with a warning (actually mistaken) that troops on board British warships were coming to reinforce Fort William and Mary, at the mouth of the Piscataqua. On this news four hundred New Hampshire men stormed the fort, confined its six defenders—who had actually resisted with cannon and small-arms fire—scooped up as much powder as they could carry, and loaded it into boats bound for local towns. And they returned the next night to remove everything but the heavy cannons.

Four months later, when the alarm of Lexington and Concord reached New Hampshire, 1,200 militiamen marched toward Boston that evening, and it is estimated that a few days later thousands more untrained New Hampshire volunteers had reached the forces gathering for the siege of Boston. At the Battle of Bunker Hill, 911 New Hampshire volunteers fought, and 107 were casualties. So it is no accident that "Live free or die," written by General John Stark, one of New Hampshire's Revolutionary War heroes, is now the state motto. During the Revolution New Hampshire men served in major and minor battles throughout the theater of war, but the home province did not suffer any fighting on its own soil.

New Hampshire men were also busy aboard privateers along the Atlantic coast and as far away as the English Channel and the North Sea. Portsmouth was an active center for shipbuilders; the *Raleigh*, the *America*, and John Paul Jones's famous *Ranger* were all built in Piscataqua shipyards. As the British continued to attack harbors and rivers, George Washington first ordered his men to build a boom of masts and chains to throw across the narrows in the Piscataqua. When the current destroyed the boom, an old ship was sent to the bottom to block the entrance.

Regions *to* Explore

COASTAL REGION

New Hampshire has just 18 miles of Atlantic seafront but in that short distance packs in stunning views, fine beaches, a network of protected harbors on the Piscataqua, and many historical sites. From Hampton Beach on the southern end to Portsmouth and New Castle on the river boundary

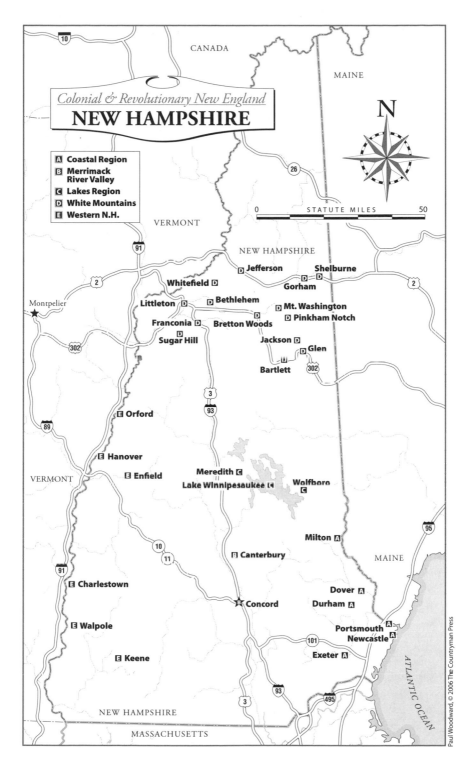

Colonial & Revolutionary New England
NEW HAMPSHIRE

A Coastal Region
B Merrimack River Valley
C Lakes Region
D White Mountains
E Western N.H.

CANADA

MAINE

N

STATUTE MILES

VERMONT

NEW HAMPSHIRE

Montpelier

Jefferson **D**
Shelburne **D**
Whitefield **D**
Gorham **D**
Littleton **D**
Bethlehem **D**
Mt. Washington **D**
Pinkham Notch **D**
Franconia **D**
Bretton Woods **D**
Sugar Hill **D**
Jackson **D**
Glen **D**
Bartlett

E Orford

E Hanover
VERMONT
E Enfield
Meredith **C**
Lake Winnipesaukee **C**
Wolfboro **C**

Milton **A**

MAINE

E Charlestown
B Canterbury
Dover **A**
Concord
Durham **A**
E Walpole
Portsmouth **A**
Newcastle **A**
E Keene
Exeter **A**

ATLANTIC OCEAN

NEW HAMPSHIRE

MASSACHUSETTS

Paul Woodward, © 2006 The Countryman Press

with Maine, the coastal strip is loaded with beach resorts and, just inland, attractive small towns dating from the colonial era. Hampton Beach has been popular with vacationers for more than a century, and Portsmouth has retained much of its historical integrity through eras of growth and change.

PORTSMOUTH

Blessed with the only large deepwater port between Newburyport in Massachusetts and Portland in Maine, Portsmouth has a proud maritime tradition going back to its founding in 1630. In successive eras it grew and prospered through fishing, the lucrative mast trade for the Royal Navy, shipbuilding, foreign trade as clipper ships fanned out through the world's oceans, and the Portsmouth Naval Shipyard, which has turned out everything from sailing frigates for the early republic to submarines for the Second World War. The compact center of the city has been renovated in recent years, and there are many historical sites to visit, including beautifully restored Georgian and Federal homes. There is also a waterfront park between the river and Strawbery Banke.

Portsmouth was much less exposed to attack from the sea than the early colony at Odiorne Point. One can imagine the delight of the first settlers when they disembarked from the *Pied Cow* and found wild strawberries growing in great profusion along the banks of the Piscataqua. With admirable directness they called their settlement "Strawbery Banke," a name that remained until 1653 when it was abandoned for the more pedestrian "Portsmouth."

HISTORICAL SITES *and* MUSEUMS
Today visitors can stroll through a living-history museum, **Strawbery Banke** (603-433-1100; www.strawberybanke.org), Marcy and Hancock Sts., occupying 10 acres in the "Puddle Dock" section of town. Open mid-Apr.–Oct. Residents wisely chose to restore the area rather than let the wrecking ball destroy an unusually rich cluster of 42 historic buildings. It is truly a "museum in progress," with archaeological digs and ongoing building restoration and historical research.

When you enter Strawbery Banke you will receive a visitor's map that indicates which houses are furnished and can be explored; others, yet to be restored, are available for external view only. There are also a number of shops where craftsmen work at colonial trades, including boatbuilding, cabinet making, cooperage, weaving, and making pottery. Take a look at the orientation film and exhibits to help get a sense of the whole museum.

You can wander into a wide range of colonial structures, including the 1695 **Sherburne House**, which has an exhibit on 17th-century construction. Features typical of a 17th-century building include a steeply pitched roof, large center chimney, and small leaded diamond-paned windows. We know that the house was built at two times because it is not symmetrical and the front door is off center. The original house had two rooms, one up and one down.

The **Shapley-Drisco House** dates from 1795 on the site of an earlier 1692 house. The right half of the house depicts family living in the 1790s, the left half, the 1950s. John Shapley was a commercial fisherman who also transported goods in the coastal trade. The family also kept a shop in the house. Shapley sold the home to James Drisco in 1800.

The 1790 **Joshua Jackson House** site was in the family from 1695 to 1800. Displays provide genealogical information and oral history about the owners.

The **Wheelwright House** belonged to Captain John Wheelwright, whose inventory included "1 sea bed, 1 quadrant, 3 sea coats and 1 old sea chest." He commanded the brig *Abigail* on eight voyages to the West Indies.

The **Jones House** dates from the early 1790s and was built on the site of an earlier structure. Jones was a jack-of-all-trades, working as a farmer, weigher of grains, truckman, and trader. He had a wife and 10 children and so needed this large home. If you're keen on archaeological digs, you can see artifacts recovered from the Marshall Pottery site, the Sherburne House, and other local sites in the Jones House.

The 1766 **William Pitt Tavern** was built by John Stavers; it was a popular gathering place for residents to exchange news, read newspapers, and conduct business. The first stagecoach service from Portsmouth to Boston, the "Portsmouth Flying Stage Coach," left from this tavern. But John Stavers was loyal to the Crown, and in 1775 an angry mob destroyed the sign in front and broke the windows. Stavers was arrested and jailed. In 1776 he signed the Association Test, which was an oath of allegiance to the colonies, and reopened his tavern. St. John's Masonic

 Recipes from the 18th century, handwritten by Mehitable Wendell, are part of the Strawbery Banke collection.

Marmalade Quince
Take the pairing and cores, cover them well with water and boil four hours, then rub it through a wire sieve. Take one-third the quantity of stewed apples strained in the same way and mix them well together. Weight it and put a pound of brown sugar to a pound of the mixture. Add the sugar and let it stand 24 hours, then boil it till clean, taking care not to let it burn, or boil it too much. The hand will have to be used in rubbing it through the sieve.

Fish Balls
Take equal quantities of potatoes and boiled halibut or cod, mix them well together with the hand — To about 4 pounds of the mixture add a tablespoonful of powdered sugar and half pound of butter, and salt and pepper to taste — Then beat up three or four eggs light and mix with it — being careful not to make it too soft make it into cakes about as large as a tea cake and fry in lard.

Lodge met here on the third floor; members of the secret society used a stairway accessible from the rear of the building. Use of the tavern for lodge meetings was briefly interrupted in 1757, when John Wentworth wrote: "Mrs. Stavers lies dead in the house of John her Husband, who, by her being there is impeded from vending his Punch, he therefore determined to put her under ground this afternoon or tomorrow . . . & then I suppose we may again assume our Lodge, that, Since last Wednesday, has been cover'd with the Show of Sorrow."

Before you leave Strawbery Banke for the center of Portsmouth, walk across the street into the attractive gardens of Prescott Park and visit the Sheafe Warehouse (ca. 1705), a remnant of the busy colonial waterfront. Here John Paul Jones supervised the outfitting of the *Ranger;* now it houses a museum of folk art.

Strawbery Banke is only one indication of Portsmouth's passion for historic preservation. While in many cities economic forces often make old houses an endangered species, that's not so in Portsmouth, and a number of the best have survived. The **Portsmouth Harbour Trail** leads you to six historic houses, which you can see in any order you like on a single ticket that is available at any one of them. Most are mansions that represent the affluence of the city's mercantile and shipping interests in the 18th century. You can take a self-guided tour or a guided tour, which is offered Thu.–Mon. from July through mid-Oct. Tours leave from the Market Square kiosk, and reservations are recommended. Call 603-436-3988.

The 1763 **Moffatt-Ladd House** (603-436-8221; www.whipple.org) is at 154 Market St. Open mid-June–late Oct. It was built as a wedding gift for Samuel Moffatt from his father, an English sea captain named John Moffatt. There may have been a tunnel from the house to the waterfront at one time. Later, John's son-in-law, William Whipple, a signer of the Declaration of Independence, lived in the house. There are three floors of 18th-century furnishings and beautifully terraced gardens. Don't forget to pause in the stairwell, to admire the murals and the carving on the staircase.

The **John Paul Jones House** (603-436-8420; www.portsmouthhistory.org), on the corner of Middle and State Sts., is large but fitted out more modestly. Open mid-May–mid-Oct. As you might expect, John Paul Jones stayed here while he was supervising the outfitting of the *Ranger* in 1777 and the *America* in 1781. The house was built by a Captain Purcell, who lived here with his wife, Sarah, niece of Governor Benning Wentworth. After Purcell's death in 1776, Sarah took in boarders, and John Paul Jones was the one most remembered today. The house contains 18th-century furniture, cookware, silver, glass, ceramics, portraits, guns, and a wooden leg—a not uncommon aftermath of naval warfare.

The **Governor John Langdon House** (603-436-3205; www.spnea.org), a Georgian mansion with an imposing facade, is on Pleasant St. Open June–mid-Oct. It was built in 1784 and contains beautiful carving. George Washington visited the house in 1789 and wrote about both the house and his host with compliments. John Langdon was a prominent statesman and patriot and a governor of New Hampshire. His fortune came from shipbuilding and privateering during the Revolution.

Another Georgian mansion, the **Wentworth Gardner House** (603-436-4406; www.seacoastnh.com) is located on Mechanic St. Open June –mid-Oct. It was built in 1760 for Thomas Wentworth, brother of John Wentworth II, the last of the royal governors. Look for the windmill spit in the great fireplace in the kitchen, Bristol tiles in blue or mulberry around most of the fireplaces, hand-painted Chinese wallpaper in the north parlor, and French wallpaper in the dining room. It has 11 fireplaces and fine carving throughout.

The **Warner House** (604-436-5909; www.warnerhouse.org) is on the corner of Daniel and Chapel Sts. Open June–Oct. It was built in 1716 for Captain Archibald MacPhaedris from brick carried as ballast in his hold. The original painted murals are still in place on the staircase, and portraits by Joseph Blackburn hang on the walls. Look for the two murals on the stair landing that portray Indians who were taken to London to meet Queen Anne in 1710.

The lightning rod on the west wall may have been installed under the watchful eye of Benjamin Franklin in 1762. The Warner House is unusual because it is one of four brick buildings in the city built before the Revolution, when New Englanders thought such construction to be damp and unwholesome.

Captain MacPhaedris was related to the Wentworth family by marriage. Benning Wentworth had been appointed royal governor by King George II in 1741, and he rented the Warner House for 10 years while building a mansion on Little Harbor. During that interval one of the parlors was used as a council chamber for the province.

In 1760 Governor Benning Wentworth married again, this time far below his station, to his 23-year-old servant. Henry Wadsworth Longfellow used the occasion as the basis for his poem "Lady Wentworth," in *Tales of a Wayside Inn*:

> And the feast went on as others do,
> But ended as none other I e'er knew.
> When they had drunk the King, with many a cheer,
> The Governor whispered in a servant's ear,
> Who disappeared, and presently there stood
> Within the room, in perfect womanhood,
> A maiden, modest and yet self-possessed,
> Youthful and beautiful, and simply dressed . . .
> Until the Governor, rising from his chair,
> Played lightly with his ruffles, then looked down,
> And said unto the Reverend Arthur Brown:
> "This is my birthday: it shall likewise be
> My wedding-day; and you shall marry me!". . .
> "Marry you? Yes, that were a pleasant task,
> Your Excellency; but to whom? I ask."
> The Governor answered: "To this lady here";
> And beckoned Martha Hilton to draw near.

The Richard Jackson House (603-436-3205), 76 Northwest St. Open June–Oct. This is the oldest surviving house in New Hampshire and Maine. It was built for a woodworker, farmer, and mariner. It has been left unfurnished to feature the 17th-century architecture.

The **Rundlet-May House** (603-436-3205; www.spnea.org), 364 Middle St. Open on the first Saturday of the month, June–Oct. This Federal mansion dates from 1807. Merchant James Rundlet furnished the home with Portsmouth-made pieces and imported wallpapers.

LODGING

THE BOW STREET INN
121 Bow St.,
Portsmouth, NH 03891
603-431-7760;
www.bowstreetinn.com
This historic B&B was a brewery in the 19th century.

THE INN AT CHRISTIAN SHORE
335 Maplewood Ave.,
Portsmouth, NH 03801
603-431-6770;
www.innatchristianshore
This Federal house dates from the early 19th century.

MARTIN HILL INN
404 Islington St.,
Portsmouth, NH 03801
603-436-2287;
www.martinhillinn.com
This historic B&B dates from the early 19th century.

THE INN AT STRAWBERY BANKE
314 Court St., Portsmouth, NH 03891
800-438-3933, 603-436-7242;
www.strawberybanke.com
A 19th-century sea captain's home in the historic district.

SISE INN
40 Court St., Portsmouth, NH 03801
877-747-3466, 603-433-1200;
www.siseinn.com
This 1880s inn is decorated in Queen Anne style.

RESTAURANTS

DOLPHIN STRIKER
15 Bow St., Portsmouth, NH 03891
603-431-5222; www.dolphinstriker.com
New American cuisine in an 18th-century warehouse.

THE LIBRARY RESTAURANT
401 State St., Portsmouth, NH 03801
603-431-5202;
www.libraryrestaurant.com
With bookcases, of course, and stone fireplaces dating from 1785.

OAR HOUSE RESTAURANT
55 Ceres St., Portsmouth, NH 03801
603-436-4025;
www.portsmouthnh.com/oarhouse
A restored 18th-century warehouse serving seafood as a specialty.

EVENTS

Strawbery Banke hosts many events; among the most popular are the 18th-century tea for children in April and Revolutionary War reenactments in June and September. Call or check the Web site (www.strawberybanke.org) for a current schedule.

INFORMATION

GREATER PORTSMOUTH CHAMBER OF COMMERCE
500 Market St., Box 239,
Portsmouth, NH 03802
603-436-3988;
www.portsmouthchamber.org

New Castle

In colonial times a fortified island, New Castle is strategically located in the middle of the Piscataqua, controlling the entrance to Portsmouth. The island town is now accessible by bridge and causeway. Its streets are lined with 18th-century homes. The Great Common, once a World War II army base, is now a recreation area with a beach and a fishing pier.

HISTORICAL SITES and MUSEUMS

Fort Constitution Historic Site (603-436-1552), NH 1A at U.S. Coast Guard Station. This fort stands on a peninsula on the northeast corner of New Castle Island. An earthwork fort, or redoubt, with four "great guns" was built here in 1632, followed by a timber blockhouse in 1666. Later named Fort William and Mary, it received cannon and military equipment from England in 1692.

Four months before Lexington and Concord, on December 13, 1774, Paul Revere rode to Portsmouth with the news that the Royal Navy was en route to reinforce lightly defended Fort William and Mary. The next day the Sons of Liberty and 400 local men stormed the fort, confined its defenders, and carried away 98 barrels of gunpowder, some of which was used at the Battle of Bunker Hill. On the following night John Sullivan and his men returned to take 16 small cannon and other military stores.

Governor Wentworth was powerless to stop the colonists. The local militia ignored him. The council members and magistrates also refused to join him. Even the crew of his personal barge refused to take him out to the fort. Only the eventual arrival of a British warship, the HMS *Scarborough*, put a stop to the patriots' depredations.

In May of 1775, in a series of confrontations, the Assembly wrested effective power from Wentworth. After an attack on his house, Wentworth, his wife, and their baby son fled to the fort to avoid capture. Two months later they sailed for Boston on the *Scarborough*.

In 1791 New Hampshire gave the United States the area where Fort William and Mary was located. The fortifications were renovated and used during later wars. Only the base of the walls remains.

LODGING

WENTWORTH BY THE SEA
Wentworth Rd., New Castle, NH 03854; 603-422-7322; www.wentworth.com
Dating from 1874 and recently renovated, this resort offers a full-service hotel and spa. It has welcomed many dignitaries over the years.

DURHAM

Durham, a few miles upriver from Portsmouth, was settled in 1635 and by 1732 had separated from neighboring Dover. A local hero, Major General John Sullivan, distinguished himself in the Revolutionary War and became a three-time governor of New Hampshire. Sullivan and other Durham patriots took the gunpowder they had seized at Fort William and Mary in New Castle to the old meetinghouse.

Today Durham is a flourishing college town, home to the University of New Hampshire. Originally the College of Agriculture and Mechanical Arts, the school had been founded in association with Dartmouth College in Hanover in 1866.

The **Durham Historical Society** (603-868-5436), Main St., is open during the summer.

LODGING

THE THREE CHIMNEYS INN
17 Newmarket Rd., Durham, NH 03824
888-399-9777, 603-868-7800;
www.threechimneysinn.com
Dating from 1649, this mansion overlooks
the Oyster River and Old Mills Falls.

RESTAURANTS

FROST SAWYER TAVERN
In the Three Chimneys Inn,
17 Newmarket Rd., Durham, NH 03824
888-399-9777, 603-868-7800;
www.threechimneysinn.com
American cuisine with an international flavor.

DOVER

Ten miles upstream from Portsmouth, the emphasis shifts from shipbuilding and seafaring to fishing, farming, and lumbering in Dover. By 1622 this was the spot David Thomson chose to set up his fishery because salmon came to spawn near Dover Point. The next year the Providence sailed into Dover Point with Edward and William Hilton and Thomas Roberts, who had grants from the Plymouth Company. A decade later, in 1633, Captain Thomas Wiggin brought settlers to Dover Neck. Farmers and fishermen were joined by loggers, including Richard Waldron, who made use of the falls of the Cochecho for lumbering. Gradually relations with the Cochecho tribe, which at first had been friendly, deteriorated, and finally exploded in the Cochecho Massacre of 1689.

Once a mill town, Dover has renovated its downtown area and the riverfront. Architectural styles range from colonial to Victorian.

HISTORICAL SITES *and* MUSEUMS

The **Woodman Institute** (603-742-1038; www.seacoastnh.com/woodman), 182–192 Central Ave. Open Apr.–Dec. It has three buildings: two brick structures and the 1675 **Damm Garrison House,** fitted with portholes for guns to defend it against Indian attacks. The museum is furnished with cooking pots, farm equipment, clothing, and colonial furniture.

LODGING

SCHOONER HOUSE INN
17 Portland Ave.,
Dover, NH 03820
877-SUITE-NH, 603-743-3435;
www.schoonerhouseinn.com
This inn overlooks the Cocheco
River. All the suites have full
kitchens.

RESTAURANTS

NEWICKS
431 Dover Point Rd.,
Dover, NH 03820; 603-742-3205
The restaurant overlooks Great Bay and offers all
kinds of fresh seafood.

INFORMATION

GREATER DOVER CHAMBER OF COMMERCE
(603-742-2218; www.dovernh.org),
299 Central Ave., Dover NH 03820.

EXETER

Farther south and not far from the sea, another early colonial settlement developed at Exeter. The moving force was the Reverend John Wheelwright, a brother-in-law of Anne Hutchinson who had been banished from Boston for his religious nonconformity. He chose to settle in Exeter and became head of the first church in town. The deed for his huge tract of land is stored at Exeter Academy, a preparatory school chartered in 1781 and one of New England's most venerable secondary education institutions.

Exeter was one of the first towns to speak openly of independence, to object to demands of the Crown, and even burn effigies of Lords Bute and North. But perhaps the most interesting act of rebellion foreshadowed the Boston Tea Party nearly forty years later.

The Mast Tree Riot took place here in 1734 when David Dunbar, surveyor for the Crown, ordered ten of his men to carve the king's arrow—a mark of royal ownership—on all trees in the Exeter mill to reserve them for the Royal Navy. In response, Exeter men disguised themselves as Indians, broke into Samuel Gilman's tavern, grabbed the surveyor's men, and tossed them out of town. Such events established the reputation of the town, and after Governor Wentworth dissolved the rebellious Assembly in 1774, Exeter effectively became the revolutionary capital of the province.

HISTORICAL SITES and MUSEUMS

The **American Independence Museum** (603-772-2622; www.independence-museum.org), 225 Water St., is in the 1721 home of the colonial governor of New Hampshire, John Taylor Gilman. Open summer and fall. Among the three Purple Hearts given during the Revolution, one rests in this house, along with an original copy of the Declaration of Independence.

The **Gilman Garrison House** (603-436-3205; www.spnea.org), 12 Water St. Also called "the old logg house," it was constructed as a fortified garrison by John Gilman in 1690. The walls were built of enormous logs, and it had pulleys to release a portcullis, or strong door, behind the main door. Peter Gilman added a wing in 1772 to make the royal governor comfortable when he chose to visit Exeter.

LODGING

THE INN BY THE BANDSTAND
4 Front St., Exeter, NH 03833
877-239-3837, 603-772-6352;
wwwinnbythebandstand
This 1809 inn has working fireplaces in every room.

If you want to be closer to the sea, you might also consider Hampton Beach.

NEW GRAYHURST
II F St., Hampton Beach, NH 03833
603-926-2584;
www.grayhurst.com
This 1890 gambrel-roof beach house has a cottage, apartment, studios, rooms, and suites.

RESTAURANTS

TAVERN AT RIVER'S EDGE
163 Water St., Exeter, NH 03833;
603-7727393;
www.thetavernatriversedge.com
This Victorian-style restaurant offers upscale entrees as well as tavern fare.

EVENTS

July: The **American Independence Festival** features colonial crafts people, troops, and more;
www.independencemuseum.org

INFORMATION

EXETER AREA CHAMBER OF COMMERCE
120 Water St., Exeter, NH 03833
603-772-2411; www.exeterarea.org

MERRIMACK RIVER VALLEY

T he second-longest river in New England, the Merrimack was used as the main mode of transportation by the early settlers along its banks. Its valley has had a resurgence as people move there to escape higher taxes and congestion in Massachusetts. Today the area is culturally and historically interesting, with colonial homes, art galleries, and a Shaker settlement to visit.

CONCORD

Lack of access to the sea and Indian troubles slowed settlement in inland New Hampshire, but development was steady along major rivers like the Merrimack. There was a trading post at the site of present-day Concord by 1660, and some colonists arrived during the succeeding years. In 1697 Hannah Dustin, who had been seized by Penacook Indians, turned the tables, scalped them, and escaped.

Settlement began in earnest in 1727 with an influx of people from Massachusetts; they called their town Penacook. They got on well with the Indians until 1746, when five men were killed in the "Bradley Massacre." They were on their way to a garrison house when a large group of Indians suddenly appeared and shot them. The **Bradley Monument**, on US 202, is inscribed with the names of those men.

In 1765 the settlement was renamed Concord. By the time of the Revolution, men from Concord came to fight at Lexington and Concord, Massachusetts.

Today, Concord is a prosperous capital city. It is the financial center of the state as well as a major industrial site and transportation depot.

HISTORICAL SITES and MUSEUMS

The **Museum of New Hampshire History** (603-228-6688; www.nhhistory.org), 6 Eagle Square. Open Feb.–Dec. Displays focus on the history of the state beginning with the Indian chief Passaconaway. Revolutionary War general John Stark and Daniel Webster are featured in the museum. You can sit in a wigwam and hear a Native American storyteller.

The **New Hampshire Historical Society** (603-228-6688; www.nhhistory.org), 30 Park St. Open year-round. The museum offers self-guided tours of its turn-of-the-20th-century building. Revolutionary War flags are on display as well as paintings and changing exhibits.

LODGING

CENTENNIAL INN
96 Pleasant St.,
Concord, NH 03301; 603-227-9000;
www.someplacesdifferent.com
This inn dates from 1892.

RESTAURANTS

THE COMMON MAN
25 Water St., Concord, NH 03301
603-228-3463; www.thecman.com

This colonial-style house is decorated with items from the past. The American cuisine includes an innovative list of entrees plus a make-your-own sandwich deli.

INFORMATION

GREATER CONCORD CHAMBER OF COMMERCE
40 Commercial St. (off I-93 exit 15),
Concord NH 03301;
603-224-2508;
www.concordnhchamber.com

CANTERBURY

The town is small, with 2,067 residents, but it has a village green with a general store, meetinghouse, church, and gazebo.

HISTORICAL SITES and MUSEUMS

Canterbury Shaker Village (603-783-9511; www.shakers.org), Shaker Rd. Open May–Dec. This is one of the best-preserved Shaker communities anywhere; 24 Shaker buildings are open as a living-history museum. (The last practicing Shaker here died in 1992.) The village was founded in 1792 as the seventh of nineteen Shaker communities. The Shakers, who practiced celibacy, devoted their "hands to work and their hearts to God." Shaker furniture includes simple but aesthetically remarkable beds, chairs, chests, work tables, benches, baskets, and more.

Visitors can watch craftsmen weaving, spinning, printing, making brooms and baskets, woodworking, and tinsmithing. You can also sign up for workshops and learn how to make brooms, herbal wreaths, and baskets, or try your hand at woodworking or weaving. When you're hungry try the Creamery Restaurant on the grounds, which serves Shaker-inspired meals.

The following recipes, courtesy of Canterbury Shaker Village, are adapted from *Seasoned with Grace: My Generation of Shaker Cooking,* by Eldress Bertha Lindsay, edited by Mary Rose Boswell (The Countryman Press, 1987):

Cold Rhubarb Tea

4 cups rhubarb stalks, unpeeled, diced   Rind of lemon or orange, grated
4 cups water   ¾ cup sugar
juice of 1 lemon or orange

Simmer rhubarb in water until very tender, about 20–25 minutes. Strain. Add juice, rind, and sugar. Stir until sugar has dissolved. Cool well and serve over ice in tall, clear glasses. Serves 4.

Rose Water Apple Pie

I two-layer pie crust, 9 inches, unbaked   5–7 tart apples
½ cup sugar   dash nutmeg
I tablespoon rose water   dash salt
   diluted in 2 tablespoons water   1 tablespoon corn starch
2 teaspoons margarine

Mix ingredients. Today's cook may want to use more sugar, ¾ cup) and less rose water (½ teaspoon to 1 tablespoon water). Add to pie shell and cover with crust. Cook at 425 degrees 5 to 10 minutes. Turn oven to 350 degrees and cook 45 minutes.

RESTAURANTS

THE SHAKER TABLE
In Canterbury Shaker Village,
288 Shaker Rd., Canterbury, NH 03224
603-783-4238; www.shakers.org
The restaurant is in a former blacksmith's shop. Traditional Shaker dishes are served.

EVENTS

Festivals, demonstrations, workshops, and classes are offered by Canterbury Shaker Village during the season.
603-783-9511; www.shakers.org

LAKES REGION

There are 273 lakes and ponds in this region, and every town and village has at least one. The largest lake is Winnipesaukee, with eight towns sharing its shoreline, which is fringed with mountains in the distance. The smaller lakes, their peninsulas and sheltered bays, home to loons, also have a special charm, as depicted elegantly in the film *On Golden Pond.*

LAKE WINNIPESAUKEE

Winnipesaukee is the biggest freshwater lake in New Hampshire and one of the largest in the United States. Its name means "Smile of the Great Spirit," a fitting tribute to its beauty. There are many ways to enjoy this magnificent lake—by lake cruise boat (originally steamships that delivered summer residents to their docks), rental motorboat, kayak, canoe, or sailboat.

This popular resort destination attracts people to its honky-tonk sections as well as quiet family-style retreats. Be forewarned—there is a huge and occasionally unruly gathering of motorcyclists in nearby Laconia every year in June. However, we have found most riders to be well behaved, though very protective of the polished chrome and paintwork of their quite beautiful machines.

MEREDITH

Meredith, on the northwestern bay of Winnipesaukee, was originally known as Palmer's town, for Samuel Palmer, who laid out most of the land around the lake. It was one of the first towns to have a charter granted by the Masonian proprietors, who had the original land grants in New Hampshire. Some of the settlers were from Salem, Massachusetts, and so the town was renamed New Salem. In 1768 it was regranted and renamed again, this time for Sir William Meredith.

LODGING

THE INNS AT MILL FALLS
312 Daniel Webster Highway,
Meredith, NH 03253
800-622-6455, 603-279-7006;
www.millfalls.com
From the windows of this early 19th-century gristmill, you can watch water cascade down through a series of channels. Four properties are included.

You might want to take a short drive up US 3 to Holderness, on Squam Lake.

THE INN ON GOLDEN POND
US 3, Holderness, NH 03245
603-968-7269;
www.innongoldenpond.com

Dating from 1879, the inn sits on 55 acres and fronts on beautiful Squam Lake, where *On Golden Pond* was filmed.

THE MANOR ON GOLDEN POND
US 3, Holderness, NH 03245
800-545-2141, 603-968-3348;
www.manorongoldenpond.com
The building, overlooking Squam Lake, looks like an English estate with carved and paneled walls and fireplaces.

INFORMATION

MEREDITH CHAMBER OF COMMERCE
US 3 and Mill St., Box 732,
Meredith NH 03253
603-279-6121, 877-279-6121
www.meredithcc.org

WOLFEBORO

This town, on the southeastern shore of Lake Winnipesaukee and adjoining Lake Wentworth, is one of the oldest summer resorts in the country. Governor John Wentworth built his summer home here in 1768 (it burned in 1820; there is a marker on the site). Maintaining its aplomb as the grand dame of the lake, Wolfeboro has become a tidy, upscale, year-round resort town, not far off the NH 16 artery and close to the White Mountains.

HISTORICAL SITES *and* MUSEUMS

The **Wolfeboro Historical Society** (603-569-4997), S. Main St. The complex includes an 1805 one-room schoolhouse, the 1778 Clark House, which is furnished with period pieces, and the Wolfeboro Historical Society Library. The Monitor Engine Company Firehouse Museum is similar to an 1862 firehouse. It has restored firefighting equipment with a horse-drawn hose wagon and an 1872 steam pumper.

Southeast of Wolfeboro, the **New Hampshire Farm Museum** (603-652-7840; www.farmmuseum.org), NH 125 off the Spaulding Turnpike at exit 18 in Milton, offers one of the most complete farm complexes anywhere. The 1780s Jones Farm house was home to Levi Jones, who came from Maine to work in a tavern owned by Joseph Plummer. He married Plummer's daughter, Betsey, and eventually became the owner of the tavern. The buildings display a variety of architectural styles from the colonial period on, and old farm implements date to colonial days as well. Visitors may tour the house, barn, blacksmith shop, cobbler shop, and country store.

LODGING

TUC' ME INN
118 N. Main St., Wolfeboro, NH 03894
603-569-5702; www.tucmeinn.com
This inn dates from 1850.

THE WOLFEBORO INN
90 N. Main St., Wolfeboro, NH 03894
800-451-2389, 603-569-3016;
www.wolfeboroinn.com
The charming original building dates from 1812; a modern three-story addition overlooks the lake.

RESTAURANTS

THE 1812 STEAKHOUSE
In the Wolfeboro Inn, 90 N. Main St.,
Wolfeboro, NH 03894

800-451-2389, 603-569-3016;
www.wolfeboroinn.com
The colonial dining room overlooks perennial gardens. Wolfe's Tavern offers a lighter menu.

EVENTS

August: Old Time Farm Days at the New Hampshire Farm Museum.

INFORMATION

WOLFEBORO AREA CHAMBER OF COMMERCE
Box 547, 32 Central Ave.,
Wolfeboro, NH 03894
800-516-5324, 603-569-1100;
www.wolfeborochamber.com
In the old railroad station.

WHITE MOUNTAINS

Now a very popular vacation destination, the White Mountains were known to early settlers as well. In 1712 Captain Thomas Baker and his men attacked and defeated a party of Indians near present-day Plymouth. Sugar Hill was settled in 1780, and a gristmill was built in Littleton in 1797.

Although the White Mountains offer few colonial and Revolutionary War–era historical sites, we have chosen to include some of the experiences visitors can enjoy in this mountain setting, the most majestic in the East. Early explorers and some hardy settlers were here!

MOUNT WASHINGTON

Darby Field climbed the peak in 1642 with the help of Indian guides, who remained below the summit in deference to the Great Spirit believed to dwell there. Field was searching for precious gems, without luck.

In 1770 white men began traveling through Crawford Notch. Timothy Nash explored the notch when he was hunting in 1771. Because the governor had promised a land grant to anyone who could bring a horse through the notch, Nash and a friend helped the horse up and down rocks with ropes. Settlers followed these trails to found towns to the north.

The Crawford family took in guests early in the 1800s. In 1819 Abel Crawford blazed a trail to the summit, supposedly for the "entertainment" of distinguished visitors like Daniel Webster, Ralph Waldo Emerson, and Nathaniel Hawthorne. After a landslide crashed down Willey Mountain, killing the Willey family, Hawthorne wrote his "The Ambitious Guest" in his *Twice-Told Tales.*

BARTLETT

This land was granted to William Stark and others for their service in the French and Indian War. The village was incorporated in 1790. It was named for Dr. Josiah Bartlett, a representative to the Continental Congress. He was the state's first governor and one of three New Hampshire signers of the Declaration of Independence. He also founded the New Hampshire Medical Society in 1791.

LODGING

THE BARTLETT INN
US 302, Bartlett, NH 03812; 800-292-2353, 603-374-2353; www.bartlettinn.com
The inn has a wraparound porch with plenty of rockers.

GLEN

Glen is located at a major junction of roads and rivers: NH 16 and US 302 intersect here, and the Saco and Ellis Rivers merge.

HISTORICAL SITES *and* MUSEUMS

Heritage New Hampshire (603-383-4186; www.heritagenh.com), NH 16. Open mid-May–Columbus Day. There are 25 theatrical sets, beginning with the earliest settlers who came from England on a ship. Then you will be introduced to some of the people who settled in New Hampshire and details from the Revolutionary War. Special effects enhance each experience.

LODGING

BERNERHOF INN
US 302, Glen, NH 03838
800-548-8007, 603-383-9132;
www.bernerhofinn.com
The 1880s Victorian-style inn is in a convenient location for touring.

COVERED BRIDGE HOUSE
US 302, Glen, NH 03838
603-383-9109; www.coveredbridge.com
The 1850 house was once a covered bridge over the Saco River and is now the gift shop for the B&B.

RESTAURANTS

RED PARKA STEAKHOUSE & PUB
US 302, Glen, NH 03838
603-383-4344
Decorations on the wall include skis from the 1930s.

GLEN JUNCTION
US 302, Glen, NH 03838
603-383-0123
A model train goes around the dining room up above your head, and there is a mural of local attractions.

JACKSON

Enter through the scenic covered bridge off NH 16 and you'll be in a very picturesque village, a center for Nordic skiing in winter and hiking in other seasons. The mountains surround the village, and access into them is easy. Jackson is one of our favorite towns in New Hampshire, largely because it has managed to maintain architectural purity while appealing to visitors who appreciate that and want active, nonmotorized sports in the surrounding mountains.

LODGING

CHRISTMAS FARM INN
NH 16B, Jackson Village, NH 03846
800-HI-ELVES, 603-383-4313;
www.christmasfarminn.com
Of the several buildings on the property, the main house dates from 1766 and a saltbox dates from 1788.

THE EAGLE MOUNTAIN HOUSE
NH.16B, Jackson, NH 03846
800-966-5779, 603-383-9111;
www.eaglemt.com
This historic hotel opened in 1879.

THE INN AT THORN HILL
Thorn Hill Rd., Jackson, NH 03846
800-289-8990, 603-383-6448;
www.innatthornhill.com
Stanford White designed this 1895 mansion. Guest rooms are available in the carriage house and cottages.

THE WENTWORTH
1 Carter Notch Rd., Jackson, NH 03846
800-637-0013, 603-383-9700;
www.thewentworth.com
The main building dates from 1900, and this elegant resort complex has spread out from there.

PINKHAM NOTCH

In 1790 Joseph Pinkham traveled to his new home here with a sled drawn by pigs. He traveled along what is now NH 16, which winds through the pass between Jackson and Gorham. Today there is much easier access to this most rugged area of New England, not only through the notch but also up to the summit of Mount Washington.

If you are bent on getting up into the high peaks of the White Mountains, don't bypass the **Appalachian Mountain Club** (603-466-2721), NH 16, Pinkham Notch. This center offers trail and weather information for the White Mountains, guided walks and lectures, and lodging at Joe Dodge's. For intrepid skiers this is the place to learn about spring skiing in fabled Tuckerman's Ravine. Be sure you want to hike up four miles carrying your skis before you tackle that one!

In summer the AMC Hiker Shuttle encircles Mount Washington, so you can plan to ride all the way around from Pinkham Notch to Crawford Depot and back. Hikers choose which trailhead to spot a car at for pickup after walking down.

Skiing Tuckerman's Ravine (aka "the ravine"), a 35- to 50-degree bowl, depending on how far you climb, is a spring ritual for many hardy New Englanders. After staying overnight at Joe Dodge's and hiking up the trail to the base of Tuckerman's, some in our group chose to sit on Picnic Rocks with cameras and a lunch. The hardy skiers trudged up as far as they dared and looked for a platform to put on their skis. Then they stared down the ravine for a long time before pushing off for abrupt, wild runs—or long falls. The crowd on Picnic Rocks cheered when someone made it down without falling, and sometimes greeted the falling skiers with friendly jeers.

Since 1861 people have enjoyed the "Road to the Sky," **Mount Washington Auto Road** (603-466-3988; www.mtwashingtonautoroad.com), NH 16, Pinkham Notch. You can take a guided tour in an Auto Road van or drive yourself to the 6,288-foot summit of Mount Washington.

At the bottom is a sign warning that you might not want to drive yourself, which we ignored after climbing many mountain roads in the European Alps. Big mistake! It's a white-knuckle ride, especially when cars pass each other and gravel on the road makes your car slide a little toward a precipice. There are no guardrails on the eight-mile road, which has many steep drop-offs, sometimes on both shoulders. We could imagine the fear the original rocking carriage ride behind horses must have inspired. But we were glad we did it—once.

In the same building as the Mount Washington Auto Road center is the **Great Glen Trails Outdoor Center** (603-466-2333; www.greatglentrails.com), NH 16, Pinkham Notch. It offers all kinds of mountain biking, walking, running, canoe, bird-watching, and winter activities as well.

LODGING

JOE DODGE LODGE
NH 16 at the AMC Pinkham Notch Visitor Center
603-466-2727; www.outdoors.org
Here is the place to sleep before a hike. Bunk beds, shared baths, and three meals a day are available.

GORHAM

Gorham is considered the gateway to the Great North Woods. The Appalachian Trail runs through the area. The town was first chartered as a part of Shelburne in 1770 and incorporated in 1836. Sylvester Davis, a resident from Gorham, Maine, suggested the name.

HISTORICAL SITES *and* MUSEUMS

Wilder-Holton House (603-788-3004), 226 Main St., Gorham. Open June–Sep. This is the home of the Lancaster Historical Society. The house dates from 1780.

If you have time to spare, a long, scenic drive up US 2 will bring you to **Groveton Old Meeting House** (603-636-2234), US 3, Groveton. Open mid-June–mid-Sep. The house dates from 1799 and is the home of the Northumberland Historical Society.

RESTAURANTS

WILFRED'S, 117 Main St., Gorham, NH 03581; 603-466-2380
For over 60 years turkey has been a specialty at Wilfred's.

SHELBURNE

The town, chartered in 1769, was named for William Petty Fitzmaurice, the Earl of Shelburne, who supported independence for the colonies. You will see a grove of birch trees as a memorial to the town's soldiers who served in World War II.

LODGING

PHILBROOK FARM INN
North Rd., Shelburne, NH 03581; 603-466-3831; www.philbrookfarminn.com
The main building dates from 1834 and has been run as an inn by five generations of Philbrooks. The Presidential Range is visible from the inn.

JEFFERSON

Jefferson was part of a land grant in 1765, but because it was largely unexplored territory, few people chose to settle here. Colonel Joseph Whipple of Portsmouth built a manor house after cutting trails through the woods. He named the town Dartmouth after William Legge, Earl of Dartmouth and patron of Dartmouth College. The colonel's brother was William Whipple, a signer of the Declaration of Independence. In 1796 Colonel Whipple renamed the town Jefferson, four years before Thomas Jefferson became president. The town has been a summer resort community since the 19th century.

LODGING

JEFFERSON INN
US 2, Jefferson, NH 03583; 800-729-7908, 603-586-7998; www.jeffersoninn.com
This 1896 inn has a veranda with mountain views.

WHITEFIELD

Whitefield was the last town to be granted a charter under the English provincial government, in 1774. The town was named for George Whitefield, an English evangelist and a friend of the Earl of Dartmouth. Other grantees were Jeremy Belknap, a historian, and John Langdon, who became governor after John Wentworth. Whitefield is now a resort town, just off the northern edge of the White Mountains, with wonderful views from some spots.

LODGING

MOUNTAIN VIEW GRAND RESORT
120 Mountain View Rd., Whitefield,
NH 03598; 866-484-3843;
www.mountainviewgrand.com
The hotel dates from 1865, but it remained closed for over 10 years and was then purchased and renovated.

SPALDING INN MOUNTAIN RETREAT
199 Mountain View Rd.,
Whitefield, NH 03598
800-368-8439, 603-837-2572;
www.spaldinginn.com
The Carriage House dates from 1860 and the main building from the turn of the 20th century.

LITTLETON

Littleton was a part of Lisbon until 1770, when it was granted a separate identity as Apthorp, named for George Apthorp, head of a mercantile business in Boston. The land was passed to other Apthorps from Newburyport, Massachusetts. Colonel Moses Little was the surveyor of the king's woods, and the town was renamed Littleton for him. Today Littleton is a commercial center for northwestern New Hampshire, with easy access to the White Mountains. Moore Reservoir offers a recreation center.

HISTORICAL SITES and MUSEUMS

Littleton Grist Mill (888-284-7478, 603-444-7478; www.littletongristmill.com), 18 Mill St., Littleton. Open year-round. This mill has a restored waterwheel dating from 1798. It still grinds out organically grown whole grain and stone-ground flours.

LODGING

BEAL HOUSE INN
2 W. Main St., Littleton, NH 03561
888-616-BEAL, 603-444-2661;
www.bealhouseinn.com
The inn dates from 1833.

THAYERS INN
111 Main St., Littleton, NH 03561
800-634-8179, 603-444-6469;
www.thayersinn.com
This 19th-century inn is in the center of town.

RESTAURANTS

BEAL HOUSE RESTAURANT
In the Beal House Inn,
2 W. Main St., Littleton, NH 03561
888-616-BEAL, 603-444-2661;
www.bealhouseinn.com
Features a copper-topped martini bar.

BETHLEHEM

The town was established in 1774 as Lloyd's Hills and incorporated as Bethlehem in 1799. It was the last of the provincial land grants in the state. Mount Agassiz was named for Jean Louis Rodolphe Agassiz, the explorer and naturalist. The town became a fashionable summer resort during the 19th century, and the long main street (US 302) is still lined with Victorian hotels and large summer homes, many of them restored.

Bethlehem is also home of the Rocks Estate (800-639-5373, 603-444-6228) on US 302. The estate has scenic trails for hiking, cross-country skiing, and wildlife viewing. Many people drive here to buy a Christmas tree.

LODGING

ADAIR COUNTRY INN
80 Guilder Lane, Bethlehem, NH 03574
888-444-2600, 603-444-2600;
www.adairinn.com
The 1927 Georgian-style mansion is handsome with antique furnishings.

THE MULBURN INN
US 302, Bethlehem, NH 03574
800-448-9557, 603-869-3389;
www.mulburninn.com
This 1908 Tudor-style mansion has wraparound porches.

SUGAR HILL AND FRANCONIA

Sugar Hill is the youngest town in New Hampshire, incorporated in 1962, but settlers had lived here long before. A popular summer resort in the 19th and early 20th centuries, it still has a number of operating historic inns. Now it is a satellite town to Franconia, famed for one of the most beautiful notches in New England, the Old Man of the Mountain—now defaced by a rock slide—a beautiful state park, and Cannon Mountain Ski Area. Although many of the grand hotels are gone, the area's rugged mountains still draw hikers, skiers, and just plain gazers from the flatlands.

HISTORICAL SITES and MUSEUMS
Sugar Hill Historical Museum (603-823-5336; www.franconianotch.org), Main St., Sugar Hill. This museum offers a genealogy library, carriage barn, sleigh shed, and changing exhibits. Displays begin with the founding of the town in 1780.

LODGING

FRANCONIA INN
1300 Easton Rd., Franconia, NH 03580
800-473-5299, 603-823-5542;
www.franconiainn.com
The inn dates from 1886, with a view that inspired Robert Frost to write "The Road Not Taken."

LOVETT'S INN
Profile Rd., Franconia, NH 03580
800-356-3802, 603-823-7761;
www.lovettsinn.com
The inn dates from 1784 and also offers cottages on the grounds.

SUGAR HILL INN
NH 117, Franconia, NH 03580
800-548-4748, 603-823-5621;

www.sugarhillinn.com
The restored 1789 farmhouse offers great views.

SUNSET HILL HOUSE
Sunset Hill Rd., Sugar Hill, NH 03586
800-786-4455, 603-823-5522;
www.sunsethillhouse.com
Mountain views from every room in this former annex to a grand hotel once on the site.

RESTAURANTS

FRANCONIA INN
1300 Easton Rd., Franconia, NH 03580
800-473-5299, 603-823-5542;

www.franconiainn.com
Offers Continental cuisine.

LOVETT'S INN
Profile Rd., Franconia, NH 03580
800-356-3802, 603-356-3802;
www.lovettsinn.com
Features fireside dining.

THE RESTAURANT AT SUNSET HILL HOUSE
Sunset Hill Rd., Sugar Hill, NH 03586
800-786-4455, 603-823-5522;
www.sunsethillhouse.com
Captures the view through its large picture windows.

BRETTON WOODS

In 1772 Bretton Woods was named for Bretton Hall, the estate of Governor John Wentworth's family in England. It was renamed Carroll in 1832 for Charles Carroll of Maryland, a signer of the Declaration of Independence. Carroll now includes Twin Mountain, Fabyan, Marshfield, and Bretton Woods. There is no town proper—just a panoramic view of Mount Washington and other peaks in the Presidential Range, a historic grand hotel elegantly restored, the oldest cog railway in the world still operating (invented by a New Hampshire native), a major ski area, and all the amenities associated with both the ski area and the hotel. Visitors are seldom disappointed!

The Mount Washington Cog Railway (800-922-8825, 603-278-5404; www.thecog.com), US 302, Bretton Woods. This cog railway, the first in the world, has been operating since 1869. It is a great way to get to the top without driving and has some fine views on trestles along the way. The cog now also operates in the winter for skiing, going up about one mile.

LODGING

THE MOUNT WASHINGTON RESORT AT BRETTON WOODS
US 302, Bretton Woods, NH 03575
800-258-0330;
www.mtwashington.com
The romantic tale of this grand hotel begins when it first opened in 1902. It was the chosen venue for the Bretton Woods Monetary Conference in 1944, which planned the postwar world financial system and established the gold standard at $35 an ounce. Purchased by New Hampshire businesspeople in 1991, the resort has been updated and expanded with several renovations. On one of our visits they were in the midst of winterizing for year-round operation—adding insulation and replacing 800 windows.

THE NOTCHLAND INN
US 302, Hart's Location, NH 03812
800-866-6131, 603-374-6131;
www.notchland.com
This 1860s granite mansion is located on 100 acres in the White Mountains National Forest. It was built by Samuel Bemis, a photographer from Boston.

RESTAURANTS

THE DINING ROOM AT THE MOUNT WASHINGTON HOTEL
US 302, Bretton Woods, NH 03575
603-278-1000;
www.mtwashington.com
Offers Continental cuisine in a room with stained-glass windows and a view of the big mountain.

FABYAN'S STATION RESTAURANT
NH 302, Bretton Woods, NH 03575
603-278-2222
On the access road for the Mount Washington Cog Railway.

THE NOTCHLAND INN
US 302, Hart's Location, NH 03812
800-866-6131, 603-374-6131;
www.notchland.com

This was once a tavern belonging to Abel Crawford, who lived just down the road.

INFORMATION

APPALACHIAN MOUNTAIN CLUB INFORMATION CENTER
US 302 north of Crawford Notch, Bretton Woods, NH 03575
603-466-2727;
www.outdoors.org
Open Memorial Day through leaf season.

MOUNT WASHINGTON VALLEY CHAMBER OF COMMERCE AND VISITORS BUREAU
Box 320, North Conway NH 03860
603-356-3171, 800-3673364;
www.mountwashingtonvalley.org

WESTERN NEW HAMPSHIRE

KEENE

Western New Hampshire was frontier territory far removed from colonial support through the 17th and much of the 18th centuries and thus considered too dangerous during the almost incessant Indian wars. Yet early settlers lived in Keene in the 1730s, after Nathan Blake built the first log cabin in 1736.

Forty families arrived in 1737 but found it hazardous to go into the fields near their homes because of Indians. In 1747 two people were killed when the fort was attacked, Nathan Blake was captured, and homes burnt. The entire population left town after too many Indian encounters, and the Indians burned the village to the ground; but by the 1750s settlers were back.

Like tourists for a century and a half, we associate Keene with Mount Monadnock and Monadnock with hiking. As a climber of Mount Fuji years ago, one of us was startled by the claim that Monadnock is second only to Fuji in number of climbers. How one would substantiate that claim is mysterious, since the mountain offers a maze of trails to its bald head. The name itself is a generic geological term, referring to a single mountain standing well above a surrounding plain, and that's what makes this mountain so visible for miles around.

Keene itself is a lively small city as the home of Keene State College and a center for services and shopping for the attractive smaller towns and villages of southwestern New Hampshire.

HISTORICAL SITES *and* MUSEUMS

The 1762 **Wyman Tavern** (603-352-5161), 399 Main St., was built by Isaac Wyman. Open June–Aug. He was a staunch patriot who led his friends to Lexington, Concord, and Boston; these Keene Minutemen met in the tavern before beginning their march. Inside the tavern visitors will see the restored taproom, two parlors, a ballroom, kitchen, office, and bedrooms.

LODGING

E.F. LANE HOTEL
30 Main St., Keene, NH 03431
888-300-5056, 603-357-7070;
www.someplacesdifferent.com
This 1890 building was once a department store.

CHESTERFIELD INN
399 Cross Rd., Chesterfield, NH 03466
800-365-5515, 603-256-3211;
www.chesterfieldinn.com
This historic country inn was a farm in the late 18th century.

RESTAURANTS

SALMON CHASE AMERICAN BISTRO
In the E.F. Lane Hotel,
30 Main St., Keene, NH 03431
603-357-7070;

www.someplacesdifferent.com
Enjoy a view of Main Street along with a meal.

THE CHESTERFIELD INN
399 Cross Rd.,
Chesterfield, NH 03466; 603-256-3211:
www.chesterfieldinn.com
Contemporary cuisine in the dining rooms, parlor, and terrace.

176 MAIN
176 Main St., Keene, NH 03431
603-357-3100; www.176main.com
This 1873 building is on the National Register of Historic Places.

INFORMATION

GREATER KEENE CHAMBER OF COMMERCE
48 Central Square,
Keene, NH 03431; 603-352-1303;
www.keenechamber.com

WALPOLE

Walpole is immersed in colonial history, and some of the houses date to the 1790s. Colonel Benjamin Bellows founded the town, and his son John Bellows was active in the Revolutionary War. Once a summer resort, the village now attracts those who appreciate the quiet beauty of its streets lined with white clapboard houses.

HISTORICAL SITES *and* MUSEUMS

Deacon Willard Lewis House (603-756-4861), Main St. This 1826 house is the home of the Walpole Historical Society. Open May–Oct., Wed. and Sat. 2–4 p.m. The collection includes antiques, paintings, photos, and furniture.

LODGING

THE INN AT VALLEY FARMS
633 Wentworth Rd.
Walpole, NH 03608
877-327-2855, 603-756-2855;

www.innatvalleyfarms.com
The 1774 colonial home offers working fireplaces and antique hardware. Cottages on the property have kitchens.

WALPOLE INN
297 Main St., Walpole, NH 03608
603-756-3320; www.walpoleinn.com
The house was built in the 1760s by
Colonel Benjamin Bellows.

RESTAURANTS

L.A. BURDICK CAFÉ
47 Main St., Walpole, NH 03608;

603-756-2882
Ken Burns and Larry Burdick have created
this popular place for lunch or dinner from
a former IGA store.

WALPOLE INN RESTAURANT
297 Main St., Walpole, NH 03608
603-756-3320; www.walpoleinn.com
A collector's artwork is displayed in the
dining room.

CHARLESTOWN

Massachusetts divided up the land in this area and chartered plantations identified by number. Plantation No. 1 was Chesterfield; No. 2, Westmoreland; No. 3,
Walpole; and No. 4, Charlestown. Those who bought property on the plantations
were "proprietors." Proprietors Stephen, Samuel, and David Farnsworth arrived
at Charlestown in 1740, and more followed. This was the most northern British
settlement on the Connecticut River, thirty miles from civilization.

A log fort was built at Charlestown on the river in 1744, at the outbreak of
King George's War, but as the northernmost white settlement it was continually
harassed by Indians. Twelve families lived in this stockaded outpost at that time.
In 1746 Abenaki Indians would not let them outside, so they eventually fled the
settlement. In April Captain Phineas Stevens and fifty of his men arrived to garrison the fort. A year later French and Indian forces attacked, but the militia inside
held on. Later the fort, called "No. 4," would be a rendezvous spot for troops on
their way to Crown Point and Bennington.

As settlers returned they built homes, which line Main Street, now a mile-long
historic district with more than sixty buildings. For those who want to seek out
towns that have maintained their heritage intact, Charlestown is a great find.

HISTORICAL SITES *and* MUSEUMS
Today visitors to **Fort at No. 4** (603-826-5700; www.fortat4.com), Springfield
Rd., will find a living-history museum of the 1740s and 1750s. Open June–Oct.
Buildings include the blacksmith shop, cow barn, great stockade, watchtower, and
several houses and lean-tos. With a map in hand visitors may wander in and out
of the buildings. Costumed guides will tell you about the daily life in the fort during this era.

LODGING

GODDARD MANSION
25 Hillstead Rd., Claremont, NH 03743
800-736-0603, 603-543-0603;
www.goddardmansion.com This 1905
mansion looks like an English manor.

HOME HILL COUNTRY INN
703 River Rd., Plainfield, NH 03781
603-675-6165; www.homehillinn.com
Before the Revolution, Home Hill belonged
to Thomas Gallup, granted to him by King
George III in 1763. It was rebuilt after a fire
and is now a Relais & Châteaux property.

RESTAURANTS

CHARLESTOWN HERITAGE DINER
122 Main St., Charlestown, NH 03603
603-826-3110
The restaurant is in a 1920s building, with rooms also in an adjoining 1820s building.

EVENTS

The Fort at No. 4 sponsors a series of events throughout the season, including the following:

June: Revolutionary War Encampment.
July: Children's Weekend.
September: Militia Muster.
October: Stark's Muster; Garrison Weekend; Pickpockets, Rogues and Highwaymen; and Rogers' Return.

INFORMATION

TOWN OF CHARLESTON VISITOR SERVICES
603-826-4400;
www.charlestown-nh.gov

HANOVER

Dartmouth College was founded in 1769 by Eleazar Wheelock at a time when only twenty families lived there. Dartmouth Row has four classroom buildings, and one of them dates from 1784. However, the first building here was a log hut.

That's a far cry from what you see now in the bustling center of Hanover, where more than five thousand undergraduate and graduate students live and learn. The college surrounds the central square and radiates outward into buildings housing major graduate schools in business, engineering, and medicine, with a research medical center serving the whole region. Always a major player in Ivy League sports, Dartmouth is now more a university than a college, and it remains the engine of Hanover's prosperity and its wealth of cultural institutions far beyond the size of the town.

HISTORICAL SITES *and* MUSEUMS

Baker Library (603-646-2560) faces the green. Open daily. It is a 1928 Georgian-style building and contains murals painted by José Clemente Orozco entitled "The Epic of American Civilization." A 17th-century edition of Shakespeare is in the collection. Nearly two million volumes are housed in the library.

Webster Cottage Museum (603-646-6529), 32 N. Main St. Open Memorial Day–Columbus Day. The Hanover Historical Society operates this museum. The house was built in 1780 for Abigail Wheelock, the daughter of Eleazar Wheelock. Daniel Webster lived here at one time, and some of his possessions remain.

LODGING

THE HANOVER INN
E. Wheelock and Main St.,
Hanover, NH 03755
800-443-7024, 603-643-4300;
www.hanoverinn.com
This Georgian building is owned by Dartmouth College. It dates to 1780, burned, and was rebuilt.

RESTAURANTS

DANIEL WEBSTER ROOM
At the Hanover Inn, E. Wheelock and Main St., Hanover, NH 03755
603-643-4300; www.hanoverinn.com
The formal dining room offers a wide selection of entrees. **Zins Wine Bistro**, also in the inn, has a lighter menu.

JESSE'S RESTAURANT
NH 120, Hanover, NH 03755
603-643-4111; www.jesses.com
Three dining rooms offer different themes:
Victorian, Adirondack, and Greenhouse.

EVENTS
For a full calendar, check with the
Hanover Area Chamber of Commerce.

INFORMATION

**HANOVER AREA CHAMBER
OF COMMERCE**
126 Nugget Building, Main St.,
Hanover 03755
603-643-3115;
www.hanoverchamber.org

ENFIELD

Two Shaker brothers from Mount Lebanon, New York, arrived in 1782 to establish a Shaker community at Enfield, now a small village along the shores of Mascoma Lake.

HISTORICAL SITES *and* MUSEUMS

Enfield Shaker Museum (603-632-4346; www.shakermuseum.org), 24 Caleb Dyer Lane, Enfield. Visitors can see a video for orientation, then tour exhibits that feature Shaker pieces. A walking tour will take you to the Shaker herb gardens. Artisans demonstrate crafts, and workshops are available.

ORFORD

Orford was chartered by the king in 1761. Historic homes along the Connecticut River date from 1773 to 1839 and are known as the "Seven Swans." The oldest house belonged to Samuel Morey, inventor of steamboat prototypes later developed by Robert Fulton. The elegance of the homes, built to Asher Benjamin's designs by local craftsmen, attests to the prosperity of the town.

RESTAURANTS

PEYTON PLACE RESTAURANT AT THE MANN TAVERN
NH 10/Main St., Orford, NH 03777
603-353-9100, www.peytonplacerestaurant.com
This 1773 tavern has a pub room and several dining rooms.

Current Information

OFFICE OF TRAVEL & TOURISM
172 Pembroke Rd., P.O. Box 1856,
Concord, NH 03302
603-271-2665
www.visitnh.gov or www.nh.com

Maine

Historical
Introduction *to the*
Maine Colony

T
he arrival of European ships in the coves and reaches of the Maine coast is a mere blip in the record of human habitation there. Centuries before, Algonquians had migrated eastward to the seacoast and remained, becoming a group of tribes referred to as the Abenaki— "people of the dawn." They had been preceded by the Red Paint People, dating from Neolithic times, who once roamed the land and disappeared, leaving behind graves containing red ocher, or powdered hematite.

Most of the graves were found near water that would have been navigable for boats, indicating a pattern of settlement that would remain constant throughout Maine's prehistory and history. Later, feisty Europeans established fishing stations, eventually settling along the coast where they could move about by water to fish and farm while trying to survive the rugged winters in a rock-bound landscape.

Sporadic Settlement

The early colonial history of Maine is fraught with uncertainty and confusion of many kinds—a tale of grandiose schemes, abandoned settlements, political maneuvering for access to its bounty of forests and fish, and almost incessant involvement in wars of European origin.

Even Maine's "discovery" by European navigators is not clearly documented, for when the Verrazano brothers sailed along its coast in 1524 they encountered

Castine Historical Society

forewarned Abenakis who apparently had dealt with Europeans before. Just after the turn of the 17th century Bartholomew Gosnold and Martin Pring made exploratory trading voyages from England to Maine, but not until 1604, when Samuel de Champlain made a survey of this complex coast of tidal rivers, rocky islands, and winding estuaries, was much known about the territory.

Early settlements were ephemeral, at best, often withdrawn after a rigorous winter or abandoned in conflicts between the French and British. The lieutenant governor of French Acadia, Pierre du Gua, Sieur de Monts, led an abortive settlement (including Samuel de Champlain) on the St. Croix River near Calais in 1604–5, and a few years later the English colony under Sir John Popham at the mouth of the Kennebec also lasted only one winter. The French tried again in 1613 by establishing Saint-Sauveur at the mouth of Somes Sound on Mount Desert Island, but they were soon driven out and set adrift in open boats by the English.

Two experienced English ship captains next visited the coast, John Smith of Virginia, who charted it in 1614, and nine years later, Christopher Levett of the Royal Navy. Both had argued that its unlimited resources of fish and timber could be more efficiently exploited through permanent settlements, and both wrote books to spread their views. But the outcome of their case for solid, permanent colonization remained ephemeral—a handful of trading and fishing outposts.

Even after the successful establishment of the neighboring Massachusetts Bay Colony in 1630, Maine remained the object of elusive settlement schemes. Many of them originated in Plymouth, England, where Sir Ferdinando Gorges had organized a joint stock company for the colonization of all New England in 1620 and took advantage of the politics before the English Civil War to get a grant from Charles I for the whole Province of Maine in 1635.

Abenaki Indians and English Fishermen

The earliest European visitors to Maine made their living by fishing and fur trading. (John Smith had been so impressed with the great variety of fish that he built a fishery on Monhegan in 1614.) The Banks of Maine had long been fished by men from southern England, especially Cornwall, Devon, Dorset, and Somerset. They found it convenient to dry and pack the fish ashore on the Isles of Shoals, Monhegan Island, and in Damariscove. By 1622 thirty ships were arriving at Mon-

---

MAINE *Time Line*

1497–99	1524	1602	1603	1604–5
John Cabot explores the coast	Giovanni da Verrazano, sailing under French flag, explores the coast	Bartholomew Gosnold reaches southern Maine	Martin Pring visits coast before heading south	French survey coast; Sieur de Monts, Samuel de Champlain, and others spend winter at mouth of Saint Croix River

hegan and Damariscove each year to export fish, fish oil, and salt fish to Europe and the West Indies.

When more permanent European settlers began arriving during the early 17th century, relations with the Indians took on greater importance. A number of Abenaki peoples lived in the area, including the Penobscots and Passamaquoddies. At first these Indians were friendly and helpful to the settlers, who needed their expertise in growing food to survive. Corn was a staple because it could be used for both animals and humans, and by 1635 several water-powered corn-grinding mills had been built along the Piscataqua River and in Berwick.

The first sawmill in the colonies was established in York in 1623. The Waldo Patent of 1630, earlier known as the Muscongus Grant, became the first timberland grant.

The King's Broad Arrow

Forests bordering the Androscoggin, Kennebec, and Penobscot Rivers were cut for all purposes, but the tall, straight pines were especially valuable to an expanding Royal Navy in need of a secure source of good timber. Lumbermen cut "mast ways," which were roads in the wilderness designed to bring out the giants without damage. Special ships were built to carry five hundred masts back to England on each voyage.

There still may be a very few giant pines left in the forests blazed with the king's broad arrow. Of course it would be extraordinary to find such an ancient pine; any tree that was large enough to be marked before 1775 must be 300 years old by now. And how could such a tree still stand after centuries of logging and battering by frequent gales and some hurricanes? Yet foresters have identified at least one that may have survived. They won't know for sure until it topples on its own and they can then check under the bark for the telltale blaze. Philip Conkling, a professional forester, wrote, "But if the tree comes down in my lifetime, I'll be there to look under the bark in the hope of finding a crow-footed blaze."

1605
George Waymouth arrives on Monhegan

1606
James I grants a charter to the Plymouth Company for land between the 41st and 45th parallels

1607
Popham colony established at mouth of Kennebec River; abandoned after a year

1609
Henry Hudson visits Casco Bay

1614
John Smith reaches Monhegan

Agents like George Tate of Falmouth (Portland) were in charge of selecting trees and transporting them to England. He marked trees that were taller than seventy-four feet and over two feet in circumference around the trunk with three slashes, the "king's broad arrow," which meant that they belonged to the king and not the colonists. Of course the colonists bridled at this restriction on rights to cut their own timber, but the Crown was not negotiable.

In fact, the Royal Navy's supremacy on world oceans was partly due to a ready source of pine masts from Maine and New Hampshire. Native timber sources in England had long since been exhausted. Sometimes, when the need for more masts was urgent, a ship would refuse its cargo in England and return to America empty to pick up more long pines. Mast ships were long and beamy to take pines more than 100 feet in length that weighed almost four tons each.

Shipbuilding

The combination of an extensive coastline, sheltered harbors, deep rivers, and abundant timber favored shipbuilding in Maine. It began early in the brief Popham settlement with the *Virginia* (1607), the first ship built in America. Several decades later John Winter started another shipyard on Richmond Island in 1632. Soon more shipyards developed on the coast and along the rivers and became a major occupation for many inhabitants. Some boats were built in unlikely places far inland—possible because of the broad tidal rivers—since the timber stood there. By 1762 William Swanton had created contract shipbuilding on the Kennebec in Bath, where yards built ships for Spain, France, and the West Indies. Shipbuilding on the Kennebec spread as far upriver as Hallowell during the early 1800s.

Wars

Along with trying to make a living in a harsh environment, Maine's inhabitants had to contend with one war after another as England and France vied to gain control of North America. By land, Maine was the frontier, exposed to raids from French-held Canada, and by sea it was vulnerable to attacks on a coast too large and intricate to be properly defended. In these continuing conflicts both sides recruited the Indians, who were struggling for survival and no longer on friendly

MAINE *Time Line*

1624	1647	1688	1703–13	1722–25
Settlement at York (called Agamenticus)	Kittery becomes the first town in Maine	Governor Andros takes Penobscot by force and fighting breaks out between the French and Indians and the English	Queen Anne's War	Lovewell's War

terms with the settlers. As early as King Philip's War (in which the French had no part), when Casco and Scarborough were destroyed in the first raids in 1675, and many other settlements met similar fates the following year, people were forced to emigrate to safer places—a pattern that continued for the next forty years.

The 18th century was not much kinder to Maine. Although permanent settlements had been established along the coast from Kittery to Casco Bay and beyond, a series of wars and frontier raids throughout the first half of the century made them constantly vulnerable. Queen Anne's War (1703–13) left only Kittery, Wells, and York intact; Lovewell's War (1722–25), a bitter guerrilla conflict, included a bloody assault on Norridgewock in which the colonists killed the French Jesuit missionary Sebastian Rasle, who was thought to be instigating Indian raids; King George's War (1744–48) led many settlers to retreat once again to other colonies. During that war William Pepperell of Kittery led a daring and successful expedition to capture the massive French fortress of Louisbourg on Nova Scotia's Cape Breton Island in 1745. The Crown's return of that fort to the French in the subsequent peace negotiations would prove a continuing source of bitterness that would add to other affronts leading up to the Revolution.

Apart from a British naval raid early in the war that obliterated Portland, and one disastrous American naval expedition, Maine was not a significant battleground during the Revolution. In 1775 Connecticut's Benedict Arnold led more than a thousand men up the Kennebec and through well over a hundred miles of wilderness to lay siege to Quebec—an amazing six-week trek that nonetheless destroyed the effectiveness of his demoralized force. And in 1779 Commodore Dudley Saltonstall brought an amphibious force of the same size against Castine in Penobscot Bay but failed to dislodge the British and had to destroy much of his own fleet when the Royal Navy arrived—one of the most disastrous expeditions in American military history.

Reaching for Independence

Maine was in effect subjected to two struggles for independence—first from Britain and then from its colonial overlord, Massachusetts. In Maine, support for the Revolution was spotty among those who were scratching out a meager living in iso-

1744-48	1754-60	1775	1775	1819
King George's War; 1745 siege of Louisbourg	French and Indian War	Benedict Arnold marches across Maine to attack Quebec	The Continental Congress divides Massachusetts into three districts, one of them Maine	Maine finally separates from Massachusetts

lated places. The rhetoric of Boston meant little to their lives; in contrast, wealthier merchants in Falmouth and other active seaports had direct connections with the vagaries of British rule in the early 1770s. In *Revolution Downeast*, James Leamon summarized the effect of the Revolution on the varied populations in Maine: "The war physically devastated Maine and polarized its people, accentuating differences between rich and poor, between interior and coastal communities, between revolutionaries and loyalists, between the establishment and dissenters, and eventually if not immediately, between Massachusetts and Maine."

At the time of the Revolution, three Massachusetts counties—York, Cumberland, and Lincoln—constituted the District of Maine. The Continental Congress reaffirmed that arrangement, and Maine would remain a part of Massachusetts until 1819. Yet forces for separation grew as Maine's interests diverged from those of Massachusetts, especially after Jefferson's embargo of 1807, the War of 1812, and Madison's embargo of 1813, all of which devastated shipowners and merchants along the Maine coast. Yet the full impetus for independence came from the growth of inland communities, where new residents sought removal of constraints from a Federalist government in Massachusetts. They began to talk about framing a constitution for a separate state in 1816 and succeeded in passing it three years later, and Maine was admitted to the Union in 1820 as part of the Missouri compromise, a politically expedient but ultimately futile attempt to balance slave and free states.

Regions *to* Explore

Maine's long, rocky peninsulas and thick forests made early road travel very difficult, and settlers usually went no further inland than about twenty miles, apart from river valleys. Why should they bother, when they could easily reach good lumbering territory along rivers and move between sections of saltwater farms by boat?

Right from the beginning, going "Down East" from Massachusetts has been a nautical affair, sailing downwind on the prevailing sou'westerlies to reach your destination in a fjordlike mixture of land and water. Even today a road trip through colonial Maine is likely to begin at the border with New Hampshire and head east along the coast, with occasional forays to the interior up major rivers like the Kennebec and Penobscot.

Our regions begin on the south coast of Maine and continue up to Machias.

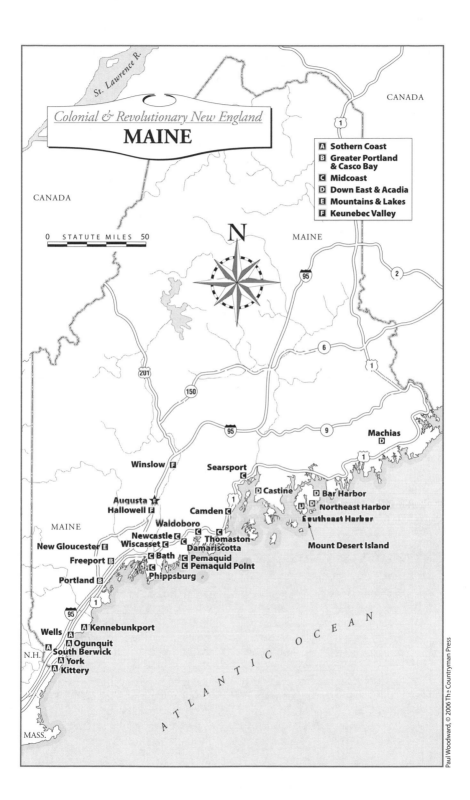

St. Lawrence R.

CANADA

Colonial & Revolutionary New England
MAINE

CANADA

A	**Sothern Coast**
B	**Greater Portland & Casco Bay**
C	**Midcoast**
D	**Down East & Acadia**
E	**Mountains & Lakes**
F	**Keunebec Valley**

0 STATUTE MILES 50

N

MAINE

95

2

6

1

201

150

9

95

Machias D

Winslow F   Searsport C

Augusta ☆   D Castine   D Bar Harbor
Hallowell F   D Northeast Harbor
                Camden C   D
MAINE   Waldoboro   Southeast Harbor
        Newcastle C   C
New Gloucester E Wiscasset C C Thomaston
        C Damariscotta
Freeport B   C Bath C Pemaquid   Mount Desert Island
                C Pemaquid Point
Portland B   Phippsburg
                95   1

Wells A A Kennebunkport
N.H. A A Ogunquit
South Berwick
A York
A Kittery

A T L A N T I C   O C E A N

MASS.

SOUTHERN COAST

Maine's southern coast up to Portland is a land of long, sandy beaches—a rarity on the remainder of the rockbound coast.

KITTERY

Maine's southernmost town, Kittery, is also the oldest town in the state, incorporated in 1647. Shipbuilding has long been the major industry here. The *Ranger*, which sailed to France under the command of John Paul Jones, was built in 1777 in a Kittery shipyard, on an island in the Piscataqua. Jones breezed out of nearby Portsmouth, New Hampshire, and made his way to France with the news that Burgoyne had surrendered. His ship received the first salute given to a ship under the American flag. Then she harassed British vessels in European waters until finally captured by the British in 1780, when she became part of the Royal Navy. A monument to John Paul Jones stands on US 1 in Kittery.

Today Kittery is best known not for its proud naval heritage but for its shopping: It has more than 120 outlet shops to entice consumers.

HISTORICAL SITES *and* MUSEUMS

The approaches to the Piscataqua were protected on the Kittery side of the river by a fort begun in 1690 and developed in the early 18th century. **Fort McClary State Historic Site** (207-384-5160, winter 207-624-6080; www.maine.gov/doc/parks) is on Kittery Point Rd. Open Memorial Day–Oct. 1. The fort provided protection against the French and Indians as well as pirates. It was named Fort William after Sir William Pepperell, a Kittery native knighted for his leadership of the Louisbourg expedition in 1745, then renamed during the Revolution, when

PIRATE LORE

✸ In colonial times, pirates and other rogues sailed all up and down the coast, and the stories about them are legion. The Isles of Shoals, actually part of New Hampshire, are located just offshore from Kittery. Mainlanders accused the islanders of housing the pirates that harassed their shipping, and also of luring ships onto the treacherous shoals by changing the location of navigation lights.

The term "mooncussers" referred to coastal residents who would place lanterns in strategic places to disorient mariners, causing them to head onto rocks while thinking they were in safe waters. Then the wreckers would salvage goods from the ship, often killing the crew. If the moon happened to shine, the would-be wreckers would cuss the light that foiled their ruse.

commemoration of a victory over the French seemed inappropriate. The hexagonal blockhouse, brick magazine, and barracks were built some years later. Photographers may want to stand below the blockhouse and look up for an unusual shot.

Maritime aficionados will want to visit the **Kittery Historical and Naval Museum** (207-439-3080), Rogers Rd. Open June–Columbus Day. Displays record the history of seafaring in Kittery and elsewhere along the coast. Models of ships, including a 13-foot replica of John Paul Jones's *Ranger*, dioramas, and a collection of shipbuilding tools, navigation instruments, and photographs portray this heritage. Shipbuilding is a major focus in the museum.

> Who owns the island? The Portsmouth Naval Shipyard sits on an island in the Piscataqua River between Kittery, Maine, and Portsmouth, New Hampshire. The states were engaged in a long-running battle over which one owned the island. It took the U.S. Supreme Court to finally settle the issue—in favor of Maine.

LODGING

HIGH MEADOWS BED & BREAKFAST
ME l0l, Eliot, ME 03903
207-439-0590
This 1736 colonial house is about 5 miles from Kittery. The house was built by Elliott Frost, a merchant-ship builder and captain.

PORTSMOUTH HARBOR INN & SPA
6 Water St., Kittery, ME 03904
207-439-4040; www.innat portsmouth.com

The building dates from 1879 and is decorated in Federal style. The spa is in the adjacent barn, which predates the house.

INFORMATION

GREATER YORK REGION CHAMBER OF COMMERCE VISITOR CENTER
1 Stonewall Lane,
York, ME 03909
207-363-4422;
www.gatewaytomaine.org

YORK

York is part of a National Historic District with many 17th- and 18th-century homes open to the public. The site was settled in 1624 as Agamenticus, named for an Indian village decimated by disease. Sir Ferdinando Gorges and his friends arrived in 1630 and called it Gorgeana. Following Gorges's death, Massachusetts claimed his lands and renamed the town York in 1652.

One of the most infamous raids of the incessant Indian wars that plagued Maine was the Candlemas Massacre during a French and Indian sweep of Maine settlements. It took place on the night of February 2, 1692, when some five hundred Abenakis killed eighty York inhabitants and burned many of the buildings. The Abenakis abandoned their snowshoes just before attacking. Snowshoe Rock is five miles north of town on Chases Pond Road, identified by a marker set into a large rock.

Today the York River is popular for boating and swimming. Agamenticus

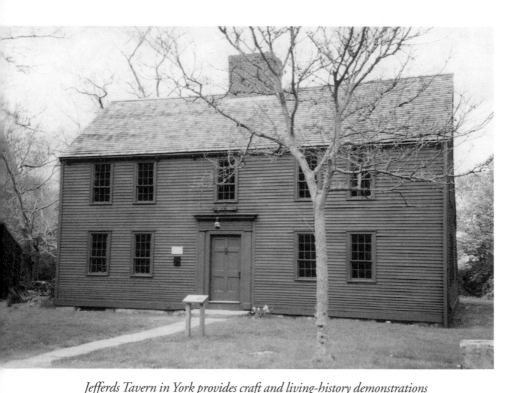

Jefferds Tavern in York provides craft and living-history demonstrations

Mountain attracts hikers and picnickers. York Harbor has a bustling waterfront. Cliff Walk begins along the boardwalk at the ocean end of Harbor Beach Road and ends on a rocky beach near Cow Beach Point. Along the way are wonderful views of the coastline, including Nubble Light to the north.

HISTORICAL SITES *and* MUSEUMS

Old York Historical Society (207-363-4974; www.oldyork.org), maintains a living-history village of seven historic buildings. Open June to mid-Oct. **Jefferds Tavern**, on Lindsay Road, is the place to get information and begin tours. The tavern, a mid-18th-century saltbox, actually started its life in Wells. Interpreters engage in a variety of craft and living-history demonstrations.

Old York village has most of the buildings that were considered essential for a settlement in the colonial era. Like to pretend you're a child in an 18th-century school? The **Old Schoolhouse** dates from 1745 and is furnished with typical school desks and benches of that era. It is one of the oldest schools in Maine.

And there's a church too, although they were extremely scarce in the beleaguered settlements of Maine until Cotton Mather cajoled young Harvard graduates to go there as missionaries in the middle of the 17th century. One of these, Samuel Moody, arrived home after the siege of Louisbourg and devoted himself to supervising the building of York's **First Parish Congregational Church** in 1747. He served as its pastor for 47 years.

Parson Moody's son Joseph Moody was the subject of one of Hawthorne's most famous short stories, "The Minister's Black Veil." Moody accidentally killed a friend while they were out hunting. He felt so guilty that he wore a handkerchief over his face for the rest of his life.

Around the bend stands the **Emerson-Wilcox House** of 1724, which was a general store, tailor shop, tavern, and home for Edward Emerson. The Emerson Tavern entertained Presidents John Quincy Adams and James Monroe, as well as the Marquis de Lafayette. It then served as a private home and is now a museum displaying the Mary Bulman collection of American 18th-century crewelwork bed hangings. Visitors will find 12 rooms to explore.

Dungeons and cells are grim reminders of what it must have been like to linger in the **Old Gaol**, but at least it was an improvement on the older Maine practice of confining prisoners in small chambers dug into the earth. Built in 1719, this gaol was once the King's Prison for Maine; both hardened criminals and debtors were held here. The gaoler's family quarters are also open.

The 18th-century **John Hancock Warehouse** offers displays on maritime traffic, industry, and life on the York River. The house was built by Thomas Donnell, then owned by John Hancock, the first signer of the Declaration of Independence and also a governor of Massachusetts.

John Hancock Wharf in Old York Village

Lucky indeed is a house that has been lived in by the same family for many generations. The **Elizabeth Perkins House**, built in 1730, still has original Perkins family pieces. Both Elizabeth Perkins and her mother, Mrs. Newton Perkins, gathered antiques from other countries, and their collections are on display.

Another old family home nearby is the **Sayward-Wheeler House**, (207-384-2454), 79 Barrell Lane Extension, York Harbor, located right on the water. Open June–Oct., first Sat. of the month. Owned by Jonathan Sayward, who was involved in the attack on the French fortress at Louisbourg, Nova Scotia, in 1745, the house has been maintained with its original family portraits and furnishings. The Society for the Preservation of New England Antiquities received the house in 1977 and found that furniture had not been moved in 200 years and was stuck to the floor. They felt lucky.

Jonathan Sayward was a Loyalist who was so worried that he kept 200 pounds sterling on hand in case he was run out of town. He had a souvenir box from King George III that revealed his politics.

Gravestone aficionados will find the **Old York Cemetery** a treasure. Some of the headstones are decorated with a death's head with wings and inscriptions using old English spelling. Don't miss the "witches grave," covered by a large stone. Some say this was done so the "witch" buried there in 1744 could never escape.

> ✸ Beverages were served during colonial times in pewter mugs, wooden "noggins," or boiled-leather mugs called black jacks. In them you would find ale, beer, wine, or rum, and sometimes hard cider. Today's Americans, who consume more water than any other nationality and expect to find it available in public places, may be surprised to learn that their colonial forebears hardly ever drank it.

In Old York Cemetery, a memorial to settlers killed in a massacre

LODGING

APPLE BLOSSOM BED & BREAKFAST
25 Brixham Rd.,
York, ME 03909; 207-351-1727;
www.appleblossombandb.com
Part of the building dates from 1717 when it was a farmhouse. The rural setting is peaceful.

DOCKSIDE GUEST QUARTERS AND RESTAURANT
Harris Island Rd., York, ME 03909
808-860-7428, 207-363-2868;
www.docksidegq.com
The 19th-century house was the original building on the property. Others include a classic New England cottage and several other units.

INN AT TANGLEWOOD HALL
611 York St.,
York Harbor, ME 0391i; 207-351-1075;
www.tanglewoodhall.com
This shingled 1880s summer mansion was once home to bandleader Tommy Dorsey.

STAGE NECK INN
8 Stage Neck Rd.,
York Harbor, ME 03911
800-222-3238, 207-363-3850;
www.stageneck.com
The inn is located on the site of the Marshall House dating from the 19th century. On a peninsula, it has great views.

YORK HARBOR INN
York St., York Harbor, ME 03911
800-343-3869, 207-363-5119;
www.yorkharborinn.com
This inn has a 1637 cabin room that was brought from the Isles of Shoals as its centerpiece. It was a private men's club in the 19th century.

RESTAURANTS

FOX'S LOBSTER HOUSE
Sawyer Park Rd.,
Nubble Point, York Harbor, ME
207-363-2643; http://216.71.193.135/
The menu includes other selections, but lobster is king.

HARBOR PORCHES
In the Stage Neck Inn, 8 Stage Neck Rd., York Harbor, ME 03911
800-222-3238, 207-363-3850;
www.stageneck.com
Seafood is the focus; vegetarian fare is also offered.

THE LOBSTER BARN
1,000 US 1, York Harbor, ME 03909
207-363-4721
The restaurant is in a New England barn with farm tools as accents. The speciality is Maine lobster.

YORK HARBOR INN
York St., York Harbor, ME 03911
800-343-3869, 207-363-5119;
www.yorkharborinn.com
Seafood is the specialty; also featured is a Sunday brunch, and the pub downstairs offers a lighter menu.

EVENTS

October. Harvestfest. A colonial-themed festival with ox roast, bean hole beans, crafts fair, and cider pressing. 207-363-4422;
www.gatewaytomaine.org

INFORMATION

MAINE TOURISM
888-624-6345, 207-623-0363;
www.visitmaine.com,
www.mainetourism.com,
www.exploremaine.org

GREATER YORK REGION CHAMBER OF COMMERCE VISITOR CENTER
1 Stonewall Lane,
York, ME 03909; 207-363-4422;
www.gatewaytomaine.org

OGUNQUIT AND WELLS

Now a popular summer beach destination, Wells was incorporated in 1653, and Ogunquit was included in the town until 1980. Although today there is not much colonial flavor in this area, one can imagine early settlers walking along the Marginal Way on the shore.

HISTORICAL SITES and MUSEUMS

The **Ogunquit Heritage Museum** (207-646-5139) traces the early settlement of Ogunquit. The **Wells Ogunquit Historic Meeting House Museum** (207-646-4775) offers historical programs and exhibits.

LODGING

ABOVE TIDE INN
66 Beach St., Ogunquit, ME 03907
207-646-7454; www.abovetideinn
The inn is on the river, with decks overlooking the changing tides.

CLIFF HOUSE RESORT & SPA
Shore Rd., Ogunquit, ME 03907
207-361-1000;
www.cliffhousemaine.com
Though the resort dates from a later era, 1872, that has its advantages: the rooms have balconies with an ocean view from Bald Head Cliff. The original building was constructed for the wife of a sea captain, with wood milled in the family sawmill in Ogunquit.

THE BEAUPORT INN ON CLAY HILL
339 Clay Hill Rd. Ogunquit, ME 03907
800-646-8681, 207-361-2400;
www.beauportinn.com
Take a look at the English paneling from 1835 and it's hard to believe that the inn is actually new—it has the feel of Old England.

RESTAURANTS

ARROWS
Berwick Rd.,
Ogunquit, ME 03907; 207-361-1100;
www.arrowsrestaurant.com
This 18th-century country house offers top-drawer cuisine, fresh food prepared with imagination. Dress code.

BARNACLE BILLY'S ETC.
70 Perkins Cove Rd.,
Ogunquit, ME 03907
207-646-4711; www.barnbilly.com
Lobster is served with flair, and the deck overlooks the harbor. The original Barnacle Billy's is still dishing up lobster next door (207-646-5575).

CLIFF HOUSE
At the Cliff House Resort & Spa,
Shore Rd., Ogunquit, ME 03907
207-361-1000;
www.cliffhousemaine.com
The menu offers a wide variety of choices, and the view can hardly be matched. Dress code.

98 PROVENCE
262 Shore Rd., Ogunquit, ME 03907
207-646-9898; www.98provence.com
The menu changes daily, and dishes from Provence are special.

INFORMATION

OGUNQUIT CHAMBER OF COMMERCE
36 Main St., Ogunquit, ME 03907
207-646-2939, 207-646-1279;
www.ogunquit.org

WELLS CHAMBER OF COMMERCE
136 Post Rd., Wells, ME 04090
207-646-2451; wellschamber.org

South Berwick

The town of South Berwick was settled in 1623 on the Salmon Falls River, and a sawmill was built there in 1634. According to local legend, a vessel appropriately named the *Pied Cow* brought the first cows to Maine in 1634, landing on the east bank of the Salmon in Vaughan Woods, off ME 236.

Today South Berwick is a quiet town with many colonial homes and spreading lawns.

HISTORICAL SITES *and* MUSEUMS

The town has a claim to fame as the home of Maine's best-known writer of fiction. Sarah Orne Jewett (1849–1909), often labeled a "local colorist" by literary historians, nevertheless has a fictional voice that rings true Down East. She gained national recognition for *A Country Doctor* (1884), remembered alongside other notable publications of that year and the next, Mark Twain's *Huckleberry Finn* and a New England classic, William Dean Howells's *The Rise of Silas Lapham.* Now you can see where she lived.

The **Sarah Orne Jewett House** (207-384-2454; www.historicnewengland.org), Portland St. Open June 1–Oct. 15. It was built about 1774 and bought a few years later by Captain Theodore Jewett. This hip-roof, dormered house has a Doric portico with fluted columns. Inside, a floral window brightens the landing. Jewett's grandfather and father filled the house with furniture from abroad, tapestries, engravings, silver, and willowware. A hidden stairway leads from the guest room to the cellar and attic.

If you've read Jewett's *The Tory Lover,* you'll recognize the setting for this historical romance: **Hamilton House**, (207-384-2454; www.spnea.org), Vaughan's Lane, off ME 236. Open June 1–Oct. 15. It was built in 1787 by shipbuilder Jonathan Hamilton. The house overlooked his lumber and shipping business on the Salmon Falls River so he could see his own ships coming around the bend. This substantial hip-roof house has four large chimneys. John Paul Jones visited a number of times.

LODGING

ACADEMY STREET INN
15 Academy St., South Berwick, ME 03908; 207-384-5633
The inn is a 1903 grand colonial-style Victorian home, with carved fireplaces, Austrian crystal chandeliers, and leaded glass windows.

Kennebunkport

There was a fishing station here as early as 1602, but Indians invaded it repeatedly. In 1719 the settlement was incorporated with the name Arundel. (Kenneth Roberts's novel *Arundel,* centering on Benedict Arnold's march to Quebec, is partly set here, where Roberts lived.) In 1821 the town's name was changed to Kennebunkport. Shipbuilding thrived and paid for the mansions built by shipbuilders and sea captains throughout the 19th century. Now tourists can stay in the lovely homes built during this prosperous era—an architectural collection unmatched along the Maine coast.

"Kennebunk" was said to be an Indian name referring to the "long-cut bank" on Gravehill Road. Others say that the name refers to "calm water."

LODGING

CAPE ARUNDEL INN
208 Ocean Ave.
Kennebunkport, ME 04046
207-967-2125;
www.capearundelinn.com
This historic home was built as a summer cottage in 1895. Walker's Point is in view, and beyond that is Cape Porpoise.

CAPTAIN FAIRFIELD INN
8 Pleasant St.,
Kennebunkport, ME 04046
800-322-1928, 207-967-4454;
www.captainfairfield.com
This 1813 mansion was given as a wedding gift to the Fairfields. Federal-style furnishings enhance the home.

THE CAPTAIN JEFFERDS INN
5 Pearl St., Kennebunkport, ME 04046
800-839-6844, 207-967-2311;
www.captainjeffersinn.com
A sea captain built this Federal-style home in 1804 as a wedding gift for his daughter.

THE CAPTAIN LORD MANSION
6 Pleasant St.,
Kennebunkport, ME 04046
800-522-3141, 207-967-3141;
www.captainlord.com
This three-story 1812 home has bedrooms named for Maine sailing vessels.

CHETWYND HOUSE INN
4 Chestnut St.,
Kennebunkport, ME 04046
207-967-2235;
www.chetwyndhouse.com
The inn was an 1840s sea captain's home.

COVE HOUSE
11 S. Maine St.,
Kennebunkport, ME 04046
207-967-3704; www.covehouse.com
This farmhouse was begun in 1793 on part of an original royal land grant.

THE INN AT GOOSE ROCKS
71 Dyke Rd.,
Kennebunkport, ME 04046
207-967-5425;
www.innatgooserocks.com
The inn, with colonial-style furnishings, is on a wooded knoll with a salt-marsh view.

THE INN AT HARBOR HEAD
41 Pier Rd., Kennebunkport, ME 04046
207-967-5564; www.harborhead.com
The home dates from 1890 and is decorated with sculptures, marine paintings, and antique furnishings.

THE KENNEBUNKPORT INN
1 Dock Square,
Kennebunkport, ME 04046
800-248-2621, 207-967-2621;
www.kennebunkportinn.com
The original building dates from 1890, and additions feature Federal-style decor.

THE MAINE STAY
34 Maine St.,
Kennebunkport, ME 04046
800-950-2117, 207-967-2117;
www.mainestayinn.com
Melville Walker, merchant sea captain, built the home in 1860.

OLD FORT INN
Old Fort Ave.,
Kennebunkport, ME 04046
800-828-3678, 207-967-5353;
www.oldfortinn.com
You'll enter the inn through an antique shop, a good place to find a remembrance of your visit. The lodge was once a barn built in the 1880s.

THE WHITE BARN INN & SPA
37 Beach Ave.,
Kennebunkport, ME 04046
207-967-2321; www.whitebarninn.com
The White Barn Inn has been operating
since the 1800s. Step into the courtyard
and you'll think you're in Europe.

1802 HOUSE
15 Locke St.,
Kennebunkport, ME 04046
800-932-5632 or 207-967-5632;
www.1802inn.com
The 1802 house is beside the 15th green
of the Cape Arundel Golf Club.

In nearby Kennebunk:

KENNEBUNK INN
45 Main St., Kennebunk, ME 04043
207-985-3351;
www.thekennebunkinn.com
The building dates from 1799, with
additions. Local folklore maintains that
the Marquis de Lafayette visited the
inn in 1825.

THE WALDO EMERSON INN
108 Summer St.,
Kennebunk, ME 04043
877-521-8776, 207-985-4250;
www.waldoemersoninn.com
Waldo Emerson (great-uncle of Ralph
Waldo Emerson) built the house in 1753.
It is the oldest remaining house in
Kennebunk.

RESTAURANTS

ALISSON'S RESTAURANT
11 Dock Square,
Kennebunkport, ME 04046
207-967-4841; www.alissons.com
Lobster rolls and chowder are favorites.

ARUNDEL WHARF RESTAURANT
43 Ocean Ave.,
Kennebunkport, ME 04046
207-967-3444; www.arundelwharf.com
Nautical decor and a casual atmosphere
make this a favorite for seafood on the
harbor.

HOLE IN THE ROOF
In the Inn at Goose Rocks, 71 Dyke Rd.,
Kennebunkport, ME 04046
207-967-5425;
www.innatgooserocks.com
Seasonal herbs and produce are grown in
the garden here.

MABEL'S LOBSTER CLAW
124 Ocean Ave.,
Kennebunkport, ME 04046
207-967-2562
Lobster is served in many different ways
for both lunch and dinner.

WHITE BARN INN RESTAURANT
At the White Barn Inn & Spa,
37 Beach Ave.,
Kennebunkport, ME 04046
207-967-2321; www.whitebarninn.com
The dining room is housed in two 19th-
century barns with displays of farm implements, tools, scales, statues of farm
animals, and barrels up in the rafters.
There is a four-course prix fixe dinner. A
jacket is required.

INFORMATION

**KENNEBUNK-KENNEBUNKPORT
CHAMBER OF COMMERCE**
17 Western Ave.,
Kennebunk, ME 04043
800-982-4421, 207-967-0857;
www.visitthe kennebunks.com

GREATER PORTLAND AND CASCO BAY

C asco Bay and the countryside around Portland provide a variety of scenic
vistas across saltwater marshes, with beaches, islands, rocky headlands,
and lighthouses for charm. The Portland Peninsula has a promontory at
each end, with the Eastern Promenade offering sweeping views over Casco Bay.

There are hiking trails and sanctuaries to enjoy.

The many islands in Casco Bay were named Calendar Islands by an early explorer who thought there was one for every day of the year. Today excursion boats and fishing charters based in Portland cruise around these islands.

PORTLAND

From an inauspicious beginning Portland developed in the footsteps of traders and explorers who liked what they saw. Portland (then called Casco) was first settled in 1623 by Christopher Levett, a captain in the Royal Navy whose *Voyage into New England* argued strenuously for permanent colonization in Maine. He built a stone house in Casco and wintered there before returning to England, leaving ten men behind in his house. The story stops because he never returned, dying at sea seven years later on a voyage from the Massachusetts Bay Colony to England.

George Cleeve arrived around 1631 and contrived to be named deputy governor of the province, until it was discovered that he had trumped up charges against earlier deputies. He returned to England and managed to find a patron who bought a patent of land at Sagadahoc, east of Casco Bay, and named him, Cleeve, deputy president of the patent. Cleeve and Sir Ferdinando Gorges fought back and forth in the courts in Boston and England over the Casco Bay colony until the Maine colonies became part of Massachusetts in 1661.

By 1675 Casco had been renamed Falmouth, and the settlement numbered about four hundred. King Philip's War broke out in southern New England that year with severe consequences for Maine, as Indians began attacking settlers virtually everywhere. In the summer of 1676 they swept through, killing colonists and burning homes.

Surviving inhabitants left by boat and secured themselves on Jewell Island; some gave up and continued on to Salem. But by 1716 new settlers came again to Falmouth after Samuel Moody built a fort there. The town flourished as a trading center, exporting fish, furs, and lumber. Shipbuilding became a major industry, and masts were exported for the Royal Navy. (Today the city's revitalized Old Port section gives a taste of the bustling waterfront warehouse district.)

> The early history of the settlement is marked by an unfortunate frontier incident. By 1628 Walter Bagnall, or "Big Walt," had moved into a hut on Spurwink River and proceeded to trade junk trinkets and liquor with the Indians for furs. As he built a fortune, the Indians began to suspect his motives and his honesty in dealing with them. An Indian chief, Squidraset, killed him a few years later.

Portland's city seal shows a phoenix rising from the ashes—a reference to the town's recovery from fires and disasters. One such calamity occurred during the early months of the Revolution, in October 1775, when four British vessels sailed into the harbor and demanded that the people turn in their arms and leave town.

This was a punitive mission under the command of Lieutenant Henry Mowat, who had orders from the Admiralty to "chastize" dissident settlements. Mowat also had unpleasant memories of an incident earlier that year in Machias, when townsmen had captured his ship and held him prisoner for a short time. Now, when the townspeople of Falmouth refused to surrender their arms, the British fleet peppered the town with bombs, grapeshot, and cannonballs. Most buildings went up in flames, and two thousand residents were left without homes.

One courageous lady, the widow Grele, refused to leave her tavern, throwing buckets of water on flames all around. Thereafter, the tavern was used for court sessions until a new courthouse could be built.

After all the ruin they had caused, the British chose not to occupy the town, so the remaining townspeople lived in the ruins and rebuilt. A few years after the war the town was renamed Portland, and commerce returned.

HISTORICAL SITES *and* MUSEUMS

George Tate, who was responsible for selecting and blazing mast trees with the "king's broad arrow," built the **Tate House** (207-774-6177; www.tatehouse.org),

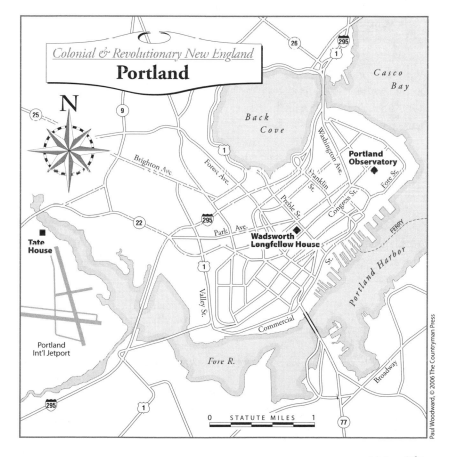

1270 Westbrook St., in 1755. Open June 15–Sep. 30. His Georgian house is unusual with its indented clerestory gambrel roof, which has a recessed windowed section above the second story. The large central chimney accommodates eight fireplaces.

Inside, the house is furnished with pieces that depict the lifestyle of a wealthy official during the 18th century. The hall contains a dogleg stairway and the original cove ceiling. Collections include pottery, porcelain, silver, and textiles; pewter and iron kitchen utensils are also on display. Family letters and memorabilia give insight into the Tate family. Outside, the raised-bed herb garden contains plants similar to those grown in the 18th century.

The first brick house built in Portland, with bricks sent from Philadelphia, was the **Wadsworth-Longfellow House** (207-774-1822; www.mainehistory.org), 485 Congress St. Open June–Oct. It was built in 1785 by Henry Wadsworth Longfellow's grandfather, General Peleg Wadsworth. Enough bricks were sent to complete one story, but the second story had to wait until another shipment arrived in 1786. And the house kept growing: To the two stories with a gable roof, a third was added after a fire damaged the roof. The house contains Wadsworth and Longfellow family furnishings, including crocheted tablecloths and needlework samplers. Other period pieces are from the collection of the Maine Historical Society.

The Longfellows and the Wadsworths were both descended from Pilgrims who came on the *Mayflower*. Henry Wadsworth Longfellow lived in the house as a child with his seven brothers and sisters, parents, and an aunt. The Maine Historical Society Summer Gallery is next door. Visitors are invited to stroll in the garden behind the house.

You can climb the 102 steps up the tower on a guided tour of the 1807 **Portland Observatory** (207-774-5561; www.portlandlandmarks.org/observatory), for fine views of Casco Bay, the White Mountains, and the country around Portland. It stands at 138 Congress St. on Munjoy Hill. Open Memorial Day–Columbus Day.

The site had been even more important in colonial days, when it was used as a lookout for incoming vessels. The hill gets its name from George Munjoy, who settled here around 1659. It is also the site of the oldest cemetery in Portland, Eastern Cemetery, with graves dating to 1670.

LODGING

ANDREWS ON AUBURN BED AND BREAKFAST

417 Auburn St.,
Portland, ME 04103;
207-797-9157
This 250-year-old colonial home is furnished with Shaker and colonial-style reproductions.

THE DANFORTH

163 Danforth St.,
Portland, ME 04102
800-991-6557, 207-879-8755;
www.danforthmaine.com
The Danforth stands at the head of Tyng Street overlooking the wharves and inner harbor. It dates from 1823 and is on the National Register of Historic Places.

INN ON CARLETON
46 Carleton St., Portland, ME 04102
800-639-1779, 207-775-1910;
innoncarleton.com
The inn is in an 1869 Victorian home, and features trompe l'oeil paintings and murals created by Charles Schumacher.

POMEGRANATE INN
46 Neal St., Portland, ME 04102
800-356-0408, 207-772-1006;
www.pomegranateinn.com
This 1880s home is decorated with works of art and antiques.

WEST END INN
146 Pine St., Portland, ME 04102
800-338-1377, 207-772-1377;
www.westendbb.com
This Second Empire–style brick townhouse dates from 1871.

In Prouts Neck:

BLACK POINT INN
510 Black Point Rd.,
Prouts Neck, ME 04074
800-258-0003, 207-883-2500;
www.blackpointinn.com

Set on nine acres at the tip of Prouts Neck, the inn reopened with new owners in April 2005. It dates from the 1870s and is a Historic Hotel of America National Trust hotel.

RESTAURANTS

FORE STREET
288 Fore St., Portland, ME 04101
207-775-2717; www.forestreet.biz
The restaurant is in a converted factory and features New England favorites, using a wood-fired grill and rotisserie.

OLD PORT TAVERN
11 Moulton St.,
Portland, ME 04101; 207-774-0444;
www.oldporttavern.com
A popular place for both locals and visitors.

INFORMATION

GREATER PORTLAND CONVENTION & VISITORS BUREAU
245 Commercial St.,
Portland, ME 04101
207-772-5800;
www.visitportland.com

FREEPORT

In nearby Freeport, now well known throughout the East as a busy shopping mecca built around an enlarged L.L. Bean store, visitors can still find some semblance of colonial atmosphere in the Harraseeket Inn on 162 Main Street. This inn began with a building in 1798, then added a new wing in 1989 to meet the increased demand. When your shopping spree is over, it's a good place to recover, take tea at four o'clock, sup in one of three dining rooms, and stay the night.

Early settlers had squabbles with the Wabanakis in the 17th and early 18th centuries. In 1725 a peace treaty with the Penobscots was signed. Freeport received a charter in 1789, dissolving its relationship with North Yarmouth.

HISTORICAL SITES *and* MUSEUMS

Harrington House (207-865-3170; www.freeporthistoricalsociety.org), 45 Main St., dates from the late 18th century. Changing exhibits detail the history of Freeport. On the same property the **Pettingill House** is an 1810 saltbox. There are 140 acres of gardens, fields, and hiking trails.

LODGING

BREWSTER HOUSE BED & BREAKFAST
180 Main St., Freeport, ME 04032
800-865-0822, 207-865-4121;
www.brewsterhouse.com
This house is an 1888 Queen Anne
Victorian furnished with antiques.

HARRASEEKET INN
162 Main St., Freeport, ME 04032
800-342-6423, 207-865-9377;
harraseeketinn.com
If you like English manor houses, you will
feel at home in the Harraseeket; the English materials were bought at auction for
the living rooms.

KENDALL TAVERN
213 Main St., Freeport, ME 04032
800-341-9572, 207-865-1338;
www.kendalltavern.com
This early 1800s farmhouse has been
restored and is decorated with antique
furnishings.

WHITE CEDAR INN
178 Main St., Freeport, ME 04032
800-853-1269, 207-865-9099;
www.whitecedarinn.com
This Victorian property was once home to
Arctic explorer Donald B. MacMillan, who
accompanied Robert E. Peary on his historic voyage to the North Pole in 1909.

ATLANTIC SEAL BED AND BREAKFAST
25 Main St., South Freeport, ME 04078
877-ATL-SEAL, 207-865-6112
This 1850 Cape Cod home has guest
rooms named for sailing vessels built in
the area. Boat cruises are available
during the season.

In nearby Durham:

**ROYALSBOROUGH INN
AT BAGLEY HOUSE**
1290 Royalsborough Rd.,
Durham, ME 04222
800-765-1772, 207-865-6566;
www.bagleyhouse.com
You'll see collections of penguins and
needlepoint in this 1772 country house. A
huge cauldron once used to make soap
and candles stands in the kitchen.

RESTAURANTS

BROAD ARROW TAVERN
In the Harraseeket Inn,
162 Main St., Freeport, ME 04032
800-342-6423, 207-865-9377;
www.harraseeketinn.com
The decor is Maine hunting lodge, with
animal heads on the wall. The open
kitchen contains a wood-fired oven and
grill. The Maine Dining Room offers fine
dining and flaming desserts. Afternoon
tea is a treat.

JAMESON TAVERN
115 Main St., Freeport, ME 04032
207-865-4196;
www.jamesontavern.com
The building dates from 1779, when it was
a private residence. The cuisine is American, with a lighter menu at lunch.

INFORMATION

FREEPORT MERCHANTS ASSOCIATION
23 Depot St., Freeport, ME 04032
207-865-1212; www.freeportusa.com

MIDCOAST

Maritime history is alive and well in this area. You can explore the traces of the Popham colony at the mouth of the Kennebec River in Phipps-burg and also head upriver to see an active naval shipbuilding indus-try at the Bath Iron Works. Two museums offer the chance to learn about Maine's shipbuilding heritage: the Maine Maritime Museum in Bath and the Penobscot Marine Museum in Searsport.

Windjammers ply the waters, and you can enjoy taking a cruise for a few hours or a few days on one of them. We cherish our memories of weeklong cruises and dining on lobster.

Drivers collect their own tours out to the end of the fingers of land that jut into the Atlantic. Try a new one and discover more harbors, fishing villages, beaches, hiking trails, festivals, photo opportunities—and more places to have a lobster roll.

BATH

Bath has been called the "cradle of shipbuilding." The demand for ships made in Maine was heavy, and Maine men were skilled at their crafts. They worked long hours for small wages but could supplement income by fishing or farming. A master builder kept control of the work from the earliest stages of cutting the trees in the forest, using patterns to find and shape the curved timbers used for frames and knees. These would be brought back to the shipyard for finishing to form the skeleton of a ship.

The planking was laid on the frame, then caulkers put oakum into the seams and applied pitch and tar to make them watertight. Painters, riggers, and men who stepped the masts all had jobs to do. Ropewalks produced the rigging and lofts cut sails. Ship carvers not only made decorative figureheads and name boards, but also decorated the houses in town with their work.

Besides ships, Bath offers a wealth of sea captains' homes in the historic district. They are not open to the public, but you can stroll by and savor their architectural styles and their gardens.

HISTORICAL SITES
and MUSEUMS

The **Maine Maritime Museum** (207-443-1316; www.mainemaritimemu seum.org), 243 Washington St., is a special place to visit. Open year-round. Over the years we have been there many times and enjoy permanent exhibits and new displays. The complex includes the Maritime History Building offering displays, photographs, paintings, tools, and galleries. On the riverfront are docks for the *Sherman Zwicker*, a Grand Banks fishing schooner, and the Percy & Small Shipyard, including a mill and joiner shop and a boat shop.

A number of years ago we made a trip to the Maine Maritime Museum to see the *Snorri*, a replica of a Viking knarr, or cargo ship, built in Phippsburg and christened at the museum. She was built to retrace the classic voyage from Greenland that led Vikings to establish a colony at L'Anse aux Meadows on the northeastern tip of Newfoundland. The reenactment was to simulate the 800-mile voyage of Leif Ericsson in A.D. 1000 or 1001. The 54-foot open vessel carried oars, 1,000 square feet of sail, and a crew of nine, led by W. Hodding Carter. A damaged rudder forced them to turn back in 1997, but on a second try they completed the voyage successfully on September 22, 1998.

A new vessel, a replica of the pinnace *Virginia*, the first ship built in the English colonies, will be built at the museum to commemorate the 400th anniversary of the Popham colony. After fund-raising and planning, the group received design approval from the U.S. Coast Guard's Marine Safety Center in Washington, D.C.

LODGING

THE GALEN C. MOSES HOUSE
1009 Washington St., Bath, ME 04530
888-442-8771, 207-442-8771;
www.galenmoses.com
This 1874 house in Italianate style was once the scene of elegant dinner parties, and features elaborate high ceilings and a grand staircase with ornate woodcarvings.

THE INN AT BATH
969 Washington St., Bath, ME 04530
800-423-0964, 207-443-4294;
www.innatbath.com
Antiques, portraits, and period furnishing fill this 1810 mansion.

FAIRHAVEN INN
118 N. Bath Rd., Bath, ME 04530
888-443-4391, 207-443-4391;
www.mainecoast.com/fairhaveninn
This 1790 home is near the Kennebec River.

RESTAURANTS

J.R. MAXWELL'S
122 Front St., Bath, ME 04530
207-443-2014
A hotel was originally in this 1840s building. The menu is eclectic, and the Boat Builder's Pub is downstairs.

KENNEBEC TAVERN & MARINA
119 Commercial St., Bath ME 04530
207-442-9636;
http://kennebectavern.com
The dining room overlooks the river and the marina. Maine seafood is the specialty.

INFORMATION

BATH/BRUNSWICK REGION CHAMBER OF COMMERCE
59 Pleasant St., Brunswick, ME 04011
207-725-8797;
www.midcoastmaine.com

PHIPPSBURG

Late in 1607 Sir George Popham brought more than a hundred colonists, including shipwrights, coopers, and carpenters, into harbor; it was late in the year, and nearly half returned to England as winter set in. The colonists managed to build a star-shaped fort, containing a warehouse and several other houses, but Popham died during the harsh winter, and Raleigh Gilbert took over as leader. After Gilbert heard from a supply ship in the spring that he had inherited a title and an estate in England, he decided to return. Others departed with him, and the colony was left without leadership. It broke up before the year was over. However, they built the first ship of the colonies, the *Virginia*.

HISTORICAL SITES *and* MUSEUMS

Fort Popham State Historic Site (207-389-1335; www.pophamcolony.org), Hunniwell's Point at Popham Beach. Open Memorial Day–Sep. The existing fort was built in 1861 near the site of the original Popham colony. Displays there interpret the history of the area—the story of Popham colony, Benedict Arnold's march through Maine, and the fort's construction.

Archaeological investigations have uncovered the remains of Fort St. George from the Popham colony. Digs have found evidence of the storehouse and Admiral Raleigh Gilbert's house. You can keep track of ongoing exploration on the Web site, www.pophamcolony.org.

LODGING

POPHAM BEACH BED & BREAKFAST
4 Riverview Ave.,
Phippsburg, ME 04562;
207-389-2409;
www.pophambeachbandb.com
This home was once a Coast Guard station, and is right on historic Popham Beach. It dates from 1883 as a lifesaving station and was taken over by the Coast Guard in 1935.

THE 1774 INN
44 Parker Head Rd.,
Phippsburg, ME 04562
207-389-1774; www.1774inn.com
The 1774 Inn is on the National Register of Historic Places as the McCobb-Hill-Minott House. James McCobb was in the lumber business. Mark L. Hill was the first U.S. congressman from Maine, and he lived in the house from 1782 to 1842.

RESTAURANTS

SPINNEY'S RESTAURANT
987 Popham Rd., Phippsburg, ME 04562; 207-389-1122
Seafood is the specialty.

THE ARNOLD TRAIL

In 1775 Benedict Arnold left from Popham on his expedition to Quebec. Not only did he get a start late in the year and have to battle wintry weather, but he was unlucky because the British received word that he was on the way, thereby destroying the element of surprise. The Arnold Trail is 194 miles long and continues from Popham to Hallowell, Skowhegan, Solon, Moscow, Stratton, Sarampus, Chain of Ponds, and Coburn Gore.

Arnold's collection of volunteers began marching at General Washington's headquarters in Cambridge and passed through Medford, Salem, and Ipswich to Newburyport. They sailed from Newburyport on September 19, 1775, on eleven schooners and sloops. Pittston, below Augusta, was the departure point for the 1,100 men who soon found themselves struggling up the Kennebec River in their 400-pound bateaux loaded with equipment.

North of Augusta they met the challenge of the Ticonic Falls, followed by Five Mile Ripples. They were able to rest at Fort Halifax in Winslow before continuing on, carrying their heavy

Rifleman George Morison wrote, "This day we left all inhabitants and entered the wilderness. It is very mountainous and covered with underwood. Little, if any part of it is fit for cultivation. The timber for the most part is composed of birch, pine, and hemlock . . . the land of nature seems to have denied to those solitary regions every good thing—and to have left it a void forever—the refuge of wild beasts."

boats up steep cliffs around waterfalls. Skowhegan Falls and Solon Falls were especially difficult. In Norridgewock, the last bit of civilization at that time, they passed the site where a Jesuit missionary priest, Father Sebastian Rasle, had been slain by the English colonists in 1724. His monument today is a granite obelisk with a cross on top.

Arnold's men reached Caratunk Falls in Solon, maneuvered through rapids, and increased their food supply by fishing. By October 10 they reached the Great Carrying Place, where they were joined by three rifle companies. They were delighted to find plentiful moose for their dinners. The next section continued through marshes, around ponds, and through a swamp. Rain had made walking difficult through the bog, but they finally reached the Dead River, where they saw mountains on both sides covered with snow.

Arnold ordered his men to abandon the boats and carry provisions on their backs. By then they were exhausted and hungry—so hungry that they ate candles, their leather shot pouches, and a beloved pet dog. After six weeks of relentless hardship they finally reached the St. Lawrence opposite Quebec on November 8 but did not attack the garrison there until December 31, 1775, with another force that had come up the easier route through Lake Champlain and the Richelieu River.

Canada's destiny might have been different if Arnold's soldiers had conquered Quebec early in 1776. But after six weeks of trudging through woodland, around rapids, and over boggy and ice-crusted marshes, the men were lucky to have emerged alive. The New Year's Eve assault during a blizzard was a disaster; hundreds of Americans were taken prisoner, and Arnold was shot through the leg. The unsuccessful siege of the heavily fortified city lasted through the early months of 1776 and was abandoned upon the arrival of a British relief fleet in May.

Those interested in this epic march can drive along US 201 and 201A to see some of the sites and read panels detailing the army's struggle. Hikers can also walk on the Appalachian Trail, map in hand, from where it joins the Arnold Trail at East Carry Pond. To do this cross over the Kennebec to the west bank at Bingham and continue north along the Kennebec to the southern tip of Pierce Pond.

WISCASSET

Settlers arrived at this site on the Sheepscot River in the mid-17th century; the town was known as Pownalborough until 1802. At one time it was the most important port in Maine. The Embargo Act of 1807 put a damper on shipping in Wiscasset.

Today Wiscasset is a picturesque town with an abundance of handsome 18th- and 19th-century mansions to stroll by. They were built by shipowners and merchants.

HISTORICAL SITES and MUSEUMS
Castle Tucker (207-882-7169; www.historicnewengland.org), Lee and High Sts. Open June 1–Oct. 15. Judge Silas Lee built this house as a present for his wife. It

has a freestanding elliptical staircase as well as original wallpaper and Federal and Victorian furniture.

Nickels-Sortwell House (207-882-6218; www.historicnewengland.org), 121 Main St. Open June 1–Oct. 15. A Maine shipmaster, Captain William Nickels, owned the house. He made a fortune in the lumber trade. This house also has an elliptical staircase, illuminated by a skylight on the third floor. Furnishings from the Sortwell family remain.

LODGING *In nearby Westport:*

SQUIRE TARBOX INN
1181 Main Rd., Westport, ME 04578
800-818-0026, 207-882-7693;

www.squiretarboxinn.com
This 1763 farmhouse was finished in 1825. Meals are available by reservation.

Damariscotta and Newcastle

The Damariscotta site was settled by John Brown in 1625 at the head of navigation on the Damariscotta River, and in 1730 three families from Boston arrived to live here. Shipbuilding was a major industry in the town.

Today Damariscotta serves as a shopping and financial center for residents and resorts along this part of the coast. The main street is a line of brick buildings erected following a fire in 1845. Colonial and Federal period homes are abundant elsewhere in town and along the river.

Fifty years ago we remember ordering lobster from Damariscotta. It came in a large garbage can packed with seaweed, and they all lived! The name brings back the vision of cooking them and savoring every bite with friends after we had finished painting their house.

HISTORICAL SITES *and* MUSEUMS
Chapman-Hall House (207-442-7863), Main St. Open July–Labor Day. It was built in 1754 by Nathaniel Chapman. The wooden house has a central brick chimney and small-paned windows. The rooms are pine paneled, with wide-board floors, and are furnished with antiques.

The **Damariscotta River Association** (207-563-1393), at 110 Belvedere Rd., has a map to its properties, including the Great Salt Bay Preserve Heritage Trail. What is a midden? A refuse heap. Native Americans left a huge heap of oyster shells when they were living in the Damariscotta-Newcastle region hundreds of years ago. You can walk down to the "Glidden Midden," which is on the National Register.

LODGING

THE FLYING CLOUD
45 River Rd., Newcastle, ME 04553;
207-563-2484; www.theflyingcloud.com
The original building dates from the 1790s,

with an 1840 addition by a sea captain. Guest rooms in this B&B are named for ports visited by the clipper ship *Flying Cloud.*

THE NEWCASTLE INN
River Rd., Newcastle, ME 04553
800-832-8669, 207-563-5685;
www.newcastleinn.com
Guest rooms are furnished with antiques
and crewel needlework by one of the owners. The inn also offers water views, and
the deck has an awning for shade.

RESTAURANTS

LUPINES
In the Newcastle Inn, River Rd.,
Newcastle, ME 04553

800-832-8669, 207-563-5685;
www.newcastleinn.com
The menu is regional with a French flair.
The restaurant also offers a four-course
fixed-price menu.

INFORMATION

**DAMARISCOTTA REGION
CHAMBER OF COMMERCE**
Box 13, Damariscotta, ME 04543
207-563-8340;
www.damariscottaregion.com

PEMAQUID POINT

Pemaquid Point is at the end of a long peninsula extending to the mouth of the Johns River, near the present-day village of New Harbor. Many journals of early explorers mention Pemaquid. David Ingram arrived in 1569, Bartholomew Gosnold in 1602. The Sieur de Monts roamed the coast with Champlain in 1605, planning settlements in the area. Raleigh Gilbert visited in 1607, and Thomas Dermer in 1619.

HISTORICAL SITES and MUSEUMS

If you enjoy archaeological digs, **Colonial Pemaquid Historic Site** (207-677-2423; www.friendsofcolonialpemaquid.org) is the place to go. Open Memorial Day–Labor Day. Foundations from the early 17th-century settlement have been uncovered near Fort William Henry just off ME 130, where artifacts including household pieces and farming implements may be seen in the adjacent museum.

Here's a place to stretch your legs with lots to explore. **Fort William Henry** is a replica of the second of three English forts on the site. A stockade called Shurt's Fort was built around 1630, then burned by Indians. Fort Charles was built in 1677. Then settlers built a third fort in 1692 to defend themselves against Indians, pirates, and the French. It was destroyed in 1696 by the French. A fourth fort, Fort Frederick, was built in 1729 and destroyed during the Revolution.

The tower of the fort contains artifacts found on the site, military equipment, and Indian deeds. You can imagine how 17th-century soldiers peered out as they guarded the entrance to the river. A stone wall encloses the old parade ground, and many cellar holes are visible. The Old Fort Cemetery just outside the fort contains old slate stones, including that of Ann Rodgers, wife of Lieutenant Patrick Rodgers, who died in 1758.

The restored 18th-century **Harrington Meeting House** (207-677-2494) is located nearby on Old Harrington Rd. Open July and Aug. Colonel David Dunbar arrived in 1696 with 200 Irish Protestants and proceeded to divide the region into three areas: Walpole, Harrington, and Pemaquid. Each was to have a meetinghouse. Later, in 1770, the Reverend Alexander McLain came to America and traveled on horseback to serve each of the three meetinghouses. You may wonder about a bit of graffiti found on a plaster layer under the Harrington Meeting House during a restoration; it reads: "McLain is a lying fool."

The building was jacked up in 1851 and moved over the present cemetery, leaving the stones intact. The box pews and galleries were removed, doors and windows relocated, and the pulpit lowered. During a renovation after 1960 the box pews were returned, the pulpit raised, and galleries replaced. A historical museum now occupies the gallery area. It houses artifacts, tools, maps, period clothing, and documents contributed by local residents. The Harrington Burial Ground contains stones dating to 1716.

Dixey Bull, a pirate who was incensed after the French seized his sloop in 1632, got another ship and resumed harassing the shipping, without much success. He arrived in Pemaquid harbor and destroyed the trading post and some houses, stealing as he went. With this upturn in his fortune, he continued to raid settlements and capture small vessels. Not surprisingly, he disappeared when a fleet left Boston to find him. No one knows if he was ever caught.

LODGING

BRADLEY INN
3063 Pemaquid Point,
New Harbor, ME 04554
800-942-5560, 207-677-2105;
www.bradleyinn.com
Guest rooms in this 1900 inn are in the main building, a carriage house, and a cottage. Perennial gardens enhance the landscaping.

THE HOTEL PEMAQUID
3098 Bristol Rd.,
New Harbor, ME 04554
207-677-2312;
www.hotelpemaquid.com
The hotel dates from 1820, when it was a farmhouse; it became a hotel in 1888. There is a large stone fireplace, and the common rooms resemble an English country house.

WALDOBORO

This town overlooking the tidal Medomak River was once known for shipbuilding. General Samuel Waldo encouraged more than fifty German families to come and farm his land. The first group arrived in 1742.

Today the town features art galleries with work by local artists. The main industries are clamming, lobstering, and sauerkraut production.

HISTORICAL SITES *and* MUSEUMS
The **Old German Church** (207-832-5100) dates from 1772. Open July and Aug. It has a wineglass pulpit. Samuel Waldo encouraged German families to settle in the area—see the inscription in the cemetery to realize their response. They came expecting to find a prosperous city but found only wilderness. Waldo promised more than he delivered.

LODGING

BLUE SKYE FARM BED & BREAKFAST
1708 Friendship Rd.,
Waldoboro, ME 04572

207-832-0300; www.blueskyefarm.com
The house dates from 1775, has stenciling
in the hall, and is furnished with antiques.

THOMASTON

In 1605 Captain George Waymouth claimed Allen's Island off the mouth of the St. Georges River for the English, and by 1630 a trading post was established there. In 1736 settlers founded Thomaston. Shipbuilding thrived, and lime processed here became an important export.

HISTORICAL SITES and MUSEUMS

The **General Henry Knox Museum** (207-354-8062; www.generalknoxmuseum .org), 30 High St. Open June–Oct. General Knox was not only a famed Revolutionary War hero and the first U.S. secretary of war, but also the son-in-law of Samuel Waldo. Knox's wife had inherited a large tract of land in the area, and upon his retirement from public service Knox built a mansion here and called it Montpelier. The house eventually fell into decline and was razed, but a replica was erected on the site in 1929, and it contains his original furnishings and possessions.

EVENTS

August: Revolutionary Encampment at Montpelier: Fifty reenactors pitch tents, chop wood, light campfires, and shoot muskets.
207-354-8062; www.generalknoxmuseum.org

CAMDEN

Captain John Smith wrote that Camden stands "under the high mountains of the Penobscot, against whose feet the sea doth beat." Champlain arrived in 1605 and called the Camden Hills the "mountains of Bedabedec" on his map. Views from the ledges of the Mount Battie South Trail are worth the climb for today's visitor, and there is also a toll road from Camden Hills State Park. Other trails favored by hikers include Mount Megunticook Trail, Tablelands Trail, Bald Rock Mountain Trail, Maiden Cliff Trail, and Ragged Mountain Trail.

The town itself is a tourist and boaters' haven and popular summer spot, with well-kept mansions lining a picture-postcard harbor. Windjammer cruises depart from here during the summer.

HISTORICAL SITES and MUSEUMS

Conway Homestead and Mary Meeker Cramer Museum (207-236-2257; www.crmuseum.org) Conway Rd. off US 1. Open July–Aug. It dates from 1770, with later additions in 1815 and 1825. The house has roof timbers fastened with treenails, or trunnels. Some of the beams in the cellar still are covered with bark, and in the kitchen there is a bake-oven built with small bricks. The entrance hall is curved and contains a "parson's cupboard."

Robert Thorndike had the original deed to the lot, and his son was one of the first white children born in the area. Several generations of Thorndikes lived in the house until it was sold to Frederick Conway in 1826. The barn houses a collection of carriages, sleighs, farm tools, and a saw to cut ice. The complex also includes a blacksmith shop, herb garden, maple sugar house, and barn. The Mary Meeker Cramer Museum houses collections of antique glass, paintings, musical instruments, furniture, costumes, quilts, and ship models.

This is the home of the Camden-Rockport Historical Society.

LODGING

THE BELMONT
6 Belmont St., Camden, ME 04843
800-238-8053, 207-236-9872;
www.thebelmontinn.com
This 1892 Edwardian-style inn is a few blocks off US 1.

BLACKBERRY INN
82 Elm St., Camden, ME 04843
800-388-6000, 207-236-6060,
www.blackberryinn.com
This Victorian property has antiques and collectibles.

CAMDEN MAINE STAY
22 High St., Camden, ME 04843
207-236-9636;
www.camdenmainestay.com
Nautical decor is a highlight in this 1802 building, including a 1935 Chris Craft model in the TV room.

NORUMBEGA
63 High St., Camden, ME 04843
877-363-4646 or 207-236-4646;
www.norumbegainn.com
This turreted and towered stone mansion looks like a castle.

WHITEHALL INN
52 High St., Camden, ME 04843
800-789-6565, 207-236-3391;
www.whitehall-inn.com
The inn dates from 1834. Edna St. Vincent Millay read her poem "Renascence" here in 1909.

In nearby Lincolnville:

THE YOUNGTOWN INN
ME 52 and Youngtown Rd.,
Lincolnville, ME 04849
800-291-8438, 207-763-4290;
www.youngtowninn.com
Dating from 1810, the building began as a farmhouse on a poultry and dairy farm and now has B&B guest rooms and a restaurant.

RESTAURANTS

BOYNTON-MCKAY FOOD CO.
30 Main St., Camden, ME 04843
207-236-2465;
www.boynton-mckay.com
The building once housed an apothecary in the 1890s. You can have a meal in one of the tall booths.

CAPPY'S CHOWDER HOUSE
1 Main St., Camden 04843
207-236-2254;
www.cappyschowder.com
This very popular pub offers lots of seafood as well as meat entrees. A bakery and coffee bar are on the lower level.

HARTSTONE INN
41 Elm St., Camden, ME 04843
800-788-4823, 207-236-4259;
http://hartstoneinn.com
A five-course dinner, prix fixe, is offered.

THE WATERFRONT RESTAURANT
Bayview St., Camden, ME 04843
207-236-3747;
www.waterfrontcamden.com
The restaurant is right on the harbor
and decorated in a nautical style.

In nearby Lincolnville:

CHEZ MICHEL
US 1, Lincolnville Beach,
Lincolnville, ME 04849
207-789-5600
French cuisine with plenty of seafood
is on the menu.

LOBSTER POUND RESTAURANT
Lincolnville Beach,
Lincolnville, ME 04849
207-789-5550
Lobster is served in many ways here.

INFORMATION

**CAMDEN-ROCKPORT-LINCOLNVILLE
CHAMBER OF COMMERCE**
2 Public Landing by the harbor,
Camden, ME 04843
800-223-5459, 207-236-4404;
www.visitcamden.com

SEARSPORT

Ships were built on the Penobscot River since 1770. The place to trace maritime history is the **Penobscot Marine Museum** (207-548-2529; www.penobscot-marinemuseum.org), US 1, Searsport. Open mid-May–mid-Oct. The museum has collections of marine paintings, ship models, scrimshaw, and boats of all kinds. There is also a lecture series. In 2005 the museum had an exhibition marking the 400th anniversary of George Waymouth's exploration of the Maine coast. A video is available of this event.

   Fort Pownall and **Fort Point State Park** are farther up the Penobscot River. The fort dates from 1759; all that is left now is earthworks. The Penobscot River was the unofficial boundary between the French and English territories.

DOWN EAST AND ACADIA

One of the prizes in Maine is this area—one of whitewater rivers, freshwater lakes, rugged promontories, and crashing waves. Hiking on Mount Desert appeals to many, and others may choose to drive around the island, stopping to see natural wonders. For history lovers, there is plenty to enjoy, with forts, museums, and a tavern where Revolutionary plans were hatched.

CASTINE

For a period of nearly 200 years Castine was fought over by the French, Dutch, British, and Americans. In 1629 the Pilgrims sent Edward Ashley here to build a trading post, which was ruined in 1631 by the French. Baron de Saint-Castin came from Quebec in 1673 to manage the trading post for the French. Castin had earlier arrived in New France at the age of 15 to claim a royal land grant belonging to his family. He canoed with several Abenaki Indians to the mouth of the Penobscot and decided to stay; Castin married the daughter of a chief. The town was named after him.

Today Castine is a popular place in the summer, with the town dock a center for ogling boats, having a picnic, and people watching.

HISTORICAL SITES *and* MUSEUMS

As early as 1626 people were protecting themselves by an early fort on the site of the present **Fort George** (Castine Historic Preservation, 207-326-8071), Wadsworth Cove Rd. Fort George was hurriedly built by the British during the Revolution, in 1779. In response to the British move, a hastily assembled American fleet of 44 ships led by Commodore Dudley Saltonstall and carrying 1,000 militiamen, including Lieutenant Colonel Paul Revere, sailed from Boston in an attempt to seize the fort. The Americans did not press the attack, and their delay proved disastrous. The British sent a fleet of reinforcements, and all the American ships were captured, scuttled, burned, or sunk. One wrecked vessel, the *Defense,* is now the object of an underwater archaeological exploration. A permanent exhibit on the disastrous Penobscot expedition can be viewed, along with other displays of regional historical interest, at the **Castine Historical Society** (207-326-4118; www.castinehistoricalsociety.org), in the restored Abbott School on the town common. Open July–Labor Day.

Also in Castine you will find the **Wilson Museum** (www.wilsonmuseum.org; 207-326-8545), 107 Perkins St. Open May-Sep. The museum contains anthropological and geological collections as well as colonial pieces. The **John Perkins House**, dating from 1763, is on the grounds. As the only pre-Revolutionary build-

Castine Historical Society

ing in the region, it holds historical interest with its hand-hewn beams. The house contains 18th-century pieces, and some come from the Perkins family. Artifacts given by local inhabitants are on display, and interpreters demonstrate the work done in the blacksmith shop. Don't overlook the interesting collection in the Hearse House.

LODGING

THE CASTINE INN
33 Main St., Castine, ME 04421
207-326-4365; www.castineinn.com
This 1890s inn has a nice mural of Castine in the dining room. Some guest rooms have a harbor view.

PENTAGOET INN
26 Main St., Castine, ME 04421
800-845-1701, 207-326-8616;
www.pentagoet.com
The inn dates from 1894 and includes a colonial-style annex.

RESTAURANTS

THE CASTINE INN
33 Main St., Castine, ME 04421
207-326-4365; www.castineinn.com
Open only for private dining; call for a reservation for a seven-course tasting dinner.

PENTAGOET INN DINING ROOM
26 Main St., Castine, ME 04421
800-845-1701, 207-326-8616;
www.pentagoet.com
Dine in the restaurant or in the Passports Pub.

MOUNT DESERT ISLAND

Samuel de Champlain found Mount Desert Island in 1604 and named it "L'isles des Monts-deserts." The barren mountains inspired his choice. French Jesuits arrived in 1613 but soon after were expelled by English explorers.

Landscape painters including Thomas Cole and Frederic Church spent their summers here, and their paintings of the area are glorious. Today, thousands of tourists flock to Mount Desert, its main resort town of Bar Harbor, and Acadia National Park, which takes up nearly half the island. Visitors can explore on foot or tour the loop by car. Mount Cadillac is the highest peak in the area at 1,532 feet, and there are dozens more mountains to scale if you wish. Many miles of hiking trails and carriage roads invite biking and hiking.

HISTORICAL SITES and MUSEUMS

The **Abbe Museum** (207-288-3519; www.abbemuseum.org), 26 Mount Desert St., Bar Harbor. Open Apr.–Dec. Exhibits include a history of the Penobsot, Passamaquoddy, Micmac, and Maliseet tribes. The "Circle of Four Directions," a circular tower, is the centerpiece of the museum. The collection includes stone tools such as projectile points, knives, axes, and fishing weights. Bone pieces include harpoons, fishhooks, combs, and needles. Seventeenth-century treasures include beads and copper tools. There's an etched powder horn thought to have belonged to chief Orono of the Penobscots. Other 18th-century pieces include pipes and jewelry.

LODGING

In Bar Harbor:

BALANCE ROCK INN
21 Albert Meadow,
Bar Harbor, ME 04609
800-753-0494, 207-288-2610;
www.barharborvacations.com
You can't miss seeing the huge rock balancing on the rocks below the house. This historic B&B dates from the turn of the 20th century.

BAR HARBOR INN
Newport Dr., Bar Harbor, ME 04609
800-248-3351, 207-288-3351;
www.barharborinn.com
Once a social club, part of the inn dates from 1887.

HEARTHSIDE BED & BREAKFAST
7 High St., Bar Harbor, ME 04609
207-288-4533; www.hearthside.com
A local doctor built this three-story weathered-shingled house around 1900.

LEDGELAWN INN
66 Mount Desert St.,
Bar Harbor, ME 04609
800-274-5334, 207-288-4596;
www.ledgelawninn.com
This inn dates from 1904, when it was built as a summer cottage for John Brigham.

MANOR HOUSE INN
106 West St., Bar Harbor, ME 04609
800-437-0088, 207-288-3759;
www.barharbormanorhouse.com
This mansion was built in 1887.

In Southwest Harbor:

THE CLAREMONT HOTEL
Claremont Rd.,
Southwest Harbor, ME 04679
800-244-5036, 207-244-5036;
www.theclaremonthotel.com
This hotel dates from 1884. Rockers await on the wraparound porch. Cottages on the property have kitchenettes.

HARBOUR COTTAGE INN AND PIER ONE
9 Dirigo Rd.,
Southwest Harbor, ME 04679
888-843-3022, 207-244-5738;
www.harbourcottageinn.com
Choose from rooms in the inn, nearby cottages with kitchens, and housekeeping units on Clark Point Road.

THE INN AT SOUTHWEST
371 Main St.,
Southwest Harbor, ME 04679
207-244-3835;
www.innatsouthwest.com
Dating from 1884, this Victorian inn has guest rooms named after lighthouses.

KINGSLEIGH INN
373 Main St.,
Southwest Harbor, ME 04679
207-244-5302;
www.kingsleighinn.com
This turn-of-the-century inn has a wraparound porch and turrets.

LINDENWOOD INN
118 Clark Point Rd.,
Southwest Harbor, ME 04679
800-307-5335, 207-244-5335;
www.lindenwoodinn.com
A sea captain built this home beside the harbor, and linden trees grace the property.

In Northeast Harbor:

ASTICOU INN
15 Peabody Dr.,
Northeast Harbor, ME 04662
800-258-3373, 207-276-3344;
www.asticou.com
This historic inn dates from 1885 and overlooks the harbor.

GREY ROCK INN
Route 3,
Northeast Harbor, ME 04662
207-276-9360;
www.greyrockinn.com
This 1910 home is next to Acadia National Park.

HARBOURSIDE INN
48 Harbourside Rd.,
Northeast Harbor, ME 04662
207-276-3272;
www.harboursideinn.com
Noted Maine architect Fred Savage
designed this shingle-style inn in the
1880s. Some of the suites have kitchens.

RESTAURANTS

Bar Harbor

**GALYN'S
RESTAURANT**
17 Main St.,
Bar Habor, ME 04609
207-288-9706
The decor is 1880s with a pressed-tin
ceiling.

THE READING ROOM
At the Bar Harbor Inn,
Newport Dr.,
Bar Harbor, ME 04609
800-248-3351, 207-288-3351;
www.barharborinn.com
The circular room has a harbor view.

TESTA'S
53 Main St., Bar Harbor, ME 04609
207-288-3327
Italian dishes are a specialty.

Southwest Harbor

THE CLAREMONT HOTEL
Claremont Rd.,
Southwest Harbor, ME 04679
800-244-5036, 207-244-5036;
www.theclaremonthotel.com
A jacket is necessary in the dining room,
and the view is spectacular. Lunch is
available in the Boathouse.

Northeast Harbor

ASTICOU INN
15 Peabody Dr.,
Northeast Harbor, ME 04662
800-258-3373, 207-276-3344;
www.asticou.com
A special treat is the buffet and dance on
Thursdays.

INFORMATION

**MOUNT DESERT CHAMBER
OF COMMERCE**
18 Harbor St.,
Northeast Harbor, ME 04662
207-276-5040;
www.acadiachamber.com

ACADIA NATIONAL PARK
ME 233, McFarland Hill,
Bar Harbor, ME 04662.
207-288-3338; www.nps.gov/acad

MACHIAS

In 1633 the English built a trading post at Machias with Richard Vines in charge,
but it was quickly destroyed by the French governor of Acadia.

The first naval battle of the Revolution took place in Machias in 1775. The
sixty families in town had had a hard winter, and they were hungry. When Captain Ichabod Jones, who had lived in Machias for only a year and was suspected of being a Tory, sailed to Boston, the townspeople thought he would bring back provisions. But

> Legend reports that the British captain of the *Margaretta* and his officers brought their weapons to church in Machias on Sunday. When the captain spotted armed men on the river, he leaped out a window, ran to his boat, made it to his vessel, and headed down to Rim Narrows. But Machias men fired on the schooner and took her.

Vice Admiral Samuel Graves, commander of the port of Boston, insisted that Jones fetch timber for the British garrison in Boston. Graves sent an armed schooner, the *Margaretta*, along with Jones, to Machias. Although a majority voted in favor of sending their lumber to Boston, others did not. As Jones distributed the provisions he had brought back, he sold them only to those who had supported his request.

The townspeople later gathered, led by Jeremiah O'Brien and Benjamin Foster, seized one of Jones's sloops, the *Unity*, and chased after the *Margaretta*. They captured her and put her guns on the *Unity*. The British later retaliated by sending several ships to ravage Machias.

Pirates used the port at Machias as early as 1675 when the pirate Rhodes arrived. Another pirate, Samuel Bellamy, managed to persuade a ship's crew, after he had captured their vessel, to join his forces. He told them that shipowners were also thieves who created laws to protect their interests; therefore crews should be able to rob as well as shipowners. He met his death after capturing a New Bedford whaler. He thought he had persauded the captain to join forces with him, and then was surprised when the captain led his ship onto the rocks, where Bellamy and his crew drowned.

Today Machias is considerably more peaceful. It is the center of commerce in Washington County. Products include lumber, seafood, and blueberries.

HISTORICAL SITES *and* MUSEUMS

Burnham Tavern Museum (207-255-4432), Main and Free Sts. Open June–Sep. The tavern is in a 1770 gambrel-roof building. Underneath each of the four cornerstones the builder, Job Burnham, placed a note reading as follows: "hospitality, cheer, hope and courage." Job and Mary Burnham lived here with their 11 children and ran the tavern. The original sign is inscribed: "Drink for the thirsty, food for the hungry, lodging for the weary, and good keeping for horses."

In 1775 the men of Machias met in this tavern to discuss action and to erect a liberty pole on the village green; here they planned their successful capture of the *Margaretta*. The tavern was also used as a hospital for the wounded. Now it is furnished with period pieces. The focus of the museum is the first naval battle of the Revolution, and it displays muskets that were used then.

LODGING

MICMAC FARM GUESTHOUSES AND GARDNER HOUSE
47 Micmac Lane,
Machiasport, ME 04655
207-255-3008; www.micmacfarm.com
Ebenezer Gardner, farmer, built his home in 1776, and it is the oldest house in town. There are three housekeeping cabins.

RIVERSIDE INN
US 1, East Machias, ME 04630
888-255-4344, 207-255-4134;
www.riversideinn-maine.com
This 1805 house offers rooms in the main building and also in the Coach House.

RESTAURANTS

HELEN'S
32 Main St., Machias, ME 04655
207-255-8423
This restaurant is very popular for home-style cooking. A specialty is pie with real whipped cream.

RIVERSIDE INN
US 1, East Machias, ME 04630
888-255-4344, 207-255-4134;

www.riversideinn-maine.com
The cuisine focuses on seafood, with other offerings as well.

INFORMATION

THE MACHIAS BAY AREA CHAMBER OF COMMERCE
12 E. Main St., Machias, ME 04654.
207-255-4402;
www.machiaschamber.org

MOUNTAINS AND LAKES

All year round residents and visitors enjoy the mountains and lakes in Maine. Fishermen look for the season in spring where brook trout and landlocked salmon wait for them. Rangeley Lake is the center of 112 small lakes and ponds that feed into it. Paddlers take to the Carrabassett for great whitewater, and families enjoy the quieter Saco for a vacation.

Skiers flock to the many ski areas and take off on Alpine skis, snowboards, and Nordic skis. Resorts range from small to large, and many families return year after year to their favorites.

NEW GLOUCESTER

HISTORICAL SITES and MUSEUMS

A living-history museum that portrays Shaker life from the 18th century to the present day is the main destination in New Gloucester. The **Shaker Museum**, (207-926-4597; www.shaker.lib.me.us), is on ME 26, at Sabbathday Lake. Open Memorial Day–Columbus Day.

The Sabbathday Lake Shaker community was founded in 1783 and formally established in 1794. It is now the sole remaining active Shaker community in the world. The meetinghouse is a two-and-a-half story clapboard building with a gambrel roof. The room for worship is on the first floor. Museum collections include furniture, textiles, tools, farm implements, and folk art. Six of the 18 buildings in the community are open to the public.

KENNEBEC VALLEY

Native Americans, French, and English all used water to get around. Invasions followed the waterways, and forts were built on them for defense. The Kennebec, one of Maine's major inland water routes, is a prime example. From the early Popham colony fort at the river's mouth to the Arnold trail that led northward to Quebec, the Kennebec is a corridor to history.

Today the river is prized by whitewater enthusiasts, and we can attest to the thrill of bouncing down the rapids. People take to rafts, kayaks, and canoes—all are invigorating.

The valley also attracts those who like to snowshoe, ski, and snowmobile in the winter and hikers and walkers in the summer.

AUGUSTA

In 1628 the Plymouth Colony founded a trading post here. Fort Western was built on the east bank of the Kennebec here at the beginning of the French and Indian War.

Augusta has been the state capital since 1827. The Maine State Library and State Museum are also here.

HISTORICAL SITES *and* MUSEUMS
The oldest wooden fort building left in New England is **Old Fort Western** (207-626-2385; www.oldfortwestern.org), City Center Plaza. Open Memorial Day–Columbus Day, Nov.–May, first Sunday of every month. Wealthy Boston merchants, proprietors of the Kennebec Purchase, built the fort in 1754. It served as a supply depot for the military garrison 17 miles upriver at Fort Halifax.

Captain James Howard, the first commander of the fort, was in charge of the 20 soldiers who were garrisoned here. After the 1763 treaty formally ending the French and Indian War, the fortifications were no longer needed. James Howard bought the fort, and generations of his family lived in the main house. Visitors can get a glimpse into 18th-century life through the costumed interpreters.

The fort's 250th anniversary was celebrated in 2004. A two-day 18th-century military encampment was held to commemorate the engagement that took place in 1754 between a wood-cutting party from the fort and 100 Indians who had been sent from New France to destroy Fort Halifax.

Fort Western has a bateau like the ones used to ferry goods from Fort Western to Fort Halifax. A boat crew was recruited to journey up the 18 miles to Fort Halifax on a resupply mission as part of the celebration. They left Fort Western on June 18, encamped at Seven Mile Island overnight, and continued to Fort Halifax. Along the way they battled rapids and current and more than once had to get out into the water and haul.

You can see the bateau in the boat-shed, and several times a summer she will be taken out for a demonstration

 In case you are called upon to row, some of the rowing commands follow:

Toss Oars!	Hold Water!
Let Fall!	Back Astern!
Give Way Together!	That's Well!
Pick Up the Stroke!	Avast!

You can guess what some of them mean.

with the crew dressed in 18th-century attire. It may be possible to board the vessel and try to row as well. Check the Web site for information on when, weather permitting, she will be in the water.

"This Land Called Maine" tells Maine's story in five natural history settings in the **Maine State Museum** (207-287-2301; www.mainestatemuseum.org). Open year-round, Tue.–Sat. Located in the Capitol Complex on State St., the museum offers a wealth of programs and displays on Maine. Visitors can see collections of gems and minerals that have been discovered in the state. Some exhibits focus on early industries, including fishing, lumbering, and shipbuilding. An archaeological exhibit entitled "12,000 years in Maine" covers prehistory and the history of Indians living in the area from 3000 B.C.

LODGING

SENATOR INN & SPA
284 Western Ave., Augusta, ME 04330
877-772-2224, 207-622-3138;
www.senatorinn.com
This building is not historic, but it has a full-service spa.

RESTAURANTS

CLOUD 9
In the Senator Inn,
284 Western Ave., Augusta, ME 04330
877-772-2224, 207-622-3138;
www.senatorinn.com
Maine seafood is special, and there is also a Sunday brunch.

EVENTS

March: Maine Maple Sunday invites visitors to see maple syrup being made. www.getrealmaine.com
July 4: Fort Western celebrates with special events and fireworks.

INFORMATION

KENNEBEC VALLEY CHAMBER OF COMMERCE
21 University Dr.,
Augusta, ME 04330
207-623-4559;
www.augustamaine.com

WINSLOW

Just across the Kennebec River from Waterville, Winslow was the site of the last frontier post on the river during the French and Indian War.

HISTORICAL SITES and MUSEUMS
Fort Halifax (207-624-6080; www.maine.gov/doc/parks), US 201, played a part in the French and Indian War. In 1754, at the beginning of the war, Indians attacked the fort but were repulsed. The French continued to urge the Indians to vanquish English settlements, but with the fall of Quebec in 1759 French power in America evaporated. Fort Halifax became a "truck house" for the Indians, a place where they brought furs and exchanged them for goods.

Today only the blockhouse from 1754 remains, a National Historic Landmark and the oldest such structure in the country. In 1987 floodwaters surrounded the blockhouse and took it completely apart. People went out in boats to recover the timbers that had floated downstream. The next year it was reassembled.

HALLOWELL

Hallowell is on the Kennebec just south of Augusta, near the head of navigation on the river. Abenaki Indians traded with colonists here since the 1600s. By the late 1700s Hallowell was an international port, and shipbuilding brought a period of prosperity in the early 1800s.

Today Hallowell is known as an antiques center with a row of shops on Water Street. It is also popular for cruising from the town docks. Hikers and cyclists will find trails in the area.

LODGING

**MAPLE HILL FARM
BED AND BREAKFAST INN**
11 Inn Rd. Hallowell, ME 04347
800-622-2708 or 207-622-2708;
www.maplebb.com
The land was cleared and settled in the late 1700s and was home to one of the founding fathers of Hallowell, William Oliver Vaughn. It is still a working farm and also offers conference facilities.

RESTAURANTS

SLATE'S
167 Water St., Hallowell, ME 04347
207-622-9575
Three buildings with a patio in the back attract locals and visitors. Sunday brunch is popular.

Current Information

MAINE TOURISM ASSOCIATION
325 Water St., Hallowell, ME 04347-2300
800-533-9595, 207-623-0363; www.mainetourism.com

MAINE OFFICE OF TOURISM
59 State House Station, Augusta, ME 04333
888-624-6345, 207-624-7483

Vermont

Historical Introduction *to* Vermont

Vermont's relatively short history is full of unsolved questions and undocumented claims, but most historians agree that Samuel de Champlain was the first European to explore the western side of the territory. In 1609, after wintering at Quebec, he proceeded with friendly Algonquians and Hurons up the St. Lawrence and Richelieu Rivers to the lake that now bears his name. When the expedition encountered a party of Iroquois Indians, a battle ensued. Champlain himself killed two Iroquois chiefs. The Iroquois never forgave him for humiliating them with "white man's lightning" and continued to fight against the French in the long struggle for domination of the territories north and west of the New England colonies.

Champlain sketched that first fight and portrayed the Indians in the nude because that is how Europeans imagined savages. He also added some palm trees—certainly a curiosity for the Lake Champlain shore—that raise some questions about his professional role as a geographer. Champlain had been appointed royal geographer by King Henry IV, and he had christened the north country around the St. Lawrence "New France" in his report to the king.

A replica of the Schooner Philadelphia, at the Lake Champlain Maritime Museum in Vergennes

MYSTERY or HOAX?

✳ Questions about Champlain's role as the first European to see the lake named after him emerged from a find in the middle of the 19th century. Near Swanton, Vermont, where the Missisquoi River joins Lake Champlain, two workmen discovered a lead tube in 1853. A note inside read:

Nov. 29 AD 1564

THIS IS THE SOME DAYE
I MUST NOW DIE THIS IS
THE 90TH DAY SINE WE
LEF THE SHIP ALL HAVE

PERISHED AND ON THE
BANKS OF THIS RIVER
I DIE TO (OR, SO) FAREWELLE
MAY FUTURE POSTERITYE
KNOWE OUR END
JOHNE GRAYE

But the claim for an earlier English presence on the lake can not be supported by any known voyage to this part of the New World. English expeditions of the time, like those of John Hawkins, were too busy with the West Indies, and Martin Frobisher's three voyages did not begin until 1576.

First Settlement

The first French settlement was that of Captain La Motte, who in 1666 built a fort and shrine to Sainte Anne on Isle La Motte, at the northern end of Lake Champlain. Next, Captain Jacobus de Warm, a Dutchman, developed an English post sixty miles south at Chimney Point, across the lake from Crown Point, in 1690. Neither of these military settlements lasted very long. Throughout the 17th century and much of the 18th, Vermont was mostly uninhabited land trod by the French and Indians on their way to attack English settlers in the south and east.

Massachusetts residents built Fort Dummer, near Brattleboro, in 1724, now considered the first permanent settlement. The French built both a fort at Crown Point on the New York side of Lake Champlain and a village on the Vermont side in 1731 but did not concentrate on settling this area. Throughout the first half of

VERMONT Time Line

1609	1666	1690	1724	1741	1764
Samuel de Champlain reaches Lake Champlain	Fort Sainte Anne built by Captain de la Motte	Captain Jacobus de Warm establishes an outpost at Chimney Point	Fort Dummer built near Brattleboro	New Hampshire claims territory that includes all of what is now Vermont, known as the New Hampshire Grants	King George III declares the western banks of the Connecticut River the boundary between New Hampshire and New York

the 18th century, England and France battled for domination of the Champlain Valley. The emphasis was still on forts, and in 1755 the French built a major one, named Carillon, at Ticonderoga to guard the strategic portage between Lake Champlain and Lake George.

The Land Grab

Vermont land was in constant turmoil over land rights as both kings and governors gave away vast tracts even while actual ownership and boundaries remained unclear. King George II in 1741 handed over to Benning Wentworth, governor of New Hampshire, land "extending due West Cross the said River [Merrimack] till it meets with our other governments."

But the "government" on the other side, that of New York, had not received word of its eastern boundary from the king. New Hampshire and New York were supposed to meet—but where? Governor Wentworth made the assumption that he had control of land as far to the west as his southern neighbors in Massachusetts and Connecticut did, according to a royal edict in 1700. That would put the border of New Hampshire on a north-south line twenty miles east of the Hudson, roughly where Vermont meets New York today. But New York's governor George Clinton opposed this expansion as an intrusion into his colony's territory, citing the earlier charter given to the Duke of York in 1664. By its terms New York extended to the western bank of the Connecticut River. Thus began one of the longest land controversies in North America—one that lasted throughout the 18th century until New York and the relatively new republic of Vermont finally came to terms in 1789.

Both governors agreed to abide by the decision of the king, which was a long time coming. And Wentworth continued to make land grants over a large portion of Vermont, which he called the New Hampshire Grants. Finally, in 1770, King George III declared "the Western Banks of the River Connecticut to be the Boundary Line between the said two Provinces of New Hampshire and New York." New York then insisted that Wentworth's grants were invalid and issued its own

1770-71	1775	1777	1777	1791
Ethan Allen and the Green Mountain Boys harass New Yorkers, claiming their land	Ethan Allen and Benedict Arnold seize Fort Ticonderoga on Lake Champlain	The only Revolutionary War battle in Vermont takes place at Hubbardton	Delegates adopt a constitution for Vermont, which becomes an independent republic	Vermont ratifies the U.S. Constitution to become the fourteenth state

New York grants for the same land.

The dispute had become hot and heavy a year earlier when New York surveyors arrived on James Breakenridge's farm in Bennington and were driven off by a large group of his neighbors. Then the king's edict and the New York response created the "unruly mob" that we remember as the Green Mountain Boys in another context. In 1770 Ethan Allen had been elected by a group called the Bennington Nine to organize the legal defense of their New Hampshire titles before the Supreme Court in Albany. When Chief Justice Robert Livingston (hardly an impartial judge, with some New York land titles in his own pocket) refused to hear the evidence, Allen had a conversation with attorneys for both sides and reportedly uttered one of the colorful phrases he was famous for: "The gods of the hills are not the gods of the valley." Then he went back to Bennington and gathered some two hundred vigilantes to protect New Hampshire grants. Thus the origin of the Green Mountain Boys had more to do with a lasting grievance against neighboring "Yorkers" than with revolutionary fervor against the king.

Ethan Allen and the Green Mountain Boys had a rough and ironic sense of humor as they warded off incursions on their land. When a New Yorker tried to claim land already settled in the New Hampshire Grants, he was often "shown the beech seal"—which meant being whipped with a beech whip. New York surveyors or sheriffs who threatened to seize homes in land grant disputes were given the "high chair treatment"—that is, suspended in the air tied in a chair!

A War Breaks Out

In April 1775, one month after a nasty fracas over land foreclosures in which two men were killed, the Cumberland County Convention at Westminster voted to petition the king for a new province. After the fighting at Lexington and Concord that same month, however, New Hampshire and New York had more important business to attend to. In May, Ethan Allen and Benedict Arnold slipped across Lake Champlain and seized Fort Ticonderoga. By September, Allen was a British prisoner, having been captured while taking part in an expedition against Canada. He was not exchanged until 1778.

Because of its position on the flank of the major north-south communications route between Canada and the middle colonies, Vermont (or what is now Vermont) played a major role in the early years of the war, when British invasions from the north sought to sever the colonies in two. In the summer of 1776, the first British invasion down Lake Champlain, under General Guy Carleton, was thwarted by the ever-active Benedict Arnold, who hastily assembled a small fleet at Skenesborough (now Whitehall, New York, on the Vermont border) and sailed north to meet the British advance. Carleton was forced to take the time to gather his own fleet, with far superior firepower, before advancing down the lake. In October, Arnold's much smaller naval force tenaciously sacrificed itself at the Battle of Valcour Island, and by the time Carleton's advance reached Ticonderoga at the bottom of the lake, ice was forming and the British were forced to call off the campaign for another year.

The following year the assembled British forces under General John Burgoyne would dwarf Carleton's earlier effort; and Burgoyne's plan called as well for simultaneous Loyalist and British advances both from the Mohawk Valley to the west and New York City to the south. After Burgoyne's seemingly unstoppable army captured Ticonderoga, British advance forces pursued the retreating Americans south to about ten miles from present-day Rutland, where on July 7 a rear guard of Continentals and militia stood its ground at Hubbardton, in the only Revolutionary battle that took place on Vermont soil. The Americans were defeated in a fierce fight, but once again the delay had bought time for their cause.

Little more than a month later, a force of German mercenaries and American Loyalists dispatched by Burgoyne to raid for supplies was defeated by New Hampshire and Vermont militia under the command of Seth Warner and John Stark at the Battle of Bennington, which actually took place just over the border in New York. Burgoyne's grand scheme had begun to collapse. An ever-increasing American army, again aided by the gallantry of Benedict Arnold, defeated Burgoyne in September and October in two battles at Saratoga, which became a turning point in the war.

The Struggle for Autonomy

After Saratoga, the theater of war moved away from Vermont. The land dispute had by now merged into the issue of separate statehood. Even after the Declaration of Independence was read in July 1776, the issue had not been settled. The New Hampshire grantees were considered the "inhabitants of Vermont" by Dr. Thomas Young, a radical from Philadelphia. He thought of the Revolution not only as a rebellion against England, but also as a chance to realign borders. He sent the radical Pennsylvania Constitution to the residents and encouraged them to form a new state. In April 1777, the constitution of New York State was published, but people in Vermont did not care for its claims, so in July of the same year, seventy delegates adopted a constitution for Vermont, with hopes that they would soon become residents of the fourteenth state in the Union.

Those hopes would remain unrealized for fourteen years, one of the most puzzling intervals in any state's history. Powerful New York interests in the Continental Congress succeeded in blocking and delaying statehood for Vermont, and in response Ethan Allen and his brothers played all the political tricks they knew (by this time, Allen had been freed in a prisoner exchange). The Vermonters first annexed sixteen towns along the eastern bank of the Connecticut River and then expelled them when the political winds blew the other way, fearing that a proposal from New York, New Hampshire, and Massachusetts to create a new boundary along the ridge of the Green Mountains would destroy their new republic. In a proactive mood, Vermont reannexed those sixteen river towns in 1781 and took in eighteen more, while also extending its land claims all the way west to the Hudson. At this point Congress stepped in and assured Vermont it would consider its admission to the Union if these aggressive land claims were abandoned—a promise not kept.

Then the most bizarre episode in this tangled web of intrigue began. The Allens, who had been fervent patriots since the taking of Fort Ticonderoga in 1775, began secret negotiations with representatives of Lieutenant General Frederick Haldimand, British governor of Canada. Frustrated with the long delays in statehood, they pursued the advantages, both in trade and status, of becoming an independent province of royal Canada. At the same time they continued the appearance of negotiations with Congress, keeping all their options open, which meant walking a tight line to allay suspicions that had reached many of their Vermont neighbors and even George Washington. So now they found reasons to delay negotiations in this geopolitical poker game, waiting for the best terms to emerge.

Britain's part in the game ended when the Peace of Paris in 1783 included Vermont within the territory of the new United States. Perhaps tired of it all, in 1789 both the New York and Vermont legislatures passed bills settling the long travail that Benning Wentworth's acquisitiveness had started a century and a half earlier, with Vermont paying New York $30,000 to vacate its claims. The final tremors of the land disputes did not subside until boundaries were drawn and Vermont was admitted to the Union as the fourteenth state on March 4, 1791.

Regions *to* Explore

CHAMPLAIN REGION

S amuel de Champlain arrived at the lake in July 1609 with two other Frenchmen and a group of Algonquian and Huron Indians. He was probably the first European to see this beautiful lake. Unfortunately, a force of Iroquois, bitter enemies of the Algonquians and Hurons, was waiting for them. Champlain's Indians attacked, and the Frenchmen joined the battle. Champlain himself killed two Iroquois chiefs with one shot of his harquebus. This action did not bode well for future relations between the French and the warlike Iroquois.

Lake Champlain was an important link in the chain of almost uninterrupted waterways that connected the St. Lawrence River in Canada with the Atlantic at the mouth of the Hudson River in New York—a highway over the centuries

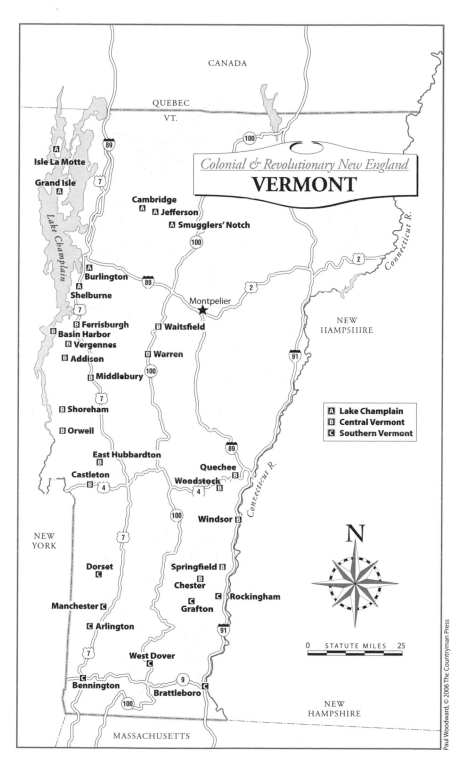

Colonial & Revolutionary New England
VERMONT

CANADA

QUEBEC

VT.

Isle La Motte

Grand Isle

Lake Champlain

Cambridge
Jefferson
Smugglers' Notch

Burlington

Shelburne

Ferrisburgh
Basin Harbor
Vergennes
Addison

Middlebury

Shoreham

Orwell

Montpelier

Waitsfield

Warren

NEW HAMPSHIRE

Connecticut R.

A Lake Champlain
B Central Vermont
C Southern Vermont

East Hubbardton

Castleton

Quechee

Woodstock

Windsor

Connecticut R.

NEW YORK

Dorset

Manchester

Arlington

Springfield
Chester
Grafton

Rockingham

N

West Dover

Bennington   Brattleboro

NEW HAMPSHIRE

MASSACHUSETTS

0 STATUTE MILES 25

for war parties, explorers, missionaries, traders, and armies. The route stretches from the Richelieu River, which empties into the St. Lawrence north of Montreal, upriver to Lake Champlain, down the lake to Ticonderoga and then to Lake George and, after a ten-mile wilderness portage, into the Hudson River near Glens Falls. During wars control of the waterway was crucial, enabling the movement of armies and supplies.

> Samuel de Champlain wrote about a creature he spotted that was twenty feet long and as thick as a barrel, with a head like a horse and a body like a serpent. Thus the legendary "Champ" was born, perhaps a descendant of Scotland's "Nessie." Times haven't changed much.

Isle La Motte was one of three sites on the lake with continuing historic importance in the colonial era; the others were Ticonderoga, controlling the passage into Lake George, and Crown Point (opposite Chimney Point), where the lake's waters are constricted to a narrow strait.

ISLE LA MOTTE

Frenchmen brought the first settlers to Isle La Motte in 1664. A Roman Catholic Mass was the first Christian religious service held in Vermont. Today cyclists prize the winding roads on the island. Orchards and farms, as well as an old marble quarry, add variety to the scenery.

HISTORICAL SITES and MUSEUMS
In 1666 Captain de la Motte and his French troops of the Carignan Regiment built **Fort Sainte-Anne** on Isle La Motte as a defense against the Mohawks, the easternmost tribe of the Iroquois Confederacy. A garrison of 300 men, including a number of Jesuits, celebrated Mass in the chapel of Fort Sainte-Anne, and in 1668 Bishop Laval of Quebec traveled by canoe to say Mass there. The fort was abandoned after eight years. Visitors to the **Shrine of Saint Anne** (802-928-3302), VT 129, will see the open-air chapel and perhaps be on hand for Mass; crowds come, especially on feast days and on Sundays. An A-frame structure covers a marble statue of Saint Anne.

A statue of Samuel de Champlain, sculpted for Expo '67 in Montreal, is located where he probably landed on Isle La Motte in 1609. He stands in a grove of trees looking out at the lake. Nearby, **Burying Ground Point** memorializes Revolutionary War soldiers who are buried there, and a plaque describes some of the history of the island.

Benedict Arnold anchored his fleet off the western shore of Isle La Motte before he engaged the advancing British forces in the **Battle of Valcour Island** on October 11, 1776. This was the first major naval battle of the Revolutionary War, and a crucial one.

The British strategy sought to split the colonies in two, with General Guy Carleton moving his army down the lake to the Hudson River and Albany. Carleton had already lost precious campaigning time when, faced with a hastily built fleet of warships commanded by Arnold, he had been forced to assemble his own, larger fleet. Arnold's little fleet included the sloops *Enterprise* and *Liberty*, the schooners *Royal Savage, Philadelphia,* and *Revenge,* and a number of smaller armed galleys and bateaux. He was outnumbered and greatly outgunned by the British fleet assembled under the command of Captain Thomas Pringle, who had two schooners and several dozen smaller ships. Sixty of Arnold's men died at Valcour Island, where the small fleet had taken defensive position.

The night after the battle, the remnants of Arnold's badly battered flotilla escaped in a dense fog by hugging the shore inside the anchored British ships. When the British awoke to an empty bay, they gave chase. Arnold held off the British in his own schooner, which he then ran ashore and burned, escaping by land, as the remainder of his ships managed to reach Fort Ticonderoga.

Because of the delay forced by Arnold, Carleton had no choice but to withdraw to Canada in the face of the rapidly approaching winter. Arnold's resistance at Valcour Island deflected a British stroke that might have won the war for the Crown.

GRAND ISLE

Vacationers like to head for Grand Isle, which has three parks for swimming, boating, and camping: Grand Isle State Park, Knight Point State Park, and North Hero State Park. There are also orchards and farm stores where you can find cheeses, jellies, apples, and gifts.

HISTORICAL SITES *and* MUSEUMS

Farther south in the Lake Champlain island chain, the **Hyde Log Cabin** (802-824-3051) stands on the main road (US 2) in **Grand Isle**. Open July–Labor Day. Dating from 1783, it is thought to be the oldest extant log cabin in the country. Jedediah Hyde Jr., who fought in the

> While architecture to the east along the coast continued to develop, houses in Vermont, a frontier territory, were made of rough-hewn logs, with unfinished pine floorboards and crude fireplaces. There were no gambrel roofs and no second-story overhangs. The houses were built simply, often without hints of any particular style.

Revolution, built the cedar cabin with a large fireplace that has been restored to its original appearance. Inside visitors will see furnishings of early colonial life collected by the Grand Isle Historical Society.

LODGING

CRESCENT BAY FARM BED & BREAKFAST
153 W. Shore Rd., South Hero, VT 05486
802-372-4807; www.crescentbaybb.com

Dating from the 1820s, the farmhouse overlooks the lake. Animals include black Angus beef cattle and llamas.

THE NORTH HERO HOUSE
US 2, North Hero, VT 05474
888-525-3644, 802-372-4732;
www.northherohouse.com
The main inn dates from 1891.

INFORMATION

**CHAMPLAIN ISLANDS
CHAMBER OF COMMERCE**
3501 US 2, North Hero, VT 05474
802-372-5683;
www.champlainislands.com

BURLINGTON

The omnipresent Allen family had been active in the Burlington area at least since 1772, when Ethan's brother Ira built ships there (while Ethan was struggling against New York land claims from Bennington). Ebenezer Allen, a cousin of Ethan, arrived in 1783 and settled on Allen's Point. He ran a ferry service for many years and in 1787 turned his home into a tavern.

Vermont's MYTHICAL HERO

Legends about Ethan Allen mix fact and fabrication, creating a mythical figure who never was. Those who believe that tall tales belong only to the American West may change their minds after hearing some of these Vermont whoppers:

Once when Ethan Allen was walking through the woods, a huge bobcat sprang and landed on his back. He reached behind and wrenched the cat onto the ground, then strangled it. When he arrived where he was going, he explained his delay by blaming the "Yorkers" for training and setting varmints against him.

Another time, he was said to have killed a bear by jamming his powder horn down the animal's throat.

Even a rattlesnake didn't get the better of him. One night after too much elbow bending, Allen and a friend stopped for a nap. A rattler coiled on Allen's chest, struck him several times, then rolled off, staggered, burped, and fell asleep. The next morning Allen complained about the pesky "mosquito" that kept biting him during the night.

Allen's drinking caused him some trouble at home, too. His wife, Fanny, finally worked out her own method for checking his sobriety. She pounded a nail high on the wall of their bedroom. In the morning, if she found his watch hanging on the nail, she knew he had come home sober; if not, he was in for it. It didn't take Allen long to put one and one together. And after a while, no matter how much he was weaving about, he'd get that watch hooked on the nail before he went to sleep.

When news leaked out of an impending real estate auction, Ethan, his brother Ira, and the sheriff announced the sale would be delayed until one o'clock the next day. And it was—until one in the morning. Just after midnight the three men met. And at the stroke of one Ethan bid a dollar for the house, barn, and hundred acres; Ira bid two dollars; and the gavel fell.

The last time Ethan Allen was seen alive was the night of February 10, 1789, when he came to Ebenezer's tavern for a load of hay. It has been surmised that they spent the night with bottles of rum, which may have contributed to Ethan's demise.

Today Burlington, Vermont's largest city, is also a popular maritime center for cruises from the Burlington Boat House. Lake Champlain ferries depart for Port Kent, New York, with a crossing time of one hour. The Burlington Bikepath is a 7.5-mile scenic route from Oakledge Park to the Winooski River.

The University of Vermont, the largest institution of higher education in the state, was founded in Burlington in 1791. The Robert Hull Fleming Museum has fine collections of European, American, African, Egyptian, and Middle Eastern art, as well as paintings by 20th-century Vermont artists.

HISTORICAL SITES *and* MUSEUMS

For a glimpse into Allen's real life, visit the **Ethan Allen Homestead** (802-865-4556; www.ethanallenhomestead.org) in Burlington (just off VT 127 northbound at the exit sign labeled NORTH AVENUE, BEACHES.) Open all year but weekends only during the winter season. Walk along a path past Fannie's garden. She planted vegetables and flowers, and the spot is still colorful during the summer season.

The house has been reconstructed and is furnished with period pieces. The Allens illuminated their home during the long Vermont winters with pine knots

Docent at the Ethan Allen Homestead in Burlington

placed in the fireplace on a flat stone. They also made candles using deer, moose, and bear fat. Rushlights were made by dipping rushes in tallow.

A bake oven in the fireplace was well known to the children in the family. They were required to put a hand in the oven and hold it there while saying a rhyme. When it became too hot to finish the rhyme the bread could be put in. Visitors can see a multimedia program and also stroll along the hiking trails.

LODGING

LANG HOUSE
360 Main St., Burlington, VT 05401
877-919-9799; www.langhouse.com
This Victorian home dates from 1881.

WILLARD STREET INN
349 South Willard St.,
Burlington, VT 05401
800-577-8712, 802-651-8710;
www.willardstreetinn.com
This Queen Anne/Georgian-revival brick mansion dates from 1881.

Near Burlington:

THE INN AT ESSEX
70 Essex Way, Essex, VT 05452
800-727-4295, 802-878-1100;
www.innatessex.com
The buildings are decorated in colonial style.

RESTAURANTS

ICE HOUSE
171 Battery St.,
Burlington, VT 05401
802-864-1800
This is in a turn-of-the-20th-century ice house with a view of Lake Champlain.

NECI COMMONS
25 Church St., Burlington, VT 05401
802-862-6324
New England Culinary Institute offers an American bistro with seasonal and local fare.

SWEETWATERS
120 Church St., Burlington, VT 05401
802-864-9800
The decor is southwestern, the setting is a former bank building.

In nearby Essex:

BUTLER'S RESTAURANT
At the Inn at Essex, 70 Essex Way,
Essex, VT 05452
802-764-1413; www.innatessex.com
Sunday brunch is offered.

THE TAVERN
At the Inn at Essex, 70 Essex Way,
Essex, VT 05452
802-764-1489; www.innatessex.com
Open for lunch and dinner.

INFORMATION

THE LAKE CHAMPLAIN REGIONAL CHAMBER OF COMMERCE
60 Main St., Burlington, VT 05401
877-686-5253, 802-863-3489;
www.vermont.org

SHELBURNE

Two German lumbermen settled Shelburne in 1768; the town was named for an English earl. Renovated farm buildings from the 1700s now house shops in the pleasant downtown area, and the large and eclectic Shelburne Museum attracts visitors from all over New England and New York.

HISTORICAL SITES *and* MUSEUMS
If you're interested in Americana collections and American folk art, head south from Burlington to the **Shelburne Museum** (802-985-3344; www.shelburne

museum.org), on VT 7. Open daily May–Oct. The 37 buildings, spread out on 45 acres, house collections of quilts, textiles, tools, glass, ceramics, scrimshaw, decoys, weathervanes, furniture, dolls, carriages, circus memorabilia, and wagons.

There are seven restored period homes; the oldest is the **Prentis House**, dating from 1733. Built in saltbox style, the house has a colonial kitchen with a large fireplace, 17th- and 18th-century furniture, plus decorative arts and textiles on display. Don't miss the crewel bed hangings.

The **Dutton House** dates from 1782; it came from Cavendish, Vermont. The **1790 Stencil House** offers colorful hand-stenciled walls.

The 1786 **Sawmill** has an operating waterwheel and an up-and-down saw. The **Stagecoach Inn** was built in 1782 in Charlotte, Vermont. Visitors will enjoy the cigar-store figures, weathervanes, whirligigs, and trade signs there.

LODGING

HEART OF THE VILLAGE
5347 Shelburne Rd.,
Shelburne, VT 05482
877-808-1834;
www.heartofthevillage.com
The house dates from 1886, when it was built by merchant Cyrus Van Vliet.

THE INN AT SHELBURNE FARMS
1611 Harbor Rd., Shelburne, VT 05482
802-985-8498;
www.shelburnefarms.org

This 19th-century country house was the home of Dr. William Seward and Lila Vanderbilt Webb, who created Shelburne Farms in 1886 as a model agricultural estate.

RESTAURANTS

THE INN AT SHELBURNE FARMS
1611 Harbor Rd., Shelburne, VT 05482
802-985-8498;
www.shelburnefarms.org
Much of the food is grown right on the estate.

CAMBRIDGE

John Spafford arrived in 1783 and became the first settler in what is now the town of Cambridge. He found good soil, rainfall for his crops, and water from the mountains. He planted corn and built a home for his family, then returned to New Hampshire for his wife and two children. Life was hard for the family, but they managed to survive.

Today vacationers enjoy the Cambridge Greenway recreation trail. It winds for just over a mile beside the Lamoille River from Jeffersonville eastward.

HISTORICAL SITES *and* MUSEUMS
The **Cambridge Historical Society** (802-365-4148; www.gmavt.net/~rgtle/), School St., Jeffersonville 05464. Displays include pictures, old town records, books, furnishings that were used in town, implements, and clothing. During the summer the society has informational programs and also a special July Fourth float.

The society is also a fine source of local human interest stories, like the following: Cora Mudgett Beebe was the granddaughter of Jesse Mudgett, who was born in 1796. Beebe told the story of the four Mudgett brothers who left Weare, New

Hampshire, and settled in Cambridge. One of them, William, worked for five years on his place and then walked back to Weare to claim his sweetheart, Hannah. They were married and walked back home across two states to Cambridge. In 1927 a Sesquicentennial Celebration Pageant was held in Cambridge with a fifth-generation descendant of William Mudgett depicting his hardy pioneer ancestor.

SMUGGLERS' NOTCH

In the last decades of the 18th century and the first of the 19th, settlers began to move farther from Lake Champlain toward the mountains. There they had to adapt to rugged terrain and roadless wilderness. Passes through the mountains, called "notches" in New England parlance, became essential lines of communication. Native Americans used a path through Smugglers' Notch, one of the steepest notches in Vermont.

In 1807 Thomas Jefferson placed an embargo on trade that effectively prevented British goods from being unloaded in the United States. They unloaded in Canada, and some of them found their way to caves up in Smugglers' Notch. There was no road there, just a horse trail.

The area later became popular as a remote place to enjoy the natural beauty of wilderness. Hikers enjoy it in summer, but don't try to drive through in winter—the road is closed.

But winter is the time to enjoy winter sports at Smugglers' Notch Resort (www.smuggs.com), which is focused on entertainment for the whole family. It offers Alpine and Nordic skiing, skating, swimming, sleigh rides, indoor tennis, and a fitness center. We recall a three-generation stay when we skied all day and then added an evening of snowboard lessons—the elder generations faded away but not the younger! As a year-round resort it has a full roster of activities in the summer too.

LODGING

SMUGGLERS NOTCH INN
55 Church St., Jeffersonville, VT 05464
800-845-3101, 802-644-2412;
www.smuggsinn.com
Part of the inn dates from the 18th century; it was once a stagecoach stop.

RESTAURANTS

HEARTH & CANDLE
At the Smugglers' Notch Resort, VT 108, Smugglers' Notch, VT 05464
802-644-1260; www.smuggs.com
American cuisine, casual family or white-tablecloth.

SMUGGLERS NOTCH INN
55 Church St., Jeffersonville, VT 05464
802-644-6607; www.smuggsinn.com
Breakfast, lunch, and dinner are offered in the Village Tavern or the main dining room. Breakfast and lunch are available in the Bakery.

THREE MOUNTAIN LODGE
VT 108, Smugglers' Notch Rd., Jeffersonville, VT 05464
802-644-5736
Offers a full menu for dinner.

INFORMATION

SMUGGLERS' NOTCH AREA CHAMBER OF COMMERCE
Box 364, Jeffersonville, VT 05464
802-644-8232; www.smugnotch.com

CENTRAL VERMONT

The Green Mountains, more rounded and wooded than the higher White Mountains in New Hampshire, support all kinds of recreational activities. One of the highlights is mountain biking, with many miles of trails for all levels of ability. Try the trails on the south side of Hogback Mountain, which also serve as Nordic trails in winter. From Ripton the Natural Turnpike is a path heading to South Lincoln and a view of Mount Abraham. Steammill Road links up with the Natural Turnpike, and sometimes moose are seen near the old steam mill.

Skiing is one of the prime activities, and enthusiasts come here from all directions. Warren and Waitsfield are especially popular destinations, with more bed and breakfasts and inns than in most other areas.

Fishing is popular on the rivers, lakes, and streams. Craft fairs abound during the summer, and festivals for music and other performing arts round out the options.

VERGENNES

Settlers arrived in Vergennes in 1766. It is a small incorporated city dating from 1788. Ethan Allen named it after Charles Gravier, Comte de Vergennes, a French supporter of the Revolution. Now it is a service and shopping center for surrounding farms. The town includes one of the most attractive small harbors on Lake Champlain, with a summer resort and a major maritime museum.

HISTORICAL SITES *and* MUSEUMS
The **Lake Champlain Maritime Museum**, (802-475-2022; www.lcmm.org), is located in Basin Harbor, 4472 Basin Harbor Rd., Vergennes. Open daily June–Oct.

Bateaux ("boats" in French) were general-purpose vessels used to transport goods and people on the rivers and lakes of French Canada and the water route through Lake Champlain and Lake George. They were built with flat bottoms for capacity, were V-shaped at stern as well as bow for maneuverability, and were usually rowed, though some were rigged with sails. During the French and Indian War and the Revolution they ranged from 25 to 35 feet in length and were used primarily as troop transports. As many as 260 of them lie buried in the mud at the bottom of Lake George, where the British sank them in the fall of 1758, hoping to recover them in the spring for the campaigns of 1759. Seven bateaux have been listed on the National Register of Historic Places.

It is home to a replica of the Revolutionary War gunboat *Philadelphia*. The real *Philadelphia*, which was sunk after the Battle of Valcour Island in 1776, was raised from the lake in 1935 and is now at the Smithsonian. A crew of more than 50 was crammed into this vessel to manage the sails and the armament of one 12-pound cannon in the bow and two 9-pound cannons amidship, as well as smaller guns. Visitors can climb all over the replica and even help hoist a sail. Call ahead to be sure the vessel is in her home port. The museum also has a replica of an 18th-century bateau, modeled on a wreck recovered from the lake. In the boat shop you can watch boatbuilders working on replicas, and a blacksmith uses his forge to make typical 18th-century boat fittings.

LODGING

BASIN HARBOR CLUB
Panton Rd. west of Vergennes,
Vergennes, VT 05491
800-622-4000, 802-475-2311;
www.basinharbor.com
The Beach family has been welcoming
guests since 1886.

THE STRONG HOUSE INN
94 W. Main St., Vergennes, VT 05491
802-877-3337;
www.stronghouseinn.com
Samuel Paddock Strong, 19th-century
businessman, built this home in 1834 in
Federal style.

RESTAURANTS

BASIN HARBOR CLUB
Panton Rd. west of Vergennes, Vergennes, VT 05491
800-622-4000, 802-475-2311;
www.basinharbor.com
Try the main dining room for lunch or dinner or the Red Mill for a lighter menu.

INFORMATION

**ADDISON COUNTY CHAMBER
OF COMMERCE**
2 Court St., Middlebury, VT 05753
800-733-8376, 802-388-7951;
www.midvermont.com

FERRISBURGH

Ferrisburgh lies just north of Vergennes in the Champlain Valley, a gently rolling landscape of Vermont farmland. The Ferriss family were among the first settlers here. (The spelling of the town's name has varied over the years.)

HISTORICAL SITES *and* MUSEUMS

Rokeby Museum (802-877-3406; www.rokeby.org), 4334 US 7. Open May–Oct. One Quaker family lived in the area from the 1790s to the 1960s. Furnishings and memorabilia are reminders of this family. They ranged from the pioneers and later farmers to Rowland E. Robinson, the 19th-century writer, illustrator, and naturalist.

ADDISON

The village of Addison sits on rolling farmland midway between Vergennes and historic Chimney Point and Crown Point on Lake Champlain.

HISTORICAL SITES and MUSEUMS

The **DAR John Strong Mansion Museum** (802-759-2309), 6656 VT 17W. Strong was one of the Green Mountain Boys. This brick house was built in 1785 to replace the cabin that was burned by Tory and Indian raiders accompanying General Burgoyne's invasion force. Open Memorial Day–Labor Day. The house contains period furnishings. Perennial and colonial herb gardens enhance the setting.

Nearby on the Champlain lakeshore, **Chimney Point**, directly across from Crown Point, New York, got its name after settlers who had been threatened too long by the English set their homes afire and left, leaving just blackened chimneys.

Dutchman Jacobus de Warm had brought a contingent of English troops here from Albany in 1690 and built a fort. By 1730 a group of French colonists arrived and rebuilt the fort, adding more homes as well.

The 18th-century **Chimney Point Tavern** (802-759-2412), VT 125, is on the Vermont side of the Lake Champlain Bridge. Archaeological artifacts found on the site are on display. The focus is on Native American and French settlers in the area.

INFORMATION

ADDISON COUNTY CHAMBER OF COMMERCE
2 Court St., Middlebury, VT 05753
800-733-8376, 802-388-7951; www.midvermont.com

WAITSFIELD AND WARREN

Over the mountains to the east of the Champlain Valley, Waitsfield and Warren are a gold mine of historic inns and B&Bs for visitors who want to transport themselves backward in time. Vacationers head for these inns, but we have no idea why there are so many—one day we visited at least ten of them.

The most interesting (but not the fastest!) way to get there from the lake takes you over the **Appalachian Gap** on VT 17, which passes between Stark Mountain and Molly Stark Mountain. The views at the summit of the pass are worth the dozens of switchbacks it takes to get there, and the whole trip will remind you how difficult traveling east or west through Vermont was in the colonial era. Early settlers quite sensibly stayed along the lake or poked up river valleys.

LODGING

Inns and B&Bs in Waitsfield:

THE INN AT THE ROUND BARN FARM
1661 E. Warren Rd.,
Waitsfield, VT 05673; 802-496-2276;
www.innattheroundbarn.com
The Joslyn Round Barn was built by dairy farmer Clem Joslyn in 1910.

LAREAU FARM COUNTRY INN
VT 100, Waitsfield, VT 05673
800-833-0766, 802-496-4949;
www.lareaufarminn.com
This 1832 Greek-revival farmhouse is next to the Mad River.

MAD RIVER INN BED & BREAKFAST
Tremblay Rd., Waitsfield, VT 05673
800-832-8278, 802-496-7900;
www.madriverinn.com
This 1860s inn offers afternoon tea.

MILLBROOK INN
533 Mill Brook Rd.,
Waitsfield, VT 05673
800-477-2809, 802-496-2405;
www.millbrookinn.com
The house dates from the 1850s.

1824 HOUSE INN
2150 Main St., Waitsfield, VT
800-426-3986, 802-496-7555;
www.1824house.com
The inn has cross-country skiing on site.

TUCKER HILL LODGE
65 Marble Hill Rd.,
Waitsfield, VT 05673
800-543-7841, 802-496-3025;
www.tuckerhill.com
This country inn features herb and flower
gardens.

WAITSFIELD INN
VT l00, Waitsfield, VT 05673
800-758-3801, 802-496-3979;
www.waitsfieldinn.com
The inn was an 1825 parsonage.

Warren lodgings:

BEAVER POND FARM INN
Golf Course Rd., Warren, VT 05674
800-685-8285, 802-583-2861;
www.beaverpondfarm.com
This farm is now a country inn with a
beaver pond and lovely views.

PITCHER INN
275 Main St., Warren, VT 05674
888-TO-PITCH, 802-496-6350;
www.pitcherinn.com
Although it looks old, the building

is new, built on the site of a structure that
had burned. Rooms suggest historical
events in town.

THE SUGARTREE INN
2440 Sugarbush Access Rd.,
Warren, VT 05674
800-666-8907, 802-583-3211;
www.sugartree.com
This B&B is very handy for skiers.

RESTAURANTS

MILLBROOK INN RESTAURANT
533 Mill Brook Rd.,
Waitsfield, VT 05673
800-477-2809, 802-496-2405;
www.millbrookinn.com
This restaurant is owned by the chef.

**CHEZ HENRI RESTAURANT
AND BISTROT**
Village Rd. in Sugarbush Village,
Warren, VT 05674; 802-583-2600
A Parisian bistrot with flair.

THE COMMON MAN
3209 German Flats Rd.,
Warren, VT 05674; 802-583-2800
This restaurant serves an international
menu.

PITCHER INN
275 Main St., Warren, VT 05674
888-TO-PITCH, 802-496-6350;
www.pitcherinn.com
Noted for its wine list; contemporary
American cuisine with European and
Pacific influences.

INFORMATION

MAD RIVER CHAMBER OF COMMERCE
4061 Main St., Waitsfield, VT 05673
800-82-VISIT, 802-496-3409;
www.madrivervalley.com

MIDDLEBURY

Middlebury was founded in 1761 but was not permanently settled until near the
end of the Revolution. Gamaliel Painter was a surveyor who arrived in the mid-
1750s. He was with Ethan Allen when they burst into Fort Ticonderoga and took
it over. The Addison County Information Center (802-388-7951), 2 Court St.,

is in his home. Middlebury College here was founded in 1800.

This attractive college town has lots of shops, including some in old mills beside the river. The Vermont State Craft Center is there. The college sponsors the Bread Loaf Writers' Conference in August.

HISTORICAL SITES *and* MUSEUMS

Henry Sheldon Museum of Vermont History (802-288-2117; www.henryshel donmuseum.org), 1 Park St., Middlebury. Open Mon.–Sat. The museum is housed in the 1829 Judd-Harris House; exhibits portray history of the region.

LODGING

In Middlebury and environs:

THE MIDDLEBURY INN
14 Courthouse Square,
Middlebury, VT 05753
800-842-4666, 802-388-4961;
www.middleburyinn.com
Nathan Wood built his brick public house in 1827. Afternoon tea is served.

THE SWIFT HOUSE INN
25 Stewart Lane, Middlebury, VT 05753
866-388-9925, 802-388-9925;
www.swifthouseinn.com
The original house was built by Samuel Swift, judge and man of letters, in 1814.

WAYBURY INN
457 E. Main St.,
East Middlebury, VT 05740
800-348-1810, 802-388-4015;
www.wayburyinn.com
This inn was originally built as a stagecoach stop. In the 1980s it was used as the exterior for the Bob Newhart show.

THE CHIPMAN INN
VT 125, Ripton, VT 05766
800-890-2390, 802-388-2390;
www.chipmaninn.com
This inn dates from 1828.

BLUEBERRY HILL INN
Ripton Rd.,
Goshen, VT 05733
800-448-0707, 802-247-6735;
www.blueberryhillinn.com
The original farmhouse dates from 1813.

THE BRANDON INN
20 Park St.,
Brandon, VT 05733
800-639-8685, 802-247-5766;
www.historicbrandoninn.com
Jacob Simons built the original tavern in 1786.

THE INN ON PARK STREET
69 Park St.,
Brandon, VT 05733
800-394-7239, 802-247-3843;
www.theinnonparkstreet.com
The style of this National Register inn is French Second Empire.

LILAC INN
53 Park St.,
Brandon, VT 05733
800-221-0720, 802-247-5463;
www.lilacinn.com
The inn dates from 1909 and features a ballroom for weddings and concerts.

SHOREHAM

Shoreham was founded in 1755. Lord Jeffery Amherst ferried soldiers across Lake Champlain here in a campaign against the French. The "Fort Ti" cable ferry goes back and forth now.

Today the town has a number of historic buildings, including the 1846 Congregational Church, the 1873 St. Genevieve Catholic church, and a general store.

LODGING

THE SHOREHAM INN
VT 74, Shoreham, VT 05770
800-255-5081, 802-897-5081;
www.shorehaminn.com
Originally built around 1790, this establishment
has served as a residence, tavern, and hotel; the
restored inn now features a "gastropub."

INFORMATION

**ADDISON COUNTY CHAMBER
OF COMMERCE**
2 Court St., Middlebury, VT 05753
800-733-8376, 802-388-7951;
www.midvermont.com

ORWELL

Mount Independence (802-948-2000; www.historicvermont.org/mountinde
pendence/), located west of VT 22A in Orwell, was once the scene of an important Revolutionary War military compound. It was planned for a garrison of twelve
thousand men in 1776, one of the largest in North America. A floating bridge
provided access across Lake Champlain to Fort Ticonderoga.

During the winter lake ice made it very difficult to send supplies there, so the
force was reduced to three thousand sol-
diers. In July of 1777 Ticonderoga and
Mount Independence were taken by Burgoyne's invasion force as the garrison
retreated. The Americans fought a rear-
guard action at the Battle of Hubbardton. Today you can see remains including
the blockhouse, gun batteries, a stockade, and a hospital. Visitors should bring
their walking shoes and enjoy the trails
in the park around the fort.

> Revolutionary War veteran
> Captain William Watson
> raised his glass at the Eagle Tav-
> ern in East Poultney, Vermont, in
> 1790 with the following toast:
> "To the Enemies of our Coun-
> try! May they have cobweb
> breeches, a porcupine saddle,
> a hard-trotting horse, and an
> eternal journey."

EVENTS

Throughout the season: Mount Independence Living History events
www.historicvermont.org/mountindependence

> Our noses traced the tantalizing scent of bacon cooking over a wood fire
> during a reenactment encampment on Mount Independence. Two
> young girls were stirring bacon in a heavy cast-iron pot over the fire in front of
> their tent. Families in Revolutionary War dress settled into their tents, and later
> some of them hauled a cannon into position, facing into the woods. Com-
> mands were called out as the men prepared to fire. We were told to open our
> mouths to protect our ears. This particular gun came south with Burgoyne. It
> is more than 200 years old and "still knows how to talk."

East Hubbardton

After General Burgoyne took Mount Independence and Fort Ticonderoga, an American rear guard met the pursuing British at Hubbardton Battlefield (802-759-2412; www.historicvermont.org/hubbardton/), Monument Rd. Open late May–early Oct. Seth Warner's Green Mountain Boys, along with two Continental regiments, covered the rear as the main army continued to escape. Warner's men were cooking breakfast on July 7, 1777, when the British burst upon them. The Americans seemed to be withstanding the redcoats' assaults until Baron von Riedesel's German soldiers arrived on the scene. The Continental regiments fought well despite heavy losses, and the battle bought precious time for the retreating main army.

The Battle of Hubbardton was the only Revolutionary War battle fought in Vermont. It was also the beginning of the end for General Burgoyne's campaign to split the colonies, leading to his defeat and surrender at Saratoga in the fall. The museum at Hubbardton has exhibits that show how this battle fits into the Revolutionary War action. Visitors can walk around the battlefield to see markers for each event. The **Hubbardton Battlefield Monument** is placed on the grave of Colonel Ebenezer Francis, who fell while leading a Massachusetts regiment.

Castleton

Zadak Remington's tavern was the place where the Green Mountain Boys planned the attack on Fort Ticonderoga in 1775. Ethan Allen and Seth Warner were the ringleaders. The tavern is no longer there.

Thomas Dake was an architect who took pride in creating the Greek-revival houses in town. They have Palladian motifs, porticoes, archways, and Ionic and Corinthian columns. Some of these homes are open during "Colonial Days," which are held every other year in the fall.

The **Higley Homestead**, on Main St., was given to the Historical Society by the last Higley to live there. The house was built in 1787, and to date three rooms have been renovated. There are collections of artifacts and furniture belonging to the Higley family.

The resort area around Lake Bomoseen is popular, and Hubbardton Battlefield State Historic Site is just seven miles north.

Woodstock

With its town green, lovely old homes, antiques shops, galleries, bookstores, and boutiques, Woodstock is one of the most attractive towns in New England. From the mid-1930s onward, Laurance and Mary Rockefeller restored historic buildings and brought the past into the present in town. Through six decades, the Rockefellers undertook many projects and established the Woodstock Foundation to oversee them. The Billings Farm and Museum opened in 1982, and the Rockefellers donated the land and buildings for a national park a decade later. The Marsh-Billings-Rockefeller National Historical Park opened to the public in 1998. You can visit Rockefeller homes in a number of places, and the mansion in Woodstock has many of the same features on a smaller scale. It opened in 2001 for tours.

HISTORICAL SITES *and* MUSEUMS

If you want to trace the thread of one family who lived in town, head for the **Dana House** (802-457-1822; www.woodstockhistsoc.org), 26 Elm St. Open mid-May–late Oct., with limited winter hours. It is also the home of the Woodstock Historical Society.

Charles Dana built his home on Elm Street in 1807. He brought his new bride, Mary Gay Swan, here. They had eight children and had to raise the roof to accommodate everyone. Mary Dana cooked in a beehive oven and the large fireplace in the kitchen. The Federal parlor houses a William and Mary–style highboy with walnut veneer dating from 1740. Upstairs you will see a 1700s wedding gown in moss green. A 1660s sampler was created with silk embroidery on linen. There's a long portrait of Titus and Clarissa Hutchinson and six of their children, painted by Thomas Ware. All are dressed in their Sunday best.

Every time we visit there is something new to see in the house. Last time we were intrigued by the 1761 charter granting 24 acres in Woodstock. It was signed by Governor Benning Wentworth of New Hampshire.

Dana House in Woodstock

LODGING

ARDMORE INN
23 Pleasant St.,
Woodstock, VT 05091
800-497-9652, 802-457-3887;
www.ardmoreinn.com
The Gillingham family built their home in 1850; they were owners of the F.H. Gillingham & Sons General Store in town.

CANTERBURY HOUSE BED & BREAKFAST
43 Pleasant St., Woodstock, VT 05091
800-390-3077, 802-457-3077;
www.thecanterburyhouse.com
This Victorian home has a large living room for socializing.

THE CHARLESTON HOUSE
21 Pleasant St., Woodstock, VT 05091
888-475-3800, 802-457-3843;
www.charlestonhouse.com
This Greek-revival home dates from 1835.

THE JACKSON HOUSE
114–3 Senior Lane,
Woodstock, VT 05091
800-448-1890, 802-457-2065;
www.jacksonhouse.com
This 1890 Victorian mansion is on the
National Register of Historic Places.

THE WOODSTOCK INN
14 The Green, Woodstock, VT 05091
800-448-7900, 802-457-1100;
www.woodstockinn.com
Captain Israel Richardson opened Richardson's Tavern on this site in 1793. The current building dates from 1969.

THE WOODSTOCKER INN
61 River St., Woodstock, VT 05091
866-662-1439, 802-457-3896;
www.woodstockervt.com
This ca. 1830 cape-style village home was once an apartment house.

KEDRON VALLEY INN
VT 106, South Woodstock, VT 05071
800-836-1193, 802-457-1473;
www.KedronValleyInn.com
This inn dates from 1828 and is 5 miles south of Woodstock.

RESTAURANTS

BENTLEY'S RESTAURANT
3 Elm St., Woodstock, VT 05091
877-457-3232, 802-457-3232;
www.bentleysrestaurant.com
Open for lunch, dinner, and Sunday brunch.

THE JACKSON HOUSE
114–3 Senior Lane,
Woodstock, VT 05091
800-448-1890, 802-457-2065;
www.jacksonhouse.com
Fine dining and a prix fixe menu. During a severe ice storm one night, when no one else had power, they graciously served everyone who came.

THE PRINCE AND THE PAUPER
24 Elm St., Woodstock, VT 05091
802-457-1818;
www.princeandpauper.com
Offering Continental cuisine.

THE WOODSTOCK INN
14 The Green, Woodstock, VT 05091
800-448-7900, 802-457-1100;
www.woodstockinn.com
Diners have a choice of the main dining room, Eagle Café, and Richardson's Tavern.

KEDRON VALLEY INN
VT 106, South Woodstock, VT 05071
800-836-1193, 802-457-1473;
www.KedronValleyInn.com
Dishes are served with Vermont flair.

INFORMATION

WOODSTOCK AREA CHAMBER OF COMMERCE
18 Central St., Woodstock, VT 05091.
888-496-6378 or 802-457-3555;
www.woodstockvt.com

WINDSOR

The Constitution of Vermont was adopted July 8, 1777, in Windsor, so this town can quite accurately be called "the birthplace of Vermont." The General Assembly met in Windsor until 1805, when Montpelier became the capital.

Today Windsor is a great place to browse for artwork. The **Vermont State Craft Center** (802-674-6729), 85 Main St., offers work by 125 artists. It also carries furniture, metalwork, jewelry, origami, photos, and handblown glass.

Speaking of glass, **Simon Pearce Glassworks** (802-674-6280) is just north of town on US 5 in the industrial park. You can watch them blowing glass and also buy some in the gift shop.

The Vermont National Bank has a painting that the artist Maxfield Parrish, who lived across the river in New Hampshire, gave to "his girls"—the friendly tellers who helped him balance his checkbook. So one day in 1950 he arrived at the bank with *New Hampshire: Thy Templed Hills*. As the bank was about to merge and the painting to be sold, a letter was found from the artist's son, saying that his father meant for the painting to stay where it was. The bank did an about-face and kept the painting in Windsor.

HISTORICAL SITES *and* MUSEUMS

Old Constitution House (802-828-3051), 16 N. Main St. Open Memorial Day weekend to Columbus Day. This former tavern was the site of the signing of the Constitution of the Free and Independent Republic of Vermont. It is a museum of Vermont history, including exhibits on this historic event.

LODGING

JUNIPER HILL INN
153 Pembroke Rd., Windsor, VT 05089
800-359-2541, 802-674-5273;
www.juniperhillinn.com

Industrialist Maxwell Evarts built his mansion in 1902, high on a hill with a great view.

QUECHEE

Quechee is in the town of Hartford, which was given a charter by King George III in 1761. Quechee Gorge must have been a challenge to early settlers, but later it became valuable as a source of water power.

Today we go to great lengths to pass through Quechee and have lunch at the Simon Pearce Restaurant. In winter the rushing waterfall spurts out from mounds of ice, and the rest of the year it is a torrent. As in Windsor, glass-blowing is featured, and the gift shop is amazing.

LODGING

**THE QUECHEE INN
AT MARSHLAND FARM**
1119 Quechee Main St.,
Quechee, VT 05059
800-235-3133, 802-295-3133;
www.quecheeinn.com
This historic inn dates from 1793, when it was built by Colonel Joseph Marsh.

RESTAURANTS

**THE QUECHEE INN
AT MARSHLAND FARM**
1119 Quechee Main St.,
Quechee, VT 05059
800-235-3133, 802-295-3133;
www.quecheeinn.com
Fine dining and a lighter menu.

SIMON PEARCE RESTAURANT
1792 Quechee Main St.,
Quechee, VT 05059
802-295-1470; www.simonpearce.com
In a restored mill with a rushing waterfall underneath, and now an active glass-blowing site, with demonstrations and original glassware for sale.

SPRINGFIELD

Once the town was active in producing tools, but the mills are not used much anymore. The town has two rivers that used to provide power—the Black and the Connecticut.

HISTORICAL SITES and MUSEUMS
The Eureka Schoolhouse (802-885-2779), VT 11, Springfield. It dates from 1785 and is now open May–Oct. as an information center.

INFORMATION
SPRINGFIELD CHAMBER OF COMMERCE
14 Clinton St., Springfield, VT 05156
802-885-2779; www.springfieldvt.com

CHESTER

The town of Chester was first chartered by Governor Benning Wentworth of New Hampshire in 1754 and named Flamstead. It received a second grant in 1763 and was renamed New Flamstead. In 1764 the first two families arrived. Shortly thereafter New York named it Chester, and the name stuck. The town has many interesting buildings, including a group of 19th-century stone houses on VT 103 at the north edge of town.

HISTORICAL SITES and MUSEUMS
The **Chester Historical Society** (802-875-6211) is on the green. Open weekends June–Oct. The society offers information on the town's history.

LODGING
HENRY FARM INN
2206 Green Mountain Turnpike,
Chester, VT 05143
800-723-8213, 802-875-2674;
www.henryfarminn.com
This 1790s farmhouse was once a stage-coach stop.

QUAIL HOLLOW INN
225 Pleasant St., Chester, VT 05143
888-829-9874, 802-875-2794;
www.quailhollowinn.com
The Great Room is a popular place after a day out sightseeing.

In nearby Weston:

THE DARLING FAMILY INN
815 VT 100, Weston, VT 05161
802-824-3223;
www.thedarlingfamilyinn.com
The house dates from the 1830s.

THE INN AT WESTON
VT 100, Weston, VT 05161
802-824-6789; www.innweston.com
The farmhouse dates from 1848.

SOUTHERN VERMONT

Variety is the spice of southern Vermont. We have explored the state and find there is always something more to discover. The Molly Stark Trail (VT 9) takes you from Brattleboro to Bennington, and you may want to take a side trip to Newfane and Townshend. Bennington has the Bennington Museum, with a superb American glass collection, Grandma Moses paintings, and the Grandma Moses schoolhouse. The Bennington Battle Monument is the tallest monument in Vermont. Manchester is home to one of the first groupings of factory outlet stores, as well as the elegant Equinox Hotel.

Ski areas abound in this region. And white-water enthusiasts savor the rushing rivers.

You can spend a day visiting the Calvin Coolidge State Historic Site in Plymouth. Besides visiting his birthplace and childhood home, you can take home some cheese from the factory that was started by his father.

ROCKINGHAM

The Vermont Country Store is the place to go for a wide range of products including canoes.

HISTORICAL SITES *and* MUSEUMS
The Old Rockingham Meeting House (802-463-3964), 11 Meeting House Rd. Open daily Memorial Day weekend to Columbus Day. This 1787 building has a high pulpit and "pigpen style" pews. The adjoining graveyard has interesting headstones.

GRAFTON

Grafton was chartered in 1756 and settled in 1780. Today its appearance is still evocative of earlier times, without any power or telephone lines aboveground. That's no accident since, like Woodstock, it has been carefully restored by a former resident, Dean Mathey, a Princeton investment banker and summer resident of the village. Starting in the 1960s the Windham Foundation set out to restore the buildings of the village, revitalize its eroded economic base, provide college scholarships for local youngsters, and help fund nonprofit organizations in the region and the state.

HISTORICAL SITES *and* MUSEUMS
The **Grafton History Museum** (802-843-1010; www.graftonhistory.org), 147 Main St. Open weekends and holidays Memorial Day–Columbus Day. Ask for information on the walking tour.

LODGING

THE OLD TAVERN
Main St. Grafton, VT 05146
800-843-1801, 802-843-2231;
www.old-tavern.com
The original building dates from 1788.

THE INN AT WOODCHUCK HILL FARM
Middletown Rd.,
Grafton, VT 05146; 802-843-2398;
www.woodchuckhill.com
This farmhouse dates from 1790.

In nearby Londonderry:

FROG'S LEAP INN
7455 VT 100, Londonderry, VT 05148
887-FROGSLEAP, 802-824-3019;
www.frogsleapinn.com
This inn dates from 1842.

LONDONDERRY INN
VT 100, South Londonderry, VT 05155
800-644-5226, 802-824-5226;
www.londonderryinn.com
The Melendy dairy farm was built in 1826
and became an inn in 1943.

RESTAURANTS

THE OLD TAVERN
Main St. Grafton, VT 05146
800-843-1801, 802-843-2231;
www.old-tavern.com
Regional American cuisine is served.

INFORMATION

**GREAT FALLS REGIONAL
CHAMBER OF COMMERCE**
17 Depot St., Bellows Falls, VT 05101
802-463-4280; www.gfrcc.org

DORSET

Dorset was chartered by Governor Benning Wentworth of New Hampshire in 1751. In 1776 the Green Mountain Boys wrote the Declaration of Independence for the New Hampshire Grants in Cephas Kent's tavern here. Signers included Thomas Chittenden, Ira Allen, Matthew Lyon, and Seth Warner. Today Dorset is an attractive town filled with colonial and Federal buildings, as well as a historic inn and a summer theater.

LODGING

THE BARROWS HOUSE
3156 VT 30, Dorset, VT 05251
800-639-1620, 802-867-4455;
www.barrowshouse.com
Some of the houses in the complex are
200 years old.

CORNUCOPIA OF DORSET
3228 VT 30, Dorset, VT 05251
800-566-5751, 802-867-5751;
www.cornucopiaofdorset.com
The main building dates from 1900.

DORSET INN
8 Church St.,
Dorset, VT 05251; 802-867-5542;
www.dorsetinn.com
The inn has been welcoming guests since
1796.

THE INN AT WEST VIEW FARM
VT 30, Dorset, VT 05251
800-769-4903, 802-867-5717;
www.innatwestviewfarm.com
The farmhouse dates from the 1870s.

RESTAURANTS

THE BARROWS HOUSE
3156 VT 30, Dorset, VT 05251
800-639-1620, 802-867-4455;
www.barrowshouse.com
Choose among the Dorset Dining Room,
the Greenhouse, and the Tavern.

DORSET INN
8 Church St., Dorset, VT 05251
802-867-5542; www.dorsetinn.com
Breakfast, lunch, and dinner; restaurant
and tavern dining.

THE INN AT WEST VIEW FARM
VT 30, Dorset, VT 05251
800-769-4903, 802-867-5717;
www.innatwestviewfarm.com
Contemporary American cuisine Thu.–Mon.

INFORMATION

DORSET CHAMBER OF COMMERCE
VT 30, Dorset, VT 05251
802-867-2450; www.dorsetvt.com

MANCHESTER

Manchester was chartered in 1761 and settled in 1764. The Historical Society does not have a phone, but the curator can be reached at 802-375-2733. Manchester Village is one of the most picturesque in Vermont, with many fine historic houses and inns. As you may know, there is a plethora of upscale shopping outlets here, and it is the home of Orvis, which offers many programs as well as fishing and other outdoor gear. The town prospered in the 19th century and has preserved many attractions, including Hildene, the house where Abraham Lincoln's son and family summered.

Like many towns in Vermont, Manchester has three parts that represent stages of growth. Manchester Village, the oldest, sits atop the hill. Manchester Center, now the site for business and shopping, is in the valley below. And to the east lies Manchester Depot, representing the growth brought as railroads poked up through the state.

LODGING

1811 HOUSE
3654 Main St.,
Manchester Village, VT 05254
800-432-1811, 802-362-1811;
www.1811house.com
The house dates from 1811, but a part of it goes back to the 1770s. There is a British-style pub inside.

THE EQUINOX
VT 7A, Manchester Village, VT 05254
800-362-4747, 802-362-4700;
www.equinoxresort.com
The inn was established in 1769 and has been transformed into a major hotel and conference center.

THE RELUCTANT PANTHER INN
West Rd.,
Manchester Village, VT 05254
800-822-2331, 802-362-2568;
www.reluctantpanther.com
This country inn is listed on the Register of Historic Places.

THE INN AT ORMSBY HILL
1842 Main St.,
Manchester Center, VT 05255
800-670-2841, 802-362-1163;
www.ormsbyhill.com
Built by Thompson Purdy in 1764, this home may have served as a hideout for Ethan Allen.

THE SETH WARNER INN
VT 7A, Manchester Center, VT 05255
802-362-3830;
www.sethwarnerinn.com
An 1880s country inn between two mountain ranges.

THE INN AT MANCHESTER
3967 Main St., Manchester, VT 05254
800-273-1793, 802-362-1793;
www.innatmanchester.com
Built as a private home in the 1880s, it became an inn in 1978.

THE VILLAGE COUNTRY INN
VT 7A, Manchester, VT 05254
800-370-0300, 802-362-1792;
www.villagecountryinn.com
This inn dates from the turn of the 20th century.

WILBURTON INN
River Rd., Manchester, VT 05254
800-648-4944, 802-362-2500;
www.wilburton.com
A Tudor-style mansion with modern
amenities.

THE INN AT WILLOW POND
VT 7A, Manchester, VT 05255
800-533-3533, 802-362-4733;
www.innatwillowpond.com
The restaurant is in a 1770s farmhouse.

In nearby Sunderland:

BATTENKILL INN
VT 7A, Sunderland, VT 05254
800-441-1628, 802-362-4213;

www.battenkillinn.com
This farmhouse dates from 1840 and
is on the Battenkill River.

RESTAURANTS

*All the inns listed above, except for the
1811 House, offer dining.*

INFORMATION

**MANCHESTER AND THE MOUNTAINS
REGIONAL CHAMBER**
5046 Main St.,
Manchester Center, VT 05255
800-362-4144, 802-362-2100;
www.manchestervermont.com

ARLINGTON

Arlington dates from 1763 when Jehiel Hawley, who was a Loyalist, settled here.
The town was known as Tory Hollow. The Tory town clerk, Isaac Bisco, destroyed
the town records and left for Canada. During the Revolution this town was the
de facto seat of government. Thomas Chittenden, the first governor of Vermont,
left Williston and moved to Arlington.

If some of the aspects of Arlington look familiar, it may be because Norman
Rockwell lived here for part of his life.

LODGING

THE ARLINGTON INN
3904 VT 7A, Arlington, VT 05250
800-443-9442, 802-375-6532;
www.arlingtoninn.com
Martin Chester Deming built this Greek-
revival mansion in 1848.

HILL FARM INN
458 Hill Farm Rd., Arlington, VT 05250
800-882-2545, 802-375-2269;
www.hillfarminn.com
The farm dates from 1905.

THE INN ON COVERED BRIDGE GREEN
3587 River Rd., Arlington, VT 05250
800-726-9480, 802-375-9489
www.coveredbridgegreen.com
This inn dates from 1792, and Ethan Allen
met his Green Mountain Boys on the green
next to the bridge. It was once the home
of Norman Rockwell.

WEST MOUNTAIN INN
River Rd., Arlington, VT 05250
802-375-6516;
www.westmountaininn.com
The original farmhouse dates from 1849.

RESTAURANTS

THE ARLINGTON INN
3904 VT 7A, Arlington, VT 05250
800-443-9442, 802-375-6532;
www.arlingtoninn.com
The chef uses fresh local ingredients in his
dishes.

WEST MOUNTAIN INN
River Rd., Arlington, VT 05250
802-375-6516;
www.westmountaininn.com
Seasonal country cuisine.

BRATTLEBORO

The slogan of this Connecticut River city is "Where Vermont Begins," because the first permanent white settlement was established here when Fort Dummer was founded in 1724. Fort Dummer State Park (802-254-2610), at 517 Old Guilford Road, two miles south of the downtown, is near the site of the fort, which was flooded when the Connecticut River was dammed in 1908. The fort was on the west bank of the river, near the present-day lumber company.

Today Brattleboro is a lively city, with a well-preserved, prosperous downtown tucked between the hills and the river.

LODGING

Two exceptional inns are near the Molly Stark Trail and Brattleboro.

THE INN AT SAWMILL FARM
VT 100 and Crosstown Rd.,
West Dover, VT 05356
800-493-1133, 802-464-8131;
www.theinnatsawmillfarm.com
The inn is in a converted 18th-century barn, with hand-hewn posts, beams, and weathered boards.

FOUR COLUMNS INN
VT 30, on the green,
Newfane, VT 05345; 802-365-7713;
www.fourcolumnsinn.com
This Greek-revival inn dates from 1832.

RESTAURANTS

The Inn at Sawmill Farm and the Four Columns Inn are both renowned for their cuisine.

INFORMATION

BRATTLEBORO CHAMBER OF COMMERCE
180 Main St., Brattleboro, VT 05301
877-254-4565;
www.brattleborochamber.org

BENNINGTON

Bennington was named after Benning Wentworth in 1749; it was the first town settled in the grants west of the Connecticut River. Ethan Allen and Seth Warner gathered the Green Mountain Boys in 1770 at the Catamount Tavern. Their aim was to get rid of the "Yorkers" who were laying claim to their lands.

During the Battle of Bennington on August 16, 1777, General John Stark of New Hampshire led the militia to victory against a strong detachment of Hessians and Loyalists sent eastward by General Burgoyne. Burgoyne wanted to replenish his army's dwindling supplies from a depot at Bennington. General Stark, Seth

John Stark wrote his wife: "Dear Molly: In less than a week, the British forces will be ours. Send every man from the farm that will come and let the haying go." She did as he asked and more; she sent two hundred townspeople along, too. As he went into battle, General Stark said, "There are the Redcoats, and they are ours, or this night Molly Stark sleeps a widow." But she didn't. He won the battle and brought home a brass cannon, one of six taken from the British.

Warner, and militia from throughout the region attacked the Hessians and Loyalists a few miles west of Bennington in Walloomsac, New York, and defeated them in a pitched battle. Burgoyne's main force met its own end less than two months later at Saratoga.

Although the battle was actually fought in what is now New York, Bennington has the monument, and it is surrounded by a handsome neighborhood of 18th- and early 19th-century homes that is well worth a visit.

HISTORICAL SITES *and* MUSEUMS

The **Bennington Battle Monument** (802-447-0550), 15 Monument Circle. Open the second weekend in Apr. through Oct. 31. At 306 feet it is the tallest structure in Vermont. Take the elevator up for a view of three states. Exhibits and a diorama depict the battle. The monument is in Old Bennington, off VT 9 (Main St.) just west of the Bennington city center.

The Bennington Museum (802-447-1571; www.benningtonmuseum.com), is at 75 Main St. (VT 9). Open daily. The many collections include an exhibit on the Battle of Bennington, plus early firearms, tools, pottery, glassware, and American art, including a large collection of Grandma Moses paintings. The 19th-century schoolhouse that Grandma Moses and other members of her family attended was moved to the grounds here. One of the earliest Stars and Stripes flags is also here.

The **Old First Church** (802-447-1223), Monument Ave., Old Bennington. Open Memorial Day weekend to Columbus Day. The church organization dates from 1762, among the oldest in Vermont. The structure dates from 1805.

The **Old Burying Ground** is next to the church. Graves include the founders of Bennington and soldiers killed in the Battle of Bennington.

John Stark statue and an exhibit inside the Bennington Museum

LODGING

ALEXANDRA BED & BREAKFAST
916 Orchard Rd.,
Bennington, VT 05201
888-207-9386, 802-442-5619;
www.alexandrainn.com
This farmhouse dates from 1859.

FOUR CHIMNEYS INN
21 West Rd., Old Bennington, VT 05201
800-649-3503, 802-447-3500;
www.fourchimneys.com
A Bennington businessman built this grand
1910 colonial-style home after the original
1783 house burned down.

THE HENRY HOUSE
Murphy Rd.,
North Bennington, VT 05257
888-442-7045, 802-442-7045;
www.henryhouseinn.com
Dating from 1769, this was the home of
William Henry, Revolutionary War hero and
participant in the Battle of Bennington.

RESTAURANTS

FOUR CHIMNEYS INN
21 West Rd., Old Bennington, VT 05201
800-649-3503, 802-447-3500;
www.fourchimneys.com
The cuisine is renowned; open for dinners.

EVENTS

August: Bennington Battle Day
Weekend. 800-229-0252 or
802-447-3311 (Bennington Area
Chamber of Commerce)

INFORMATION

BENNINGTON AREA
CHAMBER OF COMMERCE
100 Veterans Memorial Dr.,
Bennington, VT 05201
800-229-0252, 802-447-3311;
www.bennington.com

Current Information

DEPARTMENT OF TOURISM AND MARKETING
6 Baldwin St., Montpelier, VT 05602

WELCOME CENTER
134 State St., Montpelier, VT 05602
802-828-3237; www.VermontVacation.com

VERMONT CHAMBER OF COMMERCE
2 Granger Rd., Berlin, VT 04541
800-VERMONT, 802-223-3443; www.vtchamber.com

Resources

Colonial Period

Boorstin, Daniel J. *The Americans: The Colonial Experience.* New York: Random House, 1958.

Bremer, Francis J. *The Puritan Experiment: New England Society from Bradford to Edwards.* New York: St. Martin's Press, 1976.

Bushman, Richard L., *From Puritan to Yankee: Character and the Social Order in Connecticut, 1690-1765.* Cambridge, MA: Harvard University Press, 1967.

Fischer, David Hackett. *Albion's Seed: Four British Folkways in America.* Oxford: New York: Oxford University Press, 1989.

Greene, Jack P. *Pursuits of Happiness: The Social Development of Early Modern British Colonies and the Formation of American Culture.* Chapel Hill: University of North Carolina Press, 1988.

Hawke, David. *The Colonial Experience.* Indianapolis, New York, Kansas City: Bobbs-Merrill, 1966.

Kennedy, Roger G. *Rediscovering America: Journeys through Our Forgotten Past.* Boston: Houghton Mifflin, 1990.

Labaree, Benjamin W. *Colonial Massachusetts: A History.* Millwood, NY: KTO Press, 1979.

Middleton, Richard. *Colonial America: A History, 1607-1760.* Cambridge, MA, and Oxford: Blackwell, 1992.

Reich, Jerome R. *Colonial America.* Englewood Cliffs, NJ: Prentice Hall, 1989.

Schultz, Eric B., and Michael J. Tougias. *King Philip's War: The History and Legacy of America's Forgotten Conflict.* Woodstock, VT: The Countryman Press, 1999.

Revolutionary War

Bohrer, Melissa Lukeman. *Glory, Passion and Principle: The Story of Eight Remarkable Women at the Core of the American Revolution.* New York: Atria Press, 2003.

Commager, Henry Steele, and Richard B. Morris. *The Spirit of Seventy Six: The Story of the American Revolution as told by Participants.* 2 vols. New York, Indianapolis: Bobbs-Merrill, 1958.

Ellis, Joseph J. *Founding Brothers: The Revolutionary Generation.* New York: Alfred A. Knopf, 2004.

Ferling, John. *A Leap in the Dark: The Struggle to Create the American Republic.* New York: Oxford University Press, 2003.

Kelly, C. Brian. *Best Little Stories from the American Revolution.* Nashville: Cumberland House, 1999.

Labaree, Benjamin Woods. *The Boston Tea Party.* Boston: Northeastern University Press, 1964.

Leamon, James S., *Revolution Downeast: The War for American Independence in Maine.* Amherst, MA: University of Massachusetts Press, 1993.

McCullough, David. *1776.* New York: Simon & Schuster, 2005.

Raphael, Ray. *A People's History of the American Revolution: How Common People Shaped the Fight for Independence.* New York: The New Press, 2001.

Stember, Sol. *The Bicentennial Guide to the American Revolution. Volume I: The War in the North.* New York: Saturday Review Press, E.P. Dutton, 1974.

Colonial and Revolutionary General Interest

Albion, Robert G., William A. Baker, and Benjamin W. Labaree. *New England and the Sea.* Mystic, CT: Mystic Seaport Museum, 1972.

Amar, Akhil Reed. *America's Constitution: A Biography.* New York: Random House, 2005.

Bissland, Jim. *Long River Winding: Life, Love, and Death along the Connecticut.* Lee, MA: Berkshire House, 2003.

Leder, Lawrence H. *America 1603–1789: Prelude to a Nation.* Minneapolis: Burgess Publishing, 1972.

Muse, Vance. *The Smithsonian Guides to Historic America: Northern New England.* New York: Stewart, Tabori & Chang, 1989

Shalhope, Robert E. *Bennington and the Green Mountain Boys.* Baltimore: Johns Hopkins University Press, 1996.

Tree, Christina. *How New England Happened: A Guide to New England through Its History.* Boston, Toronto: Little, Brown, 1976.

Vila, Bob. *Bob Vila's Guide to Historic Homes of New England.* New York: William Morrow, 1993.

Wiencek, Henry. *The Smithsonian Guides to Historic America: Southern New England.* New York: Stewart, Tabori & Chang, 1989.

Also, each state has a *Bicentennial History* in the States and the Nation Series, published by W.W. Norton, New York. Also, each state has a *History of the American Colonies,* KTO Press (A U.S. Division of Kraus-Thomson Organization, Ltd.), Millwood, NY.

Biography

Brady, Patricia. *Martha Washington: An American Life*. New York: Viking, 2005.

Chernow, Ron. *Alexander Hamilton*. New York: Penguin, 2004.

Ellis, Joseph J. *His Excellency: George Washington*. New York, Alfred A. Knopf, 2004.

Grant, James. *John Adams: Party of One*. New York: Farrar, Straus and Giroux, 2005.

Isaacson, Walter. *Benjamin Franklin: An American Life*. New York: Simon & Schuster, 2003.

Index